A Natural History of

PEACE

A NATURAL HISTORY OF
PEACE

Edited by Thomas Gregor

VANDERBILT UNIVERSITY PRESS

Nashville and London

Publication and promotion of this book has been supported by a generous grant from
The Harry Frank Guggenheim Foundation.

First Edition 1996
96 97 98 99 00 5 4 3 2 1

This publication is made from recycled paper and meets the minimum requirements
of American National Standard for Information Sciences—Permanence of Paper
for Printed Library Materials ⊖

Library of Congress Cataloging-in-Publication Data

A natural history of peace / edited by Thomas Gregor. — 1st ed.
      p.   cm.
   Includes bibliographical references and index.
   ISBN 0-8265-1272-0 (alk. paper). — ISBN 0-8265-1280-1
(pbk. : alk. paper)
      1. Peace—History.   I. Gregor, Thomas.
JX1963.N25   1996
327.1′72—dc20   95-39462
                                              CIP

Manufactured in the United States of America

CONTENTS

ACKNOWLEDGMENTS

A Natural History of Peace reflects the thinking and research of scholars in a wide range of disciplines within the social sciences. The work was made possible thanks to a week-long conference organized by the Harry Frank Guggenheim Foundation in Charleston, South Carolina. The conference was an act of risk-taking on the part of the Foundation, in that peace is a relatively new topic to academic studies. The Foundation's role was a critical one, since it both funded the conference and provided assistance in shaping the direction of the proceedings. We are especially indebted to Karen Colvard, the grants officer of the Foundation, for both her intellectual contributions and her organizational skills. The conferees and I are deeply appreciative of her and the Foundation's support and efforts in behalf of our collaboration.

I further acknowledge the participation of my daughter, Leah Anne Gregor, as an editor and researcher for the volume, and the patience and encouragement of my family through the publication process.

INTRODUCTION

THOMAS GREGOR

What causes war? Uncertainties remain, but the large portions of the war puzzle have been solved: war exists because it meets short-term social, economic, demographic, and psychological needs. A nonaggressive culture faced with a warlike neighbor faces a bitter choice: submit or resist. Submission may lead to becoming part of a larger, warlike society. Resistance usually means imitating the aggressive methods of the warrior culture. Either way, we have learned, war turns out to be catching.

What of peace? What are its preconditions and correlates? How does an aggressive culture become a peaceful one? To what extent can the members of a society control their culture's choice of peace or war? In contrast to violence, we know all too little about peace. Peace and peace studies are relatively new to social science research. Prior to the 1980s, with the exception of a number of now classic contributions in anthropology (for example, Mead 1937; Montagu 1976) the literature was scant. Writing in 1981, Haakan Wiberg, editor of the *Journal of Peace Research*, observed, "It turns out that of the approximately 400 articles published in the *Journal of Peace Research* over seventeen years, *a single* one has been devoted to the empirical study of peaceful societies with a view to find out what seemed to make them peaceful." A more recent bibliography (Ferguson 1988) on issues of war and conflict, provides a rough quantitative measure of the imbalance between studies of peace and war. Of 361 pages of references, only four list citations of studies of peace. The first textbook on the subject of peace of necessity reflects the imbalance of research. David Barash's (1991) excellent *Introduction to Peace Studies*, although of great importance, gives less attention to peace as a phenomenon in its own right than to the causes and evolution of war, the history of the peace movement, proposals for peace through law and respect for human and environmental rights.

Today there is a rapidly growing interest in peace research, with an established worldwide organization of scholars (The International Peace Research Association) and even a U.S. government-funded agency for the promotion of peace studies (the United States Institute of Peace). Increasingly, peace research is recognized as a separate and legitimate area of inquiry, rather than a category residual to the study of war. (For current examples of work on peace, see Wallensteen [1988], Howell and Willis [1989], Rohrl, Nicholson and Zamora [1992], and Sponsel and Gregor [1994]). This volume is part of the new effort to take peace research seriously.

Recognizing the significance of research on peace, the Harry Frank Guggenheim Foundation recently convened a conference of scholars in Charleston, South Carolina, to address questions regarding the nature of human peace. The conferees represented the fields of primatology, archaeology, social anthropology, economics, political science, diplomacy, history, and psychology. They presented case studies of peaceful cultures, comparative research on peaceful societies, cross-species perspectives on the ethology of nonviolence, historical studies on the evolution of peace, and theories on the origins and nature of peaceful systems. The results of the conference, published in this volume, move forward the boundaries of what is known about peace and help set directions for future research.

Why We Know Little about Peace

Why, until recently, has peace so seldom been examined? We would do well to consider this question. An examination of the several attitudes toward peace sheds light on its nature and on our own perspective in understanding it.

Peace is hard to define and hard to find. Donald Tuzin's introductory article in this volume calls attention to the fact that peace and war have a very different status. War is real. There is no question of the existential status of human violence. Peace, however, is more of an idealization: a wished for state of human existence. In our culture, and apparently in many others, peace is seen as a yearned for but generally unattainable human condition. Hence, travelers' reports of the "gentle peoples" who live without violence turn out to be romanticized. Historical epochs of peace are brief and often end in carnage. Peace, it would seem, is a chimera, receding over the horizon just as we get closer.

Nonetheless, peace, as a wished for state of human affairs has a reality. It can be found not only in the approximations of peace in a few societies, but also, surprisingly, in the desires of warriors. As Tuzin points out, wars are often (perhaps usually) fought with the intended aim of securing peace. As he puts it, the "specter of peace" may be discovered in strange places, even in the midst of the extremely warlike New Guinea society where Tuzin has done his own research.

Peace is an assumed condition of human relationships and therefore needs no special attention. A number of scholars have suggested that we are party to an implicit logic that holds that peace is what we would possess were it not for the contagion of war. As such, war is the perturbation that needs to be explained. The same kind of reasoning shapes other sectors of the social sciences. In psychology, the focus of attention is on mental disturbance rather than our daily sense of normalcy (Galtung 1968: 487). The state of what we might call inner peace gets relatively short shrift, except perhaps in the area of humanistic psychology. Similarly, sociologists examine deviance, crime, and dysfunctional families. Research grants are in short supply for those who want to study why people do not take drugs or why they live harmoniously with their spouses. They may even face ridicule, as happened in 1976, when Senator William Proxmire awarded his "Golden Fleece Award" for a researcher's efforts to study love. Had the research focused on divorce or spouse abuse, it would have seemed reasonable. My point is that the expected state of human affairs such as peace (even though it is actually rather rare) is unexamined by the social scientist.

Peace is less exciting than war. Closely linked to the assumption that peace is the basal condition of humankind is a sense that it is less interesting than war. We know little about peace because, as Thomas Hardy once put it, "War makes rattling good history; but peace is poor reading." Even children in Western societies have the same biases, in that they are interested in war and disinterested in peace. Summarizing a variety of studies, Hakan Wiberg (1981) notes that from the perspective of children, "peace is boring" (Wiberg 1981). The same pattern is evident in other cultures. Everywhere, it would seem, war is dramatic and rich in metaphorical connections. Only rarely is peace more developed as a cultural category, as in the Hindu value of *satyagrahi* (Nakhre 1976) and the varying concepts of nonviolence reviewed by Galtung (1981). It is the exceptional and violent event that claims our attention. The institutions of peace, however, are often undramatic and quiet in their operation. Perhaps peace is often invisible to us only because it does not clamor for our attention.

Peace is impossible or unlikely, and is therefore of little interest. Although peace may be an assumed condition were it not for war, there is also a long tradition in the social sciences that sees humans as inherently fractious and violent. In Vienna, in September of 1932, for example, Sigmund Freud and Albert Einstein engaged in a historical exchange of letters in which Freud stated his death instinct theory of war and aggression:

Dear Prof. Einstein:
    . . . According to our hypothesis human instincts are of only two kinds: those which seek to preserve and unite—which we call erotic . . . and those which seek to destroy and kill, which we class together as the aggressive or destructive instinct. . . . This instinct is at work in every living being, and striving to bring it to ruin and to reduce life to its original condition of inanimate matter. Thus it quite seriously deserves to be called the death instinct. (Freud 1963: 141, 143)

According to Freud, the death instinct led to suicide when turned inward. Outwardly expressed, it led to homicide, and at a group level, to war. Freud came to this view after World War I, with its nine million deaths. Certainly the scarcity of peaceful cultures also reinforced Freud's view of human nature.

Although there is little evidence for a "death instinct," theories similar to Freud's have a wide currency in the social sciences. Many social theorists, beginning perhaps with Thomas Hobbes in the modern Western tradition, see humans as essentially aggressive. According to Hobbes, in the absence of socially given rules and the means of enforcing them, the human condition would be that of the war of one against all: "Hereby it is manifest, that during the time men live without a common power to keep them all in Awe, they are in that condition which is called War; and such a war, as is of everyman against everyman" (Leviathan). This belief finds some support in Darwinian biology, with its emphasis on competition and survival. The descendants of this intellectual tradition include the Social Darwinists of the nineteenth century (Herbert Spencer and others) and its more recent offshoots in sociobiology. That conflict is inherent in human society is central to the work of many others, including Georg Simmel, who saw discord as organically tied up with the elements that held society together and Karl Marx, who regarded violence, especially class violence, as the engine of social change. This tradition, taken together with the experience of modern warfare, leads to a kind of intellectual cynicism about peace, as in Ambrose Bierce's definition from his Devil's Dictionary: "Peace: a period of cheating between two periods of fighting." Why study peace when it is reflected neither in existing social arrangements nor social theory?

Peace is scarce and therefore difficult to study. Freud was deeply pessimistic about the (unpsychoanalyzed) human spirit. Humans were by nature so quarrelsome that he doubted that peaceful people existed:

We are told that in certain happy regions of the earth, where nature provides in abundance everything that man requires, there are races whose life is passed in tranquility and who know neither compulsion nor aggressiveness. I can scarcely believe it, and I should be glad to meet these fortunate beings. (Freud 1963: 143).

Was Freud right? In fact, he was not far off the mark. We must acknowledge that peace is unusual, even if not as scarce as Freud claimed. Researchers are hard pressed to find large numbers of peaceful societies. Richard Sipes noted in his study of war and combative sports that "relatively peaceful societies are not easy to find. I had to investigate 130 societies to find eleven, of which five were rejected because of insufficient information" (1973: 68). In a more recent and hopeful survey of the anthropological literature, Bruce Bonta (1993) locates forty-seven relatively peaceful cultures. He notes, however, that at least some of these societies are capable of considerable violence. In fact, Bonta, a careful scholar, cautiously includes "works that discredit the peacefulness" of the peoples in question (1993: 5, 6).

Bonta and Sipes's sample are primarily composed of tribal societies. When we turn our attention from small-scale cultures to state-level societies, we find that peace is even more infrequent and that war is commonplace. Thus, Arthur Westing (1982) in a study of high-fatality wars during the previous eighty years, finds that on average three such wars were occurring simultaneously, and that there was only one year in which none was waged. Twenty-five million persons died in World Wars I and II alone. Faced with such data Westing concludes, "The sad, but seemingly inescapable conclusion that I draw is that war remains as a routine, typical, and thus, in fact, normal human activity" (1982: 263).

There are investigators who believe otherwise. In chapter 4, Leslie Sponsel reviews a substantial literature and offers a more optimistic view of humankind. He shows that the evidence for violence in prehistory is not extensive, even though it is often misread as proving otherwise, and he demonstrates that there are at least some highly peaceful societies known to comparative anthropology. There are even a few societies that come close to being completely peaceful, such as the Semai of Malaysia (described by Gregor and Robarchek in chapter 6) and a number of other related societies (for example, the Chewong [Howell 1989]). Nonetheless, relative to the literature on war there is not a great deal of comparative data for the student of peace.

There are therefore good reasons why peace studies have been frustrated as a discipline. Peace is difficult to define, it is regarded as unexciting, and it is in fact scarce. Nonetheless, it exists. Even in the most violent societies, the ordinary business of human affairs demands a measure of tranquility. Moreover, peace is more than the absence of war. War is so contagious and political systems are so volatile that peace cannot endure unless special relationships, structures, and attitudes promote and protect it. We will now look at what we do know about the nature of peace.

What We Know about Peace

Human nature as peaceful. ("Men are not naturally enemies . . . nature made men happy and good."—Jean-Jacques Rousseau.) Coexisting with a view of human nature as competitive and violent is an intellectual tradition that emphasizes cooperation and peacefulness. Anthropology provides substantial support for this position in its emphasis on human culture, as opposed to instinct, as the main determinant of human behavior. Arguably, the first signs of cultural traditions in the form of primitive stone tools are two million years old. Since that early time we have evolved as beings whose behavior is shaped by culture. Admittedly, that culture is often violent. But the flexibility of human institutions and values (as opposed to biology), the existence of at least a few peaceful cultures, and the human desire for peace are powerful arguments against an inherently aggressive human nature. We have a capacity for cooperation and peacefulness as well as for warfare.

The institutions of peace are the basis for a tradition of research in the social sciences. Marcel Mauss's classic study of the gift, Durkheim's view of social solidarity, Simmel's concept of the "sociative instinct," Kropotkin's examination of mutual aid, Levi-Strauss's views of reciprocity, Freud's notion of Eros, and economists' and social psychologists' views of exchange theory all imply a view of humans who are capable of peaceful dialogue, cooperation, intermarriage, and even love. It could not be otherwise, for the fact that the species survives implies that we are able to transcend aggression. The articles in this volume demonstrate this capacity. The contributors examine both the design and operation of enduring peace systems (see the articles by Staub, Gregor and Robarchek, and Demarest) and the deliberate transformation of belligerence to peace (see the Robarcheks' description of the nearly overnight self-pacification of the Waorani and Crenshaw's study of the cessation of terrorist violence).

Looked at from the perspective of humans as molded by culture, questions of peace and war are largely about learned behavior. The most extreme version of the opposing view, in which humans are inherently violent, seems to have a projective quality: our own faults are fobbed off on our instincts, for which, presumably, we bear relatively little responsibility. More to the point, peace does exist, even if it is relatively rare. Let us now look at some of the findings of peace research to see what we have learned so far.

Absolute peace and relative peace. "Peace," Shelley once wrote, "is in the grave." If we define peace as the total absence of violence in an entire society, Shelly is correct. Perfect peace does not exist. All human societies have at least some violence. The Semai, as described by Gregor and Robarchek in chapter 6, are a group that approaches the minimum of violence. But even the Semai have had experiences with homicide (primarily in dealing with outsiders; see Dentan 1995), and there are only a few other cultures who come close to the Semai record. Also disconcerting for those who seek absolute peace is that the closer we look at peaceful societies the more violent they seem. Hunters and foragers are a case in point (see chapter 3, Knauft) as they have always appeared to be the world's most peaceful peoples. Thus, among the majority of them, war is all but unknown. Often their reaction to external threat is to flee rather then fight. Their values are peaceful, and they view violence as frightening and atypical (Dentan 1988). Recent field studies, however, show that foragers are capable of violence. Richard Lee, who has worked among the !Kung Bushmen for many years, has discovered that homicides are fairly common even if organized violence (war) is not. Based on his data, the estimated homicide rate of the !Kung (41.9 per 100,000 [Knauft 1987: 464]) is nearly four times as high as the overall rate in the United States, and almost two thirds the homicide rate of such urban areas as Detroit (58.2 per 100,000 in 1985). It is important to realize that the !Kung data are not far out of line with what we know of other small scale societies, which may reveal similar rates of homicide.

Bruce Knauft (1987) suggests that we have underreported aggression in such cultures because of their antiviolent ethic (which may have been confused with reality by some anthropologists) and a low absolute rate of aggressive encounters in any single community. In fact, many years may go by before there is a violent episode in a small tribal community. Nonetheless, Knauft calculates that the overall rate of homicide in some apparently nonviolent societies is actually higher than our own experience in the United States (see, however, chapter 4, note 7, for a critique of statistical comparisons). Further, even a low rate of interpersonal violence may have a massive impact on the psychological tranquility of a small community. This is especially the case where perpetrators and victims interact on a daily basis and are often close kin. For example, Marjorie Shostak, who describes the !Kung as essentially peaceful, nonetheless provides extended quotes from her informants that graphically describe the very high human cost of violence in a "peaceful" culture (1983).

What are we to conclude from the literature? First, there are no cultures that wholly eliminate the possibility of interpersonal violence. Second, a good number of societies, especially those at the simplest socioeconomic level, appear to have successfully avoided organized violence, that is, war. This is a significant accomplishment.

We can do better in the search for absolute peace if we drop the requirement that an entire society refrain from violence. This allows us to consider subgroups of larger societies. Here, in the United States, we may look at the Hutterites or the Amish communities whose value system is antiviolent and who are in fact incredibly peaceful. Robert Dentan comments that "no Old Order Amish person has ever been arrested for a felony . . . nor, in over 350 years, has any Hutterite slain another in a bruderhof community" (1994: 70). If we wish to look at larger segments of mass societies, there are still some reasonable choices of nearly antiviolent peoples. The most peaceful people in American culture may be the "tribe" inhabiting our own suburbs, where rates of violence and physical aggression are lower than any other easily identifiable portion of our heterogeneous society, and perhaps as low as any other culture. The lesson for us as students of human society is that we must be willing to study peace where we find it, even if it is less than perfect and crops up in unexpected places.

Would we like to be perfectly peaceful? Absolute peace is empirically nonexistent. The experience of the most peaceful societies, however, suggests what it could be like. Peaceful tribal bands are often refugee peoples (even the peaceful suburbanites have fled the cities) who have had traumatizing experiences at the hands of more aggressive societies (Dentan 1988). Peace is achieved in such groups at least as much by fear as by affection. "To be angry is not to be human; but to be fearful is," claim the Chewong of the Malay tropical rain forest (Howell 1989). Avoidance of conflict and flight from danger are their main techniques of defense. As is described in "Two Paths to Peace" (chapter 6, Gregor and Robarchek) one of the most peaceful of known societies, the Semai, achieve their status at the cost of both fear and some suppression of individual autonomy. Nonviolent subgroups, such as the Hutterites, also pay a price for peace, in that they tend to be rigid and authoritarian in their values (Dentan 1994). The experience of these peaceful groups provides us with an important lesson that shows that humans are capable of living in nearly nonviolent societies. The scarcity of such peoples implies that the suppression of all violence is not easy. Moreover, the methods of achieving near total nonviolence suggest that total peace may come at a high cost.

The fact that there are few societies that come close to an absolute definition of peace encourages us to include for study peaceful processes as well as peaceful societies. The contributors to this volume examine peace in some very quarrelsome places: reconciliation among occasionally violent nonhuman primates, the relative peace (and its collapse) of the often warlike ancient Maya, the rejection of violence by formerly terrorist groups, and the peaceful epochs that may emerge from thoughtfully concluded wars. Just as no (or few) societies are wholly peaceful, few are completely violent. Social life is simply not possible in a Hobbesian war of one against all. All societies, therefore, are potentially of interest for the student of peace.

Characteristics of relatively peaceful societies. The comparative study of peaceful societies is just beginning in the social sciences, and there are still no generally agreed upon standards as to how such cultures would be identified or how degrees of peacefulness would be measured. Indeed, for some, the whole enterprise of identifying societies as peaceful or otherwise is an illusion, since what constitutes an aggressive act in one culture may not be perceived that way in another (Heelas 1989). In contrast, our position is that the effects of violence are so massive and consequential, that we may reasonably deal with objective definitions of what constitutes peace. David Fabbro (1978) provides a sensible list of characteristics of peaceful cultures, which are also included in Bonta's (1993) bibliographic selection of peaceful societies: they do not engage in warfare; there is no standing military organization; there is relatively little interpersonal violence; and there is an ethic of interpersonal harmony. These cultures have a number of common characteristics: they are small in size, simple in technology, and socially nonhierarchical. In contrast, war and organized aggression are associated with community size and cultural development, a finding that has been replicated in numerous studies (Wright 1965; Borch and Galtung 1966; Eckhardt 1975; and Wiberg 1981). In addition to being small in scale and having a simple economy, peaceful peoples tend to be geographically isolated—living on islands, mountain tops, Arctic wastelands, and plateaus surrounded by malaria-infested jungles. In some cases this isolation is a strategic adaptation to dealing with the more aggressive societies that surround them.

Moreover, when faced with serious dissension, the response is to break up the group rather than to seek a solution. In short, many peaceful societies appear to achieve their status by evading rather than solving the problems of intertribal relations. Nonetheless, there is also evidence that peace in such groups is a positive achievement. Hence the most peaceful communities are those where children are reared nonabusively. Peoples who neglect and mistreat their children have higher frequencies of warfare and internal violence; in fact, the treatment of children is the best predictor of the presence and intensity of violence, if not the form that it takes (Ross 1993: 127).

Kinds of peace. Those who have studied peace have generally classified the institutions of peace as "positive" and "negative." Negative peace, defined simply as the absence or avoidance of war (Barash 1991: 9), is typically based on deterrence, while positive peace incorporates the notions of economic and social justice and harmony in group relations: it "is more than merely the absence of war or even the absence of violence. It refers to a condition of society in which exploitation is minimized or eliminated altogether, and in which there is neither overt violence nor the more subtle phenomenon of structural violence" (Barash 1991: 8). This last condition, the elimination of structural violence, raises issues of moral judgment. Hence, in his textbook of peace studies, Barash sees a shopkeeper who runs a segregated store or even the employees of the ill-fated pesticide plant in Bhopal, India, as contributors to "structural violence" and thereby subverters of positive peace (Barash 1991: 9).

Although the notion of positive and negative peace was a reasonable initial formulation, it may linger in the literature past its time. It positions peace studies in an evaluative and even activist stance, with a bias toward some social forms and away from others. Barash and others squarely face this issue and justify their positions by likening peace studies to the study of medicine. Who would want to speak up in favor of disease? Human institutions and their interactions, however, are more ambiguous than the relationship of biological parasite and host. Violence has been profoundly creative in human cultural evolution as well as the source of much misery. Considering that some highly peaceful societies suppress violence at the cost of individual autonomy (see chapter 6, Gregor and Robarchek), we should be cautious about prescribing for society. Even if we feel that our research urges us in that direction, categories of thought should not be merged with moral judgments. In lieu of positive and negative peace, I suggest a tripartite classification of peaceful societies and institutions: *sociative peace*, *restorative peace*, and *separative peace*.

Sociative peace. Sociative peace consists of the institutions, values, and attitudes that bind individuals in relationships of interest and sentiment. These are the most fundamental and surely the most ancient human institutions. They include reciprocity and cooperation, and the associated emotions and values of empathy and warmth. Throughout this volume these mechanisms of peace are explored in detail. Perhaps the most fundamental example is *legitimacy*, the perception that power within a society is exercised appropriately and morally. Kenneth Boulding (1989 and chapter 11 of this volume) cogently argues that this form of power may peacefully order a society by generating bonds of loyalty and a sense of community. In chapter 4, Leslie Sponsel examines evidence for sociative peace in the earliest records of archaeology and human evolution. Using a more psychological perspective, Ervin Staub, in chapter 5, demonstrates that the institutions of sociative peace require that the self be constructed in ways that are different from aggressive communities. Perceptions of out groups, willingness to take action in the interest of others, the actions of bystanders, and the cognitive and emotional maturity of the individual are inextricably linked to the development of peaceful systems. Finally, since the institutions of sociative peace are the basic fabric of social life, we find it among even the most aggressive societies and groups. Thus, in her study of terrorism in chapter 9, Martha Crenshaw shows that terrorist movements have abandoned violence simply because they came to believe it was wrong.

Restorative peace. A second class of institutions and attitudes are those I classify as restorative peace. The notion of restorative peace reflects the fact that no peace system is perfect. All societies must have ways of separating would-be belligerents, dampening the spiral of conflict, and reconciling former adversaries. Many institutions serve this purpose, including those of conflict management and conflict resolution. The most fundamental is the interpersonal process of reconciliation. In chapter 2, the primatologist Frans de Waal shows that reconciliation is not limited to human beings. Indeed, it is a critical part of the behavioral repertoire of nonhuman primates. Among humans, with our greatly elaborated cognitive processes, restoration and creation of peace is a continual process that occurs within and between groups. Many of the contributions to this volume are about restorative peace. Of special interest are extraordinary examples of how cultures and subgroups can move from intensely violent to peaceful modes of life. Clayton and Carole Robarchek describe the creation of a peaceful society among the Waorani of Ecuador, who formerly may have had the distinction of being one of the world's most violent cultures, in which sixty percent of all deaths were caused by violence. Similarly, John Vasquez demonstrates how peace may emerge from war. If peaceful epochs are to endure, however, wars must be concluded thoughtfully.

Separative peace. In an ideal world, sociative and restorative peace would be enough to maintain stable, nonviolent relationships between and within communities. It would seem, however, that more is needed. Separative peace—the peace that is maintained by evasion, disjunction, deterrence, or fear seems to provide what is missing. In its simplest form, this is the peace of nonrelationship: the peace, for example, of the Arctic Inuit and African Hottentot. Though it may seem otherwise, nonrelationship is hardly a trivial form of peace, since any relationship implies the possibility of violence. Thus, in a review article, J. David Singer (1981) maintains that diffusion and contagion of war through systems of alliance and enmity may be the most promising approach to understanding its occurrence. Moreover, he summarizes a variety of research suggesting that the frequency of war in state-level societies is directly proportional to their number of immediately adjacent neighbors. Separative peace, even if it is as simple as noncontiguity, is therefore a way of maintaining tranquility. Several of the societies described in this volume, notably the Semai and the Mehinaku (chapter 6, Gregor and Robarchek) and the Waorani (chapter 7, Robarchek) have maintained peace by keeping a substantial distance between themselves and other peoples.

Deterrence is one of the more significant forms of separative peace. Although its role in maintaining the peace during the Cold War remains a subject of debate among political scientists, it is a crucial factor in maintaining stable relationships in many societies. In this volume we will look closely at deterrence within relatively peaceful societies (see chapter 6, Gregor and Robarchek), at the role of deterrence in affecting the decision by terrorists to give up violence (chapter 9, Crenshaw), and at the impact of deterrence in forming state-level policies of peace and war (see chapter 8, Demarest, and chapter 10, Vasquez).

Sociative peace, restorative peace, and separative peace are analytically separable, but in practice they merge. For example, intermarriage among the Mehinaku of Brazil and their neighbors (see chapter 6, Gregor and Robarchek) is a mechanism of sociative peace that brings husbands and wives from different political communities together. As a result their loyalty to their home community is often in conflict with the allegiance they owe their in-laws. Divided loyalties and distant residence suggest the separation and disjunction characteristic of separative peace.

Similarly, Ervin Staub, in chapter 5, examines the psychology of peace. Quite deliberately, he focuses on the mechanisms of sociative peace, such as empathy. Yet, it turns out, one of the essential elements of interpersonal peace is the role played by bystanders. Bystanders are gentle agents of separative, deterrent peace, in that their presence is both a social sanction and a way of shaming those who would commit violent acts.

The key to peace. Sociative, restorative, and separative peace are varied and intertwined within the same culture and society. Recognizing this fact is in some ways a disappointment. We would like to discover the secret to peace. In our imagination it would be a transferable key that could unlock peace in our own culture and others. The reality turns out to be more complex. Peace, where and when it occurs, is *over-determined*. We find no single basis for peaceful relationships, but a variety of overlapping institutions, values, and attitudes that run the scale from agape, or selfless love, to skill at reconciliation, to fear of deterrence and avoidance of others. It could hardly be otherwise. Violence is so contagious and politics so volatile that only a wide range of institutions, values, and inner motives can maintain peace.

The Plan of the Volume

"Every naturall Historie is of it selfe pleasing, and very profitable"—José de Acosta, *The Natural and Moral Historie of the Indies* (1604).

In the seventeenth and eighteenth centuries there arose a manner of inquiry known as "natural history." In its broadest terms, following the Oxford English Dictionary, a natural history is "the aggregate of facts relating to the natural objects . . . of a place, or of the characteristics of a class of persons or things." In practice, natural histories brought together differing perspectives to focus a sum of scientific knowledge on a particular topic or, especially, a new phenomenon. *A Natural History of Peace* does not pretend to include the total "aggregate of facts" about peace, but through its interdisciplinary perspective and its objective approach it aims at a natural history of a relatively new object of study. The overall purpose is to examine a number of crucial questions about peace and, inevitably, about aggression, as seen by the social sciences.

The papers are introduced with a short description of the contributions of the authors and the relationship of their work to the other essays in the volume. Under the rubric *What Is Peace?* we begin with an introductory chapter by Donald Tuzin that examines the concept of peace. Exactly what is peace, how does it differ from war, and where is it to be found?

The next topic, *Broad Perspectives on Peace,* looks at the evolution of systems of peace and violence. Frans de Waal examines the process of interpersonal reconciliation, the most basic mechanism of restorative peace, among nonhuman primates. Following de Waal's contribution, Bruce Knauft looks at the evolution of systems of peace and violence through human history and across primate species. Finally, in his article, "The Natural History of Peace: A Positive View of Human Nature and Its Potential," Leslie Sponsel examines the range of evidence from anthropology (archaeology, primate studies, and comparative cultural anthropology) to make the case that peace has been an ongoing reality in the human experience. Dr. Sponsel's chapter, which provides us with more than two hundred citations of the literature, also serves as an overview of peace research in anthropology.

In the third portion of the book, *The Psychology of Peace,* Ervin Staub looks at the psychology of sociative peace. His material is drawn primarily from studies of Western subjects but the mechanisms he identifies, such as empathy and altruism, are clearly relevant to non-Western cultures as well.

The fourth section of the book, *Community-Level Case Studies of Peace,* includes the first in-depth comparison of peaceful societies. In "Two Paths to Peace," Thomas Gregor and Clayton Robarchek contrast the Mehinaku Indians of Brazil with the Semai of Malaysia. Each group has chosen a fundamentally different route toward the creation of a peaceful culture.

Finally, in *State Systems and Cycles of Peace and War,* we look at transitions between aggression and tranquility. Arthur Demarest describes the delicate peace system of the ancient Maya and its final dissolution into chaotic warfare. More optimistically, Clayton and Carole Robarchek examine the remarkably sudden move from community violence to relative peace by the Waorani Indians of Ecuador. Martha Crenshaw shows how the same process can occur among modern terrorists who make the decision to give up violence. Focusing on the process of concluding wars, John Vasquez examines how peace emerges from warfare among modern nation states. Finally, the late Kenneth Boulding, in one of his last essays, concludes with an essentially optimistic view of the human future, one in which we learn to balance opposing interests and manage conflict in ways that are peaceful and creative.

References

Barash, David B. 1991. *Introduction to Peace Studies*. Belmont, Calif.: Wadsworth.

Bonta, Bruce. 1993 *Peaceful Peoples: An Annotated Bibliography*. Metuchen, N.J.: Scarecrow.

Boulding, Kenneth E. 1989. *Three Faces of Power*. Newbury Park, Calif.: Sage.

Dentan, Robert Knox. 1988. Band-level Eden: A Mystifying Chimera. *Cultural Anthropology* 3: 276–284.

———. 1995. Bad Day at Bukit Pekan. *American Anthropologist* 97 (2): 225–230.

———. 1995a. Surrendered Men. In *The Anthropology of Peace and Nonviolence*, ed. Leslie E. Sponsel and Thomas Gregor, 69–108. Boulder, Colo.: L. Rienner.

Eckhardt, William. 1975. Primitive Militarism. *Journal of Peace Research* 9: 55–62.

Fabbro, David. 1978. Peaceful Societies: An Introduction. *Journal of Peace Research* 15: 67–84.

Ferguson, R. Brian. 1988. *The Anthropology of War: A Bibliography*. Occasional Paper No. 1. New York: Harry Frank Guggenheim Foundation.

Freud, Sigmund. 1963. "Why War?" In *Sigmund Freud: Character and Culture*, ed. Philip Rieff. New York: Collier.

Galtung, J. 1968. S.v., "Peace." *International Encyclopedia of the Social Sciences*.

———. 1981. Social Cosmology and the Concept of Peace. *Journal of Peace Research* 18: 183–189.

Howell, Signe. 1989. "To be Angry is not to be human; but to be fearful is": Chewong Concepts of Human Nature. In *Societies at Peace: Anthropological Perspectives*, ed. S. Howell and R. Willis, 45–59. London: Routledge

Howell, Signe and Roy Willis. 1989. *Societies at Peace: Anthropological Perspectives,* ed. S. Howell and R. Willis. London: Routledge.

Knauft, Bruce M. 1987. Reconsidering Violence in Simple Human Societies. *Current Anthropology* 28: 457–500.

Heelas, Paul. 1989. Identifying Peaceful Societies. In *Societies at Peace: Anthropological Perspectives*. ed. S. Howell and R. Willis. London: Routledge.

Nakhre, Amrut. 1976. Meanings of Nonviolence: A Study of Satyagrahi Attitudes. *Journal of Peace Research* 13: 185–196.

Rohrl, Vivian J., M. E. R. Nicholson and Mario D. Azmora. 1992. *The Anthropology of Peace: Essays in Honor of E. Adamson Hoebel. Studies in Third World Societies*, 47–48. Williamsburg, Va.: Department of Anthropology, College of William anmd Mary.

Ross, Marc Howard. 1993. *The Culture of Conflict: Interpretations and Interests in Comparative Perspective*. New Haven, Conn.: Yale University Press.

Shostak, Marjorie. 1983. *Nisa: The Life and Words of a !Kung Woman*. New York: Vintage.

Singer, J. David. 1981. Accounting for International War: The State of the Discipline. *Journal of Peace Research* 13: 1–18.

Sipes, Richard G. 1973. War, Sports and Aggression: An Empirical Test of Two Rival Theories. *American Anthropologist* 75: 64-86.

Sponsel, Leslie and Thomas Gregor, eds. 1995. *The Anthropology of Peace and Nonviolence*. Boulder, Colo.: L. Rienner.

Wallensteen, Peter, ed. 1988. *Peace Research: Achievements and Challenges*. Boulder, Colo.: Westview.

Westing, Arthur H. 1982. War as a Human Endeavor: The High-Fatality Wars of the Twentieth Century. *Journal of Peace Research* 3: 261–264.

Wiberg, Hakan. 1981. What Have We Learned About Peace? *Journal of Peace Research* 15: 110–149.

Wright, Q. 1965. *A Study of War*. Chicago: University of Chicago Press.

ONE

What Is Peace?

1

The Spectre of Peace in Unlikely Places:* Concept and Paradox in the Anthropology of Peace

DONALD TUZIN

■ What is peace? Donald Tuzin, a social anthropologist who works among the Arapesh people of New Guinea, finds that this is a deceptively difficult question. Peace is not simply the absence of war or a "feeling state (usually fleeting) that is marked by an absence of inner turmoil." Rather it is an idealized and probably universal view of human relationships that is seldom, if ever, fully realized in daily affairs. As such, peace is quite different from its semantic opposite, war, which is all too real. Yet, peace and war are nonetheless closely linked. Frequently, the effort to achieve peace and security motivates and explains the most aggressive behaviors. Thus, according to St. Augustine, "For what else is victory than the conquest of those who resist us? And when this is done there is peace. For every man seeks peace by waging war. . . ." In Tuzin's essay we follow "the spectre of peace" to its strangest haunts. Along the way, in this provocative and wide-ranging introduction to the nature of peace, we examine peace and war in both tribal and Western societies.

A HISTORIAN of China, Jonathan D. Spence (1985) describes how the Chinese ideograph for war, pronounced "wu," is divisible along a diagonal axis into two separate ideographs, "the upper one of which represents the word for spear, the lower a word with the sense of 'to stop' or 'to prevent.'" To imagine the ideograph divided in this fashion is to follow "a tradition among Chinese scholars reaching back almost two millennia, a tradition that allowed one to see, buried inside the word for war, the possibilities, however frail, of peace" (p. 24).

This image of peace as something "buried inside" of war captures very well the particular ontology of "peace" that is my main subject matter. My thesis is that peace belongs to a family of terms, which, unlike its congeries of opposites, refer not to material states of being, except in a special, aesthetic sense to be discussed. Rather, they refer to ideas that act as orientative, motivative, or, in Karl Popper's stronger sense, "regulative," principles. Call them what you will—ideals, values, illusions,

3

chimeras, ideological or rhetorical devices (highly consequential for behavior)—they are yet unattainable in the material form for which they are often mistaken or with which they are often mistakenly compared. Hence the characterization of peace as spectral in my title. By various means I wish to argue that the main haunt of this spectre is—paradoxically, as the Chinese knew—war.[1]

Definitions rarely make for scintillating topics, but in a volume dealing with peace the question of what peace is should not be further postponed. And postponed it has been. In the vast scholarly literature dealing with topics that bear directly or by implication on peace, surprisingly little examination is given to peace as such. Generally speaking, the nature of peace is taken for granted, in contrast to deliberate, sometimes dogged, studies of war and aggression.[2] When peace is mentioned at all, the treatment is nearly always unreflective, contradictory, or subservient to some moral or scientific doctrine. Disarray at such a basic level breeds spurious disagreements, unnecessary polarities, and misdirected arguments. Lest this mischief be compounded by the unorthodox features of my own perspective, let me situate it relative to some of the commonly held alternatives, before applying it to certain problems of peace and war in Melanesia.

* * *

To my knowledge nearly all writers on the subject—myself included—regard peace as having an intimate, indeed intrinsic, relationship with its opposite term. The opposite term is usually war, but in other than sociological contexts it may be, for example, anxiety, agitation, arousal, or argumentation. Thus we speak of being "at peace with oneself" to refer to a feeling state (usually fleeting) that is marked by an absence of inner turmoil. Furthermore, the relativistic nature of peace has evidently been recognized for a long time, for it must have been this idea that Spinoza was reacting against when he wrote, "Peace is not an absence of war; it is a virtue, a state of mind, a disposition for benevolence, confidence, justice" (*Tractatus Theologico-Politicus*, 1670). By defining peace not as a thing, nor as an absence of a thing, but as a moral condition, Spinoza disclosed a conceptual space in which peace and war—peace and any of its material opposites—can and essentially *do* exist together, because peace abides with (is "buried inside") each and every one of them. If my reading is correct, Spinoza, in saying that peace is "not an absence of war," was not denying a connection between the two. On the contrary, from his statement a case could be made that peace is not only not the absence of war, it is the *presence* of war! This surprising coexistence helps to explain, I believe, why peace has been so difficult to locate ontologically: it is buried just where we would least expect it to be—in the heart of war.

More about this later. For the moment, it is enough to suggest that a model based on a complex coincidence of peace and war is decidedly superior to the more common conception, which construes them as mutually exclusive states, each indicating the other through simple negativity. Margaret Mead (1968) gives one version of this conception—we will see others—when she observes that the "prevention of war" is the "most pressing problem of our generation," adding, "I use the term prevention of warfare rather than the term peace because the idea of peace includes the idea of war, of periods of alternation between recognized peace and recognized war" (p. 235). This construction may be colloquially valid, but it clouds the defining relationship between peace and war, because, indeed, alternativity by itself is no relationship at all. For the same reason, it is not helpful to speak of peace and war as symmetrical.

If the relationship is not one of alternativity or symmetry, neither is it a chicken-and-egg loop. Peace and war do engender one another, though in often subtle, always asymmetrical, ways. Social scientists have been slow to acknowledge that peace and war fit together, perhaps because most of them, preferring pen to sword, are reluctant to admit any kinship between the two. History's war makers have known better, however, and some have displayed impressive practical insights into the nature of peace. In particular, I refer to the notion that peace can be a principal element in war—as motive, as strategic objective, and even as tactical criterion.[3]

The idea has been around for a long time, though never to my knowledge has it been enunciated theoretically. In the fourth century, the Roman military theorist Flavius Vegetius Renatus warned, "Let him who desires peace prepare for war" (prologue to *De Rei Militari*). In a speech delivered in St. Louis on July 20, 1865, fourteen years before pronouncing that "War is all hell," General William Tecumseh Sherman observed that "the legitimate object of war is a more perfect peace."[4] "The war to end all wars"—was that not the epithet given to World War I, ennobling it with the cause most worth fighting for? And although the oratory of Sir Winston Churchill is best known for its stirring defiance of Nazi aggression,[5] in actuality his wartime speeches are progressively more laced with proposals for the organization of international peace and security in the postwar world. This rhetorical evolution reflected the growing domination of military strategies and tactics by issues of peace planning. Long before the final "race for Berlin," the whole affair had become a question of postwar political and economic arrangements. Similarly, peace-promoting institutions such as the League of Nations and the United Nations were inspired not by some peacetime idyll—since we're all friends, let's think how we can keep it that way—but by the threatening edge of the abyss, at places like Verdun and Dunkirk. Hence the asymmetry of the peace-war relationship: If peace engenders war by making it meaningful, war engenders peace by making it possible—at any rate, as possible as it can be.

Questions occur. How can men with such sanguinary careers be trusted to say anything valid or useful about *peace*? Remembering, as obvious examples, Sherman's march to the sea and Churchill's sacrifice of Coventry and revenge upon Dresden, why interpret their tender interest in peace as anything but hypocritical? Should we not retch rather than applaud when certain latter-day warlords are awarded the Nobel Peace Prize simply because they have (probably for sound strategic reasons!) stopped shooting? The temptation to cynicism is very great, but a moralizing dismissal of these cases would neglect the overdetermined character of the impulse to war, which can include a sincere desire for peace, in accord with the paradoxical nature of peace, as such, along the lines I am arguing.[6] This is why, like it or not, when peace is the issue Society seeks advice from its warriors, not its pacifists.

But not just any warrior. The moral distinction between valor and bloodthirstiness is ethnographically commonplace. The "throat-grappling instinct," as Stephen Crane called it, may be highly valued on the battlefield, but nearly all societies distrust the warrior who delights in fighting for its own sake, because too often he is perceived as morally flawed and a potential menace to his own people. Valor, on the other hand, is universally admired, even though it can be just as violent. Why? Because, I suggest, it manifests *the embodiment of peace within the war vestment*, signifying the proper (because human) retention of social goals and ideals even amid brutish practicalities.[7] Fighting for a noble cause—uniting id and superego impulses in a grand, heroic gesture—this is what constitutes the daunting glamor of war, which is the soul of the romantic tradition among Indo-European and many other peoples: the *Iliad* and the *Mahabarata*, the *chansons de geste* and the *Nibelungenlied*, modern versions such as *High Noon*, *Star Wars*, and *Rambo*—the examples are legion. But as regards the "full inwardness of the situation" (James 1911:283), from the subjective standpoint of the idealist-dreamer who imagines that war is the ultimate road to ultimate peace, none captures the phenomenon better than Stephen Crane, who, in *The Red Badge of Courage*, criticizes war through an acute awareness of its fatal allure. Consider the primitive, tragic fantasy of the protagonist, Henry Fleming, a youthful infantryman in the Army of the Potomac:

Swift pictures of himself, apart, yet in himself, came to him—a blue desperate figure leading lurid charges with one knee forward and a broken blade high—a blue, determined figure standing before a crimson and steel assault, getting calmly killed on a high place before the eyes of all. He thought of the magnificent pathos of his dead body.

These thoughts uplifted him. He felt the quiver of war desire. In his ears, he heard the ring of victory. He knew the frenzy of a rapid successful charge. The music of the trampling feet, the sharp voices, the clanking arms of the column near him made him soar on the red wings of war. For a few moments he was sublime. (Crane 1972[1894]:78–79.)

In competition with such glamor and idealism, what hope is there for the "inglorious arts of peace"?[8] It is all very well to theorize about war as the road to peace; but the many millions who have died on that road might have preferred a better way. William James advised (quoted in MacNeil 1965:v; James 1911b) that we need durable peacetime institutions that will outglorify war and be its "moral equivalent." Only then might we capture the passions of our youth—and, one must add, deflect the far more dangerous passions of their elders, if "passions" is the word to describe the icy, loveless calculations that produce the call to arms. The search for substitute institutions goes on and on. Meanwhile, the fact remains that peace is easier to *obtain* than to *sustain*. How to preserve the charisma of peace once peace is achieved and threatens to become habitual? That is the problem; that is where society always stumbles.

This dilemma has defeated peacemakers from the beginning. To speak only of this century: President Woodrow Wilson's "Fourteen Points" address, delivered to the U.S. Congress on January 8, 1918, described in ill-fated detail a plan for the guarantee of peace in the new world order. Churchill grasped the psychological dimensions of the problem when he selected the title for his famous address to Westminster College in Fulton, Missouri, on March 5, 1946. The world knows it as his "Iron Curtain" speech, picking up on one of its arresting metaphors,[9] but the author himself called it, "The Sinews of Peace." Presumably, he intended to ascribe to peace a muscularity all its own, a nobility no less virile than that of war (Churchill 1974). And yet, the oxymoronic ring of the phrase surely defeats this purpose by affirming that such an attitude toward peace is unnatural to our usual ways of thinking. Churchill himself could not sustain this attitude, not even for the duration of the

speech. Yielding to the familiar martial spirit, he closes by fondly referring to the calamitous period just ended as "the glorious years of agony"
(p. 7293). With depressing regularity, peace proves to be an unsatisfying,
insubstantial regime. All too soon the attraction of peace, like that of the
beloved or of the Holy Grail, is discovered to lie in the quest, and only
momentarily in the conquest. Thence begins the impulse toward war, for
only war can regenerate the conditions for that quest. Little else is needed
to explain why warfare is endemic in the world (cf. Montagu 1976:302).

* * *

Some scholars regard the world-historical prevalence and allure of war
as evidence for the innate aggressiveness of the species. Critics counter
that these impulses are not ingrained, but are acquired as part of a cultural
tradition. The implication is that the problem of organized armed aggression can be solved through enlightened social engineering and educational reform. If, however, I am correct about the logical, psychological,
and experiential integration of peace and war, then neither of these other
positions is warranted, and the disagreement between them is at once
irrelevant and unresolvable. Before addressing these matters directly, I
should make a few clarifying remarks about my own argument.

Returning to the original ontological question, there are writers who
use the idea of peace but deny that it can be positively defined. In effect,
this opinion aligns peace with the I-don't-know-what-it-is-but-I-know-
what-I-like school of art criticism. For example, in a discussion of war and
peace in Eskimo society, Riches (1987:18) avers that peace "is a state of
affairs which is objectively almost impossible to define, except as the
absence of something (i.e., war, violence)." The qualifier "almost" leaves
Riches's meaning slightly unclear, but one can readily appreciate the
implication that *peace* has, at the least, definitional peculiarities. A parallel case, perhaps, is *health*. Is health definable except as the absence of disease?[10]

The mistake made by phrasing the issue in these terms is to assume
that peace and war, health and disease, refer to contrarieties occurring
within the same order of things. Instead, what I have been arguing is that
peace and health exist not as objective states but as ideals contemplated
from the point of view of their opposites. One thinks about, longs for,
objectifies, and in so doing vivifies the idea of health especially during
times of sickness, peace especially during times of war.[11] We achieve
these ideals (or, more likely, experience the illusion of doing so) in the
exhilaration, relief, and sense of contentment that comes from discover-
ing that the war or the illness is *over*, the hardships and misery are behind

us. But such experiences, being aesthetic in kind, are as fleeting as they are intense. Even without the reoccurrence of conflict or illness, it is not long before peace or health, as the case may be, resumes its normal transparency. In other words, unlike the situation among nonhuman animals, who also fight and also get sick, the awareness of peace and health as imaginable alternative states informs (is "buried inside") the human experiences of war and disease, respectively. I would go further: Peace and health in these terms constitute the *consciousness* of war and disease, respectively, which is their distinctively human attribute.[12] The obverse, however, does *not* apply: peace and health are self-sufficient; they refer only to themselves. That is why they are unstable.

Please understand. In treating peace as a kind of spectral presence, I intend nothing mystical. Peace is as "real" as any of its opposites, though its reality is usually apprehended by inference (pragmatically, in the Peircean sense) rather than by direct experience. To clarify, consider another parallel case: Karl Popper's notion of the asymmetrical relationship of "truth" and "falsity," which is the cornerstone of his philosophy of science. According to Popper (e.g., 1963), truth is approached only through the elimination of error—*approached*, but never definitively attained, for we can never be sure that the next test will not falsify our present wisdom. Unlike error, which can be positively determined and can therefore be systematically eliminated, truth must always remain a vision, an ideal that orients inquiry. The reality of this vision, as in the instances of peace and health, can be demonstrated operationally. Thus, Popper (1963:226) reasons that "we search for truth, but may not know when we have found it; that we have no criterion of truth, but are nevertheless guided by the idea of truth as a *regulative principle* . . .; and that, though there are no general criteria by which we can recognize truth—except perhaps tautological truth—there are criteria of progress toward the truth. . . ."[13] Peace has these same defining properties. As with the methodological linkage of truth and falsity, we approach peace through the elimination of war; hence the paradoxical inherence of peace *within* war.

* * *

With this background, let us consider the undying question of whether humans are naturally aggressive or naturally peaceful. On one side are those who claim that the proclivity for aggression is innate in our species and that war is the collective expression of this behavioral tendency. War and aggression, then, not peace and amity, are Nature's script; remove society's restraining conventions, and humans would revert to their original brutish condition.[14] The position is familiar

enough to require no further explication here. On the other side are those
who contest the Hobbesian interpretation by pointing to the evidence of
societies that do not practice warfare.[15] Never mind that they are
extremely few—one or two dozen, at most. Never mind that they are typically minimal operations—tiny hunter-gatherer bands in which close fil-
iation affords virtually the only organizing principle. What matters is that
even one counter-example is sufficient to refute the claim of innate
aggressivism, proving that this behavior and its institutional embellish-
ments are culturally determined (Sponsel 1990). The identification of
such peoples has been cultural anthropology's singular contribution to
the issue, which, prior to this century, had been a question for philosophers.[16] Indeed, it could said that the Gentle Other is anthropology's own
version of the spectre of peace "buried inside" of war—a faint glimmer of
human possibility in an ethnographic world riven with conflict and violence (Sponsel 1990).

Throughout its long history the quality of the "innatism" debate has
suffered from distracting ideological programs. "Human nature" is perhaps the deadliest rhetorical weapon ever invented. It may also be the
most widely proliferated—used and abused from all points on the ideological compass. Anthropological appeals to human nature are always
suspect, because they are so easily (fairly or not) associated with ideological causes or cultural biases. In the present case, each side thinks it
has won the contest, and yet neither side admits defeat. This odd situation draws attention to rhetoric and *motives* and away from the quality of
evidence and arguments. Usually it happens that those of the "innate
aggressivist" camp are accused of being crypto-militarists—either apolo-
gists for warfare and aggression (because they argue for their biological
inevitability) or scientific prostitutes to repressive statist measures
intended to squelch these otherwise (supposedly) inevitable behaviors.
The innate aggressivists deny such ulterior motives, contending that their
accusers are either *themselves* ideologically motivated (e.g., as supporters
of various peace and disarmament movements) or are foolish enough to
think they can annul the bad news by shooting the messenger.

How long must this debate go on? After centuries without empirical
resolution, one must wonder whether it will *ever* be resolved within the
terms in which it is cast. If not, let it be restored to its proper place among
the philosophers and theologians. As a better alternative, I propose that
the conception of peace presented above obviates this wearisome debate
by subsuming most of its features. To recapitulate:

(1) Peace and its opposite are conceived to *co-occur*—the former being the
    end, the latter the means, in a dynamic process that is constantly

regenerating itself. Until someone identifies a normal gene governing "aggression" or "gentleness," all claims concerning ultimate "natural" priorities are undecidable.

(2) Within the integrated terms of cultural meaning and human consciousness, "peace" precedes its opposite. That is to say, the idea of peace together with the desire for peace are often the chief motivations for nonpeaceful acts. In this sense, "peace" induces peace-seeking behavior and constitutes the human significance of that behavior. In both social and psychological realms, violence that is devoid of such goals—whether fully cognized or not—may be said to be inhuman, in the strict sense.

(3) In any interpretative model, aggression and warfare must not be conflated. Although war leaders may still inflame passions and encourage hateful attitudes toward the enemy, modern warfare's chilling distinction, at least since the development of field artillery and rifled musketry, is the degree to which it has become impersonal (Wallace 1968:177-178; Holloway 1968:30; Keegan 1978:331; cf. Fornari 1975). The more we learn about "primitive warfare," the more we discover that it, too, is not totally dependent on aggressive sentiments (see no. 4). In short, warfare cannot be adequately described as a direct expression of behavioral aggression, but must be seen as also arising from a welter of social and historical contingencies.

(4) Obversely, in the absence of certain minimum levels of societal scale and organization, behavioral aggression will not produce activity recognizable as "warfare." This and the preceding point, taken together, vitiate the relevance of supposedly gentle societies (!Kung, Mbuti, Tasaday, etc.) to the problem of organized, armed conflict among industrial societies, especially on a scale that imperils life on earth.

(5) This model applies equally to sociological and psychological processes, in that both groups and individuals strive for an idealized condition of peace, if necessary, through a preemptive attack on others who are perceived to be a threat to the security of oneself or one's group. In principle, the drive for security must be seen as peace-seeking, even though war makers have been known to exploit this idea as an excuse to initiate hostilities.

* * *

The first half of this chapter proposed a theoretical perspective on peace, with special reference to its paradoxical relationship to war. My interest in this topic originated in a long-standing desire to make general sense of certain ethnographic facts and wider ethnological patterns involving peace and war in Melanesia. The remainder of this chapter will retrace those roots, in the hope of demonstrating the usefulness of the theoretical perspective they engendered.

To provide some necessary background, I should give a brief account of my ethnographic experience among the Ilahita Arapesh, a village-based horticultural society occupying the hilly hinterland of the East Sepik region of New Guinea.[17] They are closely related, linguistically, to the Mountain Arapesh—a people made famous for their gentleness by Margaret Mead (e.g., 1935, 1938, 1961). No wonder the Mountain Arapesh attracted scholarly attention: their pacifism rendered them unique in all of the large, exceedingly violent area of Melanesia. In September 1968, the year before I began my first fieldwork, Mead advised me that Arapesh-speaking groups living in the plains south of the coastal Prince Alexander and Torricelli mountains were utterly unlike the mild-mannered mountain people among whom she had worked. The plainsmen were feared as sorcerers, among other things, and were in direct contact with (and therefore likely to be influenced by) the warlike Abelam, whose not-too-remote origins were near the middle reaches of the Sepik River (see map 1).

This proved to be good advice. Outwardly, the Ilahita (one of four Arapesh-speaking peoples of the plains) displayed much the same baleful enterprise as the Abelam, Iatmul, Mundugamor, and other groups of the Middle Sepik. They subscribed to an elaborate men's cult of war (named and personified as the Tambaran) whose spirits demanded human sacrifice and whose giant house was festooned with trophies of enemy heads and other body parts. Until the Australians secured administrative control in the early 1950s, warfare concerns saturated daily life. Hostilities were interrupted only by ritual truce periods mandated by the Tambaran in tune with the initiation cycle. In addition to chronic inter-village warfare and raiding, to which I will return later in the chapter, intravillage discord was an almost daily occurrence, although there were effective social mechanisms for minimizing its severity and social divisiveness. According to arguments presented elsewhere (Tuzin 1974, 1976, 1980, 1988, 1989), these social mechanisms account for the large size and stability of villages in this region. Ilahita, the site of my research and the village after which the cultural-dialect group takes its name, had a population of 1,490 in 1970, making it possibly the largest traditional village in all of New Guinea.[18]

What is one to make of the radical difference between Mountain Arapesh and Ilahita Arapesh as regards their respective investments in peace and war? For one thing, the comparison confirms the potency of historical factors in determining such tendencies. By my reckoning, the significant divergences began fairly recently, during the final half or third of the

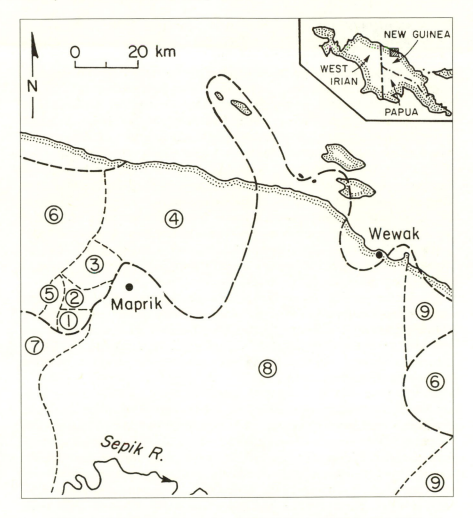

MAP 1. Major Language Groups of the East Sepik Province (after Laycock 1973)

TORICELLI PHYLUM
Arapesh Family
  Southern Arapesh
    1. Ilahita dialect
    2. Balif dialect
    3. Supari dialect
  4.Mountain Arapesh
  5. Bumbita
  6. Other Torricicelli languages

SEPIK-RAMU PHYLUM
  7. Nukuma Family, including Kwanga
    language
  8. Ndu Family, including Abelam
    language
  9. Other Sepik-Ramu languages

nineteenth century. The "ancestral" form may not have been as peaceful as the Mountain Arapesh of Mead's report, but it was certainly much closer to that pole than to the other. The split in language, geographical range, and security conditions occurred because of the disorderly predatory influx of fierce Ndu-speaking groups from the middle reaches of the Sepik River—Abelam principally, but also Boiken, in the east, and Kwanga in the west (Forge 1966; Roscoe 1989; see map 1). Some autochthonous Arapesh may have been killed or absorbed, but a large number were displaced. Of the latter, many, along with some luckless Abelam groups, fled to Ilahita and neighboring villages just beyond the fighting zone. Swelled in numbers, these settlements became a barrier to further Abelam encroachment in that direction.

All of this brought great changes to the Ilahita Arapesh. Militarism became the way of survival, both because of continuing Abelam pressures and because of secondary displacements and hostilities generated *among* the traumatized Arapesh villages. These secondary effects in turn created incentives to form alliances between Arapesh and Abelam villages, which, temporarily at least, could join against a common enemy from one or the other side of the cultural boundary. Such contacts became conduits through which the Ilahita Arapesh imported a good many elements of Abelam social and ritual organization. Most notably, the Ilahita adopted the senior grades of the Tambaran cult, those presiding over the ideology and conduct of war.

To the east, as best one can tell, the effects of Abelam encroachment on the indigenous Arapesh were very different. There, the intruders established villages well up into the foothills of the coastal range, even crossing over to the coast (map 1). While some Arapesh villages survive to this day in the lower foothills (those Mead called, somewhat misleadingly, "Plains Arapesh"), most of the Arapesh in the eastern sector found refuge in the rugged heart of the mountains. Their settlements were tiny: Alitoa, where Mead worked, was the largest, with twenty-eight houses and a human population of eighty-seven (Mead 1938:202). Chilly, misty, steep—their uncomfortable, forbidding habitat held no attractions for the land-hungry intruders, and they were left alone. If there was little or no warfare, the reasons are obvious: there was hardly anyone to fight, and hardly anything to fight over or about.[19]

Does this mean that Mountain Arapesh "gentleness" has nothing to do with their "nature" (let alone human nature in general), but instead is simply a result of historical contingency? Yes, in the sense that an accident of circumstance could have propelled the Mountain Arapesh along the same path of militarization and societal expansion followed by their

Ilahita cousins. But also, no, because of another aspect of this comparison that has not been mentioned. I referred above to Ilahita bellicosity as being "outwardly" salient. And yet, in many symbolic and behavioral areas a countercurrent is detectable—strong and steady, but reaching the cognitive surface only rarely. Difficult to define clearly, it shimmers as a kind of spectral presence within a wide range of normatively violent acts and images. At the cost of doing violence, myself, to the richness of the data on this point, let me offer a few examples, by way of illustration rather than proof.

(1) Beneath the brutal misogyny of the Tambaran, one discovers that men experience recurrent guilt over the public stances they are required to maintain. At considerable risk to themselves, they often perform surreptitious, mitigating acts of kindness toward their wives and children (Tuzin 1982). Cultural practices and the observed behavior of middle-aged men whose wives have died also appear to contain a guilt component (Tuzin 1975). These and other regular manifestations of masculine guilt, despite elaborate rationalizations available to them, indicate a shadow morality that persists as a kind of indwelling critic of outwardly affirmed standards.

(2) Although the Ilahita fought often and skillfully, there is evidence that they were "reluctant warriors" (Tuzin 1976:44 et seq.; cf. Mead 1968:216). Furthermore, battle and homicide trophies were not granted to individuals, but to the Tambaran, which was credited with all war killings. Although successful warriors were known as such, they enjoyed no particular kudos, and their deeds were prescriptively anonymous (Tuzin 1980). Valor resided in the Tambaran, not in "his" warrior-drones.

(3) All Tambaran activities (there are many different kinds) rely for their effectiveness on a magical substance, incantation, or procedure. Such magic *will fail* if all of the ritual workers are not in spiritual accord, united in their common purpose. Whether it is to raise "his" giant house, bestow renewal on all species, or insure victory in the next battle, the Tambaran will not grant success unless all resentments, grudges and dislikes (however hidden) are resolved. For the Arapesh, therefore, the extraordinary power of the Tambaran emanates from the ability of the men to lay aside all their squabblings, which is to say, to create a condition, however temporary, of peace among themselves. Furthermore, although various procedural measures are seen by the villagers to resolve or defuse conflicts (Tuzin 1972, 1974, 1976), thus arriving at peace, negatively, by the elimination of its opposite,

only the Tambaran can effect *positive* peace. This is consistent with the idea that the Tambaran, president of a cult of war, is the only force empowered to declare a truce between warring villages.

(4) The notion that magical action requires peace and spiritual unity among the actors occurs, also, in certain nontraditional ritual spheres that are by no means peculiar to the Ilahita Arapesh. A common ideational feature of "cargo cults," in Ilahita and elsewhere throughout Melanesia, is that the success of the endeavor depends upon all parties being in perfect accord. Likewise, the millenarian goals of Christian charismatic sects—one of which has blossomed in Ilahita in recent years—are widely thought to depend on perfect spiritual harmony. Note that the Ilahita (again, not uncommonly in Melanesia) perceive themselves to be inveterately fractious. (Often I would hear my friends compare their manners invidiously with those of white people, to whom they ascribed perfect civil and domestic bliss.) This implies that the preconditions set for the arrival of the Cargo or of Jesus, as the case may be, are every bit as unlikely and sensational as the sought-for event. To bring Heaven from above, one needs only to create Heaven here below! To the outside observer, there is a poignancy in these questings; because, whatever the stated external goal, one feels that the search is for an ideal that is actually buried inside themselves. It is spectral, like a childhood half-memory, or fragments of a dream, or an inner tune one can almost hear but cannot quite bring from mind to mouth. It is unqualifiedly positive. It is an image of psychical comfort and fulfillment, freedom from strife, absence of enemies inside or out—in a word, peace.

Despite, then, outward appearances to the contrary, the Ilahita Arapesh continue to be haunted by images of peace that connect them, genetically and ethnologically, with their Mountain Arapesh cousins. It would be too much to say that a tumultuous history has swept past the Ilahita without touching their character, but it would be equally erroneous to say that elements of a cultural nature—deep-seated values and orientations they share with the mountain-dwellers—have not survived these enormous events.[20] In ways diverse and often subtle, the people themselves evince awareness of a dissonance between their inner and outer requirements, and the compromises they make constitute the moral life they live. Unlike the Chinese, the Ilahita have no traditional writing system; but buried inside their world of war and emotional want, embedded in their comportment, mythology, and ritual ideas, is "the possibility, however frail, of peace" (Spence 1985:24).

The perspective on peace developed earlier in this chapter helps one to understand how two cultural groups having common ancestry, but subsequently following utterly divergent paths of historical development, can be so alike and yet so different precisely along the axis of the war and peace (pseudo-)polarity. For such a perspective to be worth its salt, however, one should expect it to do more than merely reconcile an apparent discrepancy within the narrow sphere of Arapesh studies, even if that maneuver does serve to protect anthropology's sizable investment in the Mountain Arapesh reputation for gentleness. As an additional test, I should therefore attempt a broader ethnologic purview, analytically controlled through a more specific topical focus. I will stay with Melanesia, for it is the region I know best. Since peace is least likely to be found amid war, and since New Guinea Highlanders are proverbially the most bellicose in the area, the phenomenon of warfare in the New Guinea Highlands is the obvious *pons asinorum* to be crossed by this theory of peace. For, if peace can be found "buried inside" the warfare of these Highlanders (who, unlike the Arapesh, have never been described as gentle), then the theory will have surmounted one of the most difficult tests the ethnographic world has to offer.

Altering the focus in this way involves some reorientation and repetition, for which I ask the reader's patience. The beacon may be only dimly visible at times, but it remains the idea that peace is indigenous to war and is one of its principal features. Unavoidably, I must speak more about war than about peace, both because that is where the published information is concentrated and because the idea of war as the route to peace (in practice and in concept) is intrinsic to my theoretical perspective. All of this raises a prospect that has been implicit until now: that a better understanding of peace automatically improves our understanding of war—the current anthropology of which verges on the primitive.

* * *

Most Melanesian scholars have probably never doubted the importance—perhaps paramount importance—of warfare in shaping the traditional institutions of this region. And yet, until recently, the topic labored under a fair burden of obscurity. Early accounts, often eyewitnessed, were sketchy and conceptually haphazard, while later studies were deprived of the advantages of direct observation. Among the other dazzling opportunities offered to anthropologists by the post–World War II opening of the New Guinea Highlands was the chance, long feared lost, to join the right sorts of facts, in sufficient abundance, to the right sorts of concepts, and achieve an adequate sociocultural account of warfare in

these societies.[21] By the 1970s, enough information was in hand to frame
a reasonably clear outline of institutionalized warfare in the Highlands.
What remained lacking, however, were full-bodied ethnographies specifically aimed at the sociology of war. Then came a series of studies of this
type (e.g., Gardner and Heider 1969; Heider 1970; Koch 1974), culminat-
ing in Mervyn Meggitt's comprehensive monograph on Mae Enga warfare, *Blood is Their Argument* (1977). Meggitt's book is richly furnished
with just the sort of ethnographic nooks and crannies that the spectre of
peace inclines to haunt. Let us begin there.

Meggitt's title, *Blood is Their Argument*, evokes a vivid, violent image,
but it also properly hints that the blood at issue may be of the shared as
well as the spilled variety. This is relevant to a remark made by Karl von
Clausewitz—the Alexis de Tocqueville of War—to the effect that, generally speaking, "civilized" war is an expression of hostile intentions,
whereas primitive war involves both hostile intentions and hostile feelings (Clausewitz 1943:4; orig. 1832–34; cf. Lesser 1968:95). Both types fit
Clausewitz's famous definition of war as "a mere continuation of policy
by other means" (p. 16)—hence the common element of intention—but in
the primitive case savage *emotion* is assigned equal and criterial importance. It is certainly true that warfare and violent emotion are closely
linked in New Guinea. The hyper-masculine ferocity bred into boys and
young men, often under ritual auspices, surely turns them into dedicated
throat-grapplers (Herdt 1982). But the pertinence of such behavioral predispositions to the organized aggression we call war lies in the fact that
the combatants themselves stand very close to the argument. By virtue of
limited societal scale and structural compass, it is *their* woman, *their* pig,
their garden, *their* honor that has been violated, *their* shared blood that
has been spilled. In short, it is their argument, or that of someone close to
them. Granting Clausewitz's distinction, we may say that the special
quality that sets primitive warfare apart from its civilized counterpart
owes itself less to the cultivated savagery of its combatants as to the sociological considerations of scale, along with the close juxtaposition of independent moral and political communities (cf. Hayano 1973:181, 183).

A moment ago I described how the Ilahita Arapesh preoccupation
with war coexisted traditionally with an idealized peace, evidenced in
values and actions, especially those associated with war and ritual violence. The immanence of peace as an abiding goal was analytically significant to me because it opened a way to resolving the discrepancy
between Ilahita Arapesh militarism and Mountain Arapesh pacifism—a
local puzzle gratifyingly solved, nothing more. Wider implications did
not arise, because I assumed that, for Melanesia at least, the philosophi-

cal issue of peace somehow belonged to Arapesh studies. Then came *Blood is Their Argument*, which intimated that the conclusions I had reached about the status of peace in Ilahita might have much greater generality. Specifically, Meggitt's descriptions repeatedly aroused the vagrant suspicion that the Highlanders he observed go to war for the purpose—among others, of course, but perhaps more basic than most— of providing themselves with an excuse to make peace.[22] The longer I lived with the idea, the more respectable it seemed to become, at least as mistress of a body of implications bearing on the ethnology of war and (more exotically) peace in New Guinea and, perhaps, elsewhere.

Although it amounts to a functionalist reductio ad absurdum, the idea of peace being a reason for war usefully highlights the trend of thinking which, for better or worse, has dominated the anthropology of war. Ever since anthropologists began seriously to study this topic, they have been unable to escape the unsettling conclusion that war, whatever moral and philosophic revulsion these scholars may feel toward it, has positive social functions. It adjusts population distribution in friendly accord with environmental resources; it sensibly precludes excess population growth by boosting the mortality rate; in some societies it provides the odd bit of protein; it is the crucible of experience within which "true" masculinity is annealed; finally, and closest to the anthropological heart, it promotes social solidarity among battle comrades.[23] Thus, the human tragedy that is war found intellectual redemption through functionalist interpretations, with the ironic result that peace was left unnoticed and unaccounted for, and, indeed, undefined.

Durkheimian anthropologists were by no means the first to recognize the functional significance of war. Clausewitz insisted that the character and conduct of war are deeply integrated with the wider institutional matrix.[24] In fact, one of the leading questions in his large treatise concerned the extent to which Napoleon, through his brilliantly eccentric tactical successes, may have permanently altered not only the procedures of modern combat but also and more ominously the relationship between war and the nation-state. As a military man—a general in the army of Prussia and head of the state war college—Clausewitz lived with the idea of war, had no trouble accepting its functional value, and treated the whole matter with an air of analytic detachment. This was not true of certain humane scholars, who early in this century viewed with alarm the fiendish developments in weapons technology, the reckless belligerence of world leaders, and the downright idiocy of the Spanish-American War. Still, they had to admit, in the words of William James, that war was "the gory nurse that trained societies to cohesiveness" (1911b:272; see also Sumner 1964). Their hope was that, although human aggression is probably here to stay, its organized form might be eliminated by enlarging the sphere of cohesion to include all nations—a League of Nations (as it was to be called) in which each member yielded part of its sovereignty to a higher, world authority.

As applied to the New Guinea Highlands, the idea of a mediating third party as an agent of peace was discussed by Klaus-Friedrich Koch— on the one hand, as a key to solving the problem of resurgent warfare in the Highlands;[25] on the other, as a notion which by its absence in traditional Highlands society explains the incessancy of warfare in that region (Koch 1974). The latter claim is hard to credit insofar as it rests on an imponderable contingency: if jurally constituted third parties had existed, Highlands warfare would certainly have taken a different form— but then so would everything else! For my purposes the more serious problem with this approach is that it tends to overlook the array of sociocultural agencies which, though not taking the form Koch envisioned, nevertheless set the rhythm of war and peace fairly precisely. This leads me back to the track of my argument.

* * *

The phrase "war and peace," balancing so easily on the tongue, has beguiled most writers into neglecting important sociological asymmetries between what these terms represent. Although previously discussed as a general issue, it is important to see how this asymmetry plays on the ethnographic stage. By most accounts Highlands warfare needs only a spark. Under conditions of corporate responsibility, often set against previous hostilities, an individual grievance—an incident involving oneself, one's kin, or one's property—is entirely sufficient, mutatis mutandis, to launch a thousand ships. Such a hair-trigger model requires the condition that potential enemies live in reasonably close proximity—close enough, that is, for individual offenses to occur. Among the Mae Enga and other Central Highlands groups, warfare is very much a neighborhood affair with little or no regular contact between widely separated communities. This feature likewise promotes the socially embedded quality of Highlands warfare, in which the clarity of hostile relationships is confounded by ties of marriage, trade and potential military alliance.

In contrast with war, the movement to peace is quintessentially a collective affair. Whatever may have prompted the hostilities, the weight of opinion eventually comes to favor a cessation. In this most interesting and scarcely studied moment, immediate tactical concerns are suddenly subordinated to the broader strategic objective, which is and always was *peace*—peace, of course, on terms favorable to one's own group.[26] Fight leaders surrender command to the Big Men, who must then convince their armed followers that peace is now better for them than war. This is a politically delicate business, for it requires that the Big Men successfully represent their political interests, which typically have a strong personal element, in a manner that makes them appear collectively advantageous, especially in the eyes of those closest to the argument.[27] One can hardly imagine a test more exacting of leadership skills in the Big-Man mode.

Before continuing with the war-peace asymmetry, I must digress slightly to consider one type of Mae Enga argument that seems to square badly with my own. According to Meggitt (1977:13), over one-half (57.7%) of Mae wars were fought over land. Here, we must distinguish between minor encroachments leading to wholesale conflict, as against the less frequent instances of a deliberate policy aimed at displacing an enemy from their territory. The former of these is covered by my previous remarks. The latter presents something of a problem, for it implies that war may be arise as a cold-blooded, collective calculation. Rather than set the conquest motive aside as a special case beyond the terms of my argument, I would prefer to draw a self-serving distinction between an aggressor's perceived need for additional land for subsistence, as against the perceived need for *security*. While I accept the claim (Meggitt 1977; Rappaport 1967; Vayda 1976) that war figures into the total ecological arrangement by adjusting population distributions according to available resources (especially land), and while I have no doubt that a group lacking territorial necessities for subsistence will cast about for weak neighbors to throttle, displace, or encroach upon, there are many instances in which the invasion of adjacent lands may be otherwise motivated. I refer to the tendency of densely settled groups to enhance their physical security by extending their defensible boundaries or enlarging, at the enemy's expense, a surrounding buffer zone.[28] This is shown by the widely reported (e.g., Meggitt 1977:26ff.; Rappaport 1967) pattern of conquered lands being reoccupied over a period of time by its previous inhabitants. Once the enemy has been sufficiently fragmented and humbled, reoccupation does not pose a threat; indeed, as petitioners, the vanquished are sometimes added to the ranks of the victors. If land seizure were purely a matter of subsistence need, one would expect the land to be quickly and fully occupied by the hungry aggressors. In those frequent instances where this does not occur, the peace *qua* security motive would appear to prevail.[29] Furthermore, once the matter is phrased in security terms, the potential for individual grievances to escalate reasserts itself, since other members of the group would regard the argument as an immediate threat to themselves.[30]

There is considerable evidence to support this line of interpretation. In an article correlating warfare and land shortage across a range of Papua New Guinea societies, Sillitoe (1977) concludes that wars of territorial conquest, arising from conditions of land shortage, were exceedingly rare. "Ecological explanations account for only a small number of the wars in New Guinea," he notes, "and in many places people drive the defeated off their land to achieve a resounding victory and not because they are under environmental pressure" (p. 80). Of the twenty-eight societies included in his survey, only the Abelam fought wars for the purpose of acquiring the enemy's land (see map 1 and earlier discussion). From my perch among the neighboring Ilahita Arapesh, I would only observe that the Abelam are not a pure case. Although for a complex of reasons having to do with population size, subsistence technology, and environmental limitations, the Abelam were land hungry, conquest was often the result rather than the overt cause of war, to which extent their situation resembles that of the Chimbu and Mae Enga (Sillitoe 1977:73; cf. Brown 1982a, 1982b).

Among the Ilahita Arapesh, territorial conquest was often the stated goal of offensive warfare, but for political rather than subsistence reasons. For leaders in Ilahita village, at least, military policy was explicitly aimed at enlarging the village's security zone. The strategy was to expel enemies from one's borders, disperse them amongst their own allies, and then either colonize the captured territory or offer it for settlement to landless refugees, many of whom had been displaced as a direct or indirect result of Abelam aggression and/or territorial conquest. Alternatively, the object of a conquest could be to insert a friendly settlement between two enemies, thus "breaking the [connecting] liana," that is, severing communication between them. Only once in remembered history (ca. 1938) was a banished enemy, Mamilimbi, permitted to return—not, as it happened, to their home territory, which in the intervening eighteen years had been colonized, but to another piece of land which Ilahita controlled but was not using. The arrangement ended after only four years, however, when old animosities and prior alliances reasserted themselves. During a battle with another enemy, Ilahita warriors noticed some Mamilimbi men fighting on the other side in violation of the promise of neutrality that had been a condition of the return. Angered by this display of ingratitude, Ilahita mustered its forces and drove Mamilimbi away, vowing never to make that mistake again.

Thus, although land changed hands as a result of warfare in this part of the East Sepik region, and although such transfers are intelligible in

ecological terms, attaching causal or motivational significance to either
aspect—or to both, together—not only risks mistaking effect for cause; it
neglects the overdetermined, problematic nature of warfare here and
elsewhere in Papua New Guinea. One often hears Melanesian warfare
described as *endemic* (from the Greek, meaning "peculiar to a people,"
"native," "indigenous")—a feeble, question-begging description, both
because it could apply to all but a very few societies, and because it says
nothing about warfare's place in the social and cultural orders.
"Internecine" is not much better. If either term has any utility, it is
because each carries the connotation of incessancy, a helpful notion in the
Melanesian context, for it locates warfare within the normative or prevailing conditions. If there is a meaningful distinction to be drawn
between "civilized" and "primitive" warfare (contrary to Clausewitz's
criteria of "intention" and "feeling," and see earlier discussion), it is that
the former represents a breakdown in normal relations, intentions, and
feelings, whereas the latter occurs as part of the normal state of affairs. A
vendetta—whether set in Melanesia, a university department, or between
modern nation-states—is thus prototypically "primitive" in character,
because mutual hostility between the parties is so engrained, so much a
part of normal attitudes, that a negotiated resolution seems inconceivable
without either a radical change in circumstances or the intervention of a
third party.

All the more so when institutions develop that are predicated on the
existence of war. Among the Ilahita Arapesh, warfare was structured
around two fairly stable alliances. Villages other than one's own were
either friends or enemies. In general, enemies existed to be killed,[31] and
no other excuse was necessary. Although villages sometimes switched
alliances, the structure persisted, and the status of "enemy" was a permanent, culturally embedded fixture in the life of the society. As mentioned earlier, the operations and ideas of the men's cult, the Tambaran,
depended upon enemies as preferred sacrificial victims and as a source
of trophy heads with which to adorn the interior of the spirit house. Not
that the Tambaran specifically *charged* the men to go to war, it is just that
the cult claimed the fruits of wars begun for whatever reason. Still, in its
empowering of war magic and in its mystification of village unity,
strength, and spirituality, the institution could be called a cult of war. Just
as essentially, however, the Tambaran was a cult of *peace*. This is because
its ritual cycle included regular truce intervals, during which hostages
were exchanged and enemies participated as essential actors in each others' ceremonies. This brings me back to the central theme of this chapter.

The collectively inspired nature of peace is consistent with the fact that this state is also the more socially effervescent, which probably accounts in large part for its idealized character. In contrast with the period of intense fighting, during which nearly all social activity is suspended, peace is the fleeting moment when trading and military alliances are formed or renewed; compensation payments are made to friends and recent enemies, as are marriage overtures; and arrangements are negotiated concerning large-scale coordinated engagements, such as those involved in the Highlands exchange system known as the Te.[32] Meggitt's study directly states that these social and political considerations are fully alive in the minds of tacticians and strategists during the war itself. For example, at several points he notes (pp. 68-70, 116, 117, 210) that Big Men on the enemy side are deliberately spared in anticipation of the peaceful aftermath. "'If we kill those Big Men,'" Meggitt quotes an informant as saying, "'who then will fire the bellies of our enemies afterward so they will feel impelled to meet their obligations and pay compensation for our dead?'" Continues the author: "The implication is that the Big Men on both sides, because of their long-term, mutually profitable relations in the Te and other exchanges, will work hard together to secure prompt payment of homicide compensation, which will be to their own advantage as well as to that of their clan" (p. 70; see also Knauft 1990:289).[33]

I dealt earlier with the inadequacy of the idea that war and peace are alternative states. The statement that war precedes peace would seem trivially true or, in the immediate case, merely an artifact of the tendency of ourselves and the Mae to dichotomize this feature of life into these terms. The force of the material just quoted, along with that of many other authors unquoted, urges me to suggest something more. Accepting Clausewitz's definition of war as the continuation of policy by other means, it follows that peace is the resumption of policy by its own means. In the New Guinea Highlands these means consist of the large array of economic, political, and religious activities centering on society's leaders. The point is that policy abides in the form of long-range strategic values directly affecting tactical decisions, even in the heat and bloodiness of combat. This is true whether the policy in question is being articulated by a New Guinea Big Man or a British prime minister. Furthermore (and here the suggestion becomes more daring and perhaps less universal in its application), if the "other means" afforded by war regularly affect the character of the ensuing peace, then it would not take many repetitions before the actors began to understand war as, in some sense, a necessary prelude to peace. In other words, peace, with all the social benefits that attend it, is fundamentally attainable only through war.

Although hypothetical, this formulation helps to account for a puzzling, but apparently widespread (Numelin 1950:218), custom pursued by the Ilahita Arapesh in connection with the Tambaran practices described a moment ago. At the opening of every ceremonial encounter between politically autonomous groups, the opposed parties enact a passionate and not always bloodless mock combat. My sense of it at the time was that this enabled the participants to achieve the emotional pitch appropriate to the ensuing, cooperative event. Without discarding this interpretation, I now wonder if, in addition, the convention might signify a culturally codified recognition that peace is "buried inside" war and thus requires a warlike preamble. Before giving over their sovereignty to the transcendent values implied by their social communion, before surrendering themselves to the peace of this engagement, groups need to enact that fierce martial excellence that is, tragically, in their world, their only security—the only road they know to peace.

* * *

Never before in living memory has there been a more opportune moment to examine peace—its nature and requirements. The Cold War ended a few months before this writing (September 1990),[34] and for the third time in this century the world is picking through the rubble, looking for what can be salvaged. Only this time the rubble is not bricks and mortar; it is a debris of ideas and institutions strewn about on both sides of where lately hung the Iron Curtain. The menace of thermonuclear war is a nightmare from which the world has finally awakened. The reunification of Germany, an event which three years ago would not have seemed possible in our lifetime, was accomplished with a speed and facility that set all the experts to gasping. Even the current crisis involving the Iraqi invasion of Kuwait, ominous though it was, had the good effect of prompting the United Nations Security Council to vote unanimously— for the first time in its history—to impose economic sanctions against an aggressor member nation. Such unprecedented international accord has inspired well-wishers to believe that a new world order is at hand, one in which warfare is no longer endemic. "Peace on earth" and "peace in our time" are no longer empty slogans; they seem to describe a new reality. Such world events would seem to dwarf the importance of the issues raised in this chapter, reconfirming how laughably remote war and peace in New Guinea and arcane issues of ontology are from the decisive ideas and powers of our time.

Perhaps. But if what I have been saying in this chapter has any validity, then a caveat must be delivered to those who celebrate the current news in ignorance of cultural and historical comparisons. In all previous eras peace has proved easier to woo than to live with, but this time there are impressive structural reasons for doubting that the marriage will make it out the chapel door, let alone survive the honeymoon. While many in the West jubilate over the collapse of Marxism-Leninism and the Soviet Empire, claim victory for their side, and wonder rosily how to spend the "peace dividend," others worry that our war machine is too entrenched to be so readily dismantled. We think of wars as entailing emergency mobilizations, short-lived deployments of human and material resources into sectors created or enhanced by pressing military need. An armistice signals that social life can revert quickly to the *status quo ante bellum*, because the measures that comprise a society's war footing are all explicitly temporary and dispensable. Life returns to normal. War profiteers—those unsympathetic gentlemen in frock-coats—are the only ones disturbed by the outbreak of peace. This time, however, the circumstances are different. The Cold War lasted not four years, but *forty*-four years, long enough for my generation to move from cradle to middle age, long enough for the war footing to become institutionalized in every respect, long enough for many to lose faith that this war could ever have a happy ending. In the prolonged, anxious prosperity of that era we *all* became, in a sense, war profiteers.

Of course, the adaptation the world must now undo involves far more than economic (or political or diplomatic) arrangements, which present challenges that are in principle relatively straightforward and technical. No, the situation has gone on long enough and widely enough to require a radical reshaping of society's *cultural* understandings concerning the immense cognitive domain of war and peace. More than ever before, we need to know about the nature of peace and the dynamics that connect it to its opposites. For, more than we fully realize and despite all the dancing in the streets, peace is strangely unfamiliar and frightening to us. The spectre that was amiably haunting our attic has taken flesh and moved downstairs. In the past, when this has happened, we have always seen fit to exorcise this ghost back to the attic. Let it be hoped that, this time, we will try to learn to live with it.

Notes

* My title is inspired by that of Miriam Kahn's unpublished manuscript, "The Spectre of Abundance" (Kahn n.d.).

1. This awareness is not unique to the Chinese. Consider, for example, Amos Elon's remarks (1989:27–28) about historical Jerusalem:

In the imagination of believers, Jerusalem became more than a city. She became a metaphor. Her name stood for holiness and peace—and at the same time, strangely enough, for their opposites. Faith and superstition frequently alternated and belief often degenerated into war, zealous fury, sectarian prejudice, and persecution.

The contradiction seemed embedded, somehow, in her name. In the Hebrew name *Jerushalaim*, the suffix *aim* implies a duality, a pair of things, as in *einaim* (eyes), *oznaim* (ears), *shadaim* (breasts). It was difficult not to read into this duality an implied parity between the heavenly and the earthly, peace and war, goodliness and sin.

2. In a short, pithy comment on this subject, Leeds (1968:101) quotes from Ambrose Bierce's *The Devil's Dictionary*: "Peace, n. In international affairs, a period of cheating between two periods of fighting."

3. In a tome on the sociology of war, one that includes a fifty-two-page chapter entitled "Motives," Luard (1986) completely overlooks peace as a possible candidate. Indeed, the book says almost nothing about peace, despite the many junctures at which some reference would have been appropriate. As will be seen later in this chapter, Clausewitz, who understood war in both theoretical and practical terms, was in no doubt as to the importance of the war-peace relationship.

4. Similarly, in his *Nicomachean Ethics* (10.7) Aristotle notes that we "make war that we may live in peace."

5. In conferring honorary United States citizenship on Winston Churchill, in April of 1963, President John F. Kennedy stated, "He mobilized the English language and sent it into battle."

6. When, on January 10–11, 1991, the United States Congress debated whether to grant President George Bush discretionary power to use military force against Iraq, the principal argument made by those favoring the resolution was that a political decision to wage war would be the best means to ensure peace.

7. In his study of the experience of battle, Keegan notes that the astonishing heroics of Wellington's officers at Waterloo were inspired by their concern with "the figure they cut in their brother officers' eyes" (1978:191). British middle- and upper-class ideals of honor and self-sacrifice were constitutive of valor among these officers and, importantly, those back home who were the arbiters of social standing and reputation. Far from harboring any antisocial impulse to slaughter, these officers disdained killing as "ungentlemanly" and carried weapons that had only modest lethal potential in terms of the military technology of the day. By the First World War, the British "equation of courage with morality" had progressed to the point where "the beloved captain" was the revelation of Christ himself (pp. 280–281).

8. The phrase was used by Andrew Marvell in 1650, referring to the unexciting tasks awaiting Oliver Cromwell upon his return from the Irish campaigns (*Upon Cromwell's Return from Ireland*).

9. The passage reads: "From Stettin in the Baltic to Trieste in the Adriatic an iron curtain has descended across the Continent." Interestingly, this usage was not original with Churchill. Bartlett (1968:924n.) traces the "iron curtain" metaphor to Queen Elizabeth of Belgium, who used it in 1914. Dr. Josef Goebbels, the Nazi Minister of Enlightenment and Propaganda, also preceded Churchill in its use, also with reference to the Soviet Union.

10. The UN-sponsored International Conference on Primary Health Care, held in Alma-Ata, USSR, in 1978, defined health as "a state of *complete* physical, mental, and social well-

being and . . . not merely the absence of disease or infirmity" (John Elder, M.D., personal communication). Such a condition being virtually unattainable (unlike disease or infirmity, which are all too attainable), we are left with the same definitional asymmetry that occurs in the case of peace and war.

11. O'Brien (1990:87-88) makes a similar observation in his collection of short stories about the experiences of an infantryman in the Viet Nam War.

> At its core, perhaps, war is just another name for death, and yet any soldier will tell you, if he tells the truth, that proximity to death brings with it a corresponding proximity to life. After a firefight, there is always the immense pleasure of aliveness. The trees are alive. The grass, the soil—everything. All around you things are purely living, and you among them, and the aliveness makes you tremble. You feel an intense, out-of-the-skin awareness of your living self—your truest self, the human being you want to be and then become by the force of wanting it. In the midst of evil you want to be a good man. You want decency. You want justice and courtesy and human concord, things you never knew you wanted. There is a kind of largeness to it, a kind of godliness. Though it's odd, you're never more alive than when you're almost dead. You recognize what's valuable.

12. Likewise, the consciousness and experience of being alive would be impossible without the awareness of death. And again, Judeo-Christian theodicy is canonically taken to be a doctrine that "explains" worldly suffering as endemic to a fallen world. Applying the present argument, however, a better characterization would be that the putative intervention of God's will *purposes worldly suffering in the human mode*, by rendering it meaningful—in this case, with reference to a religiously constituted ideal.

13. Popper draws an analogy between truth and a cloud-shrouded mountain peak: "A climber may not merely have difficulties in getting there—he may not know when he gets there, because he may be unable to distinguish, in the clouds, between the main summit and a subsidiary peak. Yet this does not affect the objective existence of the summit; and if the climber tells us 'I doubt whether I reached the actual summit', then he does, by implication, recognize the objective existence of the summit" (1963:226).

14. The general idea goes back to the ancients, of course, but its modern version is traceable to the ethologically oriented conjectures of Konrad Lorenz, Robert Ardrey, Desmond Morris, Robin Fox, Lionel Tiger, and others.

15. Through his own writings and in collections he has edited, Ashley Montagu has emerged as the principal opponent of the "innate aggressivist" position; see, for example, Montagu (1973, 1976, 1978). See Pollard (1974, orig. 1925) for the apparent origin of Montagu's convictions in this matter, having produced in him a "frenzy of enthusiasm" upon first reading it. "This essay had an influence upon me out of all proportion to its length," Montagu recalls, "and there is hardly a sentence in it which I have not borrowed for my own writings in the fifty years that have elapsed" (1974:421). One cannot help wondering if such certitude, persisting across a half-century filled with new scientific findings and perspectives, is something one should wish to advertise.

16. As recently as 1910, William James, who at least since 1904 had judged that "war is human nature at its uttermost," and that "society would rot without the mystical blood-payment" (James 1911a:304), could say without fear of contradiction: "We inherit the warlike type; and for most of the capacities of heroism that the human race is full of we have to thank this cruel history. Dead men tell no tales, and if there were any tribes of other type than this they have left no survivors. Our ancestors have bred pugnacity into our bone and marrow, and thousands of years of peace won't breed it out of us" (James 1911b:272). In the

light of subsequent ethnographic evidence, most modern anthropologists would probably consider this view to be overstated.

17. Fieldwork was conducted for a period of twenty-one months during 1969–72, and for a period of eleven months during 1985–86. Major funding for the first of these periods was provided by the Research School of Pacific Studies, Australian National University, with a grant-in-aid from the Wenner-Gren Foundation for Anthropological Research. Funding for the later period was provided by the National Science Foundation. I am indebted to all of these institutions for their generous support.

18. Some villages along the Papuan coast are of comparable size, but, there, the explanation almost certainly rests on the integrative capabilities of hereditary chieftainships. The Ilahita do not have chiefs and have followed a quite different course of social and political evolution.

19. It should be noted that Reo Fortune, who was Mead's husband and ethnographic collaborator among the Mountain Arapesh, published an article in 1939 with the provocative title "Arapesh Warfare" (Fortune 1939). Suffice it to say that a close comparison of his claims and Mead's shows that there is not the discrepancy that Fortune would wish the reader to believe there is. Based on personal acquaintance it seems to me that Fortune, alas, surely one of Melanesia's greatest ethnographers, allowed himself in this instance to be influenced by a personal desire to hurt and discredit Mead, to whom he was no longer married.

20. Margaret Mead's ethnographic intuitions were sometimes quite penetrating. In 1971, when she visited my wife, Beverly, and me in Ilahita—her first trip to the transmontane region of the Sepik hinterland—her comment was that everything about the place looked different from Alitoa, but the people "felt" the same. As an anthropologist whose academic teeth were cut on the concept of Culture, such continuity should not surprise me. And yet it does, perhaps because some part of me harbors a hope that experience teaches people things, changes them—for better or worse.

21. See Knauft (1990) for a comprehensive, critical review of anthropological studies of warfare in Melanesia. Although Knauft covers a much wider array of issues and variables than is being contemplated here, nothing in his excellent study contradicts my argument.

22. In discussing the old days with his Manus informants, Theodore Schwartz (personal communication) was told, "Yes, it is true that our forefathers were great war-makers; but you must understand that they were also great peace-makers." At a further comparative remove, Frans de Waal, noting the psychosocial importance of reconciliation behavior in various primate species, suggests that such animals _may fight in order to effect reconciliation_ (personal communication; see, also, this volume). The irony present in both of these statements is the central business of my chapter.

23. See also Vayda (1968) for an enumeration of functionalist hypotheses applicable to war—a list that does not include "achievement of peace."

24. See Keegan (1993) for a major criticism of Clausewitz's political theory of war—a theory which, ironically, succeeded only in arguing that "true" war serves no end but its own. In the context of advocating a cultural perspective on war, Keegan (p. 21) observes that,

> Politics played no part in the conduct of the First World War worth mentioning. The First World War was, on the contrary, an extraordinary, a monstrous cultural aberration, the outcome of an unwitting decision by Europeans in the [peaceful] century of Clausewitz . . . to turn Europe into a warrior society.

In the same sense that Karl Marx was the ideological father of the Russian Revolution, Karl von Clausewitz—another child of German idealist thinking—was the ideological father of the First World War (p. 22).

25. Paula Brown (1982a, 1982b) has voiced skepticism over the chances of successfully instituting any externally mandated third party. Without prior or corresponding changes in the political ideologies of the societies affected, such efforts, she cogently argues, would be bound to fail. Brown's assessment is consistent with the general perspective that I am developing in this chapter.

26. Clausewitz is quite specific on this point: "For strategy the victory, that is the tactical success, is primarily only a means and the things which should lead directly to peace are its ultimate object" (1943:78). See text, above, for similar views by Winston Churchill and others.

27. For more on this feature of Highlands warfare, see, in addition to Meggitt's book, Glasse's study of Huli warfare (1959), in which the author declares that this phenomenon's "jural basis . . . and its internal dynamic, is founded on what might be called the doctrine of responsibility" (p. 286). By "responsibility," Glasse is referring to ownership of the argument by an individual or a narrowly contained corporate group.

28. This is vividly illustrated by the circumstances of military conquest on the part of Ilahita village. See text, below.

29. This does not deny that large-scale, relatively decisive territorial expansions and predatory migrations do occur. Rather, I would suggest that such conquests are extremely rare in the time span accessible to ethnography and therefore do not offer a very useful paradigm for characterizing New Guinea warfare in general.

30. Hayano (1974) has shown that among the Tauna Awa of the Eastern Highlands, intermarriage with neighboring groups does not necessarily reduce concern over military security in respect of those groups.

31. And to be killed *by*. Even today, although women sometimes hang themselves, suicide among Arapesh men is unknown. Traditionally, when a man wanted his life to end he would walk to an enemy village and present himself for spearing. A lone, unarmed man would generally be allowed to pass unhindered through enemy outskirts, for sentinels would understand and respect his intentions.

32. After citing several instances of prescribed warrior purification, Turney-High concludes that, "Peace . . . seems to be the normal situation in the minds of even warlike peoples" (1971:226). That comment touches positively on the thesis of the present chapter; but from such observations it would be quite erroneous to claim, as Numelin (1950) once did, "A non-warlike character seems to be a distinctive feature of the primitive peoples in New Guinea." (p. 75).

33. It was upon reading this passage that my vagrant suspicion jumped in the boxcar and went to town!

34. To preserve the historicity and predictive thrust of this conclusion, I prefer not to revise it in the light of subsequent cataclysmic events. Later hostilities in the former Yugoslavia and former Soviet Union, in Iraq, Somalia, and Rwanda, and in countless other "hot spots"; the deadly shift to tribalism in many areas and levels of political, religious, and ethnic conflict; the growing prospect of nuclear terrorism—let the reader judge whether or not the widepread optimism in September 1990 was, as I suggested at the time, premature.

References

Bartlett, John. 1968. *Familiar Quotations*. 14th edition. Ed. Emily Morison. Boston: Little, Brown.

Brown, Paula. 1982a. Chimbu Disorder: Tribal Fighting in Newly Independent Papua New

Guinea. *Pacific Viewpoint* 23 (1): 1–21.

————. 1982b. Conflict in the New Guinea Highlands. *Journal of Conflict Resolution* 26 (3): 525–546.

Churchill, Winston, Sir. 1974. *The Sinews of Peace*. In *Winston S. Churchill: His Complete Speeches, 1897–1963*, ed. Robert Rhodes James. 8 vols. London: Chelsea House, 7:7285–7293.

Clausewitz, Karl von. 1943 (1832–34) *On War*, trans. O. J. Matthijs Jolles. New York: Modern Library.

Crane, Stephen. 1972 (1894). *The Red Badge of Courage*. New York: Washington Square Books.

Elon, Amos. 1989 *Jerusalem: City of Mirrors*. Boston: Little, Brown.

Forge, Anthony. 1966. Art and Environment in the Sepik. *Proceedings of the Royal Anthropological Institute*, 1965: 23–31.

Fornari, Franco. 1975. *The Psychoanalysis of War*. Bloomington: University of Indiana Press.

Fortune, Reo. 1939. Arapesh Warfare. *American Anthropologist* 41: 22–41.

Gardner, Robert and Karl G. Heider. 1969. *Gardens of War*. New York: Random House.

Glasse, Robert M. 1959. Revenge and Redress among the Huli: A Preliminary Account. *Mankind* 5 (7): 273–289.

Hayano, David M. 1973. Sorcery Death, Proximity, and the Perception of Out-Groups: The Tauna Awa of New Guinea. *Ethnology* 12 (2): 179–191.

————. 1974. Marriage, Alliance, and Warfare: A View from the New Guinea Highlands. *American Ethnologist* 1 (2): 281– 293.

Heider, Karl G. 1970. *The Dugum Dani: A Papuan Culture in the Highlands of West New Guinea*. Viking Fund Publications in Anthropology, no. 49. New York: Wenner-Gren Foundation for Anthropological Research.

Herdt, Gilbert H. 1982. Fetish and Fantasy in Sambia Initiation. In *Rituals of Manhood: Male Initiation in Papua New Guinea*, ed. Gilbert H. Herdt, 21–31. Berkeley: University of California Press.

Holloway, Ralph L., Jr. 1968. Human Aggression: The Need for a Species-Specific Framework. In *War: The Anthropology of Armed Conflict and Aggression*, ed. Morton Fried, Marvin Harris, and Robert Murphy, 29–48. Garden City, N.Y.: Natural History.

James, William. 1911a (1904). Remarks at the Peace Banquet. In *Memories and Studies*, 297–306. London: Longmans, Green.

————. 1911b (1910). The Moral Equivalent of War. In *Memories and Studies*, 265–296. London: Longmans, Green.

Kahn, Miriam. N.d. The Spectre of Abundance: The Cultural-Ecology of an Irrigation System in Papua New Guinea. Unpublished manuscript.

Keegan, John. 1978. *The Face of Battle: A Study of Agincourt, Waterloo and the Somme*. London: Penguin.

————. 1993 *A History of Warfare*. New York: Alfred A. Knopf.

Knauft, Bruce M. 1990. Melanesian Warfare: A Theoretical History. *Oceania* 60 (4): 250–311.

Koch, Klaus-Friedrich. 1974. *War and Peace in Jalémó: The Management of Conflict in Highland New Guinea*. Cambridge: Harvard University Press.

Laycock, Donald C. 1973. Sepik Languages: Checklist and Preliminary Classification. *Pacific Linguistics*, ser. B, no. 25.

Leeds, Anthony. 1968. General Discussion. In *War: The Anthropology of Armed Conflict and Aggression*, ed. Morton Fried, Marvin Harris, and Robert Murphy, 100–102. Garden City, N.Y.: Natural History.

Lesser, Alexander. 1968. War and the State. In *War: The Anthropology of Armed Conflict and Aggression*, ed. Morton Fried, Marvin Harris, and Robert Murphy, 92–96. Garden

City, N.Y.: Natural History.

Luard, Evan. 1986. *War in International Society: A Study in International Sociology*. London: I. B. Tauris.

McNeil, Elton B., ed. 1965. *The Nature of Human Conflict*. Englewood Cliffs, N.J.: Prentice-Hall.

Mead, Margaret. 1935. *Sex and Temperament in Three Primitive Societies*. London: Routledge & Kegan Paul.

———. 1938. The Mountain Arapesh: An Importing Culture. *Anthropological Papers of the American Museum of Natural History* 36 (3): 139–349.

———. 1961. *Cooperation and Competition among Primitive Peoples*. Boston: Beacon.

———. 1968. Alternatives to War. In *War: The Anthropology of Armed Conflict and Aggression*, ed. Morton Fried, Marvin Harris, and Robert Murphy, 215–228. Garden City, N.Y.: Natural History.

Meggitt, Mervyn. 1977. *Blood is Their Argument: Warfare among the Mae Enga Tribesmen of the New Guinea Highlands*. Palo Alto: Mayfield.

Montagu, Ashley. 1974. Comment. In *Frontiers of Anthropology*, ed. Ashley Montagu, 421. New York: G. P. Putnam's Sons.

———. 1976. *The Nature of Human Aggression*. New York: Oxford University Press.

———, ed. 1973. *Man and Aggression*. 2d. edition. New York: Oxford University Press.

———, ed. 1974. *Frontiers of Anthropology*. New York: G.P. Putnam's Sons.

———, ed. 1978. *Learning Non-Aggression: The Experience of Non-Literate Societies*. New York: Oxford University Press.

Numelin, Ragnar. 1950. *The Beginnings of Diplomacy*. London: Oxford University Press.

O'Brien, Tim. 1990. *The Things They Carried*. New York: Penguin.

Pollard, Albert Frederick. 1974 (1925). The Idea That War Is Natural Anatomized and Decently Interred. In *Frontiers of Anthropology*, ed. Ashley Montagu, 421–425. New York: G. P. Putnam's Sons.

Popper, Karl. 1963. *Conjectures and Refutations: The Growth of Scientific Knowledge*. London: Routledge & Kegan Paul.

Rappaport, Roy A. 1967. *Pigs for the Ancestors: Ritual in the Ecology of a New Guinea People*. New Haven: Yale University Press.

Riches, David. 1987. Violence, Peace, and War in "Early" Human Society: The Case of the Eskimo. In *The Sociology of War and Peace*, ed. Colin Creighton and Martin Shaw, 17–36. Houndmills, Hampshire, England: Macmillan.

Roscoe, Paul B. 1989. The Flight from the Fen: The Prehistoric Migration of the Boiken of the East Sepik Province, Papua New Guinea. *Oceania* 60 (2): 139–154.

Sillitoe, Paul. 1977. Land Shortage and War in New Guinea. *Ethnology* 16 (1): 71–81.

Spence, Jonathan D. 1985. *The Memory Palace of Matteo Ricci*. N.Y.: Penguin Books.

Sponsel, Leslie E. 1990. Ultraprimitive Pacifists: The Tasaday As a Symbol of Peace. *Anthropology Today* 6 (1): 3–5.

Sumner, William Graham. 1964 (1911). War. In *War: Studies from Psychology, Sociology, Anthropology*, ed. L. Bramson and G. W. Goethals, 205–227. New York: Basic Books.

Turney-High, Harry Holbert. 1971. *Primitive War: Its Practice and Concepts*. 2d ed. Columbia: University of South Carolina Press.

Tuzin, Donald F. 1972. Yam Symbolism in the Sepik: An Interpretative Account. *Southwestern Journal of Anthropology* 28 (3): 230–254.

———. 1974. Social Control and the Tambaran in the Sepik. In *Contention and Dispute: Aspects of Law and Social Control in Melanesia*, ed. A. L. Epstein, 317–344. Canberra: Australian National University Press.

————. 1975. The Breath of a Ghost: Dreams and the fear of the dead. *Ethos* 3 (3): 555–578.

————. 1976. *The Ilahita Arapesh: Dimensions of Unity.* Berkeley: University of California Press.

————. 1980. *The Voice of the Tambaran: Truth and Illusion in Ilahita Arapesh Religion.* Berkeley: University of California Press.

————. 1982. Ritual Violence among the Ilahita Arapesh: The Dynamics of Moral and Religious Uncertainty. In *Rituals of Manhood: Male Initiation in Papua New Guinea,* ed. Gilbert H. Herdt, 321–355. Berkeley: University of California Press.

————. 1988. Prospects of Village Death in Ilahita. *Oceania* 59 (2): 81–104.

————. 1989. The Organization of Action, Identity, and Experience in Arapesh Dualism. In *The Attraction of Opposites: Thought and Society in the Dualistic Mode,* ed. David Maybury-Lewis and Uri Almagor, 277–296. Ann Arbor: University of Michigan Press.

Vayda, Andrew P. 1968. Hypotheses about Functions of War. In *War: The Anthropology of Armed Conflict and Aggression,* ed. Morton Fried, Marvin Harris, and Robert Murphy, 85–91. Garden City, N.Y.: Natural History.

————. 1976. *War in Ecological Perspective: Persistence, Change, and Adaptive Processes in Three Oceanian Societies.* New York: Plenum.

Wallace, Anthony F. C. 1968. Psychological Preparations for War. In *War: The Anthropology of Armed Conflict and Aggression,* Morton Fried, Marvin Harris, and Robert Murphy, 173–182. Garden City, N.Y.: Natural History.

TWO

Broad Perspectives
on Peace:
The Primate Heritage,
Evolution, and
Comparative
Anthropology

2 The Biological Basis of Peaceful Coexistence: A Review of Reconciliation Research on Monkeys and Apes

FRANS B. M. DE WAAL

The little creature, which I had punished for the first time, shrank back, uttered one or two heart-broken wails, as she stared at me horror-struck, while her lips were pouted more than ever. The next moment she had flung her arms round my neck, quite beside herself, and was only comforted by degrees, when I stroked her.

—Wolfgang Köhler (1925: 261)

■ In "The Biological Basis of Peaceful Coexistence," Frans de Waal argues that social life is inherently bimodal. Just as competition for scarce resources inevitably disrupts social life, so the maintenance of the group requires methods of reconciling relationships and reducing tension. The capacity to switch between aggression and peacemaking, as well as the methods of peacemaking themselves, must have biological roots. Where better to look for them than among our primate relatives, some of whom may be no more distant from ourselves than several million years of evolution?

De Waal's and others' research shows that monkeys and apes often approach one another after a conflict and engage in behaviors that are remarkably like our own gestures of reconciliation, including a pat on the back, mouth to mouth kissing, and extending an open hand, palm up.[1] The simplest explanation of such parallel behaviors, de Waal argues, is the presence of similar, underlying intentional processes. As among humans, higher primates weigh not only the payoffs of aggressive encounters, but also the advantages of peace making and tension reduction. De Waal further demonstrates that the primates differ in their patterns of peace making and reconciliation, and he suggests that these differences may parallel contrasts among human social groups.

WHY IS IT that we tend to ascribe the aggressiveness of the human species to our "bestial" side, whereas we view peace as a victory of reason over instinct? Do we really believe that human reason has the power to create peaceful relations without assistance from biology? Humans share with many animals the ability to cooperate despite the ever-present potential of competition over food, mates, and space. This requires a psychological makeup that allows aggression and competition to be switched on and off, so to speak, dependent on previous experience and current circumstances. Human culture and rationality undoubtedly contribute to the decisions involved, but the switching ability itself is considerably older than our species.

When Konrad Lorenz (1963) compared aggressive behavior in animals and humans, he provoked a lively debate that lasts to this day. Unfortunately, but not unexpectedly, the debate focused on Lorenz's Freudian drive concept. This concept, according to which aggression is an inevitable expression of endogenously accumulated energy, did not survive the criticism of other ethologists, who argued that aggression is entirely or primarily a response to environmental stimuli (e.g., Hinde 1970: 344-349). If one is prepared to look beyond this issue, however, one will notice Lorenz's extremely important insights into the inhibitions and ritualizations that help keep aggression in check. The stage for these insights was set by his early observations of the so-called "triumph ceremony" of ducks and geese (e.g., Lorenz 1935).

These aggressive birds go through elaborate courtship rituals that serve to blunt confrontation by directing threat responses away from the partner. Combined with sexual attraction, these ceremonies have the power to turn an initially hostile relationship into a lifelong pair-bond. It is for this reason that Lorenz emphasized the mixture of motivations— including aggressive motivations—underlying love and affection rather than committing the error of some of his critics, who tried to ban aggression from the social realm by classifying it as antisocial.

Thus, a recent document by a number of experts on aggression, known as the Seville Statement on Violence, depicts aggressive behavior as an ugly trait that needs to be obliterated (Adams et al. 1987). The document's rejection of a biological component to aggression is of course highly selective and ideological. No one would even think of writing a similar manifesto questioning a genetic substrate for attachment patterns, cooperation, or sex in the human species; most people readily accept these behavioral universals as core elements of "human nature." Furthermore, the elimination of aggression is not only an unrealistic goal, it is a misguided one. A friction-free social system has yet to be found, and the ones that come closest lack the structural complexity and individual differentiation that we value so much in our own societies. A good example is a school of herrings: the fish move together without any problems, but the perfect peace that they enjoy also appears perfectly boring from the human standpoint.

Conflict is inevitable whenever demands exceed supplies. Because this is the kind of world we and most animals live in, the real question is not how to eliminate conflict and its various expressions, one of which is aggression, but how to cope with conflict, resolve it, and integrate it into otherwise beneficial relationships. This "dialectical" perspective, in which competition and cooperation are partially overlapping social domains rather than each other's antitheses, is implicit in most of the contributions to this volume and is explicitly discussed by Tuzin.

In biology, there is a long tradition of analysis in terms of dynamic equilibria. Opposites interact in feedback loops that create homeostasis within the system, whether this is an ecosystem or a social system. As previously summarized: "Just as the yang having reached its climax retreats in favor of the yin, and the yin having reached its climax retreats in favor of the yang, there exists no such thing as eternal concordance in any social system. Pure peace is like an ocean without waves and tides. Pure aggression can only bring destruction to oneself, the other, or both. It is the pendulum swing between conflict and accommodation that we observe, rather than either of the poles" (de Waal 1989a: 27).

Biologists have come a long way in their thinking about aggression since Lorenz (1963). Despite the continuing popularity of the "struggle for life" metaphor, it is increasingly recognized that there are important costs associated with open competition, hence that there exist sound evolutionary reasons for constraints on the expression of competitive tendencies (see table 1). To explain the rarity of lethal violence among animals, for example, Maynard Smith and Price (1973) proposed that the advantages of winning a fight, hence of gaining access to contested resources, are weighed against the costs of serious injury if the opponent fights for its life. Van Rhijn and Vodegel (1980) refined this model by including the role of individual recognition. They argued that animals remember against which individuals they won confrontations and against which they lost, resulting in the systematic avoidance of confrontations with stronger individuals. To these constraints we may add the value of cooperation, that is, the dependency of social animals on community life in general, and on the need for support and help from certain individuals in particular. The basic dilemma facing many animals, including humans, is that they sometimes cannot win a fight without losing a friend. This dilemma further moderates competitive tendencies (de Waal 1989a).

The evolution of behavioral mechanisms that assist the control of aggressive behavior relates to the harmful effects of aggression on the survival and reproduction of both aggressors and recipients. Three adaptive constraints on the expression aggression have been proposed:

TABLE 1. BEHAVIORAL MECHANSIMS ASSISTING CONTROL OF AGGRESSION

1. *Risk of injury and energy expenditure.* "Hawkish" competitive strategies are extremely costly if conspecifics retaliate with the same strategies (Maynard Smith and Price 1973).

2. *Individual recognition and memory of previous fights.* Losers learn to avoid confrontation with winners as reflected in accepted territories and dominance hierarchies (van Rhijn and Vodegel 1980).

3. *The value of cooperative relationships and group membership.* Aggression may endanger the benefits derived from cooperative relationships; there is a limit to the amount of aggression a relationship can endure (de Waal 1989a).

This brings me to the main topic of this chapter: the behavioral mechanisms that allow nonhuman primates either to prevent open hostilities or to repair the damage once such hostilities have occurred. One such mechanism is reconciliation. Köhler (1925) saw a "need for forgiveness" in the behavior of his juvenile chimpanzee (see epigraph). Similar stories can be heard from people who have raised apes at home. Thus, Kellogg and Kellogg (1933) experienced emotional reunions after reprimanding their infant chimpanzee and noted that she would express relief during the embrace by "heaving her great sigh, audible a meter or more away." Apes seem to perceive a conflict with their caretakers as a threat to the relationship and apparently try to control the damage by means of affectionate behavior. Although the environment of hand-reared apes is obviously unnatural, human influence does not appear to explain the phenomenon.

Reconciliation also occurs after fights in naturalistic settings in which nonhuman primates spontaneously interact amongst themselves. The present chapter reviews the evidence collected over the past decade by our team, adding recent work by others. It also pays attention to the methodology of the various studies and presents a framework for further inquiry. In doing so, the data will be considered before the theory. Conflict resolution is still very much an area of inductive research, in which every new finding stimulates our thinking.

Two Basic Hypotheses

Thus far, the principal aim of reconciliation research has been to test two alternative expectations concerning the effect of aggressive encounters on social relations.

Dispersal hypothesis: Losers of aggressive incidents tend to avoid winners. The traditional notion of aggression as a spacing mechanism (e.g., Scott 1958; Lorenz 1963) was based on experience with territorial species and on Hediger's (1941) influential concept of individual distance. It predicts a decreased probability of contact between individuals following aggressive behavior.

Reconciliation hypothesis: Individuals try to undo the damage that aggression inflicts upon valuable social relationships. This hypothesis predicts (a) an increased contact probability following aggression, and (b) the use of special reassuring and appeasing gestures during these contacts.

The reconciliation concept is supported, therefore, if individuals contact each other more frequently and with more calming gestures after aggression than in the absence of preceding aggression. Yet, it is good to realize that, strictly speaking, such a result would not demonstrate the specific function suggested by the label "reconciliation," which means the repair of a disturbed relationship. Rather than summarizing knowledge about a given behavior, or merely describing it, labels in ethology are often interpretative, and thus serve an important heuristic function (Asquith 1984). A range of testable predictions can be derived from the "reconciliation" label. One of these is that post-conflict contacts should be made selectively. Calming body contact is, in principle, possible with any social partner, whereas reconciliation requires interaction between the antagonists themselves, as they are the only ones who can mend their relationship.

The primatological literature contains numerous descriptions of reassuring and calming behavior. While initially stressing this behavior's "arousal reducing" effects on the internal state of aggressive, excited, or frightened individuals, investigators have also begun considering its social implications (Mason 1964; Ellefson 1968; van Lawick-Goodall 1968; Blurton-Jones and Trollope 1968; Poirier 1968; Lindburg 1973; Ehrlich and Musicant 1977; Seyfarth 1976; McKenna 1978). The first study explicitly dealing with the questions raised above concerned the large chimpanzee (*Pan troglodytes*) colony of the Arnhem Zoo, the Netherlands (de Waal and van Roosmalen 1979). The dispersal hypothesis could be rejected because aggressive incidents in this colony were associated with an average *decrease* in inter-individual distance. Continuous video-recording revealed that after aggression had occurred the chimpanzees were more often within two meters of one another than they were before the aggression occurred. Obviously, aggressors were avoided during the fight itself, but rapprochement often began as soon as the hostilities ceased. This was not due to a lack of space, as the group lived on an island of nearly one hectare with plenty of room for adversaries to stay out of each other's way.

Participants in aggressive episodes were observed for forty- five minutes afterwards to document their reunions. Although control procedures were not followed, the data strongly indicated that reassuring body contacts occurred relatively shortly after the conflict; were preferentially made between former opponents, and involved special behavior patterns (i.e., patterns rarely seen outside this context). Typically, contact between former opponents was initiated by an invitational hand gesture, with outstretched arm and open hand palm, often followed by mouth-to-mouth kissing (see figure 1). This intensive contact pattern was less common toward third parties. So-called consolations, in which a participant in an agonistic conflict afterwards sought contact with an uninvolved bystander, more often involved embracing than kissing (de Waal and van Roosmalen 1979; table 2).

TABLE 2

Frequencies of kissing and embracing among the chimpanzees of the Arnhem Zoo in two post-conflict contexts, i.e., reconciliation (contact between two former opponents) and consolation (contact by participants in a fight with uninvolved individuals).

Context	Kiss	Embrace
Reconciliation	23	8
Consolation	19	57

Data from de Waal and van Roosmalen (1979).

FIGURE 1A. An adult male (left) and female chimpanzee engage in a mouth-to-mouth kiss after an aggressive incident between them (reconciliation; from de Waal 1989d).

FIGURE 1B. A juvenile male (left) embraces a screaming adult male who is withdrawing from a confrontation with a rival (consolation: from de Waal 1982).

Controlled Observations

Following the above exploratory study, carefully controlled investigations of reconciliation behavior were needed. They have taken two forms: (a) observational studies comparing contact rates following aggression with contact rates during control periods, and (b) studies of experimentally provoked aggression.

Contact Rates

Increasing numbers of observational studies follow a paradigm developed by de Waal and Yoshihara (1983). This paradigm consists of a focal observation on a participant immediately following an aggressive incident (the post-conflict observation, or PC), and a control observation of the same duration on the same individual during the next possible observation day, starting at exactly the same time of day as the PC observation (the matched-control observation, or MC). This paradigm has been applied to captive groups of rhesus macaques (*Macaca mulatta*; de Waal and Yoshihara 1983), patas monkeys (*Erythrocebus patas*; York and Rowell 1988), stumptail macaques (*M. arctoides*; de Waal and Ren 1988), longtail macaques (*M. fascicularis*; Cords 1989; Aureli et al. 1989), and other species. Slightly different control procedures were followed in studies of free-ranging vervet monkeys (*Cercopithecus aethiops*; Cheney and Seyfarth 1989), captive pigtail macaques (*M. nemestrina*; Judge 1991), and captive bonobos (*Pan paniscus*; de Waal 1987).

Figure 2 shows the results of the study on stumptail macaques by de Waal and Ren (1988). A greater proportion of opponent pairs established contact after aggression than during control observations. One way to express this difference in a single measure is the so-called conciliatory tendency, i.e., the percentage of "attracted" opponent pairs. A pair is said to show attraction if the two individuals make contact during the PC observation only, or at least earlier in the PC than in the MC observation. The advantage of this measure is its built-in correction for the normal contact rate. Figure 3 compares the conciliatory tendencies of three species based on a ten minute time window, while taking nonagonistic body contact as a criterion for reconciliation. (See Veenema et al. 1994, for further refinements of the correction procedure.)

Studies of longtail macaques indicate a conciliatory tendency in the range of that of rhesus and patas monkeys (Cords 1989; Aureli et al. 1989). This means that the probability of reconciliation among stumptail monkeys is remarkably high, compared to the other monkey species investigated with controlled procedures. See Thierry (1984, 1985), however, for an uncontrolled study of another highly conciliatory monkey, the tonkeana macaque (*M. tonkeana*).

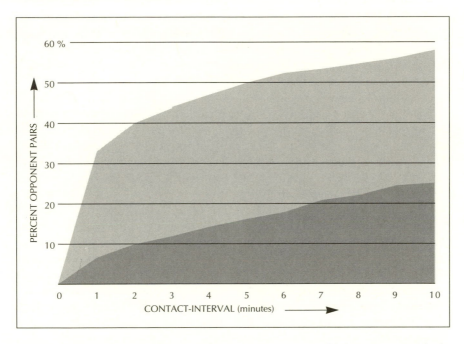

FIGURE 2. The cumulative percentage of opponent pairs that establishes nonagonistic body contact within a given time interval following aggression (Post-Conflict, or PC), or during control observattions (Matched-Control, or MC), in a captive group of stumptail macaques. From de Waal and Ren (1988).

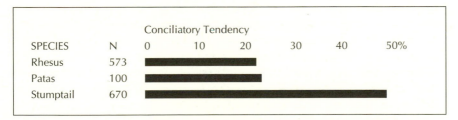

FIGURE 3. Conciliatory tendency is defined as the percentage of attracted opponent pairs, i.e., pairs making contact within a time interval following an aggressive incident that is shorter than the interval during the pair's control observation. The data concern captive groups of three monkey species, based on ten minute observations by de Waal and Yoshihara (1983), York and Rowell (1988), and de Waal and Ren (1988). N is the sample of opponent pairs.

Because in all studies the contact rates were found to be significantly higher during post-conflict as compared to control observations, the dispersal hypothesis can be safely rejected. Before favoring the reconciliation hypothesis, however, we need to exclude two obvious alternative explanations. The first one is that animals are frequently at short range from one another after an aggressive incident, because of having just interacted, which would, of course, increase the probability of contact between them if post-conflict contacts were initiated indiscriminately.

One way of excluding this explanation is to define aggressive incidents in such a way that initial spacing is likely. Thus, many of the studies required a chase or pursuit of over two meters by the aggressor. In addition, York and Rowell (1988) required proximity between individuals before initiating a control observation of them, thus excluding the possibility that the higher contact rate during PC observations was due merely to differences in spatial distribution.

This precaution was not taken in the control procedure of other studies, but de Waal and Ren (1988) did keep a record of inter-individual distances among stumptail monkeys both immediately following the aggressive incident and at the beginning of the scheduled control observation. They found no significant difference. Moreover, even individuals that were comparatively distant from one another by the end of the aggressive incident contacted one another more often following the incident than during controls.

The second alternative explanation for high contact rates among former opponents is that these rates reflect a general surge in contact following aggression, which does include participants in the incident but not on a selective basis. Several studies demonstrated, however, that the proportion of contacts involving former adversaries was greater during post-conflict periods as compared to control periods (de Waal and Yoshihara 1983; de Waal and Ren 1988; York and Rowell 1988; Aureli et al. 1989). This result includes a correction for changes in overall social activity. The conclusion is that there exists *selective attraction* between individuals who previously opposed one another in a fight.

The most rigorous control procedures, with results similar to those reported above, were followed in an observational study of the rare bonobos of the San Diego Zoo (de Waal 1987). The apes were observed continuously allowing a comparison of the following conditions: (1) the fifteen-minute block preceding aggression (pre); (2) the first fifteen-minute block following aggression (post 1); (3) the second fifteen-minute block following aggression (post 2); and (4) other times of the day, when there was no aggression and no food competition in the group (base

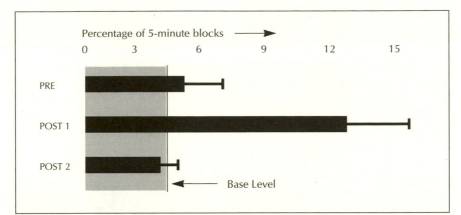

FIGURE 4. Average (± SEM) dyadic rate of interaction among captive bonobos. Rates are expressed as the percentage of five-minute time blocks in which a dyad engaged at least once in socio-sexual or affiliative behavior, excluding grooming behavior. Four conditions are compared, i.e., the three five-minute time blocks preceding aggression within the dyad (Pre), the three blocks immediately following aggression (Post 1), the three subsequent blocks (Post 2), and the base level of interaction. From de Waal (1987).

level). Data were analyzed separately per dyadic combination of individuals so that overall differences in interaction frequencies could not be due to the behavior of only a few individuals.

After aggression within a dyad, an increase occurred in the rate of affiliative and sociosexual interaction between the same individuals compared to both their base level and their pre-conflict rate (see figure 4). Since the pre-conflict rate of contact was close to the base level, a common cause for aggression and contact behavior can be ruled out. The order of events—first aggression, then an increase in contact—rather suggests a causal link between the two, as predicted by the reconciliation hypothesis.

Table 3 compares the rate of post-conflict contact for the chimpanzees of Arnhem and the bonobos of San Diego, demonstrating a higher rate in the bonobos. The ten bonobos in San Diego were divided into an all-juvenile group in a spacious enclosure, and two adult groups in a smaller "grotto" enclosure. The data are presented separately for the adult and juvenile groups in San Diego, and for the indoor and outdoor conditions in Arnhem. These results are not directly comparable to the conciliatory tendency in figure 3, because only the latter measure corrects for control contact rates. Moreover, the ten minute interval used in both analyses may not mean the same for great apes, with their longer memory span and slower pace of interaction, than for monkeys (see, e.g., Aureli et al.

1989, who defend an even shorter interval for longtail macaques).

Contact-Initiative and Aggression-Intensity

The initiative to reconciliation following clear-cut, unidirectional conflict is presented in table 4. For three macaque species, the contact initiative is compared to that during matched-control observations. Such control data are not available for the other species. Instead, table 4 shows the initiative between dominant and subordinate chimpanzees as recorded by Willemsen (1981) for contacts that were not preceded by aggression during one outdoor period in the Arnhem colony. For bonobos, the table presents the initiative to a large sample of specific contact forms (e.g., grooming, sexual mounts and matings, embracing, kissing, patting) observed in the San Diego colony. In this case as well, the dominance relationship is taken as reference point. It should be noted that all species show strong agreement between dominance and the performance of unidirectional aggression.

In three of the seven species reconciliations are mostly initiated by the aggressors, i.e., in rhesus and patas monkeys and in bonobos. Yet, there are reasons to interpret this bias differently for bonobos. Bonobos have a high rate of reconciliation (table 3) and much more elaborate patterns of reassurance behavior than rhesus and patas monkeys. Although the bonobos' control data are not directly comparable with the reconciliation data, they do suggest that the contribution of dominants to the establishment of contact increases after aggressive incidents. Such an increase is not evident in the other species. It has been suggested by de Waal and Ren (1988) that the relatively low conciliatory tendency of rhesus monkeys is due to reluctance in subordinates to approach dominants. De Waal and Luttrell (1989) have expanded on this issue by characterizing the dominance "style" of rhesus monkeys as intolerant and strict. A similar argument may apply to patas monkeys, as post-conflict interactions seem particularly tense in this species (reflected in frequent approach/avoidance interactions; York and Rowell 1988). The bias toward aggressor-initiated reconciliations therefore appears to have a different origin in the two monkey species compared to bonobos; in patas and rhesus monkeys it may be due to a fearful passivity of subordinates, and in bonobos to an increased activity of dominants.

The view that the behavior of bonobo aggressors is exceptional is supported by an analysis of the effect of aggression intensity on the probability of reconciliation. De Waal (1987) presents evidence that physical attacks among captive bonobos are more often reconciled than incidents of lower intensity and that this increase is entirely due to the increased

TABLE 3. PERCENTAGE OF RECONCILED CONFLICTS AMONG THE CHIMPANZEES OF ARNHEM ZOO AND THE BONOBOS OF SAN DIEGO ZOO.

Study		N	Percentage Reconciled
Chimpanzees	Indoors 1975–76[1]	150	34.7%
	Outdoors 1976[1]	200	29.5
	Outdoors 1980[2]	395	26.6
Bonobos	Adult subgroups[3]	333	43.8
	Juvenile subgroup[3]	179	55.9

Reconciliation is defined as nonagonistic body contact between former opponents within ten minutes of their aggressive interaction. N is the number of opponent pairs observed. Two studies in Arnhem were conducted by de Waal and van Roosmalen (1977),[1] and one by Griede (1981).[2] Data concerning the bonobos are from de Waal (1987).[3]

TABLE 4. INITIATIVE FOR THE FIRST CONTACT FOLLOWING AN AGONISTIC ENCOUNTER (RECONCILIATION) OR DURING CONTROL PERIODS.

Species	RECONCILIATIONS		CONTROL CONTACTS	
	N	% Aggressor	N	% Aggressor (or Dominant)
Patas monkey[1]	31	67.7%	—	—
Rhesus macaque[2]	142	67.6	109	65.1%
Stumptail macaque[3]	263	38.4	94	47.9
Longtail macaque[4]	88	36.4	24	58.3
Pigtail macaque[5]	162	34.6	—	—
Bonobo[6]	246	61.4	(1,795	47.4)
Chimpanzee[7]	379	44.3	(528	38.1)

N = number of contacts. % Aggressor = percentage of N in which the previous aggressor initiated the contact. Data are from York and Rowell (1988),[1] de Waal and Yoshihara (1983),[2] de Waal and Ren (1988),[3] Aureli et al. (1989),[4] Judge (1991),[5] de Waal (1987),[6] and from a combination of studies on the Arnhem chimpanzees, including de Waal and van Roosmalen (1979).[7] The control level for rhesus, stumptail and longtail macaques concerns matched-control observations on the same indiviuals; see text for an explanation of the other control levels.

contact rate of aggressors. For example, after biting another individual, aggressors would soon return to the victim to inspect the spot where they had put their teeth, and lick and clean it if an injury had resulted. The opposite relation between aggression intensity and contact initiative was found in a study of the Arnhem chimpanzees (Griede 1981). While the tendency of victims to initiate reconciliation was unaffected by the intensity of the previous conflict, aggressors were significantly less likely to initiate contact after high-intensity encounters than after low-intensity ones.

Such interspecific differences are quite puzzling and may be resolved only after a further standardization of methods and a careful differentiation as to the age and sex combination of the individuals involved in the aggression. As a further complication, Aureli et al. (1989) have demonstrated that in longtail macaques, contact initiative is different in the first three minutes than in the remaining time of the ten-minute post-conflict interval. The initiative changes from mostly by the victim to mostly by the aggressor (table 4 brings together their data over the entire interval). The authors explain the reversal of initiative as an expression of the victim's greater need for stress reduction immediately following the receipt of aggression.

Reconciliation Patterns

The greatest interspecific variability concerns the form of post-conflict reunions. Even closely related species, such as chimpanzees and bonobos, may use totally different behavior patterns. According to studies by de Waal and van Roosmalen (1979), Griede (1981), and Willemsen (1981) on the Arnhem chimpanzee colony, and also Goodall's (1986) descriptions of wild chimpanzees, reconciliations in this species typically involve kissing, embracing, outstretched-hand invitations, and gentle touching. Mounts and matings do occur in this context but do not rank among the ten most common reconciliation patterns (in the combined Arnhem studies only 2.6 percent of the post-conflict contacts involved sexual behavior). Bonobos, in contrast, typically reconcile by means of genital stimulation, and invitations for post-conflict contact are often of a sexual nature (i.e., females present their genital swelling either dorsally or while lying on their backs; males present penile erections sitting upright with legs spread apart). The reconciliation patterns described by de Waal (1987) for bonobos include: mutual penis thrusting between males; genito-genital rubbing between females (cf. Kuroda 1980); ventro-ventral and ventro-dorsal matings between the sexes; manual genital massage, and a variety of nonsexual contact forms such as ventro-ventral embracing and gentle touching. By and large, it seems that what chimpanzees do by kissing and embracing, bonobos do my means of sexual and erotic behavior.

Rhesus monkeys show a significant increase in lipsmacking and embracing during post-conflict reunions compared to control contacts (de Waal and Yoshihara 1983). Yet, while this result does support the prediction of behavioral distinctness of such reunions, less than 10 percent of the reunions involve these particular behavior patterns. This means that, most of the time, reconciliations among rhesus monkeys are relatively inconspicuous. To contrast this to the situation in stumptail macaques, de Waal and Ren (1988) have labeled the rhesus style of peacemaking *implicit* reconciliation and the stumptail style *explicit* reconciliation. That is, stumptails explicitly "refer" to the previous aggressive incident by means of conspicuous behavior patterns that they rarely show outside this context (see also de Waal 1989c).

The behavior most characteristic of reconciliations among stumptail monkeys is the hold-bottom ritual, in which one individual presents its hindquarters and the other clasps the other's haunches (figure 5). Whereas 34.3 percent of the post-conflict contacts between opponents are

FIGURE 5. After an aggressive incident three adult female stumptail monkeys engage in a clasping contact. The female in the middle squeals while holding the hips of her presenting opponent (right). The female on the left holds onto the center female, who protected her during the fight. From de Waal (1989d).

preceded by genital presentations, and 20.5 percent result in a hold-bottom, these respective behavior patterns are observed during only 1.3 percent and 0.9 percent of the control contacts. In addition, several other reassurance behaviors significantly increase in frequency after aggression among stumptails, i.e., gentle touching, mouth-to-mouth contact, genital inspection, grooming, and teeth-chattering (de Waal and Ren 1988; see also Blurton-Jones and Trollope 1968). So, stumptails combine a high conciliatory tendency (see figure 3) with a remarkably rich repertoire of reassurance gestures.

Patas monkeys do not exhibit systematic behavioral differences between reconciliations and contacts in other contexts. The failure to find such differences might be due to the relatively small sample size of the study by York and Rowell (1988). It might also reflect a general characteristic of the species, which has been said to rely on monitor/adjust behavior for social organization rather than on communication gestures and displays. Another difference is that the social hierarchy of patas monkeys is not as consistent and clear-cut as that of macaques, and is rarely expressed in ritualized status signals (Kaplan and Zucker 1980; Rowell and Olson 1983). De Waal's (1986d) model of the facilitating effect of dominance relationships on conflict resolution predicts that reconciliation behavior will be less developed in species, such as the patas monkey, with a weakly formalized hierarchy. In agreement with this prediction, post-conflict approaches in this species often lead to avoidance by the subordinate and renewed aggression by the dominant. These monkeys clearly do follow up on their conflicts, but only less than half of the approaches lead to friendly contact due to an apparent inability to overcome the resulting tensions (York and Rowell 1988).

In rhesus monkeys similar tensions are frequently observed, but in this species adversaries solve the problem by threatening low-ranking bystanders (de Waal and Yoshihara 1983; see also Cords 1988, for longtail macaques). Such redirection is relatively rare in the stumptail macaque. Possibly, all species have a need to underline status relationships after a fight, but instead of doing this in an aggressive manner, and thus endangering the peace process, some species have turned the reconciliation process itself into a status ritual. Thus, during hold-bottom interactions among stumptail monkeys, the dominant party does by far most of the clasping and the subordinate most of the presenting (de Waal and Ren 1988). In this respect, stumptails resemble male chimpanzees in that successful reconciliation requires status communication before or during the approach (de Waal 1986d).

Conclusions

Whereas the initial effect of aggression in primate groups often is dispersal, this effect is overcome within minutes by the tendency of adversaries to seek contact with one another. The increase in contact between former adversaries is both absolute and relative to contact with other individuals, i.e., there exists selective attraction between former opponents. The strength of the attraction, and its direction between aggressor and victim, differs per species. It is especially hard to generalize as even closely related species differ considerably with respect to whom will make up when.

Also, the behavior by which former adversaries resume contact is quite variable, ranging from mostly inconspicuous reconciliations among patas, rhesus, and longtail monkeys, to intensive sexual contacts among bonobos, kissing among chimpanzees, or hold-bottom rituals among stumptail monkeys. Behavioral differences between post-conflict contacts and contacts in other contexts, together with the demonstrated selective attraction, provide strong support for the reconciliation hypothesis.

Experimental Studies

Provoked Aggression

The tendency of monkeys to compete over food provides an opportunity to induce aggression experimentally and to determine the effects on subsequent relationships. This method was first applied by de Waal (1984) to small isosexual groups of juvenile rhesus monkeys. Three all-male and three all-female groups received a single piece of apple and were observed for half an hour afterwards. The behavior during these tests was compared with that during control tests without provision of extra food. In a previous study, it had been found that male rhesus monkeys in a mixed group reconciled more than females, but interpretation of this result was ambiguous because males also have a higher average dominance rank. The purpose of the experimental study was to tease apart the effects of rank and sex.

Following aggressive competition over the apple piece, and the consumption of the piece by one of the monkeys, grooming behavior and social cohesiveness increased significantly in the male groups. The female groups, in contrast, showed an insignificant decrease of the same behavior (see figure 6). This confirmed the previously found difference between the sexes in reconciliation behavior, this time unconfounded by effects of social dominance. However, it is doubtful if the apple tests measured exactly the same phenomenon. First, the increased grooming among the males was not related to the amount and direction of aggression during the initial food competition; individuals who opposed one another in a particular apple test were not necessarily the ones who did most of the subsequent grooming. Second, in another series of tests a handful of small apple pieces was spread over the cage floor. While the monkeys hurried around to fill their cheek pouches, they performed the same amount of aggression as in the tests with a single apple piece. Yet, subsequent affiliative behavior decreased in groups of both sexes. This means that it was the method of food distribution rather than the occurrence of aggression that determined subsequent affiliative patterns.

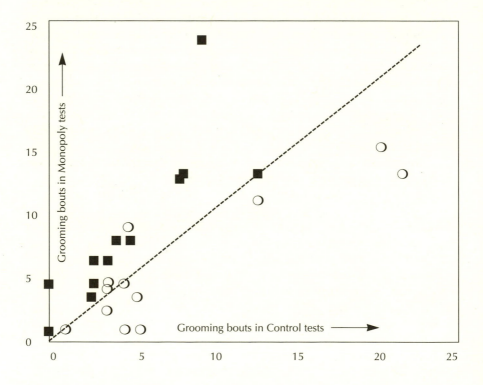

FIGURE 6. Comparison of grooming bouts performed per individual rhesus monkey during so-called Monopoly tests, in which the group received a single piece of apple, and Control tests. Data for each individual are from ten 30-minute tests of both types. Solid squares represent males; open circles represent females. Eleven of the twelve males showed a grooming increase following the food competition induced in the Monopoly tests, whereas only 3 of the twelve females did. From de Waal (1984).

For this reason, de Waal (1984) avoids the term reconciliation, speaking of "restorative" behavior instead. Such calming contact, it is argued, occurs in response to social tensions in the group, and tensions are related to the absence of food sharing. More specifically, tensions are caused by "envy" and "frustration" in non-possessors of food. Figure 7 summarizes the model.

According to this model the observed sex difference in the response of juvenile rhesus monkeys to a monopolizable food source can mean two things: either female relationships are not strained by unequal access to food, whereas male relationships are, or females are less active than males in trying to reduce the social tensions caused by unequal access.

Another experiment, involving juvenile male longtail macaques, was conducted by Cords (1988). Conflicts were provoked by giving a small tidbit to a lower-ranking male in the presence of a higher-ranking one. This was done in selected dyads at moments when they were partially isolated from the rest of the captive group to which they belonged. Three dyads consisted of matrilineally related males, and three dyads of unrelated males. Behavior was followed for fifteen minutes after the provoked aggression and compared with control observations taken on a different occasion after the same two males had interacted in a friendly or neutral manner.

Unrelated males showed attraction similar to that found in the obser-

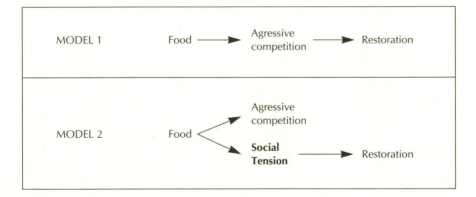

FIGURE 7. According to our initial model, restorative behavior, such as grooming, occurs in response to the disruptive effects of aggression (Model 1). The new model incorporates a hypothetical component, social tension, which is not linked to aggression but to the type of food provisioning (Model 2). According to model 2, restorative behavior occurs in response to frustrations and tensions caused by unequal access to food regardless of the amount and direction of previous aggression. From de Waal (1984).

vational studies treated before, i.e., former opponents interacted again sooner and more often after aggression than during control tests, and this did not reflect a general increase in social activity. In dyads of related males post-conflict attraction was less pronounced or absent. To explain the difference between kin and non-kin, Cords (1988) introduces the concept of the security of a social relationship, i.e., its predictability and resilience. According to this view, relationships among kin are not only of greater value but also more secure than relationships among non-kin, and may for this reason, under certain circumstances, need less repair after aggressive disturbance.

Although the concept of security seems useful, the problem is that the large majority of observational studies on monkeys indicate more reconciliation among kin than among non-kin (de Waal and Yoshihara 1983; de Waal and Ren 1988; York and Rowell 1988; Judge 1991; Aureli et al. 1989; but see Cords 1989). An alternative explanation for Cords' (1988) experimental results is given by the model in figure 7, namely that affiliative behavior after food competition depends on the mediating mechanism of social tension. Unequal access to food may create less social tension among kin than among non-kin. Although both dominant kin and non-kin make aggressive attempts to obtain the food item, there is perhaps less frustration in the loser if the winner is a relative. After all, related monkeys also show greater tolerance in competitive situations, as reflected in the amount of co-drinking and co-feeding among kin . (Yamada 1963; de Waal 1986a).

Celebrations and Food Sharing

A major difference between macaques and chimpanzees is that chimpanzees respond with reassurance behavior before or during food competition rather than, as the macaques in the above studies, afterwards. Thus, if an animal caretaker arrives with a bucket full of fruits and vegetables, the apes rush toward each other—embracing, kissing, and patting each other on the back—before coming forward to collect their share. De Waal (1989b) recorded a more than one hundred-fold increase in reassurance and appeasement behavior in chimpanzees upon the sight of attractive food. In macaques, in contrast, the same situation induces a tense, competitive atmosphere, and the monkeys immediately seek positions as close to the source of food as their dominance rank permits. It can hardly be surprising in view of this difference that noncompetitive mechanisms of food allocation are better developed in the chimpanzee than in the macaque (Goodall 1963; Nishida 1970; Teleki 1973; de Waal 1989b).

Speculating that the "celebrations" of chimpanzees reduce the probability of aggressive interaction over food, de Waal (1992) designed an experiment with two types of food delivery. One test allowed one to two minutes to elapse between the visibility of the food and its provisioning to the waiting colony; the second type allowed no such delay. The second type of provisioning gave the chimpanzees hardly any time to go through the characteristic appeasement rituals prior to food distribution. As predicted, aggressive competition over food was more common during food trials that were not preceded by such celebrations.

Similarly, in order to investigate the role of reassurance mechanisms during interactions over food in captive bonobos, de Waal (1987) recorded their behavior around feeding time, comparing it with base levels throughout the rest of the day. Upon detection of a caretaker with food, the apes would show penile erections, sexual invitations, and mounts in all possible positions and combinations. A similar sociosexual response to food has been observed in other captive bonobo colonies (e.g., Tratz and Heck 1954; Jordan 1977), and in the wild (e.g., Kano 1980; Kuroda 1980 1984; Thompson-Handler et al. 1984). Observations at the provisioning site in the forest of Wamba, Zaire, have led to a specific hypothesis concerning the functions of food-related sex, namely that it "works to ease anxiety or tension and to calm excitement" and "thus to increase tolerance, which makes food-sharing smooth" (Kuroda 1980: 190).

The fact that captive bonobos responded to food with the same sociosexual behavior as shown during reconciliations following aggression unrelated to food, suggests a shared function of the behavior, i.e., tension reduction (de Waal 1987). Moreover, some subordinates behaved considerably more assertively following sociosexual contact with dominant food possessors than without such prior contact (see figure 8). This change in self-confidence was particularly marked in one adult female vis-à-vis the dominant male. After, or sometimes even during a mating with him, this female would claim all his food. The possibility of trade of sexual favors for access to food, first suggested by Yerkes (1941) for chimpanzees and echoed by Kuroda (1984) for bonobos, is of considerable theoretical importance in connection with current scenarios of the evolution of the human family and the division of labor between the sexes (Lovejoy 1981; Fisher 1983).

Conclusions

Experimental studies confirm the paradoxical effect of aggression on affiliative behavior, i.e., an increase in affiliative behavior after, and in some species during, food-induced competition. The morphological simi-

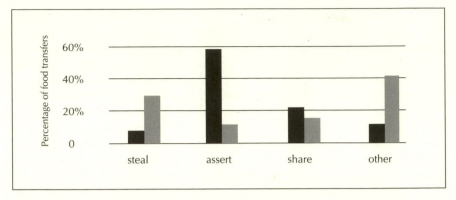

FIG. 8. Relative frequencies of four methods of food transfer from dominant to subordinate bonobos in the San Diego Zoo colony. The four types are stealing (the subordinate grabs food and runs away), assertive claiming (the subordinate calmly appropriates the dominant's food), sharing (feeding side by side on the same pile), and other types of food transfer (e.g., the subordinate waits for discarded pieces). Interactions over food preceded by affiliative or socio-sexual behavior (black) more often involved assertive claims by the subordinate than did interactions unpreceded by such behavior (gray). From de Waal (1987).

larity of this behavior to reconciliation behavior suggests a shared function. In a few species, social tensions created by the presence of attractive food may be buffered so effectively as to make food sharing possible.

Theoretical Issues

Constraints on Competition

If primates respond with reassurance behavior to social tensions, and seek reunions with former adversaries, this must mean that they value peaceful coexistence. As Kummer (1979) points out, long-term social relationships are an investment worth maintaining and defending. This insight has profound consequences for the way we view intragroup competition. It means that if two individuals compete over a particular resource, they have to take into account not only the value of the resource itself, and the risk of bodily harm, but also the value of their relationship with the competitor (see table 1). Sometimes the resource may not be worth the straining of a cooperative relationship, even if an individual could easily win the fight. This possibility considerably complicates models of competition (de Waal 1989a).

Traditionally, research on competitive relationships and social dominance has focused on the payoffs, particularly in terms of reproductive success, for the winners of combat (reviewed for primates by Fedigan 1983, and Shively 1985). Instead of this focus on the outcome of competition, however, researchers should also compare the number of opportunities for competition with the number of actual instances. Social tolerance, defined as a low competitive tendency, can be expected to correlate with a high rate of reconciliation after conflicts. The reason is that both traits—tolerance and reconciliation—supposedly serve the same function of preserving valuable relationships; the one by limiting aggression, the other by limiting the damage caused by aggression. If such a correlation can be demonstrated, this will provide a basis for more comprehensive models of conflict resolution.

A promising approach to this issue is that of comparisons between closely related species on such bases as group cohesion, the strictness of the dominance hierarchy, the symmetry of aggressive encounters, social tolerance, and conciliatory tendency. A number of comparative studies of this nature have been conducted on members of the genus *Macaca* (e.g., Thierry 1985, 1987; de Waal and Luttrell 1989). These studies explore conflict resolution and the nature of dominance relationships from the perspective of the advantages of group living and cooperation. These advantages vary per species, per environment, and per social partner, providing both proximate and ultimate reasons for variation in dominance style (de Waal 1989a; van Schaik 1989).

Social Sophistication and Cognition

Even in species with a high reconciliation rate, a large proportion of conflicts goes unreconciled. We know very little about the conditions of peacemaking. Variation across relationships has been studied by most of the investigators of reconciliation behavior. The results are often contradictory. For example, Cords (1988 1989) found more reconciliations among non-kin than among kin, whereas all other monkey studies report the opposite difference. Moreover, whereas de Waal and Yoshihara (1983) found that in rhesus monkeys the effect of kinship on conciliatory tendency disappears if social bond strength (in terms of time spent in association) is taken into account, de Waal and Ren (1988) failed to confirm an effect of bond strength on the conciliatory tendency among stumptail monkeys, finding instead that the kinship effect persists after correcting for differences in bond strength (see also Aureli et al. 1989).

Similarly, if we ask how the nature of previous aggression affects the probability of reconciliation, contradictory answers may be obtained, such as the already reported difference between chimpanzees and bonobos, i.e., in bonobos high-intensity aggression is more often reconciled by the aggressor, but in chimpanzees less often. It seems, then, that the basis on which primates decide to reconcile, or not, is a widely open area of investigation. To understand the underlying process, we may need much more subtle psychological concepts than hitherto accepted for animals. The literature suggests the following tentative lists of new concepts: rank acceptance; envy; the value and security of the relationship; the need to reduce uncertainty about the other's intentions; a distinction between reasonable and unreasonable aggression, and the withholding of reconciliation as a form of blackmail (de Waal 1982, 1984, 1986d, 1989d; Cords 1988; de Waal and Ren 1988; Aureli et al. 1989).

Several studies have systematically addressed triadic aspects of reconciliation in monkeys. De Waal and Yoshihara (1983) noted an increased grooming activity following violent aggression. Most of this grooming was aimed by the aggressor at an uninvolved third individual. This was explained as a "substitute" reconciliation resulting from two incompatible tendencies: attraction and hostility toward the opponent. In agreement with this explanation, it was found that the grooming occurred especially after fights between individuals who normally had a close relationship. The phenomenon was dubbed redirected affection.

Judge (1991), de Waal and Ren (1988), and Cheney and Seyfarth (1989) investigated the possibility that post-conflict contact with outsiders concerns individuals with a special relationship to the opponent. Thus, Cheney and Seyfarth (1989) distinguished direct reconciliation (post-conflict reunion between two opponents), simple reconciliation (post-conflict affiliation of one opponent with the kin of another), and complex reconciliation (post-conflict affiliation between kin of both opponents). Both Judge (1991) and Cheney and Seyfarth (1989) found that such triadic patterns do occur more often than expected by chance, supporting the idea that conflict and its resolution extend beyond individual opponents to their entire families (see also Cheney and Seyfarth 1986; de Waal 1989d). Yet, when de Waal and Ren (1988) expressed contact with opponent's kin as a percentage of contact partners, thus correcting for overall contact tendencies, they failed to find a difference between post-conflict and control observations.

Cheney and Seyfarth (1989) and Kummer et al. (1990) correctly point out that only experimental studies can provide the necessary controls and conditions to understand how individuals perceive the relationships among others, and how this perception influences triadic patterns of interaction. It should be added, though, that such experiments can only complement, not replace, the observation of spontaneous social interactions. Such observation remains necessary to provide insight into the function of particular cognitive capacities in daily social life and to generate new hypotheses. As an illustration, consider the following "anecdotal" evidence of social sophistication in relation to peacemaking in the Arnhem chimpanzee colony.

Deception. On six occasions a dominant female who had been unable to catch a fleeing opponent was observed to approach this individual some time afterwards with a friendly appearance, holding out her hand, only to change her behavior when the other came within reach. Reasons for believing that the female's real intention was the subsequent attack are its timing (very sudden, without warning signals), the fact that all instances concerned victims capable of outrunning the aggressor, and the intensity of the punishment (de Waal 1986c).

Opportunistic reconciliation. Reconciliation may occur in a hurried fashion if continuation of the fight would harm the interests of both individuals. For example, in the years that the Arnhem colony was ruled by a coalition of Nikkie and Yeroen, the alpha male, Nikkie, could get in serious trouble during prolonged conflicts with his partner. The third male would begin an intimidation display, initially terrorizing the females and juveniles but later displaying closer and closer to the two quarreling males themselves. Nikkie was never observed to control the third male on his own. He would first approach his opponent, Yeroen, with a large grin, seeking an embrace. Only after reestablishment of contact with his partner would Nikkie go over to the third male to subdue him. (For a photograph of one such scene see de Waal 1982: 140–141).

Third-party mediation. If, after a fight between them, two male rivals stayed in prolonged proximity without engaging in an actual physical reunion (an apparent deadlock situation), an adult female might initiate a grooming contact with one of the two. After several minutes of grooming, she would slowly walk to the other male, often followed by her grooming partner. If he failed to follow she might return to tug at his arm. After the three individuals had been together for a while, with the female in the middle, she would then get up and stroll away leaving the males alone.

Functional and Evolutionary Perspectives

Thus far, research on reconciliation behavior has aimed at demonstrating that there exists a causal connection between aggression and subsequent reassurance behavior. To further support the concept of reconciliation we now need studies on its effects. A first attempt is an unpublished study of the Arnhem chimpanzee colony by Gerard Willemsen and the author (Willemsen 1981). Comparing 127 agonistic incidents not followed by a reconciliation within half an hour with 39 reconciled incidents, we found that the probability of revival of the conflict was higher in the first category of dyads, i.e., 26.0 percent vs. 5.1 percent of the opponent pairs engaged in renewed antagonism within half an hour ($X2 = 6.6$, $p = 0.01$). This is an inconclusive result, however, as there are at least two possible explanations: (1) a friendly reunion between former opponents may cause a reduction in antagonism, or (2) a friendly reunion may reflect a low level of residual antagonism. The second explanation needs to be excluded before a conciliatory effect of reconciliation can be accepted.

One possible approach to the functional question is an experiment in which aggression-affiliation sequences among primates are interrupted in order to prevent post-conflict reunions. It has been suggested that such a procedure, if followed systematically with newly introduced monkeys, will prevent the formation of a close social bond even if there is ample time for peaceful association. The idea is that a social bond requires a formalized dominance relationship, and that aggression and subsequent reconciliation are a necessary part of the formation process (de Waal 1986d).

Cords (1990) recently reported an experiment in which affiliative contact following food-induced aggression between two monkeys could be either prevented or allowed. After this, the two monkeys would be presented with an attractive resource. Pairs that had engaged in affiliative contact showed greater compatibility, as measured by proximity during the test situation, than pairs that had not engaged in such contact. This result strongly supports a conciliatory function (i.e., the restoration of a tolerant attitude) of post-conflict reunion.

Another angle from which the function of reconciliation can be studied is through its effects on physiological and behavioral indicators of stress. Aureli et al. (1989) conducted a detailed analysis in longtail macaques of how the rate of self-scratching, a behavior assumed to correlate with sympathetic arousal, varies with the presence or absence of post-conflict reunion between former antagonists. As predicted by the reconciliation hypothesis, they found a fast reduction in scratching rate and a decrease in the reoccurrence of aggression following reconciliation. This approach, which needs further development (preferably complemented with direct physiological measures), may provide important information about the cost, in terms of stress level, associated with unreconciled aggression. Consequently, the adaptive significance of reconciliation may be illuminated from a physiological perspective.

Because reconciliation behavior has hardly been studied in the natural habitat, we do not know how the present findings extrapolate to the context in which this behavior evolved. In the field, Seyfarth (1976) observed post-conflict contacts among female baboons (*Papio cynocephalus*); Goodall (1986) studied reassurance behavior after aggression among chimpanzees, and Kuroda (1984) investigated food-related sexual interactions among bonobos. Cheney and Seyfarth (1989) applied a controlled observation paradigm to post-conflict behavior in wild vervet monkeys, confirming many of the findings of captive studies, although the observed rate of reconciliation was rather low. In view of these studies, there is no reason to assume that reconciliation behavior is limited to animals in confinement, though it would of course be surprising if the dynamics were identical under captive and free-ranging conditions.

Certain global patterns observed in captivity, such as dramatic interspecific or sex differences, probably reflect fundamental traits that are expressed under a wide variety of conditions. This has been confirmed for at least one pattern. Goodall (1986) and de Waal (1986d) independently report a higher conciliatory tendency in male chimpanzees compared to females. The first study concerned the frequency of reassurance behavior following aggression within an unspecified time interval among wild chimpanzees. The second study concerned contact between former opponents within half an hour after aggression in the Arnhem colony. Both investigators attribute the low level of peacemaking among females to the virtual absence of a clear-cut hierarchy. This is only the proximate view, however. From an evolutionary perspective we may speculate that unifying social mechanisms are more important for the reproductive success of male chimpanzees than for that of females. Males need to stick together for territorial defenses, and, in addition, their system of ever-changing coalitions requires them to stay on good terms even with rivals (Wrangham 1979; de Waal 1982; Nishida 1983; Goodall 1986).

Another general pattern, first reported by de Waal and Yoshihara (1983), is a correlation between conciliatory tendency and affiliation rate. This correlation indicates that reconciliation is most common in potentially valuable relationships, a hypothesis reviewed by Kappeler and van Schaik (1992) for a large number of primate species. Environmental pressures, such as predation and food distribution, shape the reconciliation behavior of each species to create an equilibrium between the centrifugal force of competition and the social cohesiveness required in that particular environment. On the basis of the behavior of captive stumptail monkeys, for example, we can expect this species to live in close-knit groups in its natural habitat. We do not actually know how these monkeys live, but it would not make sense for a loosely organized or widely dispersed species to possess the powerful mechanisms of physical reassurance and conflict resolution observed in captivity. Similarly, we can expect female chimpanzees to have trouble coping with competition and, as a result, to disperse, which we know happens in the wild (Nishida 1979; Goodall 1986).

Conclusions

At the proximate level, we need data on the conditions under which primates reconcile, or not. Probably, this cannot be properly understood without dramatically reconceptualizing animal psychology, including the way animals evaluate their own and others' social relationships. A broad approach to these issues would include all facets of competition, especially the conditions under which competition is suppressed or mitigated. At the functional level, we need to study the effects of reconciliation behavior on long-term relationships, and to relate mechanisms of tension regulation and social cohesiveness to the requirements of the natural environment.

Implications For Human Behavior

There is an astounding lack of systematic data on conflict resolution and reconciliation in our species. Part of the problem is that the social sciences tend to view human aggressiveness as an undesirable trait that needs to be eliminated; why pay attention to the way we cope with a behavior that we should actually get rid of?

Furthermore, the extreme emotionality surrounding the subject of aggression has hampered the development of a value-free science. By describing aggressive behavior as directed by "perpetrators" against "victims," rather than as a manifestation of a conflict of interest between two parties, aggression researchers have taxed their subject with undue moralizations. This attitude may be hard to avoid when dealing with the most extreme forms of aggression, such as rape and murder, yet we should not forget that aggression is an integrated part of many well-established relationships and rarely escalates to such violence. Whether or not aggression is a social problem depends very much on its effect on individual well-being and on long-term relationships. The consequences are not always negative: many human families manage to cohere for twenty years or more despite being veritable battlegrounds.

It is likely that many of the insights gained from reconciliation research on nonhuman primates will be applicable to our own species.

The most fruitful use of these data is for the development of hypotheses that can be tested on human behavior. The same techniques of observation developed in primate studies can be applied to human behavior—to children in the school yard, for instance—and many of the experimental techniques may, with some modification, be applicable in human research.

The most parsimonious assumption regarding the social behaviors of closely related species, such as humans and chimpanzees, is that similar behavior implies similar psychological and mental processes underlying this behavior. To propose otherwise requires the assumption of the evolution of divergent mechanisms for the production of behavior that looks and functions in much the same way. While useful in connection with distantly related species, this assumption is never made when the comparison concerns nonhuman organisms with only a couple of million years of separate evolution. Historically, our species has been considered an exception in this regard, yet arguments for this position have never been purely or even largely scientific.

Not only is there functional continuity between the post-conflict behavior of human and nonhuman primates; there exists also a remarkable morphological similarity in facial expressions and gestures (e.g., patting on the back; extending a hand; kissing; baring of the teeth in a grin or smile). Furthermore, at least in our closest relatives, we see the use of reconciliation as an internalized mechanism to prevent the emergence of aggression, making possible the sharing of prized food items. With sharing and reciprocity being one of the undisputed cornerstones of our complex societies—including our economies—this means that well-developed mechanisms of tension regulation have far-reaching consequences indeed.

The great interspecific variation observed in the rate and form of primate reconciliation behavior may be paralleled in human cultural variation. De Waal (1989d) has speculated that human cultural variation in this regard may relate to the ethnic homogeneity and level of forced proximity within a society. Cultures that place particular emphasis on compromise and consensus are found in some of the most crowded countries on the planet (e.g., the Japanese; the Dutch; the Javanese). Such a relation with population density, if true, would contradict popular extrapolations from rodents to humans, according to which aggression is expected to increase under crowded conditions. Effective mechanisms of conflict resolution seriously complicate the relation between spatial conditions and aggression in primates, both human and nonhuman, compared to species in which these mechanisms are less developed or absent (de Waal 1989c).

One of the most promising areas of future research concerns the environmental pressures that cause interspecific variation in the social organization of nonhuman primates. For example, the behavioral contrast between rhesus and stumptail monkeys, reflected in a wide variety of social characteristics, undoubtedly relates to a greater need for closely knit group life in the stumptails (de Waal and Luttrell 1989). Which aspects of the stumptails' natural environment might be responsible for increased group cohesion? Are there many predators around or serious hostilities between groups? These and similar questions can be asked in relation to human cultural variation in peacemaking tendencies, and probably the same theoretical models can be applied.

Notes

1. Upon learning of Professor de Waal's research among bonobos (pygmy chimpanzees), Kenneth Boulding was moved to compose a poem humorously summarizing the bonobo's ability to make peace. Boulding exercises artistic license in identifying the bonobo as a monkey rather than an ape, as in the title of the poem, "Monkeys Up de Waal."

> Among the major breeds of monkeys
> Some are bosses, some are flunkies,
> And yet the happiest breed we know
> Would seem to be the bonobo
>
> For these are right up to their necks
> In fairly indiscriminate sex
> In which they take such great delight
> They do not have much time to fight
>
> Monkeys will fight when they are riled
> Yet frequently are reconciled.
> No one who studies them can miss
> The great power of the hug and kiss.

It is tempting to extend de Waal's argument to human cultural groups, such as the Semai (see chapter 6, Gregor and Robarchek). In any case, de Waal and his colleagues' pioneering work shows that the arts of peace have a biological basis that we share with other species.

References

(I am grateful to Tine Griede and Gerard Willemsen for data collected in Arnhem. This research was supported by grant no. RR-00167 of the National Institutes of Health to the

Wisconsin Regional Primate Research Center, and this chapter is based on WRPRC's publication no. 27-004.)

Adams, D., et al. 1987. Statement on violence. *Medicine and War* 3: 191–192.

Asquith, P. 1984. The inevitability and Utility of Anthropomorphism in Description of Primate Behaviour. In *The Meaning of Primate Signals,* ed. R. Harr and V. Reynolds, 138–176. Cambridge: Cambridge University Press.

Aureli, P., C. van Schaik, and J. A. R. A. M. van Hooff. 1989. Functional Aspects of Reconciliation among Captive Longtailed Macaques *(Macaca fascicularis). American Journal of Primatology* 19: 39–52.

Blurton-Jones, N. G., and J. Trollope. 1968. Social Behaviour of Stump-Tailed Macaques in Captivity. *Primates* 9: 365–394.

Cheney, D. L., and R. M. Seyfarth. 1986. The Recognition of Social Alliances by Vervet Monkeys. *Animal Behaviour* 34: 1722–1731.

———. 1989. Reconciliation and Redirected Aggression in Vervet Monkeys, *Cercopithecus aethiops. Behaviour* 110: 258–275.

Cords, M. 1988. Resolution of Aggressive Conflicts by Immature Long-Tailed Macaques *(Macaca fascicularis). Animal Behaviour* 36: 1124–1135.

———. 1990. How Immature Long-Tailed Macaques Cope with Aggressive Conflict. Paper presented at the 13th Congress of the International Primatological Society, Nagoya and Kyoto, Japan.

Ehrlich, A., and A. Musicant. 1977. Social and Individual Behaviors in Captive Slow Lorises. *Behaviour* 60: 195–220.

Ellefson, J. 1968. Territorial Behavior in the Common White-Handed Gibbon, *Hylobatus lar.* In *Primates: Studies in Adaptation and Variability,* ed. P. Jay, 180–199. New York: Holt.

Fedigan, L. 1983. Dominance and Reproductive Success in Primates. *Yearbook of Physical Anthropology* 26: 91–129.

Fisher, H. 1983. *The Sex Contract.* New York: Quill.

Goodall, J. 1963. My Life among Wild Chimpanzees. *National Geographic* 117: 272–308.

———. 1986. *The Chimpanzees of Gombe: Patterns of Behavior.* Cambridge: Harvard, Belknap Press of Harvard University Press.

Goodall, J. van Lawick. 1968. The behaviour of Free-Living Chimpanzees in the Gombe Stream Reserve. *Animal Behaviour Monographs* 1 (3): 161–311.

Griede, T. 1981. Invloed op Verzoening bij Chimpansees. Unpublished research report, University of Utrecht.

Hediger, H. 1941. *Biologische Gesetzmäßigkeiten im Verhalten von Wirbeltieren.* Mitteilungen Naturforschungs Gesellschaft Bern 1940, 37–55.

Hinde, R. 1970. *Animal Behaviour: A Synthesis of Ethology and Comparative Psychology.* 2d edition. New York: McGraw-Hill.

Jordan, C. 1977. Das Verhalten Zoolebender Zwergschimpansen. Ph.D. dissertation. Goethe University, Frankfurt.

Judge, P. 1991. Dyadic and Triadic Reconciliation in Pigtail Macaques *(Macaca nemestrina). American Journal of Primatology* 23: 225–237.

Kano, T. 1980. Social Behavior of Wild Pygmy Chimpanzees *(Pan paniscus)* of Wamba: A Preliminary Report. *Journal of Human Evolution* 9: 243–260.

Kappler, P., and C. van Schaik. 1992. Methodological and Evolutionary Aspects of Reconciliation among Primates. *Ethology* 92: 51–69.

Kaplan, J., and E. Zucker. 1980. Social Organization in a Group of Free-Ranging Patas Monkeys. *Folia Primatologica* 34: 196–213.

Kellogg, W., and L. Kellogg. 1933. *The Ape and the Child*. New York: McGraw-Hill.

Köhler, W. 1959 [1925]. *Mentality of Apes*. 2d edition. New York: Vintage.

Kummer, H. 1979. On the Value of Social Relationships to Nonhuman Primates: A Heuristic Scheme. In *Human Ethology: Claims and Limits of a New Discipline*, ed. M. Von Cranach et al., 381–395. New York: Cambridge University Press.

Kummer, H., V. Dasser, and P. Hoyningen-Huene. 1990. Exploring Primate Social Cognition: Some Critical Remarks. Behaviour 112: 84–98.

Kuroda, S. 1980. Social Behavior of the Pygmy Chimpanzees. *Primates* 21: 181–197.

———. 1984. Interaction over Food among Pygmy Chimpanzees. In *The Pygmy Chimpanzee*, ed. R. Susman, 301–324. New York: Plenum.

Lindburg, D. 1973. Grooming Behavior As a Regulator of Social Interactions in Rhesus Monkeys. In *Behavioral Regulators of Behavior in Primates*, ed. C. Carpenter, 85–105. Lewisburg, Pa.: Bucknell University Press.

Lorenz, K. 1935. Der Kumpan in der Umwelt des Vogels. *Journal der Ornithologie* 83: 137–214 and 289–413.

———. 1963. Das Sogenannte Böse. Vienna: Borotha–Schoeler.

Lovejoy, C. 1981. The Origin of Man. *Science* 211: 341–350.

Mason, W. 1964. Sociability and Social Organization in Monkeys and Apes. In *Advances in Experimental Social Psychology*, ed. L. Berkowitz, 277–305. New York: Academic Press.

Maynard Smith, J., and G. Price. 1973. The Logic of Animal Conflict. *Nature* 246: 15–18.

McKenna, J. 1978. Biosocial Function of Grooming Behavior among the Common Langur Monkey (*Presbytis entellus*). *American Journal of Physical Anthropolog* 48: 503–510.

Nishida, T. 1970. Social Behavior and Relationships among Wild Chimpanzees of the Mahale Mountains. *Primates* 11: 47–87.

———. 1979. The Social Structure of Chimpanzees of the Mahale Mountains. In *The Great Apes*, ed. D. Hamburg and E. McCown, 73–121. Menlo Park, Calif.: Benjamin Cummings.

———. 1983. Alpha Status and Agonistic Alliance in Wild Chimpanzees. *Primates* 24: 318–336.

Poirier, F. 1968. Dominance Structure of the Nigiri Langur (*Presbytis johnii*) of South India. *Folia Primatologica* 12: 161–186.

van Rhijn, J., and R. Vodegel. 1980. Being Honest about One's Intentions: An Evolutionary Stable Strategy for Animal Conflicts. *Journal of Theoretical Biology* 85: 623–641.

Rowell, T., and D. Olson. 1983. Alternative Mechanisms of Social Organization in Monkeys. *Behaviour* 86: 31–54.

van Schaik, C. 1989. The Ecology of Social Relationships Amongst Female Primates. In *Comparative Socioecology: The Behavioural Ecology of Humans and Other Mammals*, ed. V. Standen and R. Foley, 195–218. Oxford: Blackwell.

Scott, J. P. 1958. *Animal Behavior*. Chicago: University of Chicago Press.

Seyfarth, R. 1976. Social Relationships among Adult Female Baboons. *Animal Behaviour* 24: 917–938.

Shively, C. 1985. The Evolution of Dominance Hierarchies in Nonhuman Primates Society. In *Power, Dominance, and Nonverbal Behavior*, ed. S. Ellyson and I. Dovidio, 67–87. Berlin: Springer.

Teleki, G. 1973. *The Predatory Behavior of Wild Chimpanzees*. Lewisburg, Pa.: Bucknell University Press.

Thierry, B. 1984. Clasping Behavior in *Macaca tonkeana*. *Behaviour* 89: 1–28.

———. 1985. A Comparative Study of Aggression and Response to Aggression in Three Species of Macaque. In *Primate Ontogeny, Cognition and Social Behaviour*, ed. I. Else and

P. Lee, 307–313. Cambridge: Cambridge University Press.

———. 1987 Coadaptation des variables sociales: l'exemple des systmes sociaux des macaques. *Colloques de l'INRA* 38: 92–100.

Thompson-Handler, N., R. Malenky, and N. Badrian. 1984. Sexual Behavior of *Pan paniscus* under Natural Conditions in the Lomako Forest, Equateur, Zaire. In *The Pygmy Chimpanzee*, ed. R. Susman, 347–368. New York: Plenum Press.

Tratz, E., and H. Heck 1954. Der afrikanische Anthropoide Bonobo, eine neue Menschenaffengattung. *Saugetierkundige Mitteilungen* 2: 97–101.

Veenema, H., M. Das, and F. Aureli. 1994. Methodological Improvements for the Study of Reconciliation. *Behavioural Processes* 31: 28–38.

de Waal, F. B. M. 1982. *Chimpanzee Politics*. London: Jonathan Cape.

———. 1984 Coping with social tension; Sex differences in the effect of food provision to small rhesus monkey groups. *Animal Behaviour* 32: 765–773.

———. 1986a. Class structure in a rhesus monkey group; the interplay between dominance and tolerance. *Animal Behaviour* 34: 1033– 1040.

———. 1986b. Conflict Resolution in Monkeys and Apes. In *Primates— the Road to Self-Sustaining Populations*, ed. F. Benirschke, 341– 350. New York: Springer Verlag.

———. 1986c. Deception in the Natural Communication of Chimpanzees. In *Deception: Perspectives on Human and Nonhuman Deceit*, ed. R. Mitchell and N. Thompson, 221–224. New York: SUNY Press.

———. 1986d. Integration of dominance and social bonding in primates. *Quarterly Review of Biology* 61: 459–479.

———. 1987. Tension Regulation and Nonreproductive Functions of Sex among Captive Bonobos (*Pan paniscus). National Geographic Research* 3: 318–335.

———. 1989a. Dominance Style And Primate Social Organization. In *Comparative Socioecology: The Behavioural Ecology of Humans and Other Mammals*, ed. V. Standen, and R. Foley, 243–264. Oxford: Blackwell.

———. 1989b. Food Sharing and Reciprocal Obligations among Chimpanzees. *Journal of Human Evolution* 18: 433–459.

———. 1989c. The Myth of a Simple Relation between Space and Aggression in Captive Primates. *Zoo Biology Supplement* 1: 141– 148.

———. 1989d. *Peacemaking among Primates*. Cambridge: Harvard University Press.

———. 1992. Appeasement, Celebration, and Food Sharing in the Two *Pan* Species. In *Topics in Primatology*, vol. 1:*Human Origins*, ed. T. Nishida et al., 37–50. Tokyo: University of Tokyo Press.

de Waal, F. B. M., and L. M. Luttrell. 1989. Toward a Comparative Socioecology of the Genus Macaca: Different Dominance Styles in Rhesus and Stumptail Monkeys. *American Journal Primatology* 19: 83–109.

de Waal, F. B. M., and R. Ren. 1988. Comparison of the Reconciliation Behavior of Stumptail and Rhesus Macaques. *Ethology* 78: 129–142.

de Waal, F. B. M., and A. van Roosmalen. 1979. Reconciliation and Consolation among Chimpanzees. *Behavioral Ecology and Sociobiology* 5: 55–66.

de Waal, F. B. M., and D. Yoshihara. 1983. Reconciliation and Re-Directed Affection in Rhesus Monkeys. *Behaviour* 85: 224–241.

Willemsen, G. 1981. Verzoeningsgedrag van de chimpansee. Unpublished Research Report, University of Utrecht.

Wrangham, R. 1979. Sex Differences in Chimpanzee Dispersion. In *The Great Apes*, ed. D. Hamburg and E. McCown, 481–490. Menlo Park, Calif.: Benjamin/Cummings.

Yamada, M. 1963. A Study of Blood Relationships in the Natural Society of the Japanese

Macaque. *Primates* 4: 43–65.

Yerkes, R. 1941. Conjugal Contrasts among Chimpanzees. *Journal of Abnormal Psychology* 36: 75–199.

York, A., and T. Rowell. 1988. Reconciliation Following Aggression in Patas Monkeys (*Erythrocebus patas*). *Animal Behaviour* 36: 502–509.

3 The Human Evolution of Cooperative Interest

BRUCE M. KNAUFT

■ Bruce Knauft points out that human evolution has been shaped by two competing forces or "imperatives." The first imperative, the biogenetic, leads to maximizing individual self-interest, often at the expense of the group. The second, a cultural imperative, is at the basis of sociality and cooperation. Although the two are often in competition, humans are distinctive occupants of a "cooperative niche" in primate evolution, in that cooperation is a crucial adaptive strategy. Knauft applies this perspective to hunters and foragers, and then, with the assistance of data on contemporary hunters and ancient Australian depictions of aggression, he projects back to earlier periods of human evolution. The result is a sweeping view of the human condition that emphasizes the propensity for cooperation as well as the capacity for aggressive individualism. As in many of the other contributions in this volume (see Chapter 7, Robarchek and Robarchek, on the transformation of Waorani violence; chapter 9, Crenshaw, on the demise of terrorist movements; and chapter 10, Vasquez, on the conditions of international peace), we see humans as significantly in control of their destinies.

HUMANS ARE "by nature" both peaceful and violent. On the one hand, humans as a species are enormously gregarious, and our forms of prosocial affiliation are elaborate and complex. Social affiliation has also been extremely important in human evolution. Widespread cooperation and exchange of information among diffuse networks of unrelated as well as related individuals are central to social functioning in all known human societies, including nomadic foragers, and likely formed an important impetus in the evolution of language (Kurland and Beckerman 1985; Knauft 1994b). As Geertz (1962) emphasized in an early essay, the symbolic systems that link unrelated people together are not add-on to human nature but an essential part of it; shared meaning systems are central to our existence as a self-domesticated species, just as a computer program is central to the operation of a computer. In contrast to most other species, human social affiliation is

71

intense among nonrelatives as well as relatives—among those whose identity is known through cultural, ethnic, or class affiliation and but weakly associated with biogenetic or breeding relationships.

Of course, culture also allows humans to cohere in oppression, disparagement, or killing, particularly of persons conceived to be deviants or members of out-groups. Moreover, if there is evidence that humans were preadapted for social gregariousness, there is equally compelling evidence that intraspecific aggression is common among primates and among mammals more generally. Particularly prominent are inter-male competition for mates and competition for resources that can confer survival and reproductive advantage. Through a wide range of social and symbolic stimuli, heightened arousal can be escalated among humans to engage the neurophysiology of aggressive rage.

With few exceptions, the balance between gregariousness and violence in *non*human species can be best explained on the basis of Darwinian postulates: behavioral pursuits maximize reproductive fitness. Given our phylogenetic heritage, it is unlikely that this Darwinian impetus is absent among humans.

But among contemporary humans, the drive toward maximizing reproductive fitness is importantly cross cut by other competing goals. Though the applicability of sociobiology to modern human populations has been hotly debated now for many years, a majority of cultural anthropologists as well as many biological theoreticians find it too narrow as a basis for explaining human behavior, particularly among contemporary populations. Neo-Darwinian emphasis on genetic selfishness can effectively explain behavior that promotes the production of many surviving offspring (and offspring of close genetic relatives). But such reasoning has difficulty accounting for the kinds of diffuse social affiliation, restrictions on sexual and aggressive behavior, and rule-governed morality that influence behavior in human societies. Depending on one's social and cultural environment, the attainment of status, prestige, and "success" may not entail the greatest reproductive advantage or inclusive fitness, and may even compromise them (e.g., Edgerton 1992). The modern demographic transition, in which industrialized countries experienced a great decrease in fertility, is but one large-scale example of this compromise (Vining 1986). Though one may debate the technicalities of this and other examples in which reproductive success and inclusive fitness are willfully compromised among humans, pragmatics speak loudly. It is increasingly untenable on empirical as well as logical grounds to assume that our desire to acquire specific goods and resources (much less the more intangible rewards of obtaining value or knowledge) is reducible to our desire to pass on as many of our genes as possible. Many things are important to us besides maximizing the number of children we and our closest genetic relatives propagate; it arbitrarily narrows human motivation to assume that our actions all funnel to this biogenetic competition. For humans, quality of life does not always boil down to quantity of life.

The standard sociobiological response to this problem is to argue that what appears to be cultural value, quality, and nonreproductive desire is a deception that masks our true motivations: quality of life is an ideology. No one would dispute that this reasoning is *partly* correct. But this is far from suggesting that *all* our cultural values, aspirations for quality of life, and nonreproductive desires are ideologies, much less that they all mask the *same* narrow and self-interested ultimate goal, i.e., biogenetic reproduction.

One of the keys that sociobiologists and behavioral ecologists use to explain the gregarious and prosocial side of human behavior is reciprocal altruism: I'm being nice to you because (and only because) you are also nice to me (see Trivers 1971, 1985). Along this view, what is apparently altruistic is in fact self-interested. Undoubtedly, as above, this is part of the story, but it is also myopic in what it excludes. The theoretical and logical validity of reciprocal altruism is predicated on tight control of cheating and deception; my being nice to you depends (unless you are a close biogenetic relative) upon my being able to know dependably that you are not cheating or deceiving me. This stricture is not hard to fill under ideal conditions—the famous "prisoner's dilemma" game—but it is much harder to satisfy in the real world of social interaction. The mathematical and logical limitations on reciprocal altruism as an evolutionarily stable strategy are more restrictive than realized by many behavioral ethologists (Boyd and Lorberbaum 1987). This confirms what experience tells us: controls on cheating are very difficult to maintain. This is true not only in complex modern societies, in which people move about constantly, but in simple human societies, such as decentralized foragers, which are characterized by flexible movement and fluid, migratory band organization that integrally includes persons who are not close biogenetic relatives. And it is among such societies that rule-of-thumb obligations for sharing of food and other resources in the community are arguably the strongest.

Closer to home, social affiliation continues in the absence of biogenetic ties. A stranger walks up and asks you the time; you look at your watch and give an honest and helpful answer. That suspicion, envy, and brutality *do* infect human relations should not blind us to the fact that most people do follow rule-of-thumb rules of social cooperation much, perhaps most, of the time. We continue to stop for red lights even when no police are watching. As social theorists and causal observers of human society have long realized, brute force and fear of retribution are simply not sufficient to account for the complex organization and functional integration of human societies. In the final analysis, then, the diverse influence of prosocial rules cannot be completely accounted for by fear of violent reprisal, by the imperative of maximal genetic reproduction, nor even by a dependable trust that those we help are not deceiving us. The man who asks the time may also go for your wallet. Yet our predisposing prosocial tendencies persist. This cooperative disposition has been rigorously documented under experimental conditions in the absence of self-interested payoffs (e.g., Caporael et. al. 1989).

If this is true of contemporary humans and in many simple societies, how long ago did the tension between biogenetic goals and the prosocial potential of cultural affiliations inflect our evolutionary past? Though it is frequently forgotten by behavioral ecologists, Darwin (1871) himself thought that it was our human instinct for "sympathy" that set us apart from all other species. And it is true that we find strikingly altruistic and even maladaptive behavior (from a genetic fitness perspective) in a number of simple human societies (e.g., Knauft 1987; 1993b: chapter 8; Moore 1990; Edgerton 1992). Maladaptiveness itself is not hard for a competitive model of human nature to account for: societies that are too maladaptive, too altruistic, or not sufficiently driven by the self-interest of individual members are out-competed or infiltrated by individuals who are more self-serving. But what if the group's values and beliefs are deeply internalized such that individuals take collective action to root out self-serving infiltrations; what if they castigate and ostracize individuals who are too self-interested?

In the simplest human societies, individuals who are too self-interested are not rewarded but shunned and may be cut off from the support of the community. And it is this community upon which their survival as well as their sense of worth depends. The costs to the individual are high, since she or he is integrally dependent upon communal networks of cooperation and protection. In many if not most simple societies, greedy or violent mates are shunned by potential spouses as well as their kin. This status levelling has been documented more specifically for a wide range of simple human societies (see Knauft 1991; Boehm 1993). Cooperation is extremely important; it is not just an ideology, applies not just among biogenetic kin, and persists despite occasional cheating. Those who are too eager to mate with others' partners, who are too domineering, and who are too self-serving are cut down to size, stripped of their esteem, and, more importantly from a sociobiological prerogative, stripped of behavioral prerogatives. This is what Boehm (1993) calls a "reverse dominance hierarchy" and what Erdal and Whiten (1994) describe as "counterdominant behavior" established through "vigilant sharing." This refusal to be dominated is the sine qua non of politically decentralized human societies, and it distinguishes us remarkably from the dominance hierarchies that characterize chimpanzees and other great apes (Knauft 1991, 1993, 1994a+b). This pattern is particularly evident among simple human societies such as decentralized hunter-gatherers, which provide our best ethnographic window on the largest part of our species' history.

Intellectual Legacy

The distinctiveness of human cooperation has generated significant interest in western social science. In his turn-of-the-century book *Mutual Aid: A Factor in Evolution*, Petr Kropotkin was one of the first to emphasize the importance of cooperative sociality in the study of human evolution (1902; see Gould 1988; cf. Vucinich 1988: chapter 10). In anthropology, the central place of sociality in early human development has a legacy in the work of, among others, Claude Lévi-Strauss (1949) on primal structures of human kinship alliance; Leslie White (1949) on evolutionary features of symbolic communication; Clifford Geertz (1962) on culture and the evolution of mind; Hockett and Ascher (1964) on "the human revolution;" and Glynn Isaac (1978, 1984) on collective hominid affiliation.

However, the importance of socially cooperative predispositions in evolution was severely questioned during 1960s and 1970s, especially in the wake of G. C. Williams's influential book *Adaptation and Natural Selection*. Williams concluded that behaviors that benefitted the group rather than the individual's genetic survival would always lose out against the stronger imperatives of individual selection, that is, the competitive self-interest of the biogenetic individual.

The 1970s and 1980s saw materialist anthropology grow increasingly into behavioral ecology, sociobiology, and, now, evolutionary psychology. However, empirical evidence of cooperative predispositions among humans did not go away. During the 1980s and 1990s, an increasing number of researchers began to question why self-interested selection should be limited to the level of the gene rather than to biochemical competition between the elements that themselves constitute the gene or, alternatively, between the groups of individuals that genes make up (e.g.,

Wilson and Sober 1989, 1994). As genetics and the study of group complexity both become more sophisticated, "the gene" is losing its status as a sacred black box; it can no longer be considered the sole and simplistically reified "unit" of selection.

Our frame of reference concerning levels of selection in human evolution took a leap forward in 1985 with the publication of Boyd and Richerson's *Culture and the Evolutionary Process*. Boyd and Richerson proposed that standard Darwinian genetic selection was not diminished but importantly complemented in humans by *another channel of selective transmission*—that of human culture. If humans are at one level a gene's way of producing another gene, as suggested by sociobiologists such as Dawkins (1989), so, too, from a cultural point of view, humans are a vehicle by which symbolic systems propagate and reproduce themselves (cf. Cullen 1993). It is the empirical relationship between these complementary processes of evolutionary selection that Boyd and Richerson seek to analyze.

The cultural side of this process is less appreciated and understood. Among humans, cultural values almost always include basic rules that enforce morality, friendship, and honesty within the social group. These rules are passed on by social learning or socialization; indeed, humans as a species are highly dependent on prolonged socialization and learning. As a result, group-cooperative dispositions among humans can be deeply internalized, effectively and quickly transmitted, and socially buttressed against more self-interested alternatives favored by processes of biogenetic selection.

None of this suggests that human behavior, and especially sexual behavior, is immune from individual self-interest. Nor does it suggest that rules of morality, prosocial affiliation, honesty, and so on, are impervious to cheating, deception, and simple disobedience. It is simply to suggest, as Freud realized decades ago, that human nature is a conflict between opposed forces that are both real, strong, and influential: the constraints of social morality, and the self-interested desires—including sexual desires—of the individual. Few but the most myopic sociobiologist would suggest that social morality has no real or independent influence on behavior, including behavior that might otherwise maximize biogenetic reproduction. Likewise, few but the most myopic cultural relativist would suggest that reproductive imperatives and their close cousin, sexual drive, have no substantive influence on culturally mediated behavior.

Given the theoretical emphasis on the self-interested side of this puzzle during the last two decades, it seems appropriate for the group-cooperative features now to be given more attention. The power of symbolic communication to bind together nonrelated individuals and establish prosocial affiliations has long been known. But with the rise of neo-Darwinian emphasis, symbolic and cultural anthropologists have moved increasingly away from the study of human evolution. Few cultural anthropologists today concern themselves with human evolution at all. Correspondingly, the theories that informed this field were left largely to the reductionist assumptions of behavioral ecology and, increasingly, sociobiology (e.g., Wilson 1975). The role of culture in the evolution of human behavior has been surprisingly neglected even as the relationship between culture, power, and history has become one of the main cutting edges of contemporary cultural anthropology.

As a corrective to these tendencies, the present chapter emphasizes the collective socialization in gregarious groups that provided a distinctive evolutionary niche for the genus *Homo*. I emphasize that this focus on culturally cooperative traits does not deny or preclude but merely *complements* biogenetically self-interested behavior among humans. With the advent of human proto-culture and then culture, altruism via group-level cultural selection never became totally determinant, but it did become an influence. Because group-advantageous strategies could be quickly and widely transmitted, deeply internalized through socialization and learning, and socially defended against infiltration, rule-of-thumb sociality was difficult to *de*-select through narrowly self-interested alternatives.

Human Evolutionary Issues

If humans harbor intrinsically competing imperatives for biogenetic and cultural transmission, to disseminate both genes and tenets of collective value, the outcome of this interface has been variable over the course of human evolution. Conflict between sexual self-interest and cooperative affiliation must have been profound during the early evolution of human social organization. Distinctive features in the social evolution of *Homo sapiens* likely included large group size, significant sexual division of labor, sharing of valuable food throughout a band of twenty-five to fifty related and unrelated individuals, high male parental investment, and exchange of information and flexible access to resources among several such dispersed but interlocking forager groups (see Rodseth et. al. 1991; Foley and Lee 1989; Foley 1987; Lovejoy 1981). This form of organization provided crucial adaptive advantages for humans relative to social carnivores, solitary and herd herbivores, and omnivorous nonhuman primates. At the same time, however, regular dispersal of individuals to exploit patchy or unpredictable food resources made mating exclusivity and paternity-certainty problematic. The human solution to this problem is arguably unique.

As Freud and the early Lévi-Strauss elucidated with complementary genius, human societies have developed symbolically mediated social and psychological constraints on sexual impulses; sexual control in humans is both psychically internalized and socially and symbolically maintained. The threat posed by immediate, disruptive, and self-interested sexual behavior in the evolution of *Homo* was to a significant extent (though by no means totally) countered by cultural prescriptions fostering sexual control and social accommodation.

How this process may have arisen out of standard natural selection is an intriguing question to which the work of Boyd and Richerson (1985) provides important insights. It is quite likely that imitative learning was strongly selected for as a rule-of thumb adaptive strategy among early humans; human infants are highly altricial and extremely dependent upon socialization as well as parental care. Both within and between generations, imitation is pronounced and behavior traits can spread rapidly. Added to this, and no doubt in causal concert with it, is the highly developed ability of humans to communicate through elaborate symbolic communication. Available evidence suggests that symbolic communication was elaborate even if not equivalent to modern language during the evolution of *Homo*.[1]

Through socialization and symbolic communication, behavioral traits can be learned and quickly spread through cultural transmission. The idiosyncrasy that sometimes occurs in cultural variation (the cultural analog of genetic mutation) couples with rapid transmission to allow the temporary spread of maladaptive customs in a population—what Durham (1991: chapter 7) calls cultural-genetic opposition. It is this feature that allows for the generation, spread, and persistence of detrimental behaviors (for instance, the smoking of nicotine- and tar-laden tobacco). In addition, however, cultural transmission allows the spread of behaviors that can favor the group over the maximimal inclusive fitness of single individuals within it. Put differently, biogenetic selection gives rise to a cultural transmission process that becomes partially decoupled from it. This does not condemn humans to biogenetic dysfunctionality; it simply adds the cultural group to the individual as a separate and competing unit of selection.

The assumption of many researchers that the individual is the sole unit of selection in human evolution is increasingly being challenged. From ethnography and demography, queries are raised by the existence of behavior patterns that systematically compromise rather than maximize the reproductive success of individual actors (e.g., Vining 1986; Knauft 1987a+c, 1989; Moore 1990). From social psychology, sociobiological assumptions have been questioned on the basis of experiments that document the existence of altruistic tendencies toward strangers in the absence of payoffs (e.g., Caporael et al. 1989; Dawes, van de Kraft, and Orbell 1988). And from theoretical biology, questions are raised by increasing realization that the conditions under which self-interested reciprocal altruism can explain cooperation are more restrictive than previously thought (e.g., Boyd and Lorberbaum 1987). At the same time, there is increasing recognition that group selection may help explain the existence of widespread reciprocity and altruism and that cultural transmission may operate through selection parameters that are nonbiogenetic, nonindividualistic, or superorganic (e.g., Wilson and Sober 1994, 1989; Boyd 1988; Boyd and Richerson 1985, 1990a+b; Rogers 1990; Richerson and Boyd 1989; Harpending and Rogers 1987; Nowak and Sigmund 1989; Durham 1991; Wilson 1989; contrast Hamilton 1964; Trivers 1971, 1985; Axelrod and Hamilton 1981).

What results is a complex coevolution between distinct behavioral transmission and selection systems, one symbolic, the other biogenetic. The increased speed and elaboration of cultural as opposed to biogenetic selection processes render symbolic effects increasingly influential on behavior over time, but the tension between them is never eradicated. Robert Paul (personal communication, cf. 1987) has suggested that a kind of "arms race" emerges between cultural constraints on sexual impulses and biogenetic selection pressures that encourage mating. This escalation may well have made humans among the sexiest and simultaneously the most sexually repressed of species.

In early human evolution, as at present, cultural control of sexual impulses was not complete; threats to band cooperation and integrity posed by illicit sexuality and its concomitant disruption were always present. The unprecedented influence on behavior and mental motivations through cultural conditioning, however, resulted in significant group-cooperative control upon sexuality. Rule-governed cultural control of sexual behavior, even if partial, could facilitate cooperation and the sexual division of labor, thus increasing the survival rate of the group as a whole.[2] This helps resolve "the problem ... [of] how exclusive sexual bonds evolved from a chimpanzee-like pattern of promiscuity" (Rodseth et al. 1991: 237). Nonsymbolic behavior selection was by itself insufficient to maintain such a mating system, since, as Wrangham (1987: 69) surmises, "unstable parties and exclusive relationships are an improbable combination unless a system such as language provides help in absentee mate-guarding."

In simple human societies such as nomadic foragers,[3] cultural appropriation of sexuality is crucially evident in (1) the institution of marriage, (2) frequent monogamy despite collective group living, (3) widespread classificatory extension of the incest taboo (elaborate exogamy), and (4) marital exchange and alliance.

Though the importance of cultural constraints on sexuality can hardly be overemphasized, there remains a poignant tension in simple societies between cultural norms and individual desires. As Collier and Rosaldo (1981) have noted, marriage and legitimate sexual access to a woman are predominant markers of male adulthood in simple societies, and these rights are fervently protected. Displacement of affinal or sexual tensions may also underlie some of the passionate and seemingly irrational violence over "trivial" issues that occurs in many simple societies.

Sexual tensions in simple societies are normally kept in check by norms of affinal harmony, group cooperation, and personal propriety. When they are ultimately galvanized, however, they are frequently quite intense, and though simple societies have a low incidence of interpersonal aggression overall, those infrequent incidents that do erupt may have a high likelihood of being lethal (Knauft 1987b). This threat is exacerbated by the absence of political leaders or authority figures who might exercise control and of institutional or formalized redress mechanisms. Indeed, violence occurs in significant degree to prevent some individuals from acquiring sexual dominance.

Violence in simple societies may be aggressively self-interested, for instance, aimed at dethroning a rival and procuring a married or unmarried woman from him as a spouse (e.g., Balikci 1970: chapter 7). However, such violence tends to be collectively disapproved of by the group at large and may result in compensatory violence at collective initiative. Moreover, if the aggressor is successful in defeating a female's legitimate mate, he can be considered an outcast because of his breach of community norms and may be unable to obtain support, even among his closest kin. In only one of the twenty-two !Kung homicides listed by Lee (1979b: 383) did the killer run off with the victim's wife, and this case is itself revealing; despite the fact that the couple had previously been lovers, the woman was frightened by the killing and soon returned alone as a result. In most simple societies, aggressively self-interested persons may be killed with the tacit consent or active collaboration of the community (see Lee 1979b: chapter 13; Balikci 1970: chapter.9). In a sense, this responsive violence is a form of execution or capital punishment (see Otterbein 1986,

1987). As Otterbein emphasizes, it tends to uphold norms (such as egalitarianism and sexual propriety) that are crucial to group survival.

Given its phylogenetic and neurophysiological underpinnings, the human aggressive potential would have been difficult if not impossible to suppress entirely, particularly for males in the context of mating competition (see Hamburg and Trudeau 1981; Blanchard and Blanchard 1984; Konner 1982: chapter 9; Valzelli 1981). However, the internalization of strong cultural norms conflicts powerfully with this impetus. What results is control of aggressive tendencies combined with sporadic expression of violence, often in an acrimonious and dysfunctional manner.

Though violence in simple societies is apt to be sudden, spasmodic, and extreme, it is also apt to subside almost as quickly as it arises (Knauft 1987b). The disputants or their survivors may move away from each other temporarily, but little else is done. Strong emphasis is placed on returning to norms of community cooperation as quickly as possible; escalation of violence is avoided. Cases in which violence erupts suddenly and goes out of control lead largely to confusion rather than to escalating rounds of collective violence between factions.

Sociality versus Collective Violence

In simple human societies, social groups are largely precluded from exclusivity and boundedness by shifting resource availability, fluid population movement, lack of fixed property, and need for interband alliance and support. Territorial rights, while often formally recognized, are rarely enforced, and permission to hunt or forage is frequently granted (Balikci 1970: 170; Lee 1979a: 87; Turnbull 1965; Woodburn 1972, 1979, 1984; see also Myers 1986; cf. Hamilton 1982). Band membership tends to be fluid, and it shifts easily to exploit available resources. Local groups also share information about resource availability, and it has been suggested that the advantage of such informationsharing was a major selective force in the evolution of human linguistic communication (Kurland and Beckerman 1985).

Even apart from cultural injunctions and affiliative needs, the shifting location and composition of bands tend to preclude a demographic basis for uniformly opposed territorial groups. Given migratory patterns and resource dispersal, resources are difficult if not impossible to defend, and the cost of such defense typically outweighs its benefit (Netting 1986: chapter 1). Likewise, the cost of defense and retaliation against aggression is usually great; it is more expeditious to move away. This dispersal tends to short-circuit the escalation of feuds, raiding, or warfare (see Woodburn 1984; Turnbull 1984; Lee and DeVore 1984; see Lee 1990).

Some authors have projected such reasoning quite far back in human evolution. Concerning *Homo erectus*, Campbell (1985b: 326) writes, "conflicts between bands, if they occurred, must have been rare in an uncrowded world.... They probably came after humans settled down on the land, became a more numerous species, and forged cultures that encouraged individual and group pride in possessions, territories, and beliefs ..." Gellner (1989) suggests that regular use of coercive force as an organizational feature of society was undeveloped prior to the advent of food storage and agriculture.

The question of territoriality and armed conflict may under specific conditions be more complicated. There is historical evidence of reciprocating collective conflict among some simple foragers, sometimes ethnically based (Balikci 1970: 182–184; Lee 1979b: 382; Clastres 1972; Hill, personal communication; Griffin 1984: 103–107). Feuding or warfare does not, however, appear pronounced except where, as among Ache, Agta, and Waorani, large-scale intrusion by agricultural societies resulted in conflict over land and internal societal reorganization (see chapter 7, Robarchek). In addition, dense rain-forest areas, where visibility is minimal, offer the potential for effective surprise raiding. However, the exploitation of these habitats was difficult in the absence of plant domestication or trade with food-producing populations and was relatively late in evolutionary terms (Campbell 1985a: chapter 2; Ichikawa 1983; Bailey et al. 1989). Apart from the influence of state societies and in selected rain forest areas, collective enmities in simple societies have tended to be minimal and to occur between groups that lie outside the extensive networks of affiliation that link adjacent bands and territories. For demographic and socioecological reasons, travel to and armed conflict against persons in such distant areas were infrequent.

* * *

The "cooperative niche" that is discernible in simple human societies needs to be more frontally considered alongside the "social carnivore niche" and the "cognitive niche" that are so often attributed to them in models of human evolution (Foley 1982; Hill 1982; Tooby and DeVore 1987; contrast Knauft 1989a, 1991; Ingold 1987). The large home range, large group size, likely sexual division of labor, and ability of social groups to maintain cohesion despite diurnal dispersion all suggest the importance of culturally mediated cooperative affiliation in human evolution.

The evolution of *Homo* is likely to have proceeded in significant part among groups that had relatively open social networks, nonhostile inter-group interactions, and a significant degree of institutionalized male-female pairbonding. A detailed review of empirical evidence undercuts the premature generalizations of Chagnon (1988: 985), Wrangham (1987; Manson and Wrangham 1991), Ghiglieri (1987), and Rodseth et al. (1991) that hypothesize high intergroup violence and competitive male domi-nance hierarchies over the long course of human evolution.

It seems highly likely that simple human societies during the evolu-tion of *Homo*, and *Homo sapiens* in particular, developed important pre-dispositions toward group affiliative behavior and communication. The large home ranges, large group size, and dispersed subsistence patterns of *Homo erectus* and early *Homo sapiens* make it likely that spread of infor-mation and connection through social networks across significant dis-tance was a crucial adaptive strategy.[4] Domestically, the ability to communicate about things not physically present facilitated the ability to establish a sexual division of labor in diurnal subsistence activities, with males and females flexibly exploiting disparate resources. This allowed more effective exploitation of home range resources that were spatially separated without compromising the integrity of the local group for pur-poses of sharing resources and nocturnal protection against predators. Communication and internalization of cultural rules also facilitated the maintenance of mating relationships despite lack of constant mate-dur-ing daily activities. And between groups, rules of conduct promoted the basis for social affiliation, trade, alliance, and transfer of members, including sexual mates, as well as transfer of information.

Simple Societies Past and Present

The range of simple societies in the archeological record is greater than those few decentralized forager groups that have been scrutinized by twentieth-century ethnographers. The latter have been strongly influ-enced by state encroachment and ecological marginalization; they cannot be taken as representative of our evolutionary history (Schrire 1984; Headland and Reid 1989). However, these changes have *reduced* rather than intensified the distinctive features discussed here; the legacy of sim-ple society characteristics was likely much stronger in the past. Historical studies document that the qualities of leadership, residential centraliza-tion, individualistic property ownership, and status competition all increase rather than decrease as foragers are subject to the trade networks and political status differentiation of horticultural and state societies (e.g.,

Cashdan 1983; Hitchcock 1987; Kent 1989; Knauft 1990b; cf. classic analysis by Murphy and Steward 1955). In contrast, decentralized leadership, diffuse and flexible interband alliance, generalized reciprocity, and adult male status equality are more common in relatively more autonomous and more decentralized foragers than in hunter-gatherers subject to greater economic interaction with state societies (e.g., Mbuti net-hunters versus Mbuti archers, !Kung San versus Basarwa [Cashdan 1980, 1986]). In terms of developmental trajectories, then, the haze of recent developments suggest that the distinctive features of simple human societies as presently discussed were much stronger in our evolutionary past than in the altered band societies of the early ethnographic present (cf. Woodburn 1988).[5]

It would be a mistake to write off our best data about simple societies as a function of Western state encroachment and projection (see Solway and Lee 1990; contrast Wilmsen 1989). Indeed, careful combination of data from ethnographic and prehistoric research, as well as primatology, is indispensable to a penetrating view of human social evolution.

Variations have certainly existed within the general category of "simple societies." For instance, patterns of violence and sociality among late Pleistocene hunters of periglacial Eurasia, who were highly dependent on very large game (offering the potential for large aggregations of consuming foragers and sizable frozen food stores), were somewhat more like those among complex hunter-gatherers than were those of foragers relying more on dispersed floral resources and smaller game (Foley 1988: 217–219; Mellars 1989: 356–357). More generally, the difference between simple- and complex-forager patterns of violence and sociality may parallel differences in resource concentration or population aggregation that potentiate them. That highly decentralized, nonintensive foraging adaptations are, on a global scale, likely to be both underrepresented in the archeological record and subject to less scholarly interest than the relatively dramatic material assemblages of more socioeconomically complex prehistoric groups should not blind us to the fact that the bulk of our genus's evolution was spent as simple foragers.

Back to Prehistory

Given the importance of empirics in future research, a concluding section with some fresh data is apposite. My scenario of sociality and violence in human evolution[6] has recently been applied by archeologists Paul Taçon and Christopher Chippindale to a detailed progression of prehistoric rock art in Arnhem Land, Northern Australia (Taçon and

Chippindale 1994; see Knauft 1994c). These renderings are particularly important because they depict interpersonal aggression and fighting. Such depictions are rare in the prehistoric rock art from any world area, and this rarity is itself significant given the copious prehistoric rendering of aggression directed against *non*human species, such as hunted animals. How rare *was* warfare in prehistory, and which types were most prominent?

Arnhem Land rock art reveals vivid differences in interpersonal aggression as portrayed over three artistic phases that stretch from over 10,000 years ago to relatively recent times. To understand and appreciate these differences, a bit of background is necessary about the fighting patterns recorded by ethnographer W. Lloyd Warner (1930, 1937) in the late 1920s among aboriginal inhabitants of Arnhem Land. Warner found multiple types of Murngin conflict and an extremely high rate of interpersonal killing—over thirty times greater than the present homicide rate in the U.S., which is itself one of the highest in the industrialized world (Warner 1937: 146f.; see Knauft 1987: 464). Moreover, much of this lethal violence occurred in collective battles and raids between rival groups, that is, it could be classified as warfare between clans or local bands.

In a cross-cultural and evolutionary perspective, the Murngin are an important example of complex rather than simple hunter-gatherers. That is, they inhabited a rich ecological environment and employed prehistorically "late" technologies that allowed them to have relatively high population densities and status differentiations, even though their society did not depend on food production, horticulture, or animal domestication. The same is true of the Tiwi, also from the lush northern coast of Australia (Hart and Pilling 1960). In these respects, Murngin and Tiwi contrast with the more dispersed and decentralized aboriginal groups that inhabited the large bulk of arid central and western Australia.

In terms of global human prehistory, complex hunter gatherer adaptations did not become prominent until 8,000 to 10,000 years ago, and they are rare before 13,000 B.P. (Henry 1985: 366; Price and Brown 1985; Zvelebil 1986). Since the genus *Homo* is certainly more than a million and a half years old, complex hunter-gatherers probably represent less than 1 percent of our genus's evolutionary history. As has long been known, trends of socioeconomic intensification that began with complex hunter-gathers eventually fostered sedentism (year-round residence in one place), an increased emphasis on material property, a greater sense of territoriality, and social exclusion of outsiders. These trends were accompanied by an increasing propensity toward warfare. Organized, inter-group fighting was common among the societies that used to be called "tribes" and was, if anything, intensified in the premodern hierarchical polities that have gone under the name of "chiefdoms" and "archaic states." In short, with the transition from "simple" to "complex" hunter-gatherers, patterns of violence intensified in organizational scale and magnitude. Warfare became more prominent as simple foragers became more sociopolitically complex (Knauft 1991).

That complex hunter-gatherers, much less "tribes" and "chiefdoms," are not representative of our species' history leaves us with an empirical conundrum. There are only a few well-documented groups of "simple" foragers to use as points of evolutionary departure. And as noted above, even these must be considered with extreme caution; evidence from archaeology, paleontology, mathematical modeling, and primatology can all become relevant as supporting parts of the evolutionary puzzle. It is in this context that evidence of prehistoric conflict in Arnhem Land, which culminated in warfare among complex hunter-gatherers, becomes particularly important.

Taçon and Chippindale found that depictions of warfare are limited to the later stages of Arnhem rock art, characterized by complex hunter-gatherer adaptations. Conflict representations dating from between 6,000 and perhaps 10,000 years ago were mostly between two individuals rather than groups. A number of details suggest that these older depictions were of armed wrestling matches or ceremonial conflicts in which the two antagonists could wound each other, but with kinsmen able to rescue an injured principal if the injuries became too severe. The conflicts did not appear subject to collective escalation. This type of controlled conflict was still present among Murngin in the early twentieth century under the name of *nirimaoi yolno* and *makarata* (Warner 1937: 156–157, 163–165). The latter were glossed by Warner as "ceremonial peacemaking fights," in which combatants were allowed a final display of antagonism to finish their anger.

Taçon and Chippindale suggest that this earlier period of Arnhem Land conflict corresponds to my characterizations of sociality and violence in simple human societies (Knauft 1991). They argue further that the ecological and archeological evidence supports the thesis that the societal organization of this period was relatively simple and socioecologically decentralized, in contrast to the "middle-range" characteristics of more complex hunter-gatherers.

However, climatic changes rendered Arnhem Land more ecologically plentiful 4,000 to 6,000 years ago. Coupled with increasing technological sophistication and socioeconomic complexity, a transition to middle-range societal characteristics is suggested by Taçon and Chippindale for this period, that is, concomitant with complex hunter-gatherer adaptations. Correspondingly, a new art style during this period exhibits a much greater incidence of collective armed conflict and, in particular, a greater incidence of severe and/or lethal wounding.

Later in the sequence, "new phase" depictions in Arnhem Land rock art point toward increasing patterns of large-scale warfare. Extremely violent conflicts are depicted, with as many as fifty-four combatants portrayed on two distinct sides, spears flying, and many gravely stricken warriors. Although one must always be wary of extrapolating behavior from prehistoric art, these latter depictions appear similar to the all-out massed warfare between two sides called *gaingar* by the Murngin who were Warner's informants (Warner 1937: 161–163). These vicious fights climaxed the building up of tensions and feuds between opposed groups across a large region of Arnhem Land and were intended to result in numerous deaths on both sides.

Certainly, further consideration of these rare and captivating rock art depictions will provide a more nuanced understanding than can be conveyed here. But basic features do suggest a relative absence of warfare among simple hunter-gatherers and its relative increase along with the increasing complexity of hunter-gatherer society and with the transition from simpler to "middle range" societal adaptations. These changes occurred in many world areas some 6,000 to 9,000 years ago during the Mesolithic (e.g., Zvelebil 1986).

The larger point is that scenarios of peace, cooperation, and violence in human evolution should be moving away from the realm of abstract argument and speculation to that of concrete application. Careful ethnographic study of aggression and affiliation among simpler human societies can dovetail with evidence from archaeology, paleontology, and primatology. Reasonable articulation of data from different sources to frame testable hypotheses will move us well beyond simple abstract argument or mathematical modeling. It will also move us beyond competing speculations based on simplistic chimpanzee-to-human analogies, or, alternatively, crude retroprojections based on select ethnographic sources. Data and creative theory from many arenas should be increasingly applied to the archeological and paleontological record.

This is a difficult task. I close, however, with a final prediction. The general role of cultural transmission and widespread social affiliation in human evolution is likely to become increasingly important in models of the spread and development of *Homo*, and *Homo sapiens* in particular, across the globe. Compared to other primate radiations, this expansion occurred with an amazing dearth of speciation. It is quite likely that diffuse social communication, trade, affiliation, and mating or marriage between groups created a chain-link network of interconnection among regional populations that favored the development of *Homo sapiens* as species with unprecedented global distribution. In the years ahead, the affiliative role of human culture will become increasingly difficult to ignore in the academic study of human evolution.

Notes

Financial support for the research upon which the present study is based is gratefully acknowledged from the Harry Frank Guggenheim Foundation. Supportive comments and critical suggestions are gratefully acknowledged from the participants of the H. F. Guggenheim Conference "What We Know About Peace," Charleston, S.C., 1990, from members of the Emory bio-cultural seminar, and from anonymous reviewers; shortcomings remain my own. This chapter was initially revised during a 1991–1992 fellowship year at the Center for Advanced Study in the Behavioral Sciences, Stanford, Calif. that was funded by their NSF research grant #BNS-8700864.

1. There is strong supporting evidence for elaborate symbolization and the existence of complex proto-language among archaic *Homo sapiens* and *Homo erectus*. Findings by paleontologists (e.g., Marshack 1981, 1985, 1989, 1990; R. White 1989), formal language origin theorists (Bickerton 1990), cultural anthropologists (Goodenough 1990), and ape-language researchers (Steklis 1985) concur on this point. Contrary to the competing predictions of Lieberman (1984) a Neanderthal hyoid "speech" bone has even been found (Arensburg et al. 1989). Even in the absence of such evidence, the findings of language researchers such as Pettito (Pettitto and Marentette 1991) suggest that the cognitive dimensions of human linguistic facility are distinct from the motor production of modern speech. The recent interest in and debate over the preponderance of anatomically modern humans in Europe at 35,000–45,000 BP (Mellars and Stringer 1989) should not obscure this larger picture.

2. Boyd and Richerson (1990a: 124) suggest that group selection for cooperative behavior is most likely for hard-to-learn traits, and Rogers (1990: 408) suggests that group selection via selective emigration is facilitated by mobility rather than by isolation of local groups.

3. In general, societies are simpler to the extent that they are socially and politically decentralized (see discussion in Knauft 1987: 478–482; 1991: 392f.). Correspondingly, material technology tends also to be simple in these societies. The simplest human societies are residentially decentralized and nomadic and lack formalized leadership roles and other forms of political subordination.

4. Unlike the earlier scenario of Isaac (1978), I do not attribute such patterns to Australopithecine adaptations.

5. Though twentiethth-century hunter-gatherers persisted in ecologically marginal areas, this does not imply that "pristine" foragers experienced ecological bounty. Because low nutritional yield per unit land is a function of technology and organization as well as of the environment per se, nonintensive human ecology needs to be viewed in evolutionary as well as in "devolutionary" terms, that is, in terms of the strategies available at earlier

periods to exploit a given habitat. Symbiotic trade between hunter-gatherers and members of horticultural or state societies (e.g., Leacock and Lee 1982: pt. 2) was absent prior to the first few millennia B.C., making the arduousness of resource reliance greater in simple societies of earlier periods. Moreover, the striking human trajectory from *Homo erectus* until quite recently has been one of expansion into environments that were at the outset "marginal" relative to ecozones previously inhabited. The prevailing economic tendency in simple societies is typically conservative: to minimize both labor and food surplus and to keep yields well below possible limits (cf. Sahlins 1972). The low-intensity human ecology associated with ethnographically known simple societies, and the associated patterns of sociality and violence presently adduced, are probably quite common in human evolution until the rise of complex hunter-gatherers, which were most common after 12,500 B.P. (Henry 1985: 366; see Price and Brown 1985).

6. See Knauft 1985, 1987, 1988, 1990a+b, 1991, 1993a+b, 1994a+b; Bowers 1988; Craig 1988; Betzig 1988; Boehm 1993; Erdal and Whiten 1993.

References

Arensburg, B., A. M. D. Vandermeersch, H. Duday, L. A. Schepartz, and Y. Rak. 1989. A Middle Paleolithc Human Hyoid Bone. *Nature* 338: 758–760.

Axelrod, R., and W. D. Hamilton. 1981. The Evolution of Cooperation. *Science* 211: 1390–1396.

Bailey, Robert C., Genevieve Head, Mark Jenike, Bruce Owen, Robert Rechtman, and Elzbita Zechenter. 1989. Hunting and Gathering in Tropical Rain Forest: Is it Possible? *American Anthropologist* 91: 59–82.

Balikci, Asen. 1970. *The Netsilik Eskimo*. Garden City, N.Y.: Natural History Press.

Betzig, Laura L., Monique Borgerhoff Mulder, and Paul Turke, eds. 1988. *Human Reproductive Behavior: A Darwinian Perspective*. Cambridge: Cambridge University Press.

Bickerton, Derek. 1990. *Language and Species*. Chicago: University of Chicago Press.

Blanchard, D. Caroline, and Robert J. Blanchard. 1984. Affect and Aggression: An Animal Model Applied to Human Behavior. In *Advances in the Study of Aggression*, ed. R. J. Blanchard and D. C. Blanchard, pp. 2–62. New York: Academic Press.

Boehm, Christopher. 1993. Egalitarian Behavior and Reverse Dominance Hierarchy. *Current Anthropology* 34: 227–254.

Bower, Bruce. 1988. Murder in Good Company. *Science News* 133: 90–91.

Boyd, Robert. 1988. The Evolution of Reciprocity in Sizable Groups. *Journal of Theoretical Biology* 132: 337–356.

Boyd, Robert, and J. P. Lorberbaum. 1987. No Pure Strategy is Evolutionarily Stable in the Repeated Prisoner's Dilemma Game. *Nature* 327: 58–59.

Boyd, Robert, and Peter J. Richerson. 1985. *Culture and the Evolutionary Process*. Chicago: University of Chicago Press.

———. 1990a. Culture and Cooperation. In *Beyond Self-Interest*, ed. Jane J. Mansbridge, pp. 111–32. Chicago: University of Chicago Press.

———. 1990b. Group Selection Among Alternative Evolutionarily Stable Strategies. *Journal of Theoretical Biology* 145: 331–342.

Campbell, Bernard G. 1985a. *Human Ecology*. New York: Aldine.

———. 1985b. *Humanking Emerging*. 4th edition. Boston: Little, Brown.

Caporael, Linnda R., Robyn M. Dawes, John M. Orbell, and Alphons J. C. van de Kragt. 1989. Selfishness Examined: Cooperation in the Absence of Egoistic Incentives. *Behav-*

ioral and Brain Sciences 12: 683–739.

Cashdan, Elizabeth A. 1983. Territoriality among Human Foragers: Ecological Models and an Application to Four Bushman Groups. *Current Anthropology* 24: 47–66.

———. 1986. Competition Between Foragers and Food-Producers on the Botletli River, Botswana.*Africa* 56: 299–318.

Chagnon, Napoleon A. 1988. Life Histories, Blood Revenge, and Warfare in a Tribal Population. *Science* 239: 985–992.

Clastres, Pierre. 1972. The Guayaki. In *Hunters and Gatherers Today: A Socioeconomic Study of Eleven Such Cultures in the Twentieth Century*, ed. M. G. Bicchieri, pp. 138–173. New York: Holt, Rinehart and Winston.

Collier, Jane F., and Michelle Z. Rosaldo. 1981. Politics and Gender in Simple Societies. In *Sexual Meanings: The Cultural Construction of Gender and Sexuality*, ed. Sherry B. Ortner and Harriet Whitehead, pp. 275–329. New York: Cambridge University Press.

Cullen, Ben. 1993. The Darwinian Resurgence and the Cultural Virus Critique. *Cambridge Archaeological Journal.* 3, no.2: 179–202.

Craig, John. 1988. Kindness and Killing. *Emory Magazine* 64, no. 4: 24–29.

Darwin, Charles. 1871. *The Descent of Man, and Selection in Relation to Sex.* Reprint; Princeton, N.J.: Princeton University Press, 1981.

Dawes, Robyn M., Alphons J. C. Van De Kragt, and John M. Orbell. 1988. Not Me or Thee but We: The Importance of Group Identity in Eliciting Cooperation in Dilemma Situations: Experimental Manipulations. *Acta Psychologica.* 68: 83–97.

Dawkins, Richard. 1989. *The Selfish Gene.* New edition. Oxford: Oxford University Press.

Durham, William. 1991. *Coevolution: Genes, Culture, and Human Diversity.* Stanford: Stanford University Press.

Edgerton, Robert B. 1992. *Sick Societies: Challenging the Myth of Primitive Harmony.* New York: Free Press.

Erdal, David, and Andrew Whiten. 1994. On Human Egalitarianism: An Evolutionary Product of Machiavellian Status Escalation? *Current Anthropology* 35, no. 2: 175–178.

Foley, Robert. 1982. A Reconsideration of the Role of Predation on Large Mammals in Tropical Hunter-Gatherer Adaptation. *Man (n.s.)* 17: 393–402.

———. 1987. *Another Unique Species: Patterns in Human Evolutionary Ecology.* New York: Longman.

———. 1988. Hominids, Humans, and Hunter-Gatherers: An Evolutionary Perspective." In *Hunters and Gatherers, vol. 1: History, Evolution, and Social Change*, ed. Tim Ingold, David Riches, and James Woodburn, pp. 207–21. Oxford: Berg.

Foley, Robert A., and C. P. Lee. 1989. Finite Social Space, Evolutionary Pathways, and Reconstructing Hominid Behavior. *Science* 243: 901–906.

Geertz, Clifford. 1962. The Growth of Culture and the Evolution of Mind. In *Theories of the Mind*, ed. J. Scher, pp. 713–740. Glencoe, Ill.: Free Press.

Gellner, E. 1989. Culture, Constraint, and Community: Semantic and Coercive Compensations for the Genetic Under-Determination Of *Homo sapiens sapiens.* In *The human revolution: Behavioral and biological perspectives on the origins of modern humans*, vol. 1, ed. Paul Mellars and Chris Stringer, pp. 514–25. Princeton, N.J.: Princeton University Press.

Ghiglieri, Michael P. 1987. Sociobiology of the Great Apes and the Hominid Ancestor. *Journal of Human Evolution* 16: 319–57.

Goodenough, Ward H. 1990. Evolution of the Human Capacity for Beliefs. *American Anthropologist* 91: 597–612.

Gould, Stephen J. 1988. Kropotkin Was No Crackpot. *Natural History* 7: 12–21.

Griffin P. Bion. 1984. Forager Resource and Land Use in the Humid Tropics: The Agta of

Northeastern Luzon, the Philippines. In *Past and Present in Hunter Gatherer Studies*, ed. Carmel Schrire, pp. 95–121. New York: Academic.

Hamburg, David A., and Michelle B. Trudeau, eds. 1981. *Biobehavioral Aspects of Aggression*. New York: Alan R. Liss.

Hamilton, Annette. 1982. Descended from Father, Belonging to Country: Rights to Land in the Australian Western Desert. In *Bands and History in Band Societies*, ed. Eleanor Leacock and Richard B. Lee, pp. 85–108. New York: Cambridge.

Hamilton, W. D. 1964. The Genetical Evolution of Social Behavior I, II. *Journal of Theoretical Biology* 7: 1–52.

Harpending, Henry, and Alan Rogers. 1987. On Wright's Mechanism for Intergroup Selection. *Journal of Theoretical Biology* 127: 51–61.

Hart, C. W. M., and Arnold R. Pilling. 1960. *The Tiwi of North Australia*. New York: Holt, Rinehart and Winston.

Headland, Thomas N., and Lawrence A. Reid. 1989. Hunter-Gatherers and Their Neighbors from the Prehistory to the Present. *Current Anthropology* 30: 43–66.

Henry, Donald O. 1985 "Preagricultural intensification: The Natufian example, in *Prehistoric hunter-gatherers: The emergence of cultural complexity*, ed. T. Douglas Price and James A. Brown, pp.365–84. Orlando: Academic Press.

Hill, Kim. 1982. Hunting and Human Evolution. *Journal of Human Evolution*. 11: 521–544.

Hitchcock, Robert K. 1987. Socioeconomic Change among the Basarwa in Botswana: An Ethnohistorical Analysis. *Ethnohistory*. 34: 219–255.

Hockett, Charles F., and Robert Ascher. 1964. The Human Revolution. *Current Anthropology* 5: 135–168.

Ichikawa, Mitsuo. 1983. An Examination of the Hunting-Dependent Life of the Mbuti Pygmies, Eastern Zaire. *African Study Monographs* 4: 44–76.

Ingold, Tim. 1987. *The Appropriation of Nature: Essays on Human Ecology and Social Relations*. Iowa City: University of Iowa Press.

Isaac, Glynn. 1978. The Food-Sharing Behavior of Protohuman Hominids. *Scientific American* 238: 90–108.

———.1984. The Archaeology of Human Origins: Studies of the Lower Pleistocene in East Africa 1971–1981. In *Advances in World Archaeology* 3:1–89. New York: Academic Press.

Kent, Susan. 1989. And Justice for All: The Development of Political Centralization among Newly Sedentary Foragers. *American Anthropologist* 91: 703–712.

Knauft, Bruce M. 1985. *Good Company and Violence: Sorcery and Social Action in a Lowland New Guinea Society*. Berkeley: University of California Press.

———. 1987a. Divergence Between Cultural Success and Reproductive Fitness in Preindustrial Cities. *Cultural Anthropology* 2: 94–114.

———. 1987b. Managing Sex and Anger: Tobacco and Kava Use among the Gebusi of Papua New Guinea. In *Drugs in Western Pacific Societies: Relations of Substance*, ed. Lamont Lindstrom, pp. 73–98. Association for Social Anthropology of Oceania, Monograph #11. Lanham, Md.: University Press of America.

———.1987c. Reconsidering Violence in Simple Human Societies: Homicide among the Gebusi of New Guinea. *Current Anthropology* 28: 457–500.

———. 1988. Reply to further *Current Anthropology* commentary on: Reconsidering Violence in Simple Human Societies. *Current Anthropology* 29: 629–633.

———. 1989a. Imagery, Pronouncement, and the Aesthetics of Reception in Gebusi Spirit Mediumship. In *The Religious Imagination in New Guinea*, ed. Michele Stephen and Gilbert H. Herdt, pp. 67–98. New Brunswick, N.J.: Rutgers University Press.

———. 1989b. Sociality versus Self-interest in Human Evolution. *Behavioral and Brain Sci-*

ences 12: 712–713.

————. 1990a. Melanesian Warfare: A Theoretical History. *Oceania* 60: 250–311.

————. 1990b. Violence among Newly Sedentary Foragers. *American Anthropologist* 92: 1013–1015.

————. 1991. Violence and Sociality in Human Evolution. *Current Anthropology* 32, no. 4: 391–428.

————. 1993a. Commentary on Christopher Boehm, "Egalitarian Behavior and Reverse Dominance Hierarchy. *Current Anthropology* 34: 243–244.

————. 1993b. *South Coast New Guinea Cultures: History, Comparison, Dialectic.* Cambridge: Cambridge University Press

————. 1994a. Culture and Cooperation in Human Evolution. *The Anthropology of Peace and Non-violence,* ed. Leslie Sponsel and Thomas Gregor, pp. 37–67. Boulder, Colo.: Lynne Rienner.

————. 1994b. On Human Egalitarianism. *Current Anthropology* 35, no. 2: 181–182.

————. 1994c. Commentary on Taçon and Chippindale, "Australia's Ancient Warriors," *Cambridge Archaeological Journal* 4: 229–231.

Konner, Melvin J. 1982. *The Tangled Wing: Biological Constraints on the Human Spirit.* New York: Harper & Row.

Kropotkin, Petr. 1902. *Mutual Aid: A Factor of Evolution.* (Reprint; New York University Press, 1972)

Kurland, Jefrey A., and Stephen J. Beckerman. 1985. Optimal Foraging and Hominid Evolution: Labor and Reciprocity. *American Anthropologist* 87: 73–93.

Leacock, Eleanor, and Richard B. Lee. 1982. Introduction. In *Politics and History in Band Societies,* ed. Eleanor Leacock and Richard B. Lee, pp. 1–20. Cambridge: Cambridge University Press.

Lee, Richard B. 1979a. *The Dobe !Kung.* New York: Holt, Rinehart and Winston.

————. 1979b. *The !Kung San: Men, Women, and Work in a Foraging Society.* New York: Cambridge University Press.

————. 1990. Primitive Communism and the Origin of Social Inequality. In *The Evolution of Political Systems: Sociopolitics of Small-Scale Sedentary Societies,* ed. Steadman Upham, pp. 225–246. Cambridge: Cambridge University Press.

Lee, Richard B., and Irven DeVore. 1984. Problems in the Study of Hunters and Gatherers. In *Man the Hunter,* ed. R. B. Lee and I. DeVore, pp. 3–12. New York: Aldine. [Original 1968.]

Levi-Strauss, Claude. 1949. *The Elementary Structures of Kinship,* tr. and ed. James Harle Bell, John Richard von Sturmer, and Rodney Needham. Boston: Beacon, 1969.

Lieberman, P. 1984. *The Biology and Evolution of Language.* Cambridge: Harvard University Press.

Lovejoy, C. Owen. 1981. The Origin of Man. *Science* 211: 341–350.

Manson, Joseph H., and Richard W. Wrangham. 1991. Intergroup Aggression in Chimpanzees and Humans. *Current Anthropology* 32: 369–390.

Marshack, Alexander. 1981. On Paleolithic Ochre and the Early Uses of Color and Symbol. *Current Anthropology* 22: 188–191.

————. 1985. *Hierarchical Evolution of the Human Capacity: The Paleolithic Evidence.* Fifty-Fourth James Arthur Lecture on the Evolution of the Human Brain, 1984. New York: American Museum of Natural History.

————. 1989. On Depiction and Language [further responses to Davidson and Noble, 1987, "The Archaeology of Perception"]. *Current Anthropology* 30: 332–335.

————. 1990. Evolution and the Human Capacity: The Symbolic Evidence. *Yearbook of Physi-*

cal Anthropology. 33.

Mellars, Paul. 1989. Technological Changes across The Middle-Upper Palaeolithic Transition: Economic, Social, and Cognitive Perspectives. In *The Human Revolution: Behavioral and Biological Perspectives on the Origins of Modern Humans*, vol. 1, ed. Paul Mellars and Chris Stringer, pp. 338–365. Princeton, N.J.: Princeton University Press.

Mellars, Paul, and C. B. Stringer, eds. 1989. *The Human Revolution: Behavioral and Biological Perspectives on the Origins of Modern Humans*. Edinburgh: Edinburgh University Press.

Moore, John M. 1990. The Reproductive Success of Cheyenne War Chiefs: A Contrary Case to Chagnon's Yanomamo. *Current Anthropology* 31: 322–330.

Murphy, Robert F., and Julian H. Steward. 1955. Tappers and Trappers: Parallel Process in Accultration. *Economic Development and Cultural Change* 4: 335–353.

Myers, Fred R. 1986. *Pintupi Country, Pintupi Self: Sentiment, Place, and Politics among Western Desert Aborigines*. Washington: Smithsonian Institution Press.

Netting, Robert McC. 1986. Hunter-Gatherers. In *Cultural Ecology*. 2d edition [by R. M. Netting]. Prospect Heights, Ill.: Waveland.

Nowak, M., and K. Sigmund. 1989. Oscillations in the Evolution of Reciprocity. *Jounral of Theoretical Biology* 137: 21–26.

Otterbein, Keith F. 1986. *The Ultimate Coercive Sanction: A Cross-Cultural Study of Capital Punishment*. New Haven: HRAF.

———. 1987. Response to Knauft, "Reconsidering Violence in Simple Human Societies." *Current Anthropology* 28: 484–485.

Paul, Robert A. 1987. The Individual and Society in Biological and Cultural Anthropology. *Cultural Anthropology* 2: 80–93.

Pettitto, Laura A., and Paula E. Marentette. 1991. Babbling in the Manual Mode: Evidence for the Ontogeny of Language. *Science* 251: 1493–1496.

Price, T. Douglas, and James A. Brown, eds. 1985. *Hunter-Gatherers: the Emergence of Cultural Complexity*. Orlando: Academic Press.

Richerson, Peter J., and Robert Boyd. 1989. The Role of Evolved Predispositions in Cultural Evolution. *Ethology and Sociobiology* 10: 195–219.

Rodseth, Lars, Richard W. Wrangham, Alisa Harrigan, and Barbara B. Smuts. 1991. The Human Community as a Primate Society. *Current Anthropology* 32: 221–55.

Rogers, Alan R. 1990. Group Selection by Selective Emigration: The Effects of Migration and Kin Structure. *American Naturalist*. 135: 398–413.

Sahlins, Marshall D. 1972. *Stone Age Economics*. Chicago: Aldine.

Schrire, Carmel, ed. 1984. *Past and Present in Hunter Gatherer Studies*. Orlando: Academic Press.

Solway, Jacqueline S., and Richard B. Lee. 1990. Foragers, Genuine or Spurious?: Situating the Kalahari San in History. *Current Anthropology* 31: 109–146.

Steklis, Horst D. 1985. Primate Communication, Comparative Neurology, and the Origin Of Language Re-Examined. *Journal of Human Evolution* 14: 157–73.

Taçon, Paul S. and Christopher Chippindale. 1994. Australia's Ancient Warriors: Changing Depictions of Fighting in the Rock Art of Arnhem Land, N.T. *Cambridge Archaeological Journal*. 4211–248.

Tooby, John and Irven DeVore. 1987. The Reconstruction of Hominid Behavioral Evolution through Strategic Modeling. In *The Evolution of Human Behavior: Primate Models*, ed. Warren G. Kinzey, pp. 183–237. Albany, N.Y.: State University of New York Press.

Trivers, Robert. 1971. The Evolution of Reciprocal Altruism. In *Readings in Sociobiology*, ed. T. Clutton-Brock and P. Harvey, pp. 189–226. San Francisco: Freeman.

———. 1985. *Social Evolution*. Menlo Park, Calif.: Cummings.

Turnbull, Colin M. 1965. The Mbuti Pygmies: An Ethnographic Survey. *Anthropological Papers of the American Museum of Natural History* 50, no. 3: 139–282.

———. 1984. The Importance of Flux in Two Hunting Societies. In *Man the Hunter*, ed. Richard B. Lee and Irven DeVore, pp. 132–137. New York: Aldine. [Original 1968.]

Valzelli, L. 1981. *The Psychobiology of Aggression and Violence*. New York: Raven.

Vining, Daniel R., Jr. 1986. Social versus Reproductive Success: The Central Theoretical Problem of Human Sociobiology. *Behavioral and Brain Sciences* 9: 167–216.

Vucinich A. 1988. *Darwin in Russian Thought*. Berkeley: University of California Press.

Warner, W. Lloyd. 1930. Murngin Warfare. *Oceania* 1: 457–494.

———. 1937. *A Black Civilization: A Social Study of an Australian Tribe*. New York: Peter Smith.

White, Leslie A. 1949. The Symbol: The Origin and Basis of Human Behavior. In *The Science of Culture*, by L. A. White: 22–39. New York: Farrar, Straus.

White, Randall. 1989. Production Complexity and Standardization in Early Aurignacian Bead and Pendant Manufacture: Evolutionary Implications. In *The Human Revolution: Behavioral and Biological Perspectives on the Origins of Modern Humans*, vol. 1, ed. Paul Mellars and Chris Stringer, pp. 366–390. Princeton, N.J.: Princeton University Press.

Williams, C. G. 1966. *Adaptation and Natural Selection*. Princeton, N.J.: Princeton University Press.

Wilmsen, Edwin N. 1989. *Land Filled with Flies: A Political Economy of the Kalahari*. Chicago: University of Chicago Press.

Wilson, David S. 1989. Levels of Selection: An Alternative to Individualism in Biology and the Human Sciences. *Social Networks* 11: 257–272.

Wilson, D. S., and E. Sober. 1989. Reviving the Superorganism. *Journal of Theoretical Biology* 136: 337–356.

———. 1994. Re-introducing Group Selection to the Human Behavioral Sciences. *Behavioral and Brain Sciences* 17: 585–654.

Wilson, E. O. 1975. *Sociobiology: The New Synthesis*. Cambridge: Harvard University Press.

Woodburn, James C. 1972. Ecology, Nomadic Movement and the Composition of the Local Group among Hunters and Gatherers: An East African Example and Its Implications. In *Man, Settlement and Urbanism*, ed. Peter J. Ucko, Ruth Tringham, and G. W. Dimbleby, pp. 293–206. Hertfordshire, U.K.: Duckworth/Garden City.

———. 1979. Minimal Politics: The Political Organization of the Hadza of North Tanzania. In *Politics in Leadership: A Comparative Perspective*, ed. William A. Shack and Percy S. Cohen, pp. 244–266. Oxford: Clarendon Press.

———. 1984. Stability and Flexibility in Hadza Residential Groupings. In *Man the Hunter*, ed. R. B. Lee and I. DeVore, pp. 103–110. New York: Aldine. [Original 1968.]

———. 1988. African Hunter-Gatherer Social Organization: Is It Best Understood as a Product of Encapsulation? In *Hunters and gatherers*, vol. 1: *History, Evolution, and Social Change*, ed. Tim Ingold, David Riches, and James Woodburn, pp. 31–64. Oxford: Berg.

Wrangham, Richard W. 1987. The Signifiance of African Apes for Reconstructing Human Social Evolution. In *The Evolution of Human Behavior: Primate Models*, ed. Warren G. Kinzey, pp. 51–71. Albany: State University of New York Press.

Zvelebil, Marek, ed. 1986. *Hunters in Transition: Mesolithic Societies of Temperate Eurasia and their Transition to Farming*. Cambridge: Cambridge University Press.

4 The Natural History of Peace: The Positive View of Human Nature and Its Potential

LESLIE E. SPONSEL

■ Leslie Sponsel argues that peace is alive, well, and frequently enough observed to justify a view of human nature that is optimistic and positive. If we have failed to see it, he suggests, it may have something to do with the myopia induced by living in a society having had more than its share of warfare and aggression. Certainly it is true that many social scientists believe that war and violence are depressingly common. As a result, to focus on peace may often require taking into view a larger context of conflict. In this volume the contributors look at mechanisms of reconciliation (de Waal), the process by which violence and peace generate one another (Tuzin, Crenshaw), and the preconditions for interludes of peace (Vasquez). Nonetheless, Sponsel makes a compelling case in this anthropological review of the evidence for peace. As he points out (supported by Knauft in chapter 3), human prehistory is relatively free of systematic evidence of organized violence, and modern hunters and foragers have low rates of nonfatal aggression. Sponsel's comprehensive review of the literature, which provides us with a useful bibliographic tool, is impressive. His documentation of peace as opposed to aggression provides a perspective on human nature that can have a profound effect on how we view and think of ourselves.

WHAT DO we know about peace?[1] One answer to this fundamental question will be developed in this chapter from a holistic anthropological perspective. From available evidence and interpretations it appears that many prehistoric and prestate societies, probably the majority, were *relatively* nonviolent and peaceful in the sense that only sporadically and temporarily did intragroup and/or intergroup aggression occur, ranging from diverse kinds of fighting, feuding, and raiding to, in some cases, warfare. Such considerations lead to the working principle underlying this chapter—the potential for the development of a more nonviolent and peaceful world is latent in human nature as

95

revealed by the natural history of peace. Here the phrase "the natural history of peace" refers to the possibility of a holistic and diachronic description of peace as the norm in most societies, which in this and other respects means that peace is natural.

Without denying the reality of many forms and occurrences of violence including warfare, this chapter purposefully focuses on nonviolence and peace for two simple reasons: (1) One necessary condition for achieving greater progress toward the realization of a more nonviolent and peaceful world is to consider nonviolence and peace directly and systematically. (2) Yet there has been a general tendency to focus on violence and war, usually to the exclusion of nonviolence and peace. Accordingly, the first part of this chapter briefly explains the systemic bias in peace studies of the negative concept of peace and then develops a working definition of the positive concept of peace. The second part surveys the major lines of evidence and interpretation regarding the natural history of peace: biology, primatology, human ethology, palaeontology, archaeology, and ethnology. In the third part, or conclusions, generalizations are drawn from this survey and a theoretical framework is outlined to suggest one approach for the development of further knowledge and understanding of nonviolence and peace.

Peace studies have flourished in recent decades as a very loosely organized interdisciplinary and multidisciplinary field of research, education, and action, which is in principle concerned with all aspects and levels of violence, war, nonviolence, peace, and related phenomena (Boulding 1978, Galtung 1985, 1986, 1988, Gulsoy 1988, Stephenson 1990, Thomas and Klare 1989, Wallensteen 1988). In practice, however, most teaching, research, symposia, and publications in the field of peace studies focus on war and other forms of violence, often to the neglect or even exclusion of nonviolence and peace. For example, anthropologist O'Nell (1989: 117) observes:

Phenomena associated with violence have long been of interest to social and behavioural scientists, including anthropologists. As a result, several theories have developed around the question of why people behave violently. It has been only recently that investigators have seriously occupied themselves with the question of why people do not behave in violent ways in response to situations appearing to provoke violence in others. So, while scientific explanations for violence have by no means become closed issues, satisfactory explanations of nonviolence have scarcely been articulated. And regrettably, the issue of peace has barely attracted serious attention.

This systemic bias is even found in major international journals devoted to the subject of peace. For example, in a review of the contents of the *Journal of Peace Research* from 1964–1980, Wiberg (1981: 113) observes, "For it turns out that out of the approximately 400 articles, research communications, etc., published over seventeen years, *a single one* has been devoted to the empirical study of peaceful societies with a view to find out what seemed to make them peaceful." (The article is by Fabbro and will be discussed later.) Wiberg (1981: 134) also notes that only about 5 percent of the material published in the journal directly concerns nonviolence.

This systemic bias is also found in anthropology. For example, in Ferguson's (1988) extensive bibliography *The Anthropology of War*, only 3.4 percent (64) of 1,888 citations directly address peace, and even then they are of varied relevance, quality, and currency. Even recent anthropological publications specifying the word *peace* in their title often have little if anything to say directly about peace (e.g., Heelas 1989, Wolf 1987).

Underlying this systemic bias is usually a *negative view* of both human nature and peace; that is, human nature is naturally aggressive, and peace is *reduced* to the absence of war (Bock 1980, Feibleman 1987, Kohn 1990, Midgley 1978, Montagu 1976). For example, in an article for a UNESCO journal, French anthropologist Balandier (1986: 499) writes:

In the beginning was violence, and all history can be seen as an unending effort to control it. Violence is always present in society and takes the form of war in relations between societies when competition can no longer be contained by trade and market.

Followers of the negative concept see a relative condition of nonviolence in society and peace between societies as achievable mainly through the reduction of violence and war after scientific research has accumulated sufficient knowledge about violence and war to control them (Konner 1982: xviii, 203, 414).

Allegiance to the negative concept of peace has far reaching and serious consequences. Most of those who follow this systemic bias effectively avoid any direct intellectual confrontation with the subjects of nonviolence and peace. Accordingly, relatively little progress has been made in advancing the knowledge and understanding of nonviolence and peace, this in sharp contrast to the large volume of studies on violence and war. This systemic bias effectively detracts attention from research, policy, and action on many of the underlying problems and issues of peace

(Barnaby 1988, Leakey and Lewin 1978: 281, Melko 1986, Smoker 1981: 149). *Yet it is as important to know and understand nonviolence and peace as to know and understand violence and war. Also it is as important to increase nonviolence and peace as it is to reduce violence and war.* In light of such considerations and for heuristic purposes the present chapter focuses as much as possible on peace, although not to the exclusion of some discussion of war.

Following the positive concept, peace may be defined ideally as the dynamic *processes* that lead to the relative *conditions* of the absence of direct and indirect violence, plus the *presence* of freedom, equality, economic and social justice, cooperation, and harmony (see Boulding 1978: 3, Webb 1986). Direct violence includes war, and indirect violence refers to structural violence such as the related phenomena of racism, poverty, and malnutrition. This positive concept of peace as an *ideal* differs from the negative concept, which reduces peace simply to the absence of war. As Boulding (1978: 8) observes, war and peace each has its attributes; neither is merely the absence or opposite of the other. Those who follow the positive concept of peace consider economic and social injustice to be the major causes of much of the violence in the modern world (Boulding 1978, Galtung 1968, 1985). From this perspective, peace is not limited to maintaining national security. (National security is usually considered to be the defense of three things: national territory from foreign invasion and occupation, strategic raw materials and economic markets, and the nation's social and political values (Barnaby 1988: 42, 210.) Rather, peace is a *relative* condition involving dynamic processes that are *life-enhancing*; that is, ideally it promotes the survival, welfare, development, and creativity of individuals within a society so that they may realize their physical, sociocultural, mental, and spiritual potential in constructive ways. Thus, peace involves at least three mutually dependent levels: individual (inner), social, and global. (For recent history, another level should be inserted between social and global, namely, national, which is the major concern of political science).

Biology

It is appropriate for an exploration of the natural history of peace to begin with nature. After all, human nature is often thought to reflect nature, given that humans are animals, whatever else they may be as well (Adler 1967). However, because of limited space it must suffice merely to raise the point that there are various natural phenomena that biologists take seriously and that clearly fall into the category of nonviolent and peaceful behavior in the broadest sense of the terms, although most biologists may not label the behavior in this way.[2]

Since Darwin, many people in Western civilization have viewed nature as fundamentally competitive and violent, with characterizations such as "the struggle for existence," "the survival of the fittest," "red in tooth and claw," and "gladiatorial arena" (Montagu 1952: 9). This characterization mirrors the social, economic, and political context of British science in the nineteenth century—mechanization, industrialization, urbanization, overpopulation, poverty, mercantile and other economic competition, colonial exploitation, racism, ethnocentrism, and warfare (Montagu 1952: 19, 27–31, 47). The view of nature held by Darwin and his followers *stressed competition to the neglect of cooperation* (Montagu 1952: 18, 34). Only in *The Descent of Man* (1871) did Darwin consider intragroup cooperation as complementary to intergroup competition (Montagu 1952: 73, 80–83).[3] Darwin also viewed warfare as an agency of natural selection in human evolution (Montagu 1952: 85, 87; also see Huxley 1896, Montagu 1942, and Pollard 1974).

Only a few evolutionists and other scholars have taken issue with the Darwinian emphasis on violence and competition; most notable is Kropotkin in his collected essays called *Mutual Aid: A Factor in Evolution* (1914). While Kropotkin did not reject the importance of competition in biological and human evolution, he argued that competition was not necessarily always violent and that cooperation and mutual aid were also important factors (Montagu 1952: 41–42). He considered competition and cooperation to be two different components of the same process of the struggle for existence (Gould 1988: 18). Moreover, Kropotkin recognized the essential mutual dependence of individuals within a community—whether plants, animals, or humans (Montagu 1952: 58). Yet only in the 1970s has mutualism begun to be recognized as an important ecological process by biologists (Boucher, James, and Keeler 1982: 318; also see Axelrod 1984, Axelrod and Hamilton 1981, van der Dennen and Falger 1990, and Montagu 1976: 137–192).

Modern sociobiology, which has much to say about aggression (Chagnon 1988, Konner 1982, Shaw 1985a, b), has also developed several concepts related to Kropotkin's ideas about cooperation and mutual aid, but using a different theoretical framework and set of terms. Sociobiologists focus on social evolution by assessing the reproductive costs and benefits of behavior. An altruistic act benefits the recipient at a cost to the actor. The exchange of altruistic acts between two individuals is called reciprocal altruism. Finally, cooperative acts benefit both actor and recipient but often have selfish components (Trivers 1985: 64–65; also see Wilson 1978: 149–167). (Kohn [1990] includes a discussion of altruism in human society in his book *The Brighter Side of Human Nature*.)

Even Lorenz (1966) in his famous book *On Aggression* considered behavior that promotes nonviolence by preventing or reducing aggression such as ritualization, appeasement, displacement, bonding, and communication. Although Lorenz and others suggested many leads, systematic research on the biology of nonviolence and peace has been greatly neglected in contrast to the attention given to the biology of aggression (Archer 1988, Groebel and Hinde 1989, Kemp 1988). Nevertheless, Kemp (1988: 118) states that "evolution has led intraspecies aggression, in the overwhelming number of species, and in all mammals, to a non-lethal and nonviolent form of behavior."

Primate Ethology

As Stevenson (1987: 130) observes, to show that the human line evolved from primates does not prove that it is nothing but a primate or that it has not evolved further. Nevertheless, primates remain relevant to the human species because, whatever else we are, we are also primates.

In recent decades several points have emerged from primate ethology that are pertinent to the natural history of peace: (1) There is a tremendous range of variation in the type, frequency, and intensity of aggressive and related behavior (Givens 1975, Itani 1983). (2) When aggression does occur, it is usually limited to highly ritualized threat displays that result in the spatial displacement of individuals but seldom in physical injury and rarely in death. (3) Aggression is avoided, reduced, or resolved by appeasement and submissive behaviors as well as through well-developed mechanisms of conflict resolution (de Waal 1982, 1986, 1989). (4) There is no hint of even the rudiments of warfare in infrahuman primates, except for our sibling species, the common chimpanzee (*Pan troglodytes*).[4]

The nonviolent behavior of infrahuman primates impresses modern primatologists as much, or even more than, their violent behavior (Fossey 1983: 56, Goodall 1986: 313–386, Smuts 1985, 1987, Strum 1985, de Waal 1982, 1986). For instance, following extensive field observations on free-ranging baboon (*Papio anubis*) troops in their natural habitat, Strum (1985: 22) concludes:

Far from being ruled by aggression and powerful individuals, this society places a premium on reciprocity, and individuals act out of enlightened self-interest.

Baboons must be nice to one another because they need one another for survival and success. It is a finely tuned system. . . . There is a politics to what baboons do and it is this social maneuvering that places a premium on baboon intelligence and creates a social smartness sometimes unmatched in human society.

After more than a quarter of a century of intensive field observations on chimpanzees in Tanzania, Goodall (1986: 357) asserts:

Chimpanzees . . . are capable of very violent behavior. Aggression, particularly in its more extreme form, is vivid and attention catching, and it is easy to get the impression that chimpanzees are more aggressive than they really are. In actuality, peaceful interactions are far more frequent than aggressive ones; mild threatening gestures are more common than vigorous ones; threats per se occur much more often than fights; and serious, wounding fights are very rare compared to brief, relatively mild ones.

Following extensive observations on how captive primates of several species avoid, reduce, and resolve conflicts, de Waal (1989: 7) states in the prologue of his book *Peacemaking Among Primates*:

My main purpose here is to correct biology's bleak orientation on the human condition. In a decade in which peace has become the single most important public issue, it is essential to introduce the accumulated evidence that, for humans, making peace is just as natural as making war. (See also de Waal 1982, 1986.)

The observations by de Waal (1989: 171–227) on reconciliation and other pacific behaviors in captive bonobos, the "pygmy chimpanzee" (*Pan paniscus*), are confirmed through studies of free-ranging bonobos in their natural habitat. According to Kano (1990: 64), bonobos are more gregarious and pacific than the common chimpanzee, and unlike the latter they have never been observed to kill members of their own species. The bonobos use grooming, sex, and other behavior to relieve group tensions and maintain social cohesion. However, although hostility is extremely rare among females, it is more common among males (Kano 1990: 66). Kano (1990: 70) concludes:

The bonobo groups of the Wamba forest are not entirely friendly or entirely antagonistic. Encounters are characterized by cautious mutual tolerance. Members of different groups use a varied sexual repertoire to reconcile and appease, and remarkably, elements of dominance do not enter into sexual activity. Bonobos have evolved systems of maintaining, at least on the surface, a pacific society.

In sum, an increasing number of modern studies of infrahuman primate behavior, both in the wild and in captivity, reveal that *nonviolence is more frequent than violence*, and that apes and monkeys have intricate *mechanisms of conflict avoidance, reduction, and resolution*. They also maintain a relatively nonviolent and peaceful society through various behaviors including, among many others, play, mating, parenting, aunting, bonding, touching, grooming, sharing, cooperation, and coalition. There is also a wide range of vocalizations, facial expressions, gestures, and body postures and movements that are nonviolent and peaceful (Goodall 1986, de Waal 1989, Silverberg and Gray 1992).

Human Ethology

A student of Konrad Lorenz, Eibl-Eibesfeldt (1989), pioneered the direct approach to human ethology through the analysis of many kilometers of film footage of naturalistic human behavior from an extremely large sample of cultures around the world. His publications also address questions of war and peace (1971, 1979, 1989: 361–422).

In his monumental compendium on human ethology that explores human nature, Eibl-Eibesfeldt (1989: 421) reaches the general conclusion that:

War, defined as strategically planned, destructive group aggression, is a product of cultural evolution. Therefore, it can be overcome culturally. It makes use of some universal innate human dispositions, such as man's aggressive emotionality and the preparedness for group defense, dominance striving, territoriality, disposition to react to agonal signals from strangers, etc. But all these traits do not lead to warfare. War requires systematic plannning, leadership, destructive weapons, and overcoming sympathy through dehumanizing the enemy in advance of the actual conflict. Man easily falls prey to indoctrination to act in supposed group interest.

To take a particular case, in his field study of the !Ko and !Kung, subgroups of the society commonly called the "Bushmen" of southern Africa, Eibl-Eibesfeldt (1975) found a diversity of types of aggressive behavior, using a very broad definition of aggression. However, he was more impressed with the ways this society *controls* aggression and with their counterbalancing friendly behavior. Eibl-Eibesfeldt describes the play and socialization of children as focused on the cultural ideal of peaceful coexistence. He also asserts that many of the patterns of bonding and the urge to bond are inborn in humans. (See also Kemp 1988.)

Human Palaeontology

The accumulated specimens of fossil hominids currently available in the collections of museums and universities throughout the world reveal that _nonviolence and peace were likely the norm throughout most of human pre-history and that intrahuman killing was probably rare._

In search of instances of intrahuman killing in the palaeontological record, Roper (1969) systematically surveyed the published reports on the remains of one or more fossil hominid individuals recovered from over 110 Pleistocene sites. Roper (1969: 448) concludes:

My own evaluation is that some intrahominid (perhaps intraspecific) killing probably occurred in Lower and Middle Pleistocene and that sporadic intraspe-cific killing probably took place among _H. sapiens_ in the Upper Paleolithic. The evidence to back up the latter statement is the four skulls with depressed frac-tures from the Upper Cave of Choukoutien in China, the drawings of human fig-ures pierced with arrows in two French caves [Pech Merle and Cougnac caves from the Aurignacian-Perigordian period], and probably the cut on the skull of the woman from Cro-Magnon. If some of the human skeletal material from Afalou-bou-Rhummel, Algeria, had exhibited mortal wounds, the contention that warfare occurred in the Upper Palaeolithic might be documented. The only other instance of possible mass killing in the Upper Palaeolithic is that of the Upper Cave of Choukoutien, and since Pei does not affirm Weidenrich's assertion that these remains were victims of a massacre it seems unwise to ascribe the term "warfare" to this situation. . . . The author's determination is that, although there seems to be sound evidence for sporadic intrahuman killing, the known data is not sufficient to document warfare.

Roper's survey of the palaeontological record of human evolution suggests (but does not prove) that intrahuman killing was a rare occur-rence. The evidence for intrahuman killing comes from only four out of more than 110 Pleistocene fossil hominid sites. Furthermore, the bulk of the available evidence for killing is limited to relatively late in prehis-tory—_Homo sapiens sapiens_ in the Upper Palaeolithic, about 30,000 to 10,000 years ago, whereas human evolution extends back at least four million years.

However, it should be noted that the amount of violence may be underrepresented in the palaeontological record because injury to soft tissues may cause death without leaving any imprint on the skeleton. Also, even indisputable skeletal evidence of prehistoric intrahuman killing cannot adduce the motivation, which may be legal or ritual rather than murder, feuding, revenge, or warfare.

Prehistoric Archaeology

As in the case of the palaeontological record, so with the archaeological record, lack of evidence is not proof of absence. Also the archaeological study of warfare suffers from many problems and limitations. It is not always possible to distinguish between hunting tools and war weapons, especially for the Palaeolithic, unlike the metal ages (Childe 1941: 127, 129, 133, Vencl 1984: 120). Weapons and fortifications of organic material are unlikely to be preserved archaeologically, except under very special climatic, geological, or other circumstances (Vencl 1984: 122). Also, even when some tools could clearly have been made for weapons, that does not necessarily mean that they were used as such in warfare (Gabriel 1990: 25 30). Some apparent fortifications may actually be retention walls (Roper 1975: 329). Some rock art depicting fighting may be ritualistic reflections of shamanistic visions rather than documenting ordinary reality (Campbell 1986: 256). Nonmaterial aspects of warfare such as political and diplomatic processes are not preserved in the archaeological record (Vencl 1984: 121–123). Such problems and limitations may bias the archaeological perspective on warfare suggesting that prehistoric societies were more pacific than they actually were (Vencl 1984: 123). Nevertheless, available evidence and interpretations are suggestive. (See Gabriel 1990 for a general review of the archaeology of warfare.)

Palaeoanthropological evidence and interpretations indicate that the human line evolved at least by 4 million years ago, agriculture about 10,000 years ago, and the state around 5,000 years ago (Gowlett 1984). During the hunter-gatherer stage of cultural evolution, which dominated 99 percent of human existence on this planet (Lee and DeVore 1968: 3), lack of archaeological evidence for warfare suggests that it was *rare or absent for most of human prehistory*. For instance, while the famous cave art from the Upper Palaeolithic of France and Spain realistically depicts the prey animals of hunters, only very rarely is human fighting illustrated and it never begins to approach warfare (Ferrill 1985: 17, Pfeiffer 1982).

Leakey and Lewin (1977) observe:

> Throughout the later stages of human evolution, from about three million years onwards, there was, however, one pattern of social behavior that became extremely important, and we can therefore expect the forces of natural selection would have ensured its becoming deeply embedded in the human brain: this is cooperation ... (p. 245).

Because the mixed economy of hunting and gathering brings with it a much more efficient exploitation of resources in the environment and also sharpens the edge of social interactions—both of which enhance adaptability of the human animal—evolutionary forces favored its development. It is probably the single most important factor in the emergence of mankind. And cooperation was an essential element of its success. More than any other piece of social behavior, the motivation to cooperate in group effort is a direct legacy of the nature of human evolution (p. 248).

The earliest evidence for anything that could properly be labeled warfare comes from the fortifications surrounding some Neolithic sites such as Jericho about 9,500 to 9,000 years ago (Eisler 1988: 48–58, Gabriel 1990: 23, Gowlett 1984: 160, Roper 1975: 329, Vencl 1984: 120–121). Roper (1975: 330–331) argues that in the Near East during the Neolithic the control of strategic trading sites was the catalyst for warfare. Turning to Europe, Keeley and Cahen (1989) interpret fortifications around the villages of the first agricultural colonists in Belgium about 6,300 to 6,000 years ago as defenses against raids by indigenous Mesolithic hunter-gatherers. Yet the existence of weapons and/or fortifications does not indicate how widespread and frequent warfare might have been (Gabriel 1990: 30).

As culture evolves toward the state level of sociopolitical organization, war appears to become inevitable (Carneiro 1970, 1978, Cohen 1984, Gowlett 1984: 175, Lewellen 1983, Paynter 1989, Wright 1977). This inevitability is not simply a theoretical assumption; it is evident at some phase in the archaeological sequence of the evolution of every state (Gowlett 1984: 175, 178–179, 186–189, 194). Cohen (1984: 338) argues that: "War helps to make states, states make war, and therefore states are in part, and always must be, war machines." He observes that war is more frequent in the earlier stages of the state than in its later stages when the society is more organized politically and has a standing army (p. 354). Yet *even at the state level war is not ubiquitous*, because comparative historical studies document extended periods of relative peace sometimes lasting centuries or even millennia (Melko 1973, 1990, Melko and Hord 1984, Melko and Weigel 1981).

With the evolution of the state level of sociopolitical organization, more than ever before, and especially in contrast to egalitarian foraging societies, social stratification is highly developed, and becomes an important form of indirect (structural) violence (Berreman 1981, Paynter 1989, Webb 1986).

Eisler (1987) developed a new feminist interpretation of cultural evolution that she calls cultural transformation theory. According to this theory, cultural diversity overlays two elemental models of society that have profound systemic consequences.

The *partnership model* is based on linking people in an egalitarian society that does not evaluate differences hierarchically. This model generates an affiliative, cooperative, and nurturing society with a technology of production, a religion of reproduction, and a relatively nonviolent and peaceful life.

The *dominator model* is based on ranking differences, beginning with those most fundamental in our species—male and female. These and other differences are interpreted in terms of superiority and inferiority, and the sociocultural system is structured around various hierarchies backed by authoritarian threat and force. Members of both sexes are conditioned to equate masculinity with fighting power and dominance. This model generates warfare and other forms of direct violence as well as indirect (structural) violence (pp. xvii–xix). This is correlated with the development of a technology and religion of confrontation and destruction.

Eisler concentrates on European prehistory and reviews archaeological and other evidence to argue that both foraging and farming stages of cultural evolution were based on the partnership model. Only after a period of chaos triggered by peripheral invaders, beginning around 7,000 years ago, did the transformation to the dominator model occur in Europe (pp. 43–45).

Regardless of the validity of Eisler's interpretations and models of European prehistory, the idea that there is a *positive correlation between gender equality and nonviolence/peace* is sustained by ethnographic cases like the Semai, Chewong, Buid, and Piaroa, among others (Howell and Willis 1989: 22, 24–25, 36, 46, 68, 81–82, 87, 95; also see Adams 1983, Burbank 1987, Divale and Harris 1976, Lee 1982, Mitsherlich 1987, Rosenberger 1973, Turnbull 1982, and Whyte 1978).

In summary, interpretations of the accumulated evidence available from prehistoric archaeology suggest that *relative nonviolence and peace prevailed for most of human prehistory. Warfare in cultural evolution is a relatively recent development that emerged in some phase of the evolution of agriculture and subsequently flourished with the rise of the state* (cf. Keeley 1995).

Because the development of war in human prehistory is determined by cultural rather than biological evolution, this raises the possibility that societies can transcend previous cultural stages including warfare to evolve very different cultural systems (Mead 1964, 1968). Indeed, the transformation of warlike societies into peaceful ones has occurred repeatedly in human history, such as in Melanesia with pacification under the pressures of European colonialism (Rodman and Cooper 1979).

Ethnology and Ethnography

Many analyses of the ethnographic record indicate that, in general, nonviolence and peace prevail in hunter-gatherer societies, although some cases of homicide and feuding have been reported (Palmer 1965, Knauft 1987, Wolf 1987).[5] That warfare would be absent or negligible in most foraging societies is not only *plausible* but also *probable*, if one considers that they are largely occupied with subsistence, lack sufficient food surplus to sustain a military organization and its adventures, and do not have political leadership and organization to direct warfare (cf. Wolf 1987). Also among foragers, the possession of group territory that might be defended through the development of warfare against other groups is quite variable, depending on resource distribution, abundance, and predictability (Dyson-Hudson and Smith 1978). The typical foraging lifestyle emphasizes mobility, kinship, egalitarianism, cooperation, generalized reciprocity, social harmony, and nonviolent mechanisms of conflict resolution such as fissioning, if for no other reason than that their survival and adaptation depend on such attributes (Leakey 1978, 1981, Lee 1979, 1982; Turnbull 1961, 1983).[6] In addition, many societies have fairly well developed institutionalized mechanisms for conflict resolution and social justice, such as mediation (Greenhouse 1985, Marshall 1961).

Several cross-cultural studies support the characterization of foragers as, in general, relatively nonviolent and peaceful. For instance, in a quantitative analysis comparing 652 nonliterate societies, Broch and Galtung (1966: 33) found that 4 percent were pacific engaging only in defensive wars, 53 percent fought as a social ritual with relatively little bloodshed, 26 percent had economic war, and 7 percent had political war. (For 10 percent of the societies the pattern of war was unknown.) Broch and Galtung (1966: 40–41) conclude that belligerence increases with increasing civilization and also with greater contact and that territory and the state are closely related to this process. They confirm Wright's (1942) previous general conclusion that "primitive" societies are more peaceful than "civilized" ones. (See also Leavitt 1977.)

Fabbro's (1978) seminal analysis compared seven supposedly nonviolent and peaceful societies: Semai, Siriono, !Kung San, Mbuti, Copper Eskimo, Hutterites, and Islanders of Tristan da Cunha. The first five are mainly foragers while the last two are agrarian societies. Table 1 lists the attributes that were either absent or present in all seven of these societies.

These characteristics approximate those indicated in the ideal definition of positive peace discussed earlier.

TABLE 1. FABBRO'S NONVIOLENT SOCIETIES

Attributes absent
- intergroup violence or feuding
- internal (civil) or external war
- threat from external enemy group or nation
- social stratification and other forms of structural violence such as sorcery or witchcraft
- full-time political leader or centralized authority
- police and military organizations

Attributes present
- small and open communities with face-to-face interpersonal interactions
- egalitarian social structure
- generalized reciprocity
- social control and decision making through group concensus
- nonviolent values and enculturation

Most of these characteristics are also reflected to some degree in additional ethnographic cases of relatively nonviolent and peaceful societies as documented in four sources. *Societies At Peace*, edited by Howell and Willis (1989), focuses on indigenous theories of human nature, egalitarian gender relations, nonviolent values, and enculturation for the Buid, Chewong, Piaroa, Semai, and Zapotec, among others. *Learning Non-Aggression*, edited by Montagu (1978), concentrates on cases of enculturation for nonviolence among the Inuit, !Kung San, Mbuti, Semai, Tahitians, and others. Sponsel and Gregor (1994) include case studies of nonviolent and peaceful aspects of the Semai, Zapotec, Inuit, Kinga, Xingu, and Yanomami, while Bonta (1993) published an annotated bibliography of forty-seven peaceful societies.

The Semai of Malaysia are the best documented case of a pacific society. Dentan (1968) lived with the Semai in 1962–1963 and 1976, while Clayton and Carole Robarchek (1977a, b, 1981, 1989a, b) lived with them in 1973–1974 and 1979–1980. Although Dentan and the Robarchek's worked independently at different periods with the Semai, they are in basic agreement that the society is essentially nonviolent and peaceful. They describe in detail the nonviolent ethos and lifestyle of the Semai.

Semai

Part of the enculturation process of the Semai is for children to learn to be nonviolent through the kinds of games they play and other means (Dentan 1978). (For more on nonviolent enculturation and play see Montagu [1978] and Royce [1980].)

However, some others, who have not lived with the Semai, such as Paul (1978), have asserted that the Semai are really bloodthirsty killers, at least latently, and that this confirms the innate aggressiveness of human nature. Such arguments have been successfully refuted in a joint article by Robarchek and Dentan (1987).

It would be remiss not to mention the Tasaday of the Philippines, because they are famous as an "ultraprimitive" case of an extremely pacific society and therefore of considerable interest to the history of anthropological aspects of peace studies and the theme of the natural history of peace (Sponsel 1992). However, to be objective, any support the Tasaday case might provide for the basic argument of this chapter must be suspended until the controversy over their authenticity is resolved one way or another (Headland 1992). Briefly, the Tasaday are supposed to have no weapons or enemies, as well as no words for anger, murder, war, or enemy. Nance (1975: 447) described the Tasaday as follows:

Although we could not or would not emulate them and may never extract new principles of behavior from them, we could treasure them as reminders of what was humanly possible, as inspiring emblems of social peace and harmony, of simply, love.

Similarly MacLeish (1972: 248) wrote:

[The Tasaday are] perhaps the simplest of living humans, and those closest to nature . . . gentle and affectionate. . . . Our friends have given me a new measure of man. If our ancient ancestors were like the Tasaday, we come from far better stock than I had thought.

The apparently "ultraprimitive" status of the Tasaday was interpreted as a reflection of the *elemental pacific qualities of human nature*. The Tasaday provided a precedent and model of a nonviolent and peaceful egalitarian community living by group consensus in freedom and in harmony with nature (Sponsel 1990b, 1992). Unfortunately, no more can be said of this intriguing case in the present context until the controversy is resolved, which may depend on further research, especially from archaeology, ethnohistory, genetics, and linguistics.

There are also cross-cultural studies that challenge the view of hunter-gatherers as relatively nonviolent and peaceful. Ember (1978) compared fifty societies of hunter-gatherers throughout the world and found that 64 percent had warfare at least once every two years, 26 percent had warfare somewhat less often, and only 10 percent had no, or almost no, warfare. She asserts that this dispels the myth that hunter-gatherers are typically peaceful. However, the broad definition of warfare used by Ember is inadequate and inflates the frequency. (Also see the discussion of Ferguson's ideas, below in this chapter).

More recently, Knauft (1987) extracted and interpreted data from some of the literature on what he calls "simple" human societies to compare estimates of annual homicide rates per 100,000 people (cf. Palmer 1965). He finds that these societies have high rates of homicide, in some cases even several times higher than the average for the United States. However, homicide should not be confused with warfare. That is, a society can be violent in the sense of having a high rate of homicide yet still be peaceful, in the negative sense, by lacking warfare. These societies include the Central Eskimo, Hadza, !Kung Bushmen, Mbuti, and Semai, who have usually been described as relatively nonviolent and peaceful! But note the statements indicated with added emphasis in Knauft's (1987: 459) conclusion:

> Especially in egalitarian societies, there may be a pattern of social life that is *generally peaceful and tranquil* but is punctuated by aggression which, when it does occur, is unrestrained and frequently homicidal. This may result in a high ratio of lethal violence to aggression despite a *low overall incidence of aggression*.[7]

One problem with the comparative studies by both Ember and Knauft is that they may not give sufficient attention to the specific details of motivations and context as well as external influences. For example, Broch and Galtung (1966: 42) early advocated analyzing the relationship between societies rather than studying a society as an isolate. Recently Ferguson (1990a) identified the neglected factor of Western contact as triggering or at least intensifying much of indigenous warfare through social stress and depopulation from epidemic disease, territorial displacement, competition for resources (especially Western trade goods), and so on. (Blick [1988] independently developed a parallel argument). If the argument is valid in general, then *much of what some ethnographers have taken for granted as traditional endemic violence and warfare may actually have often been precipitated, or at least intensified, by direct or indirect Western contact*. Moreover, the supposed chronic endemic warfare and other forms of violence in so-called primitive societies may have been substantially less in precontact times than many anthropologists have believed. In the light of this new argument the ethnographic record of warlike societies needs to be reassessed, and this may be assisted by more ethnohistorical research on the contact situation. (It should also be noted that contact with Western societies has sometimes led to the pacification of societies in which warfare was formerly endemic (Rodman and Cooper 1979, Robarchek and Robarchek 1989, Scheffler 1964, Willis 1989).

In light of the above it is of interest that San rock paintings depicting fighting are common in southern Africa and may reflect millenia of conflict with other African societies and centuries of conflict with European colonial society (Campbell 1986). Also in the case of the Maasai pastoralists of eastern Africa, Jacobs (1979) debunks their reputation for bellicosity and argues that it was contrived by outsiders to exploit their land, first by African and Arab farmers and later by Europeans (cf. Evans-Pritchard 1940: 150–151; also see Bodley 1990).

This contact argument has even been applied to a reinterpretation of Yanomami aggression by Ferguson (1990b, 1991, 1992). The Yanomami are an Amazonian tribal society that for decades have been consistently characterized as "the fierce people" in numerous publications by Chagnon (1968: 1–2, 1988, 1990), and are therefore of special relevance to the natural history of peace as another extreme case and as a polar opposite of the Tasaday (Sponsel 1983, 1991). But in recent years several anthropologists, who have also conducted fieldwork for many years with Yanomami, have begun to question openly the reality of the ethnographic image created by Chagnon (Albert 1989, 1990, Albert and Ramos 1989, Colchester 1987: 8, Lizot 1985: xiv, Good 1991: 73–74, Ramos 1987, Smole 1976: 16). These anthropologists are reconsidering the violence in Yanomami society.

Here it must suffice to summarize briefly the pertinent aspects of the most recently published reports of fieldwork with the Yanomami, in this instance from the very extensive research by Good (1989, 1991). So far, Good has lived in Yanomami villages for a total of sixty-eight months over a period of fourteen years (1989: 4–5). In particular, he illuminates one of the factors helping to explain the fierce reputation of the Yanomami—the high visibility of violence in villages. The Yanomami village (*shabono*) is a large circular communal house with no walls other than the one around its perimeter. In this circular house, virtually all activity is visible or audible from any other location. Good was impressed that, in sharp contrast to family and community violence in his own country (United States), in a Yanomami village there is so little privacy that almost everything is public including violence (1991: 73).

Instead of concealing anger, the Yanomami openly vent it (pp. 70–72), for example, through public complaint speeches (p. 208) and public insult (p. 74).

Good was also impressed by how harmonious communal life actually was, considering that seventy-five or more people fairly regularly live day and night in one giant room (the *shabono*), and they have no institutionalized government, police, or military to maintain order and settle disputes (p. 69). Good observed that despite disease and occasional fights and infrequent raids, the Yanomami are basically happy people living in a harmonious society (pp. 82, 174–175). Kinship and friendship are important factors maintaining social cohesion (pp. 293, 317). Also daily life in the community is permeated by laughter, joking, and clowning, which relieves tension (p. 51). When aggression occurs it is usually highly ritualized (p. 69). Finally, Good mentions that the Yanomami he observed never engaged in anything even close to open warfare (p. 44). Of course Good's observations in one region do not refute the occurrence of warfare elsewhere in this society, but like other field-workers his observations indicate that warfare is not ubiquitous among the Yanomami, despite Chagnon's characterizations. In fact, Good hints that the term *warfare* may not be appropriate to describe Yanomami aggression.

The above points also bear on more general considerations. In one of the most widely read ethnographies, Chagnon (1983: 213) states, "Warfare among the Yanomamö—*or any sovereign tribal people*—is an *expectable* form of political behavior and no more requires special explanation than do religion or economy" (emphasis added]). Furthermore, embedded in a sociobiological interpretation of his detailed quantitative data on the Yanomami in the prestigious journal *Science*, Chagnon (1988: 985) asserts, "Violence is a potent force in human society and may be *the principal* driving force behind the evolution of culture" (emphasis added]). Although a reader might be impressed by the many years Chagnon has studied the Yanomami and by his use of extensive quantitative data on other matters, actually he does not adequately marshall arguments or evidence to sustain these two opinions. Moreover, their fallibility should be clear from the foregoing review of diverse lines of evidence on the natural history of peace (e.g., Eisler 1987, Gabriel 1990). It appears that in many prehistoric and "primitive" societies, probably even the majority, nonviolence and peace were prevalent in daily life, only sporadically and temporarily interrupted by intagroup or intergroup aggression, ranging from diverse kinds of fighting, feuding, and raiding to, in some cases, warfare. (See also Lizot 1994).

As part of the revisionism that has become fashionable in contemporary cultural anthropology in recent years, *scholars are challenging previous ethnographic images of societies as either nonviolent/peaceful or violent/warlike.* Although in recent years the increased quantity and quality of anthropological contributions to peace studies is heartening, it may take considerable time, effort, and personnel before a consensus and/or synthesis emerges. In any case, the idea that war is *not* a cultural universal remains intact. But there is a need to identify more systematically and precisely and to explore in research, both on etic (scientific and generalizing) and emic (particular native views) grounds, the meaning of *nonviolence, peace, violence,* and *war.* Some scholars even assert that using such words as general labels for cultures is very problematic (Campbell 1989, Heelas 1989). Moreover, Albert (1990: 561) even goes so far as to assert that the characterization of any social interaction as "violent" is culture bound. Thus, "tribal violence" is an ethnocentric concept because in Western civilization the idea of violence is inseparable from its association with the transgression of a social norm (see also Howell and Willis 1989: 6–7). In this connection it is interesting that two distinct neighboring ethnic groups in the Philippines, the Buid and Tausug, use the same word (*maisug*) for aggression, but give it exactly the opposite moral evaluation (Gibson 1989: 67).

Finally, of special interest are formerly violent/warlike societies that for various reasons have been transformed into relatively nonviolent/peaceful ones in Melanesia (Rodman and Cooper 1979, Scheffler 1964), Africa (Willis 1989), and Amazonia (Robarchek and Robarchek 1989). The conditions and processes involved in such transitions merit much more research, especially as they bear on the possibilities of developing a more nonviolent and peaceful world.

Conclusions

What do we know about peace? This chapter reviewed the natural history of peace within the holistic framework of diverse lines of evidence: biology, primate ethology, human ethology, human palaeontology, prehistoric archaeology, ethnology, and ethnography. Two trends in particular stand out from this review of diverse lines of evidence. (1) In recent years the *revisionist* fashion has stimulated the reassessment of the ethnographic images of societies portrayed as either nonviolent/peaceful or violent/warlike. (2) It appears that the natural and social sciences may be on the verge of a *paradigm shift*—to include nonviolence and peace as well as violence and war as legitimate subjects for research, and eventually to balance the historic and current systemic bias of the disproportionate ount of attention given to violence and war in contrast to nonviolence and peace. This paradigm shift will not be easy because it must surmount the obstacles in the history and culture of Western civilization, which may be most pronounced in American society and which in various ways tend to value violence and war over nonviolence and peace (Graham and Gurr 1969, Hofstadter and Wallace 1971, Iglitzin 1972, Palmer 1972, Toplin 1975). *Peace appears to be elusive not because relatively nonviolent and peaceful societies are so rare—they are not—but instead because so rarely have nonviolence and peace been the focus of research in anthropology and other disciplines, including even the field of peace studies. The deficiency lies in the research, including the ethnographic record, and not in human nature.* Overall the two trends of revisionism and the paradigm shift are healthy if the field of peace studies, like science in general, is to be a genuinely critical, analytical, and self-correcting process. Perhaps nonviolence and peace are finally becoming legitimate subjects for research and teaching, thereby opening a new frontier with all the excitement, challenges, and promises of exploration.

This chapter has focused on nonviolence and peace as a heuristic exercise simply because elsewhere it has been so neglected. Certainly it is extremely important to conduct research on violence and war with the hope of contributing to their understanding, reduction, and control. While this type of research is necessary, alone it is not sufficient to develop a more nonviolent and peaceful society and world. Progress in that direction will remain very limited until we seriously, systematically, and intensively directly consider nonviolence and peace. To put it simply and undeniably—you cannot understand or achieve something by ignoring it.

Although space allows for presentation of only some of the highlights of each line of evidence, this conclusion will emphasize five points that are often neglected.

(1) Although *conflict is inevitable and ubiquitous, violence is not*. There are nonviolent and peaceful ways to reduce and resolve conflict, even in monkey and ape societies (e.g., Howell and Willis 1989: 3, 15, 19).
(2) *Human nature has the psychobiological potential to be either nonviolent/peaceful or violent/warlike.*
(3) *Nonviolence and peace appear to have prevailed in many prehistoric and prestate societies.*
(4) *War is not a cultural universal.* In particular, war seems to be most frequent and intense in the state level of sociopolitical organization, a relatively recent and short phase of cultural evolution that may even-

tually be transcended through further evolution. Nevertheless, there are civilizations that have experienced centuries or even millennia of relative peace.

(5) *The potential for the development of a more nonviolent and peaceful world is latent in human nature as revealed by the natural history of peace* (e.g., Kohn 1990). Humans have evolved both biological and cultural behavioral mechanisms to promote nonviolence and peace as well as to avoid, reduce, and resolve conflict and violence. Indeed ethnography does provide *heuristic precedents and models* of sociocultural systems that are relatively nonviolent and peaceful (Bonta 1993, Fabbro 1978, Howell and Willis 1989, Montagu 1978, Sponsel and Gregor 1994).

In this chapter, peace is considered to be a relative (rather than absolute) *condition* involving dynamic life-enhancing *processes* operating in relation to *ideals*. While it may be necessary first to experience war, or know about the existence of war, in order to conceptualize it explicitly and articulate a preference for peace instead, it is not necessary to have war first in order to value peace. A society, either peaceful or warlike, reflects cultural values, whether explicit or implicit. Interpretations of the palaeontological and archaeological records strongly suggest that peace occurred prior to war in human prehistory and cultural evolution. From ethnology and ethnography it is clear that relatively nonviolent and peaceful societies may value peace quite independently of any experience or knowledge of war. Thus, war is not necessarily prior to peace on either theoretical or experiential grounds. An analogy would be to assert the necessary prior occurrence of sickness for health, hate for love, or death for life. Considerations like these expose the reductionism and absurdity of such etic ideas as those that conflict resolution or ritualized warfare are peace, or peace is the residual category that includes whatever remains after war.

This exploration of the natural history of peace closes by urging the understanding that a *theory of human nature* is inevitably associated with theories of peace and war, regardless of whether it is explicit or implicit, and whether it has been developed in a systematic, informed, and critical manner. The importance of a theory of human nature in influencing beliefs and actions is stressed by Stevenson (1987: 3):

What is man? This is surely one of the most important questions of all. For so much else depends on our view of human nature. The meaning and purpose of human life, what we ought to do, and what we can hope to achieve—all these are fundamentally affected by whatever we think is the "real" or "true" nature of man. (See also Berry 1989, Eisenberg 1972: 124, Nelson and Olin 1979, and Roosevelt 1990).

Notes

This chapter is substantially revised from a paper presented at the Guggenheim conference on "What We Know About Peace," and the author is very grateful to the participants for their critical but constructive discussion of the original paper and in particular to the conference organizer and book editor, Thomas Gregor. The Spark M. Matsunaga Institute for Peace at the University of Hawaii awarded a Faculty Research Grant, which, among other things, supported a thorough literature search by Ram Cheddtri as some of the background for this chapter. Of course, only the author is responsible for any errors or deficiencies.

1. Some of the points in this chapter are discussed in more detail in Sponsel (1989, 1990a, 1994).

2. A curious but feeble attempt has been made by Lackner (1984) to consider some of the peaceful aspects of nature.

3. This principle has been applied by Bigelow (1969: 4–7) in his account of the evolution of human nature and war where he considers social cooperation as necessary for defense and offense against other groups in the struggle for survival. (Also see Knauft 1994). Parallel ideas are applied in analyses by Murphy (1957) of the Mundurucu and Overing (1989) of the Piaroa, both societies in Amazonia. Also see the cross-cultural study of the relationship between internal and external conflict by Ross (1985).

4. Despite the above, Goodall (1986: chapters 12 and 17) also sees in chimpanzees the rudiments of warfare. Following vivid descriptions of adult males on patrol along the perimeter of their territory, where they cooperated in violently attacking and killing members of an adjacent group, apparently without provocation, and other observations, Goodall (1986: 534) concludes:

> The chimpanzee, as a result of a unique combination of strong affiliative bonds between adult males on the one hand and an unusually hostile and violently aggressive attitude toward nongroup individuals on the other, has clearly reached a stage where he stands at the very threshold of human achievement in destruction, cruelty, and planned intergroup conflict. If ever he develops the power of language—and, as we have seen, he stands close to that threshold, too—might he not push open the door and wage war with the best of us?

5. Fabbro's analysis is one of a number of attemps to consider the pacific nature of "primitive" society, although some are now mainly of historical interest: Collins (1981), Ellis (1919), Howell and Willis (1989), Kang (1979), Kropotkin (1914: chapter 3), Melotti (1987), Montagu (1978), Nance (1975), Perry (1917), Smith (1929: chapters 5–6), Van Velzen and Wetering (1960), Wright (1942).

6. It should be noted that there are exceptional cases of foraging societies without agriculture that had warfare, such as the Kwakiutl of the Northwest Pacific Coast who engaged

in intense competition and even had slavery, but they involved quite special circumstances (Ferguson 1984).

7. There are many problems with Knauft's use of homicide rates, despite the magical appeal of statistics. (1) The average homicide rate for the United States as a whole is almost meaningless because of the enormous variation in homicide rates from urban to rural areas, among different "racial" and ethnic groups, and between regions in such a large and heterogeneous society. (2) If the killing of other humans by Americans during wars, such as in the dropping of the atomic bombs on Nagasaki and Hiroshima during WWII, were included in Knauft's calculations, then the rates for the United States would certainly be elevated very substantially. If he is intent on an objective measure of violence, then the reason for excluding war statistics in the case of the United States is unclear. If the quantification of violence in the form of homicide rates among ethnographic groups like the Yanomami includes those in the context of warfare (internal and/or external), then there does not seem to be any justification for treating the U.S. any differently. (3) Also it is questionable to compare the homicide rates of a large, complex, multicultural society like the United States with those of small and fairly homogeneous societies. (4) Furthermore, some of Knauft's estimates of homicide rates may not be accurate. For example, Dentan (1988a: 626) asserts that the homicide rate of the Semai is somewhere around 0.56 per 1/100,000 in contrast to Knauft's (1987: 458) estimate of 30.3 per 100,000. (5) Albert (1990: 561) is also critical of Knauft's attempt to assess degree of violence through quantitative comparisons that completely ignore the specifics of the situation, cultural context, and meaning of any particular homicide. He asserts that there is no value-free and cross-culturally valid definition of violence.

References

Adams, David B. 1983. Why There Are So Few Women Warriors. *Behavior Science Research* 18, no.3: 196–212.

Adler, Mortimer J. 1967. *The Difference of Man and the Difference it Makes*. New York: World.

Albert, Bruce. 1989. On Yanomami "Violence": Inclusive Fitness or Ethnographer's Representation? *Current Anthropology* 30, no. 5: 637–640.

———. 1990. On Yanomami Warfare: Rejoinder. *Current Anthropology* 31(5): 558–563.

Albert, Bruce, and Alcida Rita Ramos. 1989. Yanomami Indians and Anthropological Ethics. *Science* 244: 632.

Archer, John. 1988. *The Behavioural Biology of Aggression*. New York: Cambridge University Press.

Axelrod, Robert. 1984. *The Evolution of Cooperation*. New York: Basic Books.

Axelrod, Robert, and William D. Hamilton 1981 The Evolution of Cooperation. *Science* 211: 1390–1396.

Balandier, Georges. 1986. An Anthropology of Violence and War. *International Social Sciences Journal* 38, no. 4: 499–512.

Barnaby, Frank, ed. 1988 *The Gaia Peace Atlas: Survival into the Third Millennium*. New York: Doubleday.

Berry, Christopher J. 1989. *Human Nature*. Atlantic Highlands, N.J.: Humanities Press International.

Berreman, Gerald D. 1981. Social Inequality: A Cross-Cultural Analysis. In *Social Inequality: Comparative and Developmental Approaches*, ed. Gerald D. Berreman, pp. 3–40. New York:

Academic.

Bigelow, Robert. 1969. *The Dawn Warriors: Man's Evolution Toward Peace.* Boston: Little, Brown.

———. 1975. The Role of Competition and Cooperation in Human Evolution. In *War: Its Causes and Correlates,* ed. Martin A. Nettleship et.al. pp. 235–261. The Hague: Mouton.

Blick, Jeffrey P. 1988. Genocidal Warfare in Tribal Societies as a Result of European Induced Culture Conflict. *Man* 23, no.4: 654–670.

Bock, Kenneth. 1980. *Human Nature and History: A Response to Sociobiology.* New York: Columbia University Press.

Bodley, John H. 1990. We Fought with Spears. In John H. Bodley, *Victims of Progress,* pp. 42–56. Mountain View, Calif.: Mayfield.

Bonta, Bruce M. 1993. *Peaceful Peoples: An Annotated Bibliography.* Metuchen, N.J.: Scarecrow.

Boucher, D. H., S. James, and K. H. Keeler. 1982. The Ecology of Mutualism. *Annual Review of Ecology and Systematics* 13: 315–347.

Boulding, Kenneth E. 1978. *Stable Peace.* Austin: University of Texas Press.

Broch, Tom, and Johan Galtung. 1966. Belligerence among The Primitives. *Journal of Peace Research* 3: 33–45.

Burbank, Victoria K. 1987. Female Aggression in Cross-Cultural Perspective. *Behavior Science Research* 21, nos. 1–4: 70–100.

Campbell, Alan. 1989. Peace. In *Societies at Peace: Anthropological Perspectives,* ed. Signe Howell and Roy Willis, pp. 213–224. New York: Routledge.

Campbell, C. 1986. Images of War: A Problem in San rock Art Research. *World Archaeology* 18, no. 2: 255–268.

Carneiro, Robert. 1970. A Theory of the Origin of the State. *Science* 469: 733–738.

———. 1978. Political Expansion as An Expression of the Principle of Competitive Exclusion. In *Origins of the State: The Anthropology of Political Evolution,* ed. Ronald Cohen and Elman Service, pp. 205–223. Philadelphia: Institute for the Study of Human Issues.

Chagnon, Napoleon A. 1968. *Yanomamo: The Fierce People.* New York: Holt, Rinehart and Winston.

———. 1983 *Yanomamo: The Fierce People.* 3d edition. New York: Holt, Rinehart, and Winston.

———. 1988. Life Histories, Blood Revenge, and Warfare in a Tribal Population. *Science* 239: 985–991.

———. 1990. Reproduction and Somatic Conflicts of Interest in the Genesis of Violence and Warfare among Tribesmen. In *The Anthropology of War,* ed. Jonathan Haas, pp. 77–104. New York: Cambridge University Press.

Childe, V. Gordon. 1941. War in Prehistoric Societies. *The Sociological Review* 32: 127–138.

Cohen, Ronald. 1984. Warfare and State Formation: Wars Make States and States Make Wars. In *Warfare, Culture, and Environment,* ed. R. Brian Ferguson, pp. 329–358. New York: Academic.

Colchester, Marcus. 1987. Book Review: *Tales of the Yanomami: Daily Life in the Venezuelan Forest,* by Jacques Lizot. *Survival International News* 16: 8.

Collins, James X. 1981. An Anthropological Understanding of Non-Aggressive Social Systems. In *Applying Systems and Cybernetics,* ed. G. E. Lasker, pp. 553–557. New York: Pergamon.

Darwin, Charles R. 1871. *The Descent of Man.* London: John Murray.

van der Dennen, Johan M. G., and Vincent S. S. Falger, eds. 1990. *Sociobiology and Conflict: Evolutionary Perspectives on Competition, Cooperation, Violence and Warfare.* New York: Chapman and Hall.

Dentan, Robert K. 1968. *The Semai: A Nonviolent People of Malaya*. New York: Holt, Rinehart and Winston.

———. 1978. Notes on Childhood in a Nonviolent Context: The Semai Case (Malaysia). In *Learning Non-Aggression: The Experience of Non-Literate Societies*, ed. Ashley Montagu, pp. 94–143. New York: Oxford University Press.

———. 1988a. On Reconsidering Violence in Simple Societies. *Current Anthropology* 29, no. 4: 625–629.

———. 1988b Reply to Paul. *American Anthropologist* 90, no, 2: 420–423.

Divale, William, and Marvin Harris. 1976. Population, Warfare, and the Male Supremacist Complex. *American Anthropologist* 78: 521–538.

Dyson-Hudson, Rada, and Eric Alden Smith. 1978. Human Territoriality: An Ecological Assessment. *American Anthropologist* 80 no. 1: 21–41.

Eibl-Eibesfeldt, Irenaus. 1971. *Love and Hate: The Natural History of Behavior Patterns*. New York: Holt, Rinehart and Winston.

———. 1975. Aggression in the !Ko-Bushmen. In *War, Its Causes and Correlates*, ed. Martin A. Nettleship et.al., pp. 281–296. The Hague: Mouton Publishers.

———. 1979. *The Biology of Peace and War: Men, Animals, and Aggression*. New York: Viking Press.

———.1989. *Human Ethology*. New York: Aldine de Gruyter.

Ellis, Havelock. 1919. The Origin of War. In Havelock Ellis, *The Philosophy of Conflict And Other Essays in War-Time*, pp. 42–56. London: Constable and Company.

Eisenberg, Leon. 1972. The Nature of Human Nature. *Science* 176, no. 4031: 123–128.

Eisler, Riane. 1987. *The Chalice and the Blade: Our History, Our Future*. San Francisco: Harper and Row.

Ember, C. 1978. Myths about Hunter-Gatherers. *Ethnology* 17: 439–448.

Evans-Pritchard, E. E. 1940. *The Nuer: A Description of the Modes of Livelihood and Political Institutions of a Nilotic People*. New York: Oxford University Press.

Fabbro, David. 1978. Peaceful Societies: An Introduction. *Journal of Peace Research* 15, no. 1: 67–83.

Feibleman, James Kern. 1987. *The Destroyers: The Underside of Human Nature*. New York: Peter Lang.

Ferguson, R. Brian, ed. 1984. A Re-Examination of the Causes of Northwest Coast Warfare. In *Warfare, Culture, and Environment*, ed. R. Brian Ferguson, pp. 267–328. New York: Academic.

———. 1988. *The Anthropology of War: A Bibliography*. Occasional Papers of the Harry Guggenheim Foundation, No. 1. New York: Harry Frank Guggenheim Foundation.

———. 1990a. Blood of the Leviathan: Western contact and Warfare in Amazonia. *American Ethnologist* 17, no. 2: 237–257.

———. 1990b A Savage Encounter: Western Contact and the Yanomama War Complex. In *War in the Tribal Zone: Expanding States and Indigenous Warfare*, ed. R. Brian Ferguson and Neil L. Whitehead, pp. 199–227. Santa Fe, N.M.: School for American Research Press.

———. 1992. "Tribal Warfare." *Scientific American* 266, no. 1: 108–113.

———. 1994. Yanomami Warfare: A Case History. Santa Fe, N.M.: School for American Research Press.

Ferrill, Archer. 1985. Prehistoric Warfare. In Archer Ferrill, *The Origins of War*, pp. 9–31. New York: Thames and Hudson.

Fossey, Dian. 1983. *Gorillas in the Mist*. Boston: Houhgton Mifflin.

Gabriel, Richard A. 1990. The Archaeology of War. In Richard A. Gabriel, *The Culture of War: Invention and Early Development*, pp. 19–34. Westport, Conn.: Greenwood.

Galtung, Johan. 1968. Peace. *International Encyclopedia of Social Sciences*, vol. 2: 487–496.

Galtung, Johan 1985 Twenty-Five Years of Peace Research: Ten Challenges and Some Responses. *Journal of Peace Research* 22, no. 2: 141–158.

———. 1986. Peace Theory: An Introduction. In *World Encyclopedia of Peace*, ed. Ervin Laszlo and Jong Youl Yoo. New York: Pergamon Press, 2:251–260.

———. 1988. The Next Twenty-five Years of Peace Research: Tasks and Prospects. In *Peace Research: Achievements and Challenges*, ed, Peter Wallensteen, pp. 242–263. Boulder, Colo.: Westview.

Gibson, Thomas. 1989. Symbolic Representations of Tranquillity and Aggression among the Buid. In *Societies At Peace: Anthropological Perspectives*, ed. Signe Howell and Roy Willis, pp. 60–78. New York: Routledge.

Givens, R. Dale. 1975. Aggression in Nonhuman Primates: Implications for Understanding Human Behavior. In *War: Its Causes and Correlates*, ed. Martin A. Nettleship et al., pp. 263–280. The Hauge: Mouton.

Good, Kenneth. 1989. Yanomami Hunting Patterns: Trekking and Garden Relocation as an Adaptation to Game Availability in Amazonia, Venezuela. Ph.D. diss., University of Florida.

Good, Kenneth, with David Chanoff. 1991. *Into the Heart: One Man's Pursuit of Love and Knowledge among the Yanomama*. New York: Simon and Schuster.

Goodall, Jane. 1986. *The Chimpanzees of Gombe: Patterns of Behavior*. Cambridge: Harvard University Press.

Gould, Stephen Jay. 1988. Kropotkin Was No Crackpot. *Natural History* 97, no. 7: 12, 14, 16–18, 21.

Gowlett, John. 1984. *Ascent of Civilization: The Archaeology of Early Man*. New York: Knopf.

Graham, Hugh Davis, and Ted Robert Gurr, eds. 1969. *Violence in America: Historical and Comparative Perspective*. New York: Bantam.

Greenhouse, Carol J. 1985. Mediation: A Comparative Approach. *Man* 20, no. 1: 90–114.

Groebel, Jo, and Robert A. Hinde, eds. 1989. *Aggression and War: Their Biological and Social Bases*. New York: Cambridge University Press.

Gulsoy, Tanses. 1988. *Why the Fight over Peace Studies?* Occasional Papers of the Harry Guggenheim Foundation, No. 2. New York: Harry Frank Guggenheim Foundation.

Headland, Thomas N., ed. 1992. *The Tasaday Controversy: An Assessment of the Evidence*. Washington, D.C.: American Anthropological Association Special Publication.

Heelas, Paul. 1989. Identifying Peaceful Societies. In *Societies at Peace: Anthropological Perspectives*, ed. Signe Howell and Roy Willis, pp. 225–243. New York: Routledge.

Hofstadter, Richard, and Michael Wallace, eds. 1971. *American Violence: A Documentary History*. New York: Random House.

Howell, Signe, and Roy Willis, eds. 1989. *Societies At Peace: Anthropological Perspectives*. New York: Routledge.

Huxley, Thomas Henry. 1896. The Struggle for Existence in Human Society. In his Thomas Henry Huxley, *Evolution and Ethics and Other Essays*, pp. 195–236. New York: AMS.

Iglitzin, Lynne B. 1972. *Violent Conflict in American Society*. San Francisco: Chandler.

Itani, Junichiro. 1983. Intraspecific Killing among Non-human Primates. In *Law, Biology and Culture: The Evolution of Law*, ed. Margaret Gruter and Paul Bohannan, pp. 62–74. New York: Oxford.

Jacobs, Alan H. 1979. Maasai. Inter-Tribal Relations: Belligerent Herdsmen or Peaceable Pastoralists. In *Warfare among East African Herders*, ed. Katsuyoshi Fukui and David Turton, pp. 33–52. Seri Ethnological Studies, no. 3. Osaka: National Museum of Ethnology.

Kang, Gay. 1979. Exogamy and Peace Relations of Social Units: A Cross-Cultural Test. *Eth-*

nology 18, no. 1: 85–99.

Kano, Takayoshi. 1990. The Bonobo's Peaceable Kingdom. *Natural History* 11: 62–71.

Keeley, Lawrence H., and Daniel Cahen. 1989. Early Neolithic Forts and Villages in NE Belgium: A Preliminary Report. *Journal of Field Archaeology* 16, no. 2: 157–176.

———. 1995. *War Before Civilization: The Myth of the Peaceful Savage.* New York: Oxford University Press.

Kemp, Graham. 1988. Nonviolence: A Biological Perspective. In *A Just Peace Through Transformation: Cultural, Economic, and Political Foundations for Change,* ed. Chadwick Alger and Michael Stohl, pp. 112–126. Boulder, Colo: Westview.

Kohn, Alfie. 1990. The Brighter Side of *Human Nature: Altruism and Empathy in Everyday Life.* New York: Basic Books.

Konner, Melvin. 1982. *The Tangled Wing: Biological Constraints on the Human Spirit.* New York: Holt, Rinehart and Winston.

Knauft, Bruce M. 1987. Reconsidering Violence in Simple Human Societies. *Current Anthropology* 28, no. 4: 457–500.

———. 1994 Culture and Cooperation in Human Evolution. In *The Anthropology of Peace and Nonviolence,* ed. Leslie E. Sponsel and Thomas Gregor, pp. 37–67. Boulder, Colo.: Lynne Rienner.

Kropotkin, Petr. 1914. *Mutual Aid: A Factor of Evolution.* Boston: Extending Horizons Books.

Lackner, Stephan. 1984. *Peaceable Nature.* New York: Harper and Row.

Leakey, Richard E. 1981. The Making of Aggression. In Richard E. Leakey, *The Making of Mankind,* pp. 219–237. New York: E. P. Dutton.

Leakey, Richard E., and Roger Lewin. 1977. Origins: *What New Discoveries Reveal about the Emergence of Our Species.* London: Macdonald and Jane's.

———. 1978 An End To The Hunting Hypothesis. In Richard E. Leakey and Roger Lewin, *People of the Lake: Mankind and Its Beginnings,* pp. 251–282. Garden City, N.Y.: Anchor / Doubleday.

Leavitt, Gregory C. 1977. The Frequency of Warfare: An Evolutionary Perspective. *Sociological Inquiry* 47, no. 1: 49–58.

Lee, Richard B. 1979. Conflict and Violence. In Richard B. Lee, *The !Kung San: Men, Women, and Work in a Foraging Society,* pp. 370–400. New York: Cambridge University Press

———. 1982. Politics, Sexual and Non-Sexual in an Egalitarian Society. In *Politics and History in Band Societies,* ed. Eleanor Leacock and Richard Lee, pp. 37–59. New York: Cambridge University Press.

Lewellen, Ted C. 1983. The Evolution of the State, In Ted C. Lewellen, *Political Anthropology,* pp. 41–62. South Hadley, Mass.: Bergin and Garvey.

Lizot, Jacques. 1985. *Tales of the Yanomami: Daily Life in the Venezuelan Forest.* New York: Cambridge University Press.

———. 1994 Words in the Night: The Ceremonial Dialogue—One Expression of Peaceful Relationships Among the Yanomami. In *The Anthropology of Peace and Nonviolence,* ed. Leslie E. Sponsel and Thomas Gregor, pp. 213–240. Boulder, Colo.: Lynne Rienner.

Lorenz, Konrad. 1966. *On Aggression.* New York: Bantam.

Marshall, Lorna. 1961. Sharing, Talking, and Giving: Relief of Social Tensions among !Kung Bushmen. *Africa* 31: 231–249.

MacLeish, Kenneth. 1972. Stone Age Men of the Philippines. *National Geographic* 142, no. 3: 219–250.

Mead, Margaret. 1964. Warfare: It's Only an Invention—Not a Biological Necessity. In Margaret Mead, *Anthropology: A Human Science,* pp. 126–133. Princeton: D. Van Nostrand.

———. 1968. Alternatives to War. In War: *The Anthropology of Armed Conflict and Aggression,* ed. Morton Fried et.al., pp. 215–228. Garden City, N.Y.: Natural History Press.

Melko, Matthew. 1973. *52 Peaceful Societies*. Oakville, Ontario: Canadian Peace Research Institute.

———. 1984 Peaceful Societies. *World Encyclopedia of Peace,* ed. Ervin Laszol and Jong Youl Yoo. New York: Pergamon Press, 2:268–270.

Melko, Matthew. 1990. *Peace In Our Time*. New York: Paragon House.

Melko, Matthew, and John Hord. 1984. *Peace in the Western World*. Jefferson, North Carolina: McFarland & Company.

Melko, Matthew, and Richard D. Weigel. 1981. *Peace in the Ancient World*. Jefferson, North Carolina: McFarland & Company.

Melotti, Umberto. 1987. War and Peace in Primitive Human Societies: The Effects of Exogamy. *The Mankind Quarterly* 27, no. 4: 371–378.

Midgley, Mary. 1978. *Beast and Man: The Roots of Human Nature*. Ithaca, New York: Cornell University Press.

Mitscherlich, Margarete. 1987. *The Peaceable Sex: On Aggression in Women and Men*. New York: Fromm International.

Montagu, Ashley. 1942. The Nature of War and the Myth of Nature. *Scientific Monthly* 54: 342–353.

———. 1952. *Darwin, Competition and Cooperation*. New York: Henry Schuman.

———. 1976 *The Nature of Human Aggression*. New York: Oxford University Press.

———. ed. 1978 *Learning Non-Aggression: The Experience of Non-Literate Societies*. New York: Oxford University Press.

Murphy, Robert F. 1957. Intergroup Hostility and Social Cohesion. *American Anthropologist* 59: 1018–1035.

Nance, John. 1975. *The Gentle Tasaday: A Stone Age People of the Philippine Rain Forest*. New York: Harcourt, Brace, Jovanovich.

Nelson, Keith L., and Spencer C. Olin, Jr. 1979. *Why War? Ideology, Theory, and History*. Berkeley, Calif.: University of California Press.

O'Nell, Carl W. 1989. The Non-violent Zapotec. In *Societies At Peace: Anthropological Perspectives,* ed. Signe Howell and Roy Willis, pp. 117–132. New York: Routledge.

Overing, Joanna. 1989. Styles of Manhood: An Amazonian Contrast In tranquillity and Violence. In *Societies At Peace: Anthropological Perspectives,* ed. Signe Howell and Roy WIllis, pp. 79–99. New York: Routledge.

Palmer, Stuart. 1965. Murder and Suicide in Forty Non-Literate Societies. *Journal of Criminal Law, Criminology, and Police Science* 56: 320–324.

———. 1972. *The Violent Society*. New Haven, Conn.: College and University Press Publishers.

Paul, Robert A. 1978. Instinctive Aggression in Man: The Semai Case. *Journal of Psychoanalytical Anthropology* 1, no. 1: 65–79.

Paynter, Robert. 1989. The Archaeology of Equality and Inequality. *Annual Review of Anthropology* 18: 369–399.

Perry, William. 1917. The Peaceable Habits of Primitive Communities: An Anthropological Study of the Golden Age. *The Hibben Journal* 16: 28–46.

Pfeiffer, John. 1982. *The Creative Explosion: An Inquiry into the Origins of Art and Religion*. New York: Harper and Row.

Pollard, Albert F. 1974. The Idea That War Is Natural Anatomized and Decently Interred. In *Frontiers of Anthropology,* ed. Ashley Montagu, pp. 421–425. New York: G.P. Putnam's Sons.

Ramos, Alcida Rita. 1987. Reflecting on the Yanomami: Ethnographic Images and the Pursuit of the Exotic. *Cultural Anthropology* 2, no. 3: 284–304.

Richard, Alison F. 1985. *Primates in Nature*. San Francisco: W. H. Freeman.

Robarchek, Clayton A. 1977a. Semai Nonviolence: A Systems Approach to Understanding. Ph.D. diss., University of California, Riverside.

———. 1977b Frustration, Aggression, and the Nonviolent Semai. *American Ethnologist* 4: 762–779.

———. 1981. The Image of Nonviolence: World View of the Semai Senoi. *Journal of the Federated States Museums* 25: 103–117.

———. 1989. Primitive Warfare and the Ratomorphic Image of Mankind. *American Anthropologist* 91, no. 4: 903–920.

———. 1989b. Hobbesian and Rousseauan Images of Man: Autonomy and Individualism in a Peaceful Society. In *Societies At Peace: Anthropological Perspectives*, ed. Signe Howell and Roy Willis, pp. 31–44. New York: Routledge.

Robarchek, Clayton A., and Robert Knox Dentan. 1987. Blood Drunkenness and the Bloodthirsty Semai: Unmaking Another Anthropological Myth. *American Anthropologist* 89, no. 2: 356–365.

Robarchek, Clayton A., and C. J. Robarchek. 1989. The Waorani: From Warfare to Peacefulness. *The World and I* 4, no. 1: 625–635.

Rodman, Margaret, and Matthew Cooper, eds. 1979. *The Pacification of Melanesia*. Ann Arbor: University of Michigan Press.

Roosevelt, Grace G. 1990. *Reading Rousseau in the Nuclear Age*. Philadelphia: Temple University Press.

Roper, Marilyn Keyes. 1969. A Survey of the Evidence for Intrahuman Killing in the Pleistocene. *Current Anthropology* 10, no. 4: 427–458.

———. 1975. Evidence of Warfare in the Near East from 10,000–4,300 B.C. In *War, Its Causes and Correlates*, ed. Martin A. Nettleship et.al., pp. 299–343. The Hague: Mouton Publishers.

Rosenberger, Lizzi. 1973. Women's Role in Aggression. In *Pyschological Bases of War*, ed. Heinrich Z. Winnik, Rafael Moses, and Mortimer Ostow, pp. 43–58. New York: Quadrangle.

Ross, Marc Howard. 1985. Internal and External Conflict and Violence: Cross-Cultural Evidence and a New Analysis. *Journal of Conflict Resolution* 29, no. 4: 547–579.

Royce, Joseph. 1980. Play in Violent and Non-violent Cultures. *Anthropos* 75: 799–822.

Scheffler, Harold. 1964. The Social Consequences of Peace on Choiseul Island. *Ethnology* 3: 398–403.

Shaw, R. Paul. 1985a. Humanity's Propensity for Warfare: A Sociobiological Perspective. *The Canadian Review of Sociology and Anthropology* 22, no. 2: 158–183.

———. 1985b. Merging Ultimate and Proximate Causes in Sociobiology and Studies of Warfare. *The Canadian Review of Sociology and Anthropology* 22, no. 2: 192–201.

Silverberg, James, and J. Patrick Gray, eds. 1992. *Aggression and Peacefulness in Humans and Other Primates*. New York: Oxford University Press.

Smith, G. Elliot. 1929. *Human History*. New York: Norton.

Smoker, P. 1981. Small Peace. *Journal of Peace Research* 18, no.2: 149–157.

Smole, William J. 1976. *The Yanoama Indians: A Cultural Geography*. Austin: University of Texas Press.

Smuts, Barbara. 1985. *Sex and Friendship in Baboons*. New York: De Gruyter Aldine.

———. 1987. What Are Friends For? *Natural History* 6, no. 2: 36–45.

Sponsel, Leslie E. 1983. Yanomama Warfare, Protein Capture, and Cultural Ecology: A Critical Analysis of The Arguments of the Opponents. *Interciencia* 8: 204–210.

————. 1989. An Anthropologist's Perspective on Peace and Quality of Life. In *Peace and Development: An Interdisciplinary Perspective,* ed. Daniel S. Sanders and Jon K. Matsuoka, pp. 29–48. Honolulu: University of Hawaii School of Social Work.

————. 1990a The Mutual Relevance of Anthropology and Peace Studies. *Human Peace Quarterly* 7, nos. 3–4: 3–9.

————. 1990b. Ultraprimitive Pacifists: The Tasaday as a Symbol of Peace. *Anthropology Today* 6, no. 1: 3–5.

————. 1992. Our Fascination with the Tasaday: Anthropological Images and Images of Anthropology. In *The Tasaday Controversy: An Assessment of the Evidence,* ed. Thomas N. Headland, Washington, D.C.: American Anthropological Association Special Publications.

————. 1994. The Mutual Relevance of Anthropology and Peace Studies. In *The Anthropology of Peace and Nonviolence,* ed. Leslie E. Sponsel and Thomas Gregor, pp. 1–36. Boulder, Colo.: Lynne Rienner.

Sponsel, Leslie E., and Thomas Gregor, eds. 1994. *The Anthropology of Peace and Nonviolence.* Boulder, Colo.: Lynne Rienner.

Stephenson, Carolyn. 1990. *Peace Studies: The Evolution of Peace Research and Peace Education.* Occasional Paper No. 1. Honolulu: University of Hawaii Institute for Peace.

Stevenson, Leslie. 1987. *Seven Theories of Human Nature.* New York: Oxford University Press.

Strum, Shirley C. 1985. Baboons May Be Smarter Than People. *Animal Kingdom* 88, no. 2: 12–15.

Thomas, Daniel C., and Michael T. Klare, eds. 1989. *Peace and World Order Studies: A Curriculum Guide.* Boulder, Colo.: Westview.

Toplin, Robert B. 1975. *Unchallenged Violence: An American Ordeal.* Westport, Conn.: Greenwood.

Trivers, Robert. 1985. *Social Evolution.* Menlo Park, Calif.: Benjamin / Cummings.

Turnbull, Colin M. 1961. *The Forest People.* New York: Simon and Schuster.

————. 1982. The Ritualization of Potential Conflict between the Sexes among the Mbuti. In *Politics and History in Band Societies,* ed. Eleanor Leacock and Richard Lee, pp. 133–155. New York: Cambridge University Press.

————. 1983. *The Mbuti Pygmies: Change and Adaptation.* New York: Holt, Rinehart and Winston.

Van Velzen, H. U .E., and W. Van Wetering. 1960. Residence, Power Groups And Intra-Societal Aggression: An Enquiry Into The Conditions Leading To Peacefulness Within Non-Stratified Societies. *Internationales Archiv fur Ethnographie* 49: 169–200.

Vencl, S. 1984. War and Warfare in Archaeology. *Journal of Anthropological Archaeology* 3: 116–132.

de Waal, Frans. 1982. *Chimpanzee Politics: Power and Sex Among the Apes.* New York: Harper and Row.

————. 1986. Conflict Resolution in Monkeys and Apes. In *Primates: The Road to Self-Sustaining Populations,* ed. Kurt Benirschke, pp. 341–350. Chicago: Aldine.

————. 1989. *Peacemaking among Primates.* Cambridge: Harvard University Press.

Wallensteen, Peter, ed. 1988. Peace Research: *Achievements and Challenges.* Boulder, Colo.: Westview.

Webb, Keith. 198.6 Structural Violence and the Definition of Conflict. In *World Encyclopedia of Peace,* ed. Ervin Laszlo and Jong Youl Yoo. New York: Pergamon, 2:431–434.

Whyte, Martin King. 1978. *The Status of Women in Preindustrial Societies.* Princeton, N.J.: Princeton University Press.

Wiberg, Hakan. 1981. JPR 1964–1980—What Have We Learnt about Peace? *Journal of Peace*

    Research 18, no. 2: 111–148.
Willis, Roy. 1989. The "Peace Puzzle" in Ufipa. In *Societies At Peace: Anthropological Perspec-
    tives,* ed. Signe Howell and Roy Willis, pp. 133–145. New York: Routledge.
Wilson, Edward O. 1978. *On Human Nature.* Cambridge: Harvard University Press.
Wolf, Eric. 1987. Cycles of Violence: The Anthropology of War andPeace. In *Waymarks,* ed.
    Kenneth Moore, pp. 127–150. Notre Dame: University of Notre Dame Press.
Wright, Quincy. 1942. *A Study of War.* Chicago: University of Chicago Press.
Wright, H. 1977. Recent Research on the Origin of the State. *Annual Review of Anthropology*
    6: 379–397.

THREE

The Psychology of Peace

5 The Psychological and Cultural Roots of Group Violence and the Creation of Caring Societies and Peaceful Group Relations

ERVIN STAUB

■ What are the qualities of motivation and relationship that make peace possible? Ervin Staub examines the roots of violence between groups, including social conditions, group relations, culture, and the evolution of antagonism and violence. He then develops a psychology of sociative peace, maintaining that peaceful societies foster prosocial behavior—caring about others' welfare, trust, empathy, cooperation, and a sense of shared humanity. Bystanders play a particularly crucial role in Staub's psychology of peace. By their capacity to witness and react to others, they may constrain violence and reward peaceful, prosocial conduct. Staub examines the many ways in which peace is linked to positive values and the legitimate use of power. His version of the peaceful society is one in which we would like to live. In other contributions to this volume (notably those of Demarest in chapter 8, and Gregor and Robarchek in chapter 6) we shall see that peace is possible under conditions that are far less attractive than the ideally peaceful society that Staub implicitly describes. However, as suggested by Tuzin (chapter 1) and Crenshaw's study of terrorists that give up violence (chapter 9), prosocial values are likely to be found in all cultures, no matter what their level of aggression. By highlighting this aspect of behavior, Staub's psychology of prosocial values becomes an essential part of our understanding of peace.

IN THE FIRST part of this chapter I will examine the characteristics of and psychological reactions in individuals and groups that lead to hostility and violence against other groups. I will also discuss what activates these characteristics and gives rise to the psychological reactions that lead a group to turn against another at a particular time. By "group" I mean the subgroups of a society, like ethnic, racial, religious, or even political groups and groups differentiated by their status and power in society (as in the case of the disappearances in Argentina [see Staub 1989 a]), as well as nation states. I will focus on internal problems in groups, what I call difficult life conditions, as important activating or instigating conditions for group violence. In the second part of the chapter, I will consider how individual and group characteristics can be developed that promote positive group relations and peace.[1]

Difficult Life Conditions and Basic Needs

Conflict and violence arise either from characteristics of groups or from conditions affecting groups; most often they arise from the combination of the two (Staub 1989a). Certain conditions may be regarded as instigating conditions for aggression: they give rise to motives that make aggression probable. These conditions can be external to groups, relational, or internal. Attack or threat of attack by another group can be purely external, although it is often the outcome of an evolution in the relationship between two groups. Competition and conflict with another country, for example, over territory or in trade, are relational. Within a society a history of differences may exist between subgroups concerning power and privilege. Their respective positions in society and their relationship to each other can be instigating conditions for mutual aggression.

Difficult life conditions within a society—such as economic problems and deprivation, political conflict or political violence, and great and rapid social change—are also important instigating conditions for violence. They tend to generate material and psychological needs in people that enhance the likelihood of aggression.

Human beings have many motives, from the biological need for food to the spiritual need for transcending the self. Certain psychological needs are so important, so basic, that some degree of their fulfillment is necessary for normal functioning. This suggestion is in the spirit of a number of psychological theories proposing either universal human motives (Maslow 1962) or basic requirements for maintaining the self (Epstein 1980) or basic human needs (Staub 1989a; 1996). Basic needs are more fundamental than the learned motives that guide many of our actions in everyday life, which I call personal goals (Staub 1978, 1980, 1989a).

Difficult life conditions may threaten people's material well being and at times even their survival. They threaten their need for security. But severe economic problems, political turmoil and conflict, or profound social change, as well as the disorganization and social chaos that result from them, can deeply threaten and frustrate a number of basic psychological needs beyond security. In such circumstances, the foundation of people's individual self-concept is threatened: their values, their ways of life, their view of themselves as competent people who can exercise control and provide for themselves and their families. Their group self-concept is also threatened, their positive view of their group and their belief that their group can and will protect and support them. People's comprehension of reality is also undermined: their view of the world, of how to live life, of their place in the world. To hold a usable comprehension of reality is a profound human need (Epstein 1980; Janoff-Bulman 1985); to regain a usable comprehension of reality will strongly motivate action. Connections to other human beings, also a profound need, are weakened, due to competition for scarce resources and self-focus, at a time when support and connection are most needed. Finally, intense need for hope, for belief in a better future, will be generated.

People will be strongly motivated to defend and elevate individual and group self-concepts—including their sense of competence and power to influence events—to gain a comprehension of reality, to regain support and connection, and to regain hope in the future (Staub, 1989a; 1996). Threat by another group can also activate these and/or other needs. In the case of outside threat, the need for security and the need to defend a positive societal self-concept can be especially important.

How can groups fulfill these needs? They can work to improve life conditions, which is frequently a slow and difficult matter. They can work to resolve conflict with other groups by peaceful means. But the stronger that certain cultural-societal characteristics are, the more likely the group will attempt to fulfill basic needs in ways that lead to group violence. Primary among these ways are adopting and creating ideologies that promise a better future but also identify enemies (see later section on "modes of responding").

My analysis of instances of genocides and mass killing—including detailed examination of the Holocaust, the genocide in Turkey, the "autogenocide" in Cambodia, and the disappearances in Argentina—shows that in every instance life conditions were extremely difficult (Staub 1989a). For example, in Germany between the end of World War I and 1933 when Hitler came to power, there was a revolution, tremendous inflation, then severe depression with many people out of work, and intense political conflict with private armies fighting each other on the streets and in the countryside. There were also great changes in social mores. These changes were partly an outcome of difficult life conditions, a form of social disorganization, but also added an element to the difficult conditions of life. In Turkey life problems were even worse, if possible, before the government initiated the policy of genocide against the

Armenians. In the former Yugoslavia as well, the collapse of communism and the political and other uncertainties that followed represented difficult life conditions (Staub, 1996).

Group Characteristics and the Evolution of Conflict

Certain characteristics of groups represent a predisposition for group violence. The greater the extent a society possesses these predisposing characteristics the more probable it becomes that the dominant group or the government will turn against a subgroup of society, or against an external enemy, in response to difficult life conditions. These characteristics affect the intensity and nature of needs that arise, making it probable that these needs will be fulfilled in ways that lead the group to turn against another. They also affect the response to conflict or threat and can at times themselves generate conflict and hostility. My analysis of the four genocides and mass killings listed above (Staub, 1989a) and my less extensive analysis of the violence in the former Yugoslavia (Staub, 1996) indicate that the pattern or combination of characteristics that I describe below were present in every instance—with variation in their exact form.

Devaluation and Ideology of Antagonism

One predisposing characteristic for group violence is a history of devaluation of another group. Human beings have a strong potential to differentiate between "us," members of an ingroup, and "them," members of an outgroup. This potential is shown in infants, as they develop strong positive bonds (attachment) to caretakers, while at the same time show fear of strangers (Ainsworth 1979). Experience strongly shapes the differentiation between us and them. For example, infants who are more securely attached to their primary caretakers and who have a wider range of experience with other people show less anxiety around strangers (Schaffer 1988). Unfortunately, in most groups, children are taught to differentiate strongly between a positively valued ingroup and those who belong to other groups, devaluing outgroups and their members (Allport 1954; Piaget and Weil 1951). Devaluation, in turn, makes hurting others easier and more likely (Bandura et al. 1975; Staub 1989a).

People in many societies evolve strong devaluative stereotypes and negative images of at least some other groups, which can be subgroups of the society, outside groups, or both. Such devaluation has many functions. It helps to elevate the self and to create cohesion within the group. At times leaders actively create antagonism toward others, which usually increases internal cohesion and enhances support for the leaders. But devaluation of others does not seem necessary to create group cohesion. Research on cooperation, primarily with children, indicates that working together can build positive group ties, even a positive orientation toward those outside the cooperating group (Heber and Heber 1957; Johnson et al. 1981).

Devaluation also "preselects" a scapegoat, a group that is blamed in difficult times or that is identified as an ideological enemy. The intense devaluation of internal groups, frequently less powerful subgroups of a society, usually has two components: a purely devaluative component, which depicts the group as less worthy—less industrious, intelligent, or good—and a representation of the group as a threat to the ingroup.

The Jews in Germany and the Armenians in Turkey had been devalued for centuries, before the advent of those leaders that guided these societies to genocide. Strong rifts exist in many societies, which can give rise to devaluation. This was the case in Cambodia, with a rift between the peasants in the countryside and the officials, merchants, and educated people in the cities. In Russia before the 1917 revolution, there was a similar rift between the wealthy nobility and the poor.

Devaluation can justify the exploitation or poverty of a subgroup of society. Dominant, powerful, or wealthy groups need to justify their status. They tend to do so by devaluing the groups that serve them and by developing ideologies that make their own privileged role acceptable and even right. As a result, demands of the less privileged will be resisted, not only because they threaten status and privilege but also because they are contrary to the world view of the privileged. This makes it more difficult to resolve conflicts of interest in peaceful ways.

Just as internal groups can be devalued, so the devaluation of external groups can become part of a culture. Devaluation and hostility may be an outcome of past conflict and violence. An "ideology of antagonism" may develop, which focuses on the other's hostility and defines the other as a threat to the group's existence. An aspect of such an ideology is the belief that strength and superiority over the other are required to ensure the group's safety. In extreme cases an important part of the group's self-concept may become its enmity toward the other. Such an ideology is frequently the result of a history of conflict and violence between groups, with persisting memories of that history and its wounds deeply embedded in each group's culture. The emergence of ethnic violence in the former Soviet Union between, for example, Azerbaijainis and Armenians, and the violence between groups in the former Yugoslavia seem to be based on mutually held ideologies of antagonism.

The speedy change in attitudes in the United States toward the Soviet Union was possible probably because little violence had taken place between the two countries, and no deep physical or psychic wounds had been inflicted. The conflict was based on a clash of ideologies and perceived interests. The change in the ideology, in the international conduct, and in the internal conditions of the Soviet Union eliminated both the ideological clash and the conflict of interests and made the U.S. a victor and potential benefactor. In addition the strong affirmation that American policy and political culture received in this process was a likely contributor to the speed of attitudinal change.

Discrimination, persecution, and violent actions against a devalued group maintain and enhance its devaluation. Sometimes groups relate to each other in a mode of conflict. Each engages in behavior that harms the interests of the other, even if at a cost to itself. Gain by the other is experienced as frustration and even as provocation. Apparently, rumors that Armenians were receiving housing and other benefits touched off the violence against them in Azerbaijan in 1989. Until Gorbachev's revolution this zero-sum-game mentality seemed to characterize U.S.-Soviet relations.

Once devaluation has become part of a culture—its literature, media, and verbal exchange among people—it is likely to persist even during periods when it has no special psychological function. The persistence of devaluation and ideologies of antagonism is evident in Eastern Europe and the former Soviet Union where, after the repressive rule of communism lifted, old antagonisms actively emerged. To overcome devaluation and antagonism that has become part of the deep structure of a culture requires active steps. The mere passage of time is insufficient.

A strong us-them differentiation and a negative view of others makes aggressive behavior by groups more likely. However, it is a combination of characteristics, not a single characteristic, that creates the predisposition for group violence. The Semai have a highly peaceful society, even though they hold a negative view of outsiders, who are seen as hostile and feared greatly. But this negative view of others is accompanied by a strong self-definition as a peaceful people. The Semai avoid conflict, amongst themselves and with others, and yield rather than fight (See Gregor and Robarchek, chapter 6).

A peaceful adaptation that is essentially passive can be successful if one's neighbors are not violent and warlike. But peace may be best served by an active approach, the building of positive connections, cooperation, and shared goals.

Authority, Obedience and a Monolithic Society

Strong respect for authority and the tendency to obey authorities is another predisposing characteristic for group violence. Given this characteristic, in the face of difficult life conditions or external threat members of the group will be more dependent on guidance by authorities. When leaders take actions that might lead to increasing conflict with or violence against others, members of the group will be less likely to speak out or act in opposition.

Similar consequences follow from monolithic rather than pluralistic culture and society. The terms *monolithic* and *pluralistic* have different meanings among different disciplines and different authors (Fein 1990). I will use *monolithic culture* to mean a culture in which a limited set of values is dominant and freedom of the expression of varied values and beliefs is limited. I will use *pluralistic society* to suggest a society of varied values, beliefs, and interests, where potential or actual conflicts among the groups or subgroups holding them are worked out in the public domain. An aspect of pluralism is the participation of all subgroups in the life of a society. In heterogeneous societies, like many modern nation states, the exclusion of certain groups from public life is usually tied to their devaluation. Without equal rights and equal voice, their influence will be limited, and they themselves can become victims. In this perspective, the defining character of a pluralistic society is not varied groups, but the possibility of participation by groups with their varied values and interests in the public domain.

This view suggests that strongly established hierarchical arrangements are potentially harmful, especially in complex, heterogeneous human societies with varied subgroups that can turn against each other. Among primates (see chapter 2, de Waal) a stable dominance hierarchy reduces violence, and this can happen in small human groups as well. Under stable conditions, hierarchical, obedience-oriented or monolithic societies may be as peaceful as pluralistic ones. But when stress, threat, life problems, or social change bring forth leadership that moves the group toward violence against others, a multiplicity of beliefs and values makes it more likely that opposition will arise that inhibits this movement. Wide ranging participation by people in the public domain can balance the leaders' influence and limit the arbitrary use of power.

My analysis of the Holocaust, of the genocide of the Armenians, and of the genocide in Cambodia (Staub 1989a) suggests that all these societies were highly authority oriented and traditionally monolithic. There has been strong authority orientation in the groups of the former

Yugoslavia as well (Staub, 1996). In Argentina the society as a whole was less monolithic. But the armed forces, which developed the policy of disappearances—the kidnapping, torture, and killing of "enemies," a category which over time became increasingly loosely defined—was a highly authority-oriented and monolithic system (Staub 1989a).

Cultural-Societal Self Concepts

Individuals have both individual self-concepts, the way they see themselves, and group self-concepts, which members of a group tend to share. The way members see their group affects their response to life problems and to conflicts with other groups.

While all groups tend to be ethnocentric, viewing themselves more positively than others (Allport 1954), in some groups there is an especially strong view of the group as good, worthy, and superior (Staub 1989a). For groups as well as individuals, such a superior self-concept may be defensive in nature (Staub 1993), a result of past difficulties and wounds, like a history of defeat and dominance by others or of poverty and deprivation. However, even when defensive, the elevation of the group can employ realistic components, such as a past history of national greatness and power over others or extraordinary natural resources or great literary or artistic achievements. A belief in its superiority can lead a society, or its members, to feel justified in conquest, whether of territory or by spreading beliefs and ideals.

A feeling of superiority may frequently be accompanied by an underlying sense of vulnerability. When both characteristics are present, the impact of difficult life conditions can be especially strong. They threaten the belief in superiority and activate or awaken feelings of vulnerability. Given a belief in one's group's superiority, threat by another group may give rise to aggression, motivated partly by "macho pride" (White 1984).

My analysis of genocides, mass killings, and disappearances (Staub 1989a; 1996) confirms the role of societal or group self-concept. For example, Germany has historically manifested a strong belief in its superiority, partly based on its military prowess and its cultural and artistic achievements. At the same time, a history in which they have suffered military devastation, with very great loss of life, has also led Germans to a feeling of deep vulnerability. These two aspects of the German self-concept played a role in the Nazis coming to power and in the subsequent genocide and external violence that led to World War II.

A superior group self-concept may also account for some U.S. policies and actions, including a history of subversion or armed invasion in Latin America, especially Central America, to create governments that are to our liking. But this sense of superiority is relatively easily shaken. In the U.S., in my view, there have been "difficult life conditions" for the last two to three decades, not primarily in terms of severe economic problems or intense political conflict, usually two of the main sources of it, but in terms of a third source—great social changes and attendant social disorganization (see Staub 1989a; for the alternative concepts of normative breakdown and disorientation, see Fein 1990). Assassinations, social movements, and changed norms about human relationships, changes in families and single parenting, as well as change in the U.S. economic status and role in the world, are among the constituents of these difficult life conditions. The moderately difficult life conditions in the U.S. have been long lasting and would be expected to give rise to strong needs and feelings of self-doubt. This may explain why the American people found intense satisfaction in the war against and victory over Iraq. It reaffirmed a group or societal self-concept of strength, power, and superiority (Staub 1991b).

The "content" of the societal self-concept can also be important. As in the case of the Semai, a group can identify itself as peaceful and avoid conflict and violence. Or the group's self-definition may include certain territories. Conflict between neighboring groups may arise from claims to land that are part of both group's societal self-concept. As in the Falklands war, the territory need not have material significance, in terms of population or natural resources.

A History of Aggressiveness

A group may have a history of hostility and war and of resolving conflict in aggressive ways. This shapes the culture and the nature of its social organization and makes future aggression more likely.

A past history of aggressiveness is likely to lead to the assumption that aggression is inevitable in human affairs or that it is the normal mode of conflict resolution (Heusmann and Eron 1984; Staub 1989a). As part of such a world view, other groups will be seen as aggressive, which requires aggressive self-defense. Institutions are likely to develop that serve aggression; their existence, in turn, makes aggression more likely. Such a history will shape culture and is likely to lead to socialization practices that, in turn, imbue children with personal characteristics that generate hostility and aggression. These characteristics include viewing people and the world as hostile, promoting skills for fighting and war, and even valuing aggression.

U.S.?

For example, Germany had a long history of internal aggression and war, and Nazi thinking idealized aggression (Hitler 1923; Staub 1989a).

The U.S. has also frequently engaged in armed conflict. Just considering the period following World War II, in addition to many landings and stationings of Marines, the U.S. has engaged in war in Korea and Vietnam, bombed Libya, and invaded Grenada and Panama. All this made turning to war against Iraq easier and more likely, limiting efforts at peaceful solutions.

There are, of course, conditions and experiences that change societies: their organization, political system, culture, institutions, and the individuals in them. Societies can change with regard to aggressiveness and other characteristics. Examples include Germany and Japan, which, as a result of defeat and external influences, have undergone great changes. Another example is South Africa. However, deeply set elements of culture also show great persistence. The attacks on foreign residents of Germany may be an example of a persistent tendency to devalue "outgroup" members. In Germany, lack of deep exploration of the past may have limited cultural change (Bar-On 1989).

Group Motives and Values

It is often assumed that groups act to further their "rational" self-interest, primary among which are security and material well-being. Pursuit of these goals can lead to a genuine conflict of interest between groups. Each of two parties might claim the right to territory important for its security, existence, or material well-being, as in the earlier stages of the Palestinian-Israeli conflict. However, what is regarded as an important interest is a function of a group's characteristics, including its values and motives. Groups that greatly value wealth, power, and prestige are more likely to define their interests in ways that bring them into conflict with others than groups that strongly value caring, cooperation, and positive relations. The experience of threat from others and past harm inflicted by others can generate both a motive for self-defense and a purely aggressive motive: anger, feelings of hostility, and the desire to harm.

Dissociation and Integration

Among individuals as well as groups the different aspects of the self can be well integrated, or some aspects can be "dissociated." Dissociation means lack of awareness in oneself of feelings, desires, and needs. Psychoanalytic thinking, in which the concept of dissociation originated, identifies sexuality and aggression as the feelings and desires of individuals that are usually denied, repressed, and thereby dissociated from the self. But any aspect of the experience of the individual or society can be dissociated, depending on what is acceptable or unacceptable for an individual or a group in light of its values and self-concept.

One author (Lewis 1978), for example, has suggested that in the U.S. a strong ideological belief in equality of opportunity has led people to ignore and deny the reality of inequality of opportunity. As a result people blame themselves for their failures even when those failures originate in the structures of society that limit opportunity for members of some groups.

Societies can make integration within persons easier or more difficult. In addition to the personal level, culture, institutions, and the political system may be more or less integrated. The less conducive the culture to personal integration and the less psychologically integrated the society, the more likely it is that instigating conditions will give rise to tensions or forces that fuel hostility between groups.

Modes of Responding to Conditions That Trigger Violence

Instigating conditions for aggression can be dealt with peacefully. However, given group characteristics that predispose toward violence, it becomes likely that such conditions will give rise to psychological reactions and modes of thinking that turn one group against another. Difficult life conditions tend to give rise to scapegoating (Allport 1954; Staub 1989a). Typically, some group is identified as responsible for the life problems. This relieves people of feelings of responsibility for events, offers comprehension, and affords the possibility of control by acting against or eliminating the scapegoat.

Ideologies frequently arise, offering a vision of a better life and, thus, both new comprehension of reality and hope for the future. The ideology can be primarily nationalistic, offering a better life for the group, or it can apply to all humanity, offering a better life for all. The Pan-Turkish ideology with its ideals of renewed national greatness and purity that preceded the genocide of the Armenians was a nationalistic ideology; Communism offered a better world ideology; frequently ideologies are mixed. Whatever their nature, however, they almost invariably identify an enemy that supposedly stands in the way of the ideology's fulfillment. The movements that arise to fulfill the ideology frequently turn against the enemy.

The Evolution of Group Violence

An important component of the conception of group violence presented here is evolution or change in groups. Actions have consequences. They affect others' behavior. A cycle of actions and reactions can lead to violent conflict—or positive relations. But individuals and groups also change as a result of their own actions. Their evolution is, to an important degree, a function of the actions they themselves initiate and engage in.

A subgroup of society becomes the victim of mass killing or genocide usually as the outcome of an evolution, what I have called *steps along the continuum of destruction* (Staub 1989a). Psychological research shows that people learn by doing. As people help or harm others, they become increasingly helpful or capable of inflicting increasing harm. For example, I have found that children who were led to engage in helpful acts, such as teaching younger children or making toys for poor, hospitalized children, were subsequently more helpful themselves (Staub 1975, 1979, 1988). On the other hand, people who participated in experiments where, in order to teach others, they were told to administer electric shocks to a learner making mistakes on the task, progressively increased the level of shock over the course of the task (Buss 1966; Goldstein et al. 1975).

The evolution of helping and harmdoing is also apparent in real life. Many heroic rescuers of Jews in Nazi Europe started out intending to help an acquaintance for a short time, but then became increasingly helpful and committed (Oliner and Oliner 1988; Staub 1989a, 1993). Helpful actions create psychological change in the actor. People usually help others only if they see them in at least a somewhat positive light. But as they act, their positive evaluation of those they help and their concern for their welfare tends to increase. Their self-concept and values change; they come to see themselves as willing to make sacrifices for other people. In the end, they can develop intense commitment to helping.

Concern about others may focus on certain people but can also generalize and extend to all human beings. For example, the Mothers of the Plaza de Mayo first demonstrated, with great danger to themselves, to protest the disappearance of their own children, partly in the hope of getting information about them. Over time they became concerned with all the disappeared and with injustice and inhumanity in general (Elshtain 1986; Staub 1989a).

Similarly, in mass killings and genocides perpetrators usually start with limited acts of persecution or violence. But they change, as a result of their actions. Their motivations to harm evolve, and their inhibitions decline. They become capable of increasing violence.

When people harm others, they come to devalue their victims and become less concerned with their welfare. They tend to engage in "just-world thinking," which is based on the human tendency to believe that the world is a just, fair place. They come to view those who suffer, and even those they themselves have harmed, as deserving their suffering (Lerner 1980). Progressively, those who inflict harm may so intensely devalue their victims that they exclude them from the moral realm. The perpetrators come to see themselves as willing and capable of harming and even destroying the victims, for justifiable reasons. Along the way the whole society changes, societal norms change, and institutions develop that serve the victims' destruction.

The evolution may also take the form of mutual acts of hostility. Reciprocity is basic in human relations, a deeply set and apparently universal norm, at least in the interactions of individuals (Gouldner 1960; Staub 1978). It apparently operates at the group level as well. Acts of hostility by one group usually lead to reciprocal acts by the other. Unfortunately, individuals and groups are often unaware of their own role in reciprocal hostility. They don't see the impact of their behavior on the other, but focus on the other's hostile actions and consider their own behavior as a justifiable reaction.

Given predisposing characteristics to violence, another's actions may be interpreted as hostile, even if they are not. A cycle of hostility may follow, ending in overt violence. As noted earlier, deep-seated conflict may develop over time that becomes part of the group's self-definition: "I am, among other things, the enemy of this other."

The Role of Bystanders

Bystanders are extremely important in determining a group's course. By bystanders I mean members of a society who are themselves neither victims nor agents of violence. Frequently bystanders constitute a large majority. If they remain passive in the face of increasing mistreatment of a subgroup of society or in the face of increasingly hostile words and acts toward an outside group, they confirm the leaders in the rightness of their actions.

Moreover, if bystanders remain passive, they themselves change. It is difficult to see others suffer. To reduce their empathic distress and justify their passivity, people tend to devalue victims. Over time, bystanders may change into perpetrators. For example, a group of psychoanalysts in Berlin first passively accepted and rationalized the removal and persecution of their Jewish colleagues, then began to change psychoanalytic theory to fit Nazi ideology. Then some of them became involved with the euthanasia killings, the killing of mentally ill, retarded, and physically handicapped Germans. Some of them later participated in the extermination of Jews (Staub 1989b).

There are many reasons why bystanders tend to remain passive, including fear of those in power and a focus on their own needs in difficult times. A further reason is a shared culture with perpetrators that creates also in bystanders some predisposition for the violence that perpetrators engage in (Staub 1989a). Whatever the reason, the bystanders' passivity encourages perpetrators.

So does the passivity of *external* bystanders, such as nations. Nations often remain passive and even support those nations that harm and kill subgroups in their own society or that attack other countries. There are many reasons for this, including definitions of self-interest that are devoid of broader values, and a self-view as an "entity" that is not a moral agent.

Other nations continued normal relations with Germany in spite of the murder of members of opposition groups and the increasing persecution of Jews. In 1936 the whole world affirmed Nazi Germany by participating in the Berlin Olympics. Before its invasion of Kuwait many countries provided economic support and arms to Iraq, in spite of its attack on Iran, and the killings of internal "enemies" and Kurds. It is not surprising that, affirmed in its aggression, Iraqi aggression continued.

The Power of Bystanders

Bystanders have tremendous potential influence on events. Passivity by some people creates passivity in others and decreases helpfulness in emergencies (Latane and Darley 1970). An active response by one person increases helping by others. A person verbally identifying a situation as one in which help is needed increases action by others, while defining the situation as one in which no action is needed decreases action by others (Bickman 1972; Staub 1974).

Real life events also show the potential power of bystanders. In the village of LeChambon, in Vichy France, heroic help of refugees by villagers influenced members of the Vichy police, who began to make anonymous telephone calls to warn the village of impending raids. Even a German officer was influenced by their heroism and in turn persuaded his superior not to destroy the village (Hallie 1979). In other European countries as well, bystander actions affected the feelings and actions of other bystanders, activated the victims in their own behalf, and even influenced the behavior of some Nazi occupiers (Fein 1979; Staub 1989a).

The power of nations as bystanders is evident in the new political realities in South Africa. There is much scholarly discussion about the extent to which the international boycott affected South African politics. My view, based partly on conversations with influential South Africans, is that the progressive and wide ranging response of the world community, ranging from the refusal to allow South African athletes to participate in international sports events to the boycott and sanctions, had a substantial role.

The conditions for effective influence by other nations need to be specified. Early responses by the community of nations to discrimination and violence against people, before the perpetrators are committed to an ideology and to the destruction of their victims, are most likely to be effective. They can reinstate moral consideration in relation to the victims and give rise to the concern of perpetrators for the consequences to themselves of their actions.

Creating Caring Societies and Peaceful Group Relations

Caring within groups and peaceful relations with other groups need not go together. For example, it is possible for members of a group to develop a positive orientation toward each other while devaluing and feeling hostility towards outgroups. Moreover, less-caring relations within a group do not exclude the possibility of peaceful relations with other groups; group level behavior is not identical to the behavior of individuals. However, positively valuing people in one's own group and caring about their welfare can be extended to people outside the group. Such valuing and caring, therefore, represent a good starting point for the creation of attitudes, values, and institutions that promote and maintain peace. How might we foster individual and group characteristics, as well as relations between groups that promote and maintain peace?

A relatively small group of abolitionists in the mid-nineteenth century contributed a great deal to abolishing slavery by their committed and courageous actions. Those who possess the required values and commitment can take actions that transform other bystanders. These include social scientists, who can disseminate information to foster parental child rearing that promotes caring. Parents in turn can influence schools to create classroom environments that promote caring, helping, and positive relations among children across group lines.

A Positive View of Human Beings and Other-Oriented Motives
People can devalue outgroups, or they can become aware of their shared humanity with others. Positive evaluation of human beings, or at least of the human potential, seems a precondition for the development

of motives that lead people to help others or to take action for the common good.

One of these motives is empathy, the vicarious experience of others' emotions. Research indicates that there are various types of empathy. One type, which may be called sympathy, tends to lead people to help others. Sympathy includes not only the experience of distress in response to the distress of another person, but also concern about the welfare of the other. Observers who feel sympathy want to diminish others' distress or improve their welfare (Eisenberg 1992; Batson 1989; Staub and Feinberg 1980).

Caring about others' welfare can also be based on beliefs and values, rather than empathic emotion. The development of these values probably requires empathy *with the child* on the parts of parents and other important adults (Staub 1991a). A prosocial value orientation, which is a combination of positive evaluation of human beings, caring about their welfare, and a feeling of personal responsibility for others' welfare, is associated with people helping others in both physical (Staub 1974) and psychological (Feinberg 1978; Grodman 1979; see Staub 1978) distress, and with self-reports of a wide range of helpfulness and socially responsible actions (Staub 1990).

There can also be motivations for helping, and sources of social responsibility that do not require a positive evaluation of people and a feeling of connection to them. One of these is the desire to create a safe social system, which protects one's own security and well-being. Another is a class of motives that I have called moral rule-orientations (Staub 1986; 1990). Moral rules can be specific—like prescribing help for others in physical distress—or fairly general, like principles of justice. Although such rules are originally created to protect and promote human welfare, individuals can learn them as group norms without acquiring genuine concern for the welfare of others. As a result rules can become absolutes that diminish human welfare—for example, a belief in justice that leads to a focus on punishment and revenge.

A positive evaluation of human nature or human beings seems also required for trust. Trust is a precondition for cooperative arrangements and peaceful conflict resolution. It refers to the belief that others will reciprocate our positive efforts, contribute their share, abide by agreements. Obviously, trust cannot be commanded; when it does not exist, it must evolve, through the processes that will be described below. Taking at least minimal risks in trusting others and being trustworthy are important building blocks for trust in both individual and group relations.

It is possible for people to develop a positive view of human beings but apply this view only to members of their own group. If peace is to prevail, it is essential that groups come to see the humanity of other groups and their members and to include them in the moral domain. It is necessary for people to place a high value on cooperation and positive relations relative to power or dominance over others. Wealth, power, dominance, and status are self-oriented motives. They bring pleasure but also security and, in a society that highly values them, a positive sense of self as well. Difficult life conditions create insecurity and activate and intensify self-aggrandizing motives. The development of positive group relations can be an important source of security and trust.

A variety of other individual tendencies and group characteristics contribute to caring and peaceful behavior. They include positive but moderate rather than superior self concepts; reasonable respect for authority combined with the capacity and willingness of individuals to question it; self-awareness; a pluralistic society; and an evaluation of group behavior partly in terms of its effects on the well-being of future generations.

Resolving Deep-Seated Hostility

The appropriate starting point for creating caring groups and positive group relations depends on the existing characteristics of groups and their relations to others. For example, resolving historical animosity is extremely difficult but can be an essential first step. Some recent approaches in group dynamics offer hopeful possibilities (Volkan 1988; Montville 1987).

In "dialogue" groups a small number of people from two hostile groups come together. They can be ordinary citizens or often influential members of each group who want to break with the past. Participants might describe the harm suffered and the pain experienced at the hands of the other group. To make this mutually tolerable, and an avenue for change, members of each group must progress to recognizing and acknowledging their own group's role and responsibility in the conflict. Beyond mourning and assuming their share of responsibility, the process is more effective if participants can offer each other forgiveness for the harm they have caused. There are many variants of such an approach, some focusing on problem solving and on resolving issues of conflict between groups, in addition to or as a way of overcoming hostility. For example, small groups of Israeli Jews and Palestinians have been meeting for a number of years (Kelman 1995). Some of the participants have later become involved in the official peace negotiations.

As I noted, the awareness of one's shared humanity with others is an important building block for peace and positive relations. Seeing the humanity of members of another group is especially important when they have been historically devalued, possibly to such a degree that they have been excluded from the moral domain (Opawa 1990). Education about the other must be part of the process, coming to know the other's characteristics and ways of life. To be effective such education requires concrete information about the lives of others, and information about their history that makes their culture and personal experiences meaningful.

The process that I have briefly described—sharing one's pain, acknowledging one's responsibility, coming to mutual forgiveness and problem solving along the way—can begin between small groups from each side in the conflict, but it must be brought to the larger community if change is to occur. Participants in the small groups can engage in public discussion, modeling the process they had privately engaged in. A difficult requirement is that they retain credibility and minimize wrath against themselves by members of their own groups, who are still rooted in deep hostility. Progressively, the other processes for creating positive connections that are described below can be introduced.

Socialization, Stability, and Ideals

The socializing experiences to which children are exposed are important in creating caring, connection, and nonviolent ways of resolving conflict. I have discussed optimal or "positive" socializing practices elsewhere (Staub 1979, 1981, 1986, 1989a, 1992), together with the characteristics they tend to shape. These include empathy and a prosocial value orientation; role taking and competencies; a positive but not "superior" self-concept; connected but not embedded selves; and a critical consciousness, which means the ability to use one's own judgment, and critical loyalty, the kind of loyalty to one's group that makes it possible to oppose policies and practices that are contrary to one's values (Staub 1989a).

Other-oriented values must be sufficiently important in a society for members to value positive socialization practices, and exert effort to institute them. Currently in most societies the importance of these values is at best moderate relative to self-related values like power, wealth, and achievement. Therefore, changes in societal values and socialization practices must progress together.

The central positive socializing practices are warmth and affection rather than coldness, indifference and hostility; the use of reasoning rather than authoritarian setting of rules; pointing out to children the consequences of their behavior toward others, both negative and positive; firm but nonforceful guidance that ensures that children fulfill important values and standards; and guiding children to act in helpful and caring rather than hostile and aggressive ways. The examples of adults' behavior are also clearly important (Grusec 1981; Eisenberg 1992; Radke-Yarrow et.al. 1983; Staub 1979, 1981, 1986, 1989a, 1992).

Guiding children to act in prosocial ways does not mean constant interference. Children should be allowed substantial autonomy, including the opportunity to work out conflicts. However, their personal characteristics, including their orientation to others and strategies of interaction, are shaped by their experiences of interaction (Dodge 1980; Staub 1979; 1992). Guidance that helps them resolve conflict in nonaggressive ways and limits the amount of aggression in peer groups will affect the kind of persons children become.

To use positive socialization, parents and teachers require supporting conditions, such as physical and material security, and reasonably ordered lives. Societal conditions and social institutions that provide stability are important (Staub, 1996). So is a vision of reality that recognizes the possibilities of caring and cooperation among people. Such a vision can also mobilize people for actions that contribute to the evolution of caring societies and positive groups relations.

The Need for a Positive Vision

Economic problems, political conflict, and great social changes are recurring aspects of group life. To create psychological stability in the midst of deprivation and turmoil, it is necessary to have a positive vision. Nationalistic ideologies, what I have called "better-world" ideologies like communism, and mixed ones like Nazism offer "ideals" and a "positive" vision for followers. But either this vision is absolutist in nature, or embedded in the ideology is the identification of enemies, or both. This combination leads ideological movements to disregard the welfare of individuals and groups of people as they turn against enemies of the ideology, often artificially created. The focus on enemies usually intensifies as the ideology proves difficult to fulfill, since blaming enemies explains failure and creates internal cohesion.

It seems essential to create a positive vision based on humanistic and inclusive ideals without an inherent destructive potential. This vision can focus on the possibility of, and satisfactions inherent in connection to, community and peace. It can lead people to fulfill basic needs by turning towards and joining with others. Respect for the rights and welfare of all human beings can be furthered by awareness of the inescapable inter-connectedness of life on earth: a shared humanity based on respect for the environment, shared interests in avoiding nuclear destruction, economic interconnection, and visions of an increasingly global community.

The Evolution Of Positive Group Relations

Cross-Cutting Relations

Morton Deutsch (1973) has proposed, and I have adopted and adapted (Staub 1989a), the concept of *cross-cutting relations*. It has long been held that contact between members of different groups can reduce devaluation or prejudice. But for this to occur, a number of conditions must be fulfilled (Allport 1954). For example, contact must be deep rather than superficial, and there must be equality within the context of the interaction (Staub 1989a). I believe that prior education about members of the other group, including information that helps to process the others' behavioral and communicative style, is also very important. Without that, mutual misperceptions can reactivate devaluation. Superficial con-tacts like tourism or integration in housing without real relations among people (Deutsch and Collins 1951) do not reduce prejudice or overcome devaluation across group lines.

Cooperative learning procedures in schools are one example of cross cutting relations. They were originally introduced to deal with failures of school integration in the U.S., as minority children continued to perform poorly and evince poor self-concepts. Cooperative learning practices lead children to learn in an interactive and mutually supportive way. In some forms of it the children play both teaching and learning roles. Coopera-tive learning practices tend to enhance the academic performance and self-esteem of minority children and the prosocial—cooperative and helpful—behaviors of all participating children (Aronson, et al. 1978; Johnson et al. 1981).

Positive actions and Systems of Positive Reciprocity

When individuals and groups act in a cooperative, helpful, or caring way toward others, they tend to generate positive reciprocity. In addi-tion, as I have noted, one's own behavior creates changes in oneself. A person who helps another, a nation that reaches out to another, will cre-ate changes in the self. The more unusual this reaching out, the greater the change might be. Following the Cuban missile crisis, Kennedy and Kruschev, the U.S. and the USSR, took a number of positive, reciprocal actions, such as limiting nuclear testing, to reduce the nuclear danger.

While reciprocity appears to be a universal norm present in all societies (Gouldner 1960), this does not mean that individuals or groups always follow the norm. A person's or group's actual response to another's positive actions depends on many factors. Reciprocity is less likely if the recipient believes that the motive underlying a helpful act was self-interest—for example, the intention to induce reciprocity (Shopler 1970; Staub 1978). The relationship to the other affects the interpretation of the other's intentions. Presumably, the attribution of selfish intention is more likely if the relationship to the other had been hostile. When positive acts appear to be based on genuine caring for the interests of the recipient or to genuinely promote mutual interests, reciprocity is more likely.

Joint Projects and Superordinate Goals

Initiating positive actions can lead to a system of positive reciprocity. A step beyond this is the creation of joint, cooperative projects. Community projects, for example, can bring together members of different subgroups of society. In Amherst, Massachusetts, many segments of the community joined in building a playground at one of the elementary schools. Inspired by their example, a year later members of the university community and the town joined to clean up and repaint the twenty-four-story library building at the university (Staub 1989a). Individuals and subgroups can overcome devaluative stereotypes and form ties in the course of such cooperative projects. I had the strong impression that in Amherst ties between students and faculty from the same department who worked together, and relations between faculty and members of the physical plant who guided the library cleanup, strongly improved. But without continued interaction such improvement will be temporary.

Members of subgroups of societies, and of nations, can join in alliances against third parties; but they can also join in constructive projects. Joint projects can range from business enterprises, to cultural and educational activities, to space exploration, to research on significant problems like AIDS. But when there is deep hostility between groups, the members who enter into joint projects can become the objects of ostracism and harassment. Preparation of the community can diminish risk.

While the positive acts that individuals or groups initiate are ends in themselves, even more importantly they are avenues for creating peace. Positive attitudes, feelings of connection, and shared goals that are superordinate to separate and conflicting goals can evolve.

Transforming and Mobilizing Bystanders: Creating Self-Awareness

Leadership can be important, but leaders frequently do not act in behalf of peace. Ordinary members of groups, the people I have called bystanders, must be instrumental in creating the evolution toward caring and peaceful societies. Part of the process must be the development of self-awareness. This can be promoted in the schools, in workshops, or in television programs. Knowledge of the characteristics of groups that make antagonism and violence more likely can heighten the awareness of these characteristics in one's own group.

Awareness of what makes it difficult for individuals to speak out against a direction their group has taken, even if this direction is contrary to their values and even their interests, is important (See Staub 1989a). Because people define themselves to a substantial degree by their membership in groups—ethnic, racial, religious, or national—fear of ostracism and punishment can powerfully inhibit speaking out in opposition. This is understandable given that groups, even in pluralistic societies, do frown upon and punish deviation. Ideally groups would encourage opposing voices, which inform members about processes and actions that carry destructive potentials. The development of a critical consciousness is an essential component of being a responsible, active bystander. Critical consciousness consists of the questioning and independent evaluation of the meaning and consequences of events in one's group. Critical loyalty, which consists of commitment both to the ultimate welfare of the group rather than to its current course and to the welfare of all human beings, and the resulting willingness to oppose destructive policies, is also central to active bystandership.

Knowledge of the potential power of bystanders and of what specific things people can do that might make a difference is also important. Research findings suggest that both a perception of threat and "empowerment" or people's belief in their capacity to make a difference, are important determinants of nuclear and environmental activism. When both exist, people are more likely to take action (McKenzie-Mohr and Laurier 1992).

Societies and relations between groups are difficult to change. Without a belief that their actions will have real, even if small, impact it is unlikely that people will turn from the many demands of everyday life and the pursuit of self-related motives. Accepting limited goals may be important, as well as the belief that one's actions contribute to a spread of activism and the creation of a process of change. It also seems important to mobilize people not only in response to threat, but also in the pursuit of the fulfillment of a positive vision.

An individual alone cannot create social change. Working with others is essential, both to increase the chance of effectiveness and to provide mutual support in the face of limited progress. The abolitionists were able to proceed in the face of ridicule and abuse partly because of group support. Commitment to principles also maintains morale. Even if people possess values and goals that lead them to action in behalf of the social good, strong commitment usually evolves as people engage in action to fulfill their values and goals (Locatelli and Holt 1986).

A study based on seven thousand questionnaires returned by *Psychology Today* readers (Staub 1989c, 1990), examined the relationships among different constellations of values and the self-reports of different kinds of helpful behaviors, including social action. Using varied information about people's values and goals, I constructed four "worldviews." *Actively caring people* were concerned about others' welfare, felt personal responsibility for others' welfare and responsibility for the social good, and felt competent to help. They reported frequent helpfulness of many kinds, including working for social causes. Those with a *liberal world view* felt a limited degree of personal responsibility for the welfare of other individuals, but felt intense social responsibility, that is, responsibility for the common good. Their helpfulness consisted primarily of work for social causes. People with a *religious world view* were strongly guided by rules. They helped others in several ways but did not work for social causes. Finally, *materialistic-competitive* people were unhelpful.

People who have different bases for caring help in different ways. An actively caring orientation to people and the world, which was associated with many forms of helpfulness, requires some of the socialization practices noted above (Staub 1975, 1979, 1981, 1992, 1996).

The Role of Institutions

It is important to create institutions that can be instrumental in building and maintaining positive group relations through the vicissitudes of events. They are needed to promote positive socialization in the schools; to create education in self-awareness; to attend to the peaceful resolution of emerging group conflicts; and to initiate joint projects among subgroups and with other nations. They can evaluate the potential impact of new policies and practices.

Summary

The evolution of peaceful societies requires action on a number of levels: the creation of a positive vision, joint projects across different groups and cross-cutting relations in their creation and execution, increasing self-awareness and awareness of the group's characteristics and functioning; the positive socialization of children; citizens who take action; and the involvement of leaders and people with potential influence on the public. The more of these domains are addressed, the more likely that a cumulative process of change will begin. Change must be relational, taking place not only within groups but in the relationship between groups. Nations and the community of nations need to become active bystanders and to react early—in words and actions, nonviolently if possible—to aggression directed at any group, whether a subgroup of society or a nation. For change to persist, it is important to create institutions that embody, maintain, and continue to further positive group relations.

Notes

1. The discussion of the origins of group conflict is based primarily on *The Roots of Evil: The Origins of Genocide and Other Group Violence* (Staub 1989a). In that book a conception is presented of the psychological and cultural origins of group violence. Then it is applied to the detailed analysis of a number of genocides and mass killings, and extended to a consideration of war.

References

Aronson, E., C. Stephan, J. Sikes, N. Blaney, and M. Snapp. 1978. *The Jigsaw Classroom*. Beverly Hills, Calif.: Sage.

Ainsworth, M. D. S. 1979. Infant-Mother Attachment. *American Psychologist* 34: 932–937.

Allport, G. 1954. *The Nature of Prejudice*. Reading, Mass.: Addison-Wesley.

Bandura, A., B. Underwood, and M. E. Fromson. 1975. Disinhibition of Aggression through Diffusion of Responsibility and Dehumanization of Victims. *Journal of Research in Personality* 9: 253–269.

Bar-On, D. 1989. *The Legacy of Silence: Encounters with Children of the Third Reich*. Cambridge: Harvard University Press.

Batson, D. 1990. How Social an Animal? The Human Capacity for Caring. *American Psychologist* 45: 336–347.

Bickman, L. 1972. Social Influence and Diffusion of Responsibility in an Emergency. *Journal of Experimental and Social Psychology* 8: 438–445.

Buss, A.H. 1966. The Effect of Harm on Subsequent Aggression. *Journal of Experimental*

Research in Personality 1: 249–255.

Deutsch, M. 1973. *The Resolution of Conflict: Constructive and Destructive Processes.* New Haven, Conn.: Yale University Press.

Deutsch, M., and M. E. Collins. 1951 *Interracial Housing: A Psychological Evaluation of a Social Experiment.* Minneapolis: University of Minnesota Press.

Dodge, K. A. 1980. Social Cognition and Children's Aggressive Behavior. *Child Development* 51: 162–170.

Elshtain, J. 1986. Reflections on Political Torture and Murder: Visits with the Mothers of the Plaza del Mayo. Invited talk, Department of Psychology, University of Massachusetts, Amherst.

Eisenberg, N. 1992. *The Caring Child.* Cambridge: Harvard University Press.

Epstein, S. 1980. The Self-Concept: A Review and the Proposal of an Integrated Theory of Personality. In *Personality: Basic Aspects and Current Research*, ed. E. Staub. Englewood Cliffs, N.J.: Prentice-Hall.

Fein, H. 1979. Accounting for Genocide: Victims and Survivors of the Holocaust. New York: Free Press.

———. 1990. Genocide: A Sociological Perspective. *Current Sociology* 38: 1–126.

Feinberg, J. K. 1978. Anatomy of a Helping Situation: Some Personality and Situational Determinants of Helping in a Conflict Situation Involving Another's Psychological Distress. Unpublished doctoral dissertation, University of Massachusetts, Amherst.

Goldstein, J. H., R. W. Davis, and D. Herman. 1975. Escalation of Aggression: Experimental Studies. *Journal of Personality and Social Psychology* 31: 162–170.

Goulder, A. W. 1960. The Norm of Reciprocity: A Preliminary Statement. *American Sociological Review* 25: 161–179.

Grodman, S.M. 1979. The Role of Personality and Situational Variables in Responding to and Helping an Individual in Psychological Distress. Unpublished doctoral dissertation, University of Massachusetts, Amherst.

Grusec, J. 1981. Socialization Processes and the Development of Altruism. In *Altruism and Helping Behavior*, ed. J. P. Rushton and R. M. Sorrentino. Hillsdale, N.J.: Lawrence Erlbaum Associates.

Hallie, P. P. 1979. *Lest Innocent Blood be Shed: The Story of the Village of Le Chambon, and How Goodness Happened There.* New York: Harper & Row.

Heber, R. F., and M. E. Heber. 1957. The Effect of Group Failure and Success on Social Status. *Journal of Educational Psychology* 48: 129–134.

Hitler, A. 1925. *Mein Kampf*, tr. Ralph Manheim. Boston, Mass.: Houghton Mifflin.

Huesmann, L. R., and L. D. Eron. 1984. Cognitive Processes and the Persistence of Aggressive Behavior. *Aggressive Behavior* 10: 243–251.

Janoff-Bulman, R. 1985. The Aftermath of Victimization: Rebuilding Shattered Assumptions. In *Trauma and Its Wake*, ed. C. R. Figley. New York: Bruner/Mazel.

Johnson, D. W., et al. 1981. The Effects of Cooperative, Competitive and Individualistic Goal Structures on Achievement: A Meta Analysis. *Psychological Bulletin* 89: 47–62.

Kelman, H. 1995. The Role of Nationalism and Patriotism in Israeli-Palestinian Relations. In *Patriotism*, ed. E. Staub and D. Bar-Tal. Chicago: Nelson-Hall.

Latane, B., and J. Darley. 1970. *The Unresponsive Bystander: Why Doesn't He Help?* New York: Appleton-Crofts.

Lerner, M. 1980. *The Belief in a Just World: A Fundamental Delusion.* New York: Plenum.

Locatelli, M. G., and R. R. Holt. 1986. "Antinuclear Activism, Psychic Numbing and Mental Health." In Mental Health Implications of Life in the Nuclear Age. *International Journal of Mental Health* 15: 143–162.

Lewis, M. 1978. *The Culture of Inequality*. New York: New American Library.

Maslow, A. H. 1962. *Toward a Psychology of Being*. 2d edition. New York: Van Nostrand.

McKenzie-Mohr, D., and W. Laurier. 1992. Understanding the Psychology of Global Activism. In *In Our Hands: Psychology and Social Responsibility in a Global Age*, ed. S. Staub and P. Green. New York: New York University Press.

Montville, J. V. 1987. Psychoanalytic Enlightenment and the Greening of Diplomacy. *Journal of the American Psychoanalytic Association* 37: 297–318.

Oliner, S. B., and P. Oliner. 1988. *The Altruistic Personality: Rescuers of Jews In Nazi Europe*. New York: Free Press.

Opawa, S. 1990. Moral Exclusion and Injustice. *Journal of Social Issues* 46: #1.

Piaget, J., and A. Weil. 1951. The Development in Children of the Idea of the Homeland and of Relations with Other Countries. *International Social Science Bulletin* 3: 570.

Radke-Yarrow, M. R., C. Zahn-Waxler, and M. Chapman. 1984. Children's Prosocial Dispositions and Behavior. In *Carmichael's Manual of Child Psychology*, ed. P. H. Mussenvol. 4th edition. New York: Wiley & Sons.

Shaffer, D. R. 1994. *Social and Personality Development*. Monterey, Calif.: Brooks-Cole.

Schopler, J. 1970. An Attribution Analysis of Some Determinants of Reciprocating a Benefit. In *Altruism and Helping Behavior*, ed. J. Macaulay and L. Berkowitz. New York: Academic Press.

Staub, E. 1974. Helping a Distressed Person: Social, Personality, and Stimulus Determinants. In *Advances in Experimental Social Psychology*, ed. L. Berkowitz. New York: Academic Press.

———. 1975. To Rear a Prosocial Child: Reasoning, Learning by Doing, and Learning by Teaching Others. In *Moral Development: Current Theory and Research*, ed. D. DePalma and J. Folley. Hillsdale, N.J.: Erlbaum.

———. 1978. *Positive Social Behavior and Morality: Social and Personal Influences*, vol. 1. New York: Academic Press.

———. 1979. *Positive Social Behavior and Morality: Socialization and Development*, vol 2. New York: Academic Press.

———. 1980. Social and Prosocial Behavior: Personal and Situational Influences and Their Interactions. In *Personality: Basic Aspects and Current Research*, ed. E. Staub. Englewood Cliffs, N.J.: Prentice-Hall.

———. 1981. Promoting Positive Behavior in Schools, in Other Educational Settings, and in the Home. In *Altruism and Helping Behavior*, ed. J. P. Rushton, and R. M. Sorrentino. Hillsdale, N.J.: Erlbaum.

———. 1986. A Conception of the Determinants and Development of Altruism and Aggression: Motives, the Self, the Environment. In *Altruism and Aggression: Social and Biological Origins. Cambridge*, ed. C. Zahn-Waxler. New York: Cambridge University Press.

———. 1988. "The Evolution of Caring and Nonaggressive Persons and Societies." In *Positive Approaches to Peace*, ed. R. Wagner, J. DeRivera, and M. Watkins, *Journal of Social Issues* 44: 81–100.

———. 1989a. The Roots of Evil: *The Origins of Genocide and Other Group Violence*. New York: Cambridge University Press.

———. 1989b. Steps Along the Continuum of Destruction: The Evolution of Bystanders: German Psychoanalysts and Lessons for Today. *Political Psychology* 10: 39–53.

———. 1989c. What Are Your Values and Goals? *Psychology Today* 10.

———. 1990. The Power to Help Others. Unpublished manuscript.

———. 1991a. Altruistic and Moral Motivations for Helping and Their Translation into Action. *Psychological Inquiry* 1: 150–153.

————. 1991b. The Persian Gulf Conflict War Reflective of Stormy Undercurrents in the U.S. Psyche. *Psychology International,* Spring, 1–9 (Washington, D.C.: American Psychological Association).

————. 1992. The Origins of Caring, Helping and Nonaggression: Parental Socialization, the Family System, Schools, and Cultural Influence. In *Embracing the Other: Philosophical, Psychological, and Historical Perspectives on Altruism,* ed. S. Oliner, P. Oliner, et al. New York: New York University Press.

————. 1993. Individual and Group Selves, Motivation and Morality. In *The Moral Self,* ed. W. Edelstein and T. Wren. Cambridge: MIT Press.

————. 1996. Cultural-Societal Roots of Violence: The Examples of Genocidal Violence and of Contemporary Youth Violence in the United States. *American Psychologist* 51: 117–132.

Staub, E., and Feinberg, H. 1980. Regularities in Peer Interaction, Empathy, and Sensitivity to Others. Presented at the Symposium: Development of Prosocial Behavior and Cognitions. American Psychological Association Meetings, Montreal.

Tversky, A., and D. Kahneman. 1974. Judgment Under Uncertainty: Heuristics and Biases. *Science* 185: 1124–1131.

Volkan, V. D. 1988. *The Need to Have Enemies and Allies.* Northvale, N.Y.: Jason Aronson.

White, R. K. 1984. *Fearful Warriors: A Psychological Profile of U.S.-Soviet Relations.* New York: Free Press.

FOUR

Community-Level
Case Studies of Peace

6 Two Paths to Peace: Semai and Mehinaku Nonviolence

THOMAS GREGOR AND CLAYTON A. ROBARCHEK

We don't fight people. We fight the trees and animals of the forest.
—An old Semai man.

We are Xinguanos. We don't shoot or club people. We trade, and wrestle,
and attend each others' rituals, and that is good.
—A Mehinaku Chief

■ Peaceful societies are rare and even more rarely studied. Even rarer are comparative studies of peace with an eye to winnowing out how cultures manage to live without violence. "Two Paths to Peace" is a step in the direction of the comparative study of peace. One of the societies in the comparison, the Mehinaku, is an example of a relatively peaceful society. War and most interpersonal aggression is unknown, but execution of suspected witches occurs. The Semai are one of the world's most peaceful cultures, where physical aggression is tabooed. The Mehinaku achieve their flawed peace through a series of incentives and institutions. The Semai do it through repression. The comparison of the two experiences raises many questions and suggests a number of answers about the nature of peace. The Semai provide us with evidence that something close to absolute peace could be a reality. The comparison with the Mehinaku and the discussion of the costs for the Semai, however, raise a vexing question: is it worth it?

THE LAST twenty years have seen a burgeoning of anthropological research on issues of war and peace. One of the important empirical findings to emerge from this research is that violence is nearly ubiquitous. Not only are there no utopias, but even many well-known cases of "peaceful" societies turn out to have their share of interpersonal violence, if not warfare (see Introduction). From the point of view of theory, our knowledge of war and violence is advancing; many of their sources are now apparent. The volatility of political systems, the social, psychological, and ecological payoffs of aggression, and the tendency of armed conflict to spread contagiously within geographic regions make violence a commonplace. The real puzzle for social scientists is not war and violence, but a more unusual phenomenon: peace.

Our own research begins a comparative study of peace by examining two peaceful small-scale tropical-forest societies, the Mehinaku of the Xingu River in Brazil and the Semai of the Central Malay Peninsula (West Malaysia).[1] Both exemplify the simple societies described by Bruce Knauft, in his discussion of the evolution of peace and violence (chapter 3). To a greater degree than many such societies, however, the Mehinaku and the Semai reject violence. This is surprising, given that most of their neighbors in the Asian and Amazonian tropical regions are warlike and there is a positive correlation between simple tropical-forest societies and warfare.[2]

There are striking similarities in these two societies half a world apart. Both are horticulturalists whose subsistence systems are based on the cultivation of manioc, primarily by women, and on hunting and fishing, mostly by men. Villages are small and relatively impermanent, abandoned periodically as the available garden land is exhausted. Both have flexible, bilateral systems of kinship in which the nuclear family, the marriage bond, and the sibling relationship are the central organizing features. Both are endogamous to a significant degree but have ties to other communities with whom they trade and intermarry. In both cases, the village is a politically autonomous unit.

Crucial to our concerns here is that the dynamics of the Semai and Mehinaku peace are very different. As we see it, there are two ways of sustaining peace: through internalized psychological restraints and through external socio-cultural constraints. In general, the social sciences give primary emphasis to the role of institutions or the external environment in structuring issues of peace and violence. In this volume, for example, the cessation of terrorist violence described by Crenshaw illustrates the significance of the external political environment. The Semai, however, achieve peace primarily through internalized restraints that create a personality for which violence is catastrophic and to be avoided at all costs. In contrast, the Mehinaku build restraints—albeit imperfectly and incompletely—against violence into institutions more than personalities. For them, peace is more a matter of policy than of psychological necessity. And yet, although the Semai and the Mehinaku have followed different paths, they have arrived at a common destination: a world where human relations are carried on largely free from violent confrontations. Our objective in this chapter is to explore the ways in which these two societies have achieved peace.[3]

The Semai and the Mehinaku

The Semai

There are about fifteen thousand Semai, most of whom live in small bands scattered along the mountainous spine of the Malay Peninsula. Each band occupies a defined territory, usually a small river valley or a segment of a larger one. Subsistence is based on the cultivation of man- ioc and rice, supplemented by hunting and fishing.[4] A typical band con- sists of one or two closely-related settlements of no more than one hundred people who are closely related as a consequence of cognatic descent and frequent band endogamy. Semai society is also marked by relative equality between the sexes and a sense that men and women have similar temperaments and characters.

Political authority is based on the headman, who is the "first among equals." Traditionally, the bands were politically autonomous, although occasionally a charismatic headman would come to exercise some authority over neighboring groups. While intervillage visiting is com- mon, there is very little formal contact between them beyond the occa- sional interband marriage or dispute resolution.

Violence within and between Semai communities is nearly nonexis- tent. Husbands do not beat their wives nor parents their children. Neigh- bors do not fight with one another, nor do communities contest violently. There are no reliable reports of Semai engaging in intergroup or intra- group warfare or raiding.[5] Over the past three or four decades, there are fewer than a half-dozen reliable reports of homicides in the entire popu- lation, and nearly all of these, in one way or another, involved outsiders (see Dentan 1988).

Semai oral history recalls a (perhaps mythical) time when they were actively at war with the Malays. The tales recount ambushes and battles, which the Semai invariably won. In more recent times, continuing into the early years of this century, Semai settlements were subject to slave raids by Malays and others. Neither Malay nor colonial histories nor the oral history of the Semai themselves report active resistance to these incursions. The Semai response was always a disorganized and headlong flight into the forest.

The Mehinaku

The Mehinaku are a tribe of 130 tropical forest Indians living along the headwaters of the Xingu River, in the Xingu National Park in Central Brazil. First contacted in 1884 by the German explorer Karl von den

Steinen, they retain an intact culture and autonomy over village affairs. Culturally, they are representative of many other small-scale sedentary communities in the South American lowlands that are organized around fishing, hunting, and the horticulture of manioc. This technological base and many other aspects of their culture are similar to the Semai. The major organizational difference between the two societies is in the relative complexity of Mehinaku institutions and the simplicity of those of the Semai. In sharp contrast to the Semai the Mehinaku community is highly sex-dichotomized and organized around an elaborate "men's house complex" (Gregor 1978), in which the women are restrained from participating in social and religious activities by the threat of organized gang rape.

The Mehinaku also contrast with the Semai in how they participate in an intricate system of peaceful intertribal relations. For the more inwardly directed Semai, such contact is an uneasy ad hoc affair based on the need to settle disputes, arrange marriages, or devise strategies for dealing with outsiders. For the Mehinaku, intertribal relations is a cultural focus. Interacting with nine other tribes in the Xingu basin representing three different major language groups and five mutually unintelligible subdialects, they have forged a rich intertribal culture based on the trade of specialty goods, intermarriage, and attendance at each other's rituals. The process of native acculturation promoted by this interaction has produced a relatively homogeneous "Xinguano" culture, in which the separate village-tribes resemble localized and autonomous ethnic groups.

What is truly striking, and quite unlike most of the other tropical forest peoples in South America, is that the intense interaction of the Xinguano tribes has been largely free of violence. Admittedly, the peace has been marred by instances of witchcraft killings and rare (though bloody) defensive raids against the predatory tribes beyond the boundaries of the Xingu basin. What is lacking in the Xingu, however, is a tradition of violence. Indeed the value systems of these communities is "antiviolent." Prestige is awarded those who avoid conflict; there are currently no roles for warriors; religious sanctions inhibit aggression; and methods of disciplining children discourage displays of anger. The pattern of intense, peaceful engagement between communities speaking different languages is nearly unprecedented in Native South America and extremely rare throughout the world.

The Semai and the Mehinaku represent two fundamentally different strategies for organizing peacefulness: those that internalize barriers to violence and those that rely on external sanctions. [The Semai build peace-fulness into the personalities of individuals by making conflict feared to such a degree that violence is almost unthinkable. The Mehinaku build peace into the organization of society so that when the villagers pursue their own interests, they enlarge and intensify the scope of the peace system.]

Dependence and Danger: Semai Social Personality

The Danger / Dependency Complex

Perhaps the most fundamental feature of Semai social personality is the centrality of both fear and what we call a danger/dependency complex. To a degree, this pattern reflects a political reality among the Semai, as they have historically been at the mercy of more powerful peoples. What is of interest, however, is that fear among the Semai now goes well beyond a rational perception of their environment. Fear, danger, and dependency are acquired in the course of child rearing. Those acquisitions shape a self-view and world view in which individuals see themselves as helpless in a hostile and malevolent environment that is almost entirely beyond their control (Robarchek 1979b, 1986, 1989). Virtually every activity, such as gardening, hunting, and even children's play, is circumscribed by taboos whose observance, the community hopes, will forestall the dangers inherent in daily life. In this world the only sanctuary is the band: a hundred or so others with whom one's life is intertwined from birth to death.

Situations that are potential sources of conflict, over such matters as sex, food, and cooperation, are regarded as occasions of danger. Frustration and anger, and indeed all strong feelings that might threaten band unity, are defined as threatening. Individuals thereby learn to be afraid of their own emotions. With the sole exception of fear, open or intense expression of emotion seldom occurs (Robarchek 1979b). Angry outbursts are extremely rare, and visibly angry individuals deny their feelings (cf. Dentan 1968); grief is restrained; open expression of sexuality is never seen; even laughter and expressions of joy are subdued. Above all, anger is especially dangerous. When speaking of it, the band members exaggerate the potential consequences to the object of anger. They claim, for instance, that striking a spouse or spanking a child can result in death. They say that even relatively mild conflicts between kindreds or communities may precipitate mass killings. In language and symbolism, band members equate the violent potential of unrestrained emotions with the danger of tropical thunderstorms that occasionally visit destruction and death on Semai communities.[6]

Semai concepts of what is good and bad are closely linked to their fear of disruptive emotions. For the band members, "goodness" is defined positively in terms of the nurturance of the group, while "badness" is defined negatively in terms of aggressiveness, violence, and other behaviors inimical to affiliation. These normative ideals are largely realized in behavior: most Semai are generous, unassuming, unassertive, nonaggressive, and, above all, nonviolent.

This ideal is essentially the same for both men and women. There is no rigid sexual division of labor; no tasks that are forbidden to either men or women; no knowledge that is restricted to one or the other gender. The picture presented by Gregor (1985) of the Mehinaku man who went hungry rather than do the woman's work of manioc processing would seem foolish to a Semai. There is, in short, no polarization of gender roles and no basis for an assertive masculine image. Such commonly "masculine" qualities as bravery, strength, and aggressiveness have no special value to the Semai.

The danger/dependency complex, the ubiquity of fear, and the perception of personal lack of power are symbolically expressed in, among other things, attitudes toward food. For the Semai, food and sharing are equivalent to nurturance. Within a settlement, widespread sharing of food is a matter of course. So strong is the obligation to share that even wage labor and a cash economy have not overcome it. On the contrary, men who have no gardens now go into debt with traders and shopkeepers in order to buy rice to share with their neighbors and kin.[7]

As important as food sharing is economically, its symbolic role in expressing nurturance may be even more significant. Band members constantly remind one another of the necessity of nurturance by the group and the moral obligation to nurture and share. Any formal gathering begins and ends with the headman and elders reciting the past aid they have given the group and received from it. The message is clear: everyone is dependent on everyone else; no one can survive alone. The members of the band must either deal with one another or live in an anarchical world of selfishness, quarreling, and murder (cf. Robarchek 1989, 1990).[8]

Pehunan: The Dangers of Frustration

The equivalence of food sharing and nurturance, the dependence of individuals on the group, and the danger of rejection can be seen in the concept of *pehunan*, a state of danger resulting from the frustration of desire. A person is spoken of as having "incurred" *pehunan*, much as one incurs an injury. In *pehunan*, one is in danger of accidents, illness, and death. A band member may incur *pehunan* as the result of an unfulfilled desire for such things as sex, tobacco, or even jewelry, although more typically it is the result of hunger for a specific food. At the heart of the concept of *pehunan* is a sense of the interdependence of band members and their duty to assist one another. Hence the danger is particularly acute after a person voices his desire, which transforms it from individual need to a social obligation. Expressed in the *pehunan* complex is the helplessness and vulnerability of the individual facing a hostile and threatening world. Only through the security of the band, symbolized by food sharing and nurturance, is life possible. To be rejected and denied is to be condemned to death.

One of the corollaries of group dependence is the near absence of competition, boasting, or other forms of overt self-aggrandizement. Openly seeking to gain superior rank would be, at best, unseemly (cf. Dentan 1968). Competitive games and sports are nonexistent, except as introduced through schools in the more acculturated communities. There are no contests based on strength, speed, skill, intelligence, or on any other personal quality. There are no occasions where individuals are placed in direct competition with one another on the basis of strength, dress, body painting, dancing, or singing.[9] Comparisons of people on almost any grounds are in bad taste. Open reference to someone's alleged physical peculiarities (e.g. "she has big eyes") is highly insulting and can be grounds for a formal dispute settlement. Institutionalized competition, such as Mehinaku wrestling matches, is completely foreign to the Semai.[10]

Because of the crucial role of the group as the only refuge from ubiquitous danger, Semai culture stresses band unity. Conflict is especially frightening since it calls into question the band as the source of nurturance and security in a malevolent world. A clear demonstration of the threatening nature of conflict can be seen in the responses to a sentence-completion test that Robarchek employed to elicit attitudes and values. One item asked the respondent to complete the phrase "more than anything (s)he is afraid of. . . ." The modal response, more common than the combined frequencies of "spirits," "tigers," and "death," was "a conflict" (of the sort that precipitates a formal settlement).

Individualism and Self Expression: Mehinaku Social Personality

The Semai ideal personality is generous, unassuming, unassertive and, most of all, nonviolent. Anger, like all other strong emotions, is translated into fear or is repressed due to the intense anxiety it generates.

The constraints on anger and aggression are largely internal to the personality, rooted in psychologically primitive cognitive and affective orientations. Conflict is so threatening and arouses such anxiety that most people will go to great lengths to avoid it. In contrast, the Mehinaku are far more expressive and independent. They are emotionally more capable of feeling anger and engaging in acts of violence. It is primarily the institutional context that restrains overt conflict.

Growing up Mehinaku

Mehinaku children grow up in a world that appears relatively manageable. Initially at the center of a caring network of kin, they are fed on demand and their cries are attended to. As is characteristic of many tribal peoples, the pattern of intense nurturance is abruptly reversed with the birth of a new sibling, but even then the child's world is a relatively controllable and forgiving place. Parents often accede to their young children's demands, and children are expected to express a range of intense emotions, from anger to sexuality. At no point in the process of development are children conditioned, in the fashion of the Semai, to erect barriers against intense emotion or to equate anger with fear. The ideal personality type that emerges from the Mehinaku process of socialization is described as *ketepepei,* a term that implies an individual who is outgoing, optimistic, and friendly. To an extent, this orientation is reminiscent of the Semai, where affiliation is the root meaning of that which is good. Among the Mehinaku, however, the nurturant dimension of belonging to the group is largely missing. Distant kin, those beyond first-cousins, may be open competitors for resources, spouses, and prominence. Only within the circle of primary kin do the villagers feel enveloped in warmth and community.

Expressiveness and Sexuality

Perhaps the most visible difference between Mehinaku and Semai social personalities is the dramatic nature of Mehinaku self-expression. Being *ketepepei* means being expressive: whooping when a fisherman returns to the village, adorning oneself with feathers and brightly colored body paints and hair pigments, and laughing at the other villagers' jokes. The men's house in the center of the village is the best place to observe this kind of conduct. "In the men's house," it is said, "there is no shame." Here the respect owed affinal kin and the older generation is partly dropped, and the men interact as if they all participated in the joking relationships that are more normally characteristic of cross-cousins.

The relatively anxiety-free period of early socialization leaves the villagers in touch with more problematic emotions than those suggested by being *ketepepei*. Sexuality, greed, jealousy, and anger are all recognized as powerful emotions, and are part of the Mehinaku ethnopsychology of personal motivation. The men describe themselves as perpetually libidinous. Nearly all of the villagers participate in what is surely one of the more extravagantly developed networks of sexual intrigue yet documented (Gregor 1985). The gossip network hums with stories of assignations and sexual jealousy. Undeniably, Mehinaku sexuality is also clouded with anxiety, but in contrast to the more restrained Semai pattern, the villagers are exuberantly sexual.

Individualism and the Economy

Although in many ways the Mehinaku share the Semai ethic of generosity and sharing, there are limitations. Especially significant is the frequency of theft. Among the Mehinaku, theft is more common and morally less problematic than among the Semai. According to the villagers, the thief steals for aggressive and self aggrandizing motives: "he steals because he wants it." In response, the villagers lock their doors at night, hoist boxes of valued possession into the rafters of their houses, conceal their canoes in the swamp around the village, and cache tools in hiding places in their fields.

In contrast to the Semai, the acquisitiveness and envy of others' possessions suggested by the existence of theft infuses the Mehinaku economic system. Though the Mehinaku live in a technologically simple society, they have a well-developed sense of property, riches, poverty, and trade. Unlike the Semai, where selling and bartering within the band are considered almost indecent (Robarchek 1988), the Mehinaku trade high-status exchange goods, such as shell necklaces and belts, ceramic pots and western manufactures. These transactions often bypass the network of reciprocity that ideally links close kin and, nowadays, may even be for cash.

Patterns of food sharing, so crucial in defining nurturance and group dependence among the Semai, take on a different function among the Mehinaku. Like the Semai, the Mehinaku villagers must share to survive. But unlike the Semai, the boundaries of sharing are drawn more narrowly. Manioc flour, the staple of village life, is never distributed beyond the village households. Fish are passed along through the network of kinship, but when the catch is small, a family may eat by itself. Equally telling, the villagers grumble about the "glutton" who secretly eats by himself and the stingy man who sneaks fish into the village after dark, so that he does not have to share.

Standing Out

Since the individual cannot depend on the group for security and nurturance, he must depend on himself and the kinsmen he can draw into his orbit. In this milieu, the successful man parlays skills into a secure political base. Above all, such a man stands out. He is not only a public speaker, (as a Semai may be) but he is many things no Semai would ever seek to be: the strongest wrestler, the handsomest man, the maker of the best arrows, the most prestigious chief, the richest villager, the most powerful shaman, the most knowledgeable teller of myths . . . the list could be extended indefinitely.

At times the hunger for status provokes the villagers to do outlandish things and go to great lengths to be recognized. The more ego-hungry dress absurdly for certain rituals, build their houses in the style of despised Indian tribes, make up stories of supernatural events to impress their fellows, and fabricate evidence of witchcraft and the supernatural to make a name for themselves as shamans. The attention-craving mentality that makes *The Guinness Book of Records* a thriving business for Americans would be entirely comprehensible to the Mehinaku. Among the Semai, such conduct would simply be bizarre.

Corresponding to this competition for recognition is a belief that each villager controls his own destiny. Those who fail, it is believed, have some fundamental flaw of personality that keeps them from achieving. Hence villagers who lack ritually important property (shell belts and necklaces) are poor because they are lazy. Those who are weak wrestlers failed to take medicines and scarify their bodies when they were in adolescent seclusion. Those who end up short and sickly have themselves to blame because they have engaged in excessive sexual contact with women. In contrast with the Semai, who attribute personal misfortune and failure to the malevolence of spirits and ghosts, or see it as the result of human frailty in a hostile world, the Mehinaku regard each individual as responsible for his or her fate. With this sense of control comes a heavy burden: there seems to be no failing in life that is not blamed on the individual.

Anger and Aggression

There is one major limitation to the larger pattern of individualism, self-assertiveness and competition for esteem: anger is regarded as a dangerous and inappropriate emotion. Much like the Semai, the Mehinaku metaphorically equate anger with things that are violent, unpredictable, and potentially lethal. A raging fire in a garden, a thunder storm, and even a species of hot pepper that leaves anyone foolish enough to eat it writhing on the ground in agony, are all said to be "angry." The good citizen, according to the villagers, and above all a chief, must never display anger. An angry confrontation, for the villagers, can be worse than the serious act that may have provoked it.

An angry boy is of concern to his parents, who discipline the child with scarifier to correct his conduct. He is likened to the hated "wild" Indians beyond the borders of the Xingu reservation, and a variety of magical cures are administered to change his temperament. One of the village women specializes in a form of "breath magic" (*ejekeki*) that is said to cure anger. In return for a small gift, she blows on the child and intones a spell designed to drain him of angry feelings. The same kind of breath magic is also used to pacify dangerous white men and "wild" Indians when they are encountered outside the reservation.

The Mehinaku social personality is relatively individualistic and expressive. The villagers are aware that neither breath magic nor sanctions can wholly eliminate anger. They feel anger and often express it, despite the sanctions against it. They are sensitive to even small indications of moodiness in others that may signal resentment and irritation. Under circumstances that we will describe, however, they are capable of violence and even cruelty. Unlike the Semai, the internalized rules against violence are not enough to keep the peace. As we shall see, the Mehinaku rely on external incentives and sanctions.

The Symbolic Construction of Peacefulness

In chapter 1, Donald Tuzin usefully points out that the most warlike societies yearn for tranquillity and security: the "specter of peace," as he puts it, may be found in "unlikely places." In general, however, warlike societies have values that extol violence. Values of "antiviolence" are less frequently documented, partly because they are less frequent but also because they are less conspicuous. Peace, it would seem, is more taken for granted than war. Nonetheless, peace systems, if they are to survive, must be sustained by antiviolent values. Both the Semai and Mehinaku have an explicit ethics of antiviolence. In both cultures, this ethic surfaces directly in the spontaneous statements of informants: "We don't fight people," says an old Semai man, "we fight the trees and animals of the forest." "We are Xinguanos," said one of the Mehinaku. "We don't shoot or club people. We trade, and wrestle, and attend each others' rituals, and that is good." Just as revealing as these statements, however, is the Semai and Mehinaku preoccupation with the out-groups that do not meet their standards. In surprisingly parallel ways, both groups dramatize their own peaceful ideals by casting outsiders as negative role models. Violence and nonviolence are thereby boundary markers that set the peaceful, civilized Semai and Mehinaku apart from the animal-like "savages" without.

The Semai View of Outsiders

Among Semai, one commonly hears statements such as, "The Malays and Chinese are always fighting, but we sit impassively." This statement reflects the division of the human world into two components: *hii'* (inclusive *we*) and *mai* (*they*). The former are kin and band members, those who can be trusted and upon whom one can depend for support; the latter are everybody else. Only among *hii'* can one feel secure; the intentions of *mai* can never be known for certain, and relations with them should be circumspect. The potential malevolence of *mai* can be seen in the notion of "mai kahnoh kuui," the cutting-off-head-strangers. These are *mai:* Malays, Chinese, Indians, even Semai from other bands, who are believed to hide in ambush along forest paths. They kill and decapitate the unwary in order to sell the severed heads as charms to be buried under buildings, dams, and other new constructions.

The contrast between *hii'* and *mai*, between co-villagers and strangers, can be seen in the supernatural world of dangerous spirits (*mara'*) and protective, familiar spirits (*gunik*). *Mara'* are "they that eat us"—murderous "spirits" who inhabit trees, waterfalls, hilltops, graves, or who simply wander about seeking human prey to kill and eat. No offense is necessary to precipitate an attack. Like the tiger, *mara'* kill by nature, and, by nature, humans are their prey. Occasionally, however, the *mara'* may come to someone in a dream and indicate a wish to be adopted by the dreamer, to become a member of his or her family, to become a *gunik*. The *mara'* teaches the dreamer a song by means of which the *mara'* (now a *gunik*) can be called during the "sings," seances held to summon the band's *gunik* to treat illnesses by repelling the attacks of "foreign" *mara'*.

These paired, isomorphic images of "we" and "they," of "protective spirit" and "dangerous spirit" are charged with condensed meanings that appear at many levels of Semai culture. Thus the contrast of *hii'*/*mai* and *gunik*/*mara'* is equivalent to that of insiders/outsiders, co-residents/strangers, kin/non-kin, nurturant/benevolent, protector/attacker, nonviolence/violence, and good/evil. Consistent throughout is the equation of nonviolence with good and violence with evil. As the nurturance, benevolence, and protection of "we" is reified and given cultural expression in the image of the *gunik* protective spirit, so the unpredictability and homicidal malevolence of "they" is terrifyingly objectified in the *mara'* spirits and in the "cutting-off-head-strangers."

The Mehinaku View of the Outsider

The Mehinaku perspective on the outside world is similar to that of the Semai in that the social world is dichotomized into good and evil, largely on the basis of perceived aggressiveness. In keeping with the more complex Xinguano world, however, the Mehinaku view of humanity is composed of more social categories. These include the Mehinaku villagers and other Xingu Indians, who are called *putaka* (a term that is a cognate of the word for village and hospitality); the white men (*kajaiba*); and the *wajaiyu*, or the "wild," Indians beyond the borders of the Xingu reservation. *Putaka*, or Xinguanos, are regarded as human, as "Children of the Sun." They are cultured and civilized and at least pay lip service to a common community of nurturance and concern: "We weep for one another when we die." No one, however, weeps for the *wajaiyu* or wild Indian, who in malicious tales is said to be the offspring of snakes and rodents. Like an animal, the villagers say, he sleeps on the ground, defecates in the water, fornicates in strange positions, crawls with vermin, and reeks with the odors of animals. He attacks unpredictably and without provocation:

He beats his children. He rapes his wife. He shoots arrows at the white man's planes. He splits people's heads with clubs. He kidnaps children and burns villages. He kills his own kin. War for him is a festival.

Like the feared *mai* and *mara'* among the Semai, the *wajaiyu* is a potent symbol, in this case condensing emotions associated with dirt, animality, and death. Recently, these stereotypes have softened. The process is slow since there is an element of truth to some of these pejorative stereotypes. The Indians surrounding the Xingu basin include societies who, in the past, attacked the Xinguanos, killing men, kidnapping women and children, ransacking villages, and committing acts of random terror. In the thoughts of the Xingu villagers the image of the wild Indian has become the most single powerful symbol of what no Xinguano wants to be. Let a man edge in that direction through aggressive acts, and others are quick to bring him back into line. Quarrelsome persons are gossiped about and occasionally taunted as resembling a *wajaiyu* whom the villagers find repulsive. Disobedient children are warned that they too will grow up to be like him. Like the *mai* and the *mara'* among the Semai, the wild Indian is a negative role model. He stands as a dramatic moral counterpoint to the ideal of peaceful behavior. The crucial distinction is that the Mehinaku's fears have had a basis in real experience. Semai fear of the violence of outsiders has had some real basis in the recent past (see Robarchek and Dentan 1987; Dentan 1992), although that fear is exaggerated. Far more than is the case among the Mehinaku, the world view of the Semai is constructed of their own fantasies and projections.

The Institutional Basis of Peace

The Isolation of the Semai and the Internal Politics of Disputes

The traditional Semai band was relatively isolated and self-sufficient. There was little in the way of institutionalized interaction among the bands, such as trade, formal visits, rituals, or village festivals.[11] As a result, Semai identity has always been firmly rooted in the natal band, even when a person had to live elsewhere. When, for example, a man or woman marries into another band, there is a formal meeting involving the headmen of the two groups. Each headman affirms his "responsibility" for the good behavior of his band member. If there is discord between the couple or conflict between the in-marrying spouse and community members, this is reported to the headman and to the kindred, and it is their obligation to pressure their kinsman to mend his ways. Failing that, the headmen are obliged to represent their band members in the *becharaa'* hearing that will be convened to resolve the dispute. Without the support of his natal group and its leader, an individual would be entirely on his own, a prospect that is extremely threatening.

This fear illustrates the role of the headman as spokesman for his group and symbol of its nurturance. He has no coercive authority, yet he is respected. He is often addressed as "parent's younger brother," and he represents the emotional security that the community's "elders," real and symbolic parental figures, provide. To the sentence-completion item "When there are no elders present, we feel . . .," the modal response was "like we are alone."

The Mehinaku and Intertribal Relations in Brazil's Upper Xingu

For most Semai, life alone and away from the band is almost unthinkable. For the Mehinaku it is a daily option. Boredom, quarrels with other villagers, or simply a desire to be away from it all are sufficient reasons for "wandering" off through the forest. Usually the trips last no more than a day, but longer separations are also common. At least once each year most families take up residence far from the community in their own temporary "dry season" villages. Potentially, these settlements are the nucleus for factional splits that threaten the larger community. In the past, they sometimes became established villages that attracted groups of kin and friends. Unlike the Semai, the boundaries of the community are permeable.

The openness of the group is further reflected in the pattern of visiting. Hardly a day passes without some kind of contact with members of different tribes. Visitors come to trade specialty goods, to participate in one another's rituals, to intermarry, to visit a powerful shaman, to visit kin, or to seek refuge from allegations of witchcraft in the home tribe. So developed is the culture of hosting that virtually any outsider can count on a warm reception, a place for his hammock, firewood, water, and food. Superficially, the same pattern of hosting exists among the Semai, but their motives are different. They will entertain a visitor, but mainly because they fear that denying his needs would place him in a state of *pehunan* or provoke conflict with his band. For the Mehinaku, offering hospitality is part of being a good citizen. It not only expresses generosity but cements valued relationships with members of other tribes.

The permeability of group boundaries among the Mehinaku is reflected in their concept of tribal identity. While among the Semai band membership is fixed at birth,[12] among the Mehinaku it is a more fluid concept that depends on a mix of parentage, language skills, residence, and the opinion of others. One of the villagers, whose parents came from both the Mehinaku and Waura tribes, drew an imaginary line down the center of his body: "This side," he said, "Mehinaku. That side is Waura." Far less allegiance is owed the group than among the Semai, and emotionally diffuse (and peaceful) relationships are extended well beyond tribal boundaries.

The role of the chief. Corresponding to the tradition of visiting and hospitality is an elaborate and historically ancient system of intertribal relations. To a large extent, this system is built around the interaction of village chiefs, whose inaugurations and deaths are commemorated by major intertribal ceremonies. At these rituals the chiefs ceremonially greet one another and offer presents of prestige goods (necklaces, ceramic pots, hardwood bows) that are representative of each tribe's trade specialty.

Although the chief has little real authority, he represents in his behavior the values of peaceful intertribal relations. Ideally, he never expresses anger. Each day, in formal speeches made at dawn on the village plaza, he admonishes the community to avoid gossip and quarrels. Like the Semai headman, he is a paternal figure who, in a least two of the Xingu languages, refers to the villagers as "the children." The chief's example of restrained behavior and his daily lectures are seen by the villagers as essential to peace. A village filled with acrimony is said to be a village in which the chief has failed to "admonish his people." The Mehinaku chief thereby symbolizes many of the values that make the peace system function, but he can only lead his miscreant "children" by example.

Incentives for Peace

The intertribal peace system in the Upper Xingu works because there are incentives that motivate the villagers to enlarge and intensify the system. Specifically, there is no better route to personal fame than recognition by other tribes: a champion wrestler wins his laurels in matches with other tribes; a wealthy man is rich because he controls trade goods acquired in other villages; a powerful shaman is recognized by his intertribal reputation; and a leader of locally powerful factions enhances his status with supporters and kinsmen in other tribes.

Interaction that is destructive of relationships with other tribes—such as stealing from their fish traps, pilfering small items on visits, and participating in acts of casual vandalism—is characteristic of immature adolescents and the socially marginal. These so-called "trash yard people" are despised not only because such acts are contrary to the ethic of the Xingu peace, but because they invite retaliation in which everyone suffers. More to the point, tension between the tribes threatens the prominent status of the most powerful men in the community. Chiefs, shamans, wrestlers, and craftsmen are diminished in stature if they are not respected by other villagers. The incentives structured into the Xingu system thereby strongly favor the leader who builds positive intertribal relationships.

Generosity, Disputes, and Dampening the Conflict Spiral

Pehunan and Waritya

The sources of many disputes are similar for Semai and Mehinaku (and, for that matter, for the rest of humanity): sexual jealousy, territorial infringement, stinginess, theft, and gossip being among the most prominent. Tensions arising from conflicts in these areas are intensely felt. The values that restrain conflict among the Semai and the Mehinaku are also similar even though the institutional bases of peace are quite different. Perhaps the most striking convergence involves beliefs pertaining to food sharing and the fulfillment of desire. The Semai concept of *pehunan* holds that an individual whose wants are frustrated is at risk. Since the band members do not wish to be responsible for harm that befalls their fellows, they accede to reasonable requests. On the other hand, since voicing a want increases the danger of *pehunan*, requests that are likely to be denied will not be made. As a result, individuals rarely come into direct conflict over material goods (Robarchek 1977a).

A surprising parallel can be seen in the Mehinaku notion of *waritya*, a term that is best translated as "frustrating and endangering." Like *pehunan*, *waritya* is a state induced by being denied food, sex, or a material item. As in the case of *pehunan*, denial of food, with its implications of loss of nurturance, is the most common source of the problem. An individual who has been denied is vulnerable to injury, sickness, or assault by a witch or spirit. If any of these should occur, the rejecting individual is the one responsible. Precisely in accord with the Semai *pehunan* belief, the villagers' fear of frustrating their fellows encourages generosity with food and possessions.

Forest Sirens and Sexual Frustration

Both the Semai and the Mehinaku include sexual frustration as sources of potential danger. In surprisingly similar ways, they elaborate these beliefs further in their fear of forest sirens who are drawn to their victims by sexual longing. For the Semai, a broken promise for an assignation or simply a high level of unfulfilled desire attracts a *sasoo* woman (or man). The *sasoo* is a spirit that assumes the form of the missing lover and possesses the body and mind of the frustrated victim. After an act of intercourse the *sasoo* spirit merges with the flesh and bones of the frustrated lover and drives him or her mad. While the hazards of sexual frustration and *sasoo* do not compel acquiescence to sexual overtures, they do give them a certain legitimacy (cf. Dentan 1968). One old man, Robarchek was told, had married his wife at the urging of his kindred primarily because she wanted him so badly (and hence was endangered).[13]

The Mehinaku have a similar belief in the forest siren. Men on the trail who day-dream of wife or mistress will attract an "Angry Woman Spirit" (*japujaneju*). Gregor was frequently warned not to think of his wife while on the path, lest a woman appear to him who looked just like her. Brief encounters or sightings of Angry Woman Spirit leave her victim weakened and maddened. If he has sexual relations with her, she will carry him off to her forest house, never allowing him to return to his home and family. For both the Mehinaku and the Semai, the forest siren is a warning about the hazards of intense desire. "Sex," as one Mehinaku put it, "is not good." Similarly, an elder advised Robarchek, "One should not want a woman too much . . . there is danger [of *sasoo*]. In contrast with the Semai, however, the Mehinaku seem better able to respond to the danger. Not only is Angry Woman Spirit survivable, but the villagers can take evasive action. In the mythic past they have successfully fought back.[14]

As in other contrasts between the two groups, the Mehinaku appear to have greater mastery of their social environment, and a greater sense of confidence in coming to terms with it.

The Sanctions That Enforce Generosity

One effect of Mehinaku and Semai beliefs about frustrated desire is to cause people to be sensitive to the wishes of others. They are willing to accede, or at least they are apprehensive about the consequences if they do not. For both tribes, these attitudes express an ethic of generosity, in which an individual's good name is dependent on his willingness to offer food and sociability to others. So taken for granted is this ethic among the Mehinaku that "generosity" is a linguistically unmarked category. The only way to refer to it is "not stingy." Significantly, for both groups, generosity is so much the normal expectation that there is no expression for "thank you." An attempt to repay a gift of food is slightly insulting because it implies that the gift was not freely given, but was calculated with the expectation of return.

Sources of conflict over material goods are also reduced in both societies by means of sanctions that compel generosity. Semai values, as we have seen, define generosity as the primary attribute of "goodness." Nurturance and affiliation, as expressed in sharing, are the core values of Semai society. If band members are ungenerous, they will lose standing within the community. They may also fall victim to *tinghaa'*, a supernatural punishment for failing to have nurtured a deceased band member. The victim of *tinghaa'* is persistently unlucky in the food quest: gardens fail, traps go empty, and poisoned darts miss their mark (see Robarchek 1986). At one level *tinghaa'* appears to be an external sanction that motivates generosity. But its supernatural nature and the emotional intensity associated with issues of sharing suggest otherwise. Generosity is far more than good policy for the Semai. It is deeply internalized within the personality and springs from a sense of vulnerability and dependence upon the band.

Mehinaku generosity is superficially like that of the Semai. It is composed of both fear of the magical consequences of denying others and a desire to contribute to a common good. To a larger extent than is the case among the Semai, however, Mehinaku generosity reflects a conscious desire to maintain one's good standing in the community and to avoid the anger of those who are turned down. Unlike a Semai, a Mehinaku is not simply generous; he is *conspicuously* generous. Hence the generous man plants corn and publicly calls the whole village to harvest it. After a fishing trip he brings a good share of his catch out to the men's house to be divided among his comrades. In exchange, he is highly regarded by the villagers. For him, generosity may not be so much a reflection of inner values as it is an expression of wise policy.

Avoiding Confrontations

Both Semai and Mehinaku will go to great lengths to avoid an open confrontation. For the Semai, becoming involved in a public dispute is overwhelmingly threatening, since such disputes challenge the supportive relationships that are the foundations of personal security. Band members are usually willing to copmpromise personal interests and tolerate annoyances rather than precipitate a conflict and risk an open confrontation (Robarchek 1979a).

Semai sensitivity to conflict extends well beyond overt violence. Symptoms of conflict that would be ignored among the Mehinaku are grounds for community action. Gossip or even a few sharp words are a serious matter and grounds for a formal *becharaa'* hearing. The responsibility for dealing with even these minor symptoms of conflict rests, at least in principle, with the community as a whole. Anyone who has knowledge of ill feeling between members of the group should bring it to the attention of the headman, who summons the kindreds to a *becharaa'* to resolve the matter. In practice, a considerable amount of gossip and backbiting are tolerable, and even add a little spice to daily life. When even a minor confrontation occurs, however, a *becharra'* will be convened to settle the matter.

Among the Mehinaku, confrontations are also distressing. An "angry," confrontational man is avoided and despised by his fellow villagers, who may even use a special class of magic to pacify him. He is said to be like the homicidal "wild Indians" beyond the borders of the Xingu reservation, and to court illness from nursing "anger in his belly." Far better to maintain a statesmanlike image in public and accept a minor transgression than risk being labeled as angry. Nonetheless, the villagers feel anger and engage in a variety of surreptitious measures to strike back at those who offend them. The victim of theft, for example, loudly declares, "Let the thief have my possession" but may try to exact revenge by stealing an item of even greater value, having sex with the thief's wife, or at least gossiping about him. He is careful to "add pepper" to whatever tale he launches into the gossip network so that it will sting all the more when it gets back to its intended victim. Hence Mehinaku public life is relatively tranquil, but the village may seethe with bitter gossip.

Methods of Dispute Settlement

The Semai becharaa'. Whenever the issues are serious or, more commonly, when feelings run strong, the Semai conduct a *becharaa'*, a public airing. The *becharaa'* is an emotionally therapeutic event. In practice, it is something like a marathon encounter group (sometimes lasting for several days and nights), where all interested parties discuss the affair to the point of exhaustion. By repeatedly retelling and reexperiencing the event, its affective content dissipates to a point where the issues no longer can elicit a reaction. At this point, when everyone is suitably numb, the headman voices the consensus that has emerged. A reconciliation of the antagonists is possible, and normal social relations may be resumed.[15]

Although it has the form of a hearing, the *becharaa'* is more a therapeutic than a legal event. It does not produce rulings or significant external sanctions. These are built into Semai personalities. The *becharaa'* reemphasizes the cultural values of nurturance, affiliation and interdependence that were called into question by the dispute, and it reenvelops the disputants within the sheltering group. By submitting to the will of the band, the wrongdoer is accorded forgiveness and thus feels a sense of relief. In the words of one Semai, "When a person commits an offense, he should inform his kindred and be reprimanded by the elders. Then he can feel good again."

Avoiding conflict and restraining violence among the Mehinaku. The *becharaa'* derives its power from the internalized image of the band as a source of inclusion and nurturance. Among the more individualistic Mehinaku, the tribe holds no one in its emotional thrall. In the absence of political authority to enforce rules against violence, the system relies heavily on motivating individuals to avoid confrontation and maintain the appearance of harmony. Ultimately, this system works because the villagers can, if necessary, leave the tribe and avoid a showdown. Indeed, the most probable solution to a serious conflict is that the weaker party will leave. The destination may be a small "dry-season" village for a month's sojourn, another tribe where there are close kin, or, in an extreme case, a backwoods Brazilian settlement. On Gregor's last trip to the Mehinaku, there was one such visitor from a another tribe who was fleeing witchcraft allegations in his home community. At the same time, one of the Mehinaku, a victim of gossip and much bad feeling, was about to leave the village for an extended stay in another community. Unlike the Semai, where a permanent departure may be almost equivalent to social death, the Mehinaku can pack their bags and leave their conflicts behind.

At times, the villagers engage in conflicts that cannot be resolved so easily. Among the most dangerous of these are episodes of pushing and shoving that have broken out immediately after deaths allegedly caused by witchcraft. These melees, called *japujaki* (literally, "big anger"), are rare events and frightening to those who participate. Even in the thick of the battle, however, the villagers do not anticipate more serious violence or armed conflict. Such battles are for wild Indians and white men.

The only regular form of violence among adult men is witch killings and ritualized gang rape. The killings (three in the last thirty years) are bloody affairs in which the victim is cut down, usually outside the village, with machetes, guns, and arrows. The killer takes no pride in his act. He is, in fact, contaminated by the blood (a dangerous and disgusting fluid from the perspective of the villagers), which magically enlarges his face and abdomen. Such men, so called "fiends for killing," were pointed out to me as examples of repulsive individuals whom no woman wanted to marry and who were best avoided. One such killer, who described his act in considerable detail, told me of magical methods by which he tried to wipe himself clean of his victim's blood. His description of the event, filled with self-justification, is now a highly polished narrative, perfected before uncomfortable audiences of kin and residence mates. As among the Semai, it is clear that some inhibitions to violence are built into the Mehinaku personality and reinforced by supernatural sanction. The difference is that the barriers are less central to the personality and are more readily breached. The Mehinaku are therefore more dependent than the Semai on social sanctions against conflict and on positive incentives to avoid it.

Conflict and the Abyss of Violence

Both Mehinaku and Semai see disputes as the brink of an abyss into which all may ultimately be drawn. For the Semai, however, the fear is extravagantly exaggerated, so that even controllable conflicts are seen as a prelude to violence. When, for example, members of one kindred were found to be planting fruit trees in territories claimed by others, people insisted that "we must get this settled or there will be fighting; people will start cutting down each others' trees and shooting each other with poisoned darts." On another occasion, when asked by the Malaysian authorities to give evidence against a notoriously dishonest headman in another band, people said, "If we send him to jail, his relatives will come here and kill us all; they will shoot us with blowpipes through the walls of our houses." That any such actions were unlikely in the extreme was irrelevant; the statement expressed the Semai perception that any conflict has the potential to plunge society into unrestrained violence (Robarchek 1990).

For the Mehinaku, violence is also threatening. Unlike the Semai, however, they are able to put their concerns into perspective so that they can actually enjoy certain kinds of aggressive encounters. Perhaps most shocking to a Semai visitor would be the daily wrestling matches during which the Mehinaku vigorously pit themselves against their fellows. From the Mehinaku perspective this kind of interaction is aggressive, but also therapeutic: "When our bellies are `hot with anger' we wrestle and then the anger is gone."

This acceptance of a measure of conflict also makes it possible for the Mehinaku to view their system from the perspective of an outside observer, and attempt, thereby, to control it. Some thoughtful Xinguanos feel that a revenge killing following a death from witchcraft is an atavistic breach of the Xingu ethic of peacefulness. In the early 1990s one of the tribal leaders, a man whose own father was killed as a witch, conducted a crusade against revenge: "I would not kill a witch even if he killed my sons. There is no way to know with certainty who is guilty. Most of those who have been killed were needlessly killed." The villagers are thus able to evaluate their institutions and respond to them in deliberate ways. The Mehinaku peace, like that of the Waorani or of the terrorists who give up violence (See Robarchek and Crenshaw, this volume) is a conscious and self-aware choice.

Peace and the Supernatural: Mehinaku Witches and Semai Ghosts

Mehinaku Witchcraft and the Role of Fear in Restraining Conflict

Among the Mehinaku, factionalism and allegations of witchcraft divide and subdivide the community. From the perspective of any adult, two-thirds of the other villagers, generally distant kin and members of other residences (Gregor 1978), are suspected of witchcraft and malevolent intent. Although it is doubtful that any of the villagers practice witchcraft, the fear is palpable. Village gossip is filled with allegations, and a special class of shamans (*yakapa*; see Gregor 1978) divine the identity of witches and manufacture evidence of their guilt. When they are very anxious at night, the villagers lock their doors to keep out the witches who would shoot them with invisible arrows or work lethal spells.

The system is potentially explosive, but on a daily basis it functions to apply a veneer of courtesy to ordinary life. Requests for food, possessions, and even sex may be honored out of fear of witchcraft. Thus the villagers smile, part with their possessions, and accept all manner of indignities (especially from visitors from other communities) because they are frightened they will become the victims of sorcery.[16]

Socially, fear of witchcraft serves to keep the Xingu system decentralized, and curbs the power of the chiefs and heads of village factions. Potentially, these leaders could use their positions to rally support in conflicts with other tribes. In practice, their authority is limited by fear. One of the Xingu chiefs lives in chronic anxiety:

Let us say that I distribute gifts. I keep nothing for myself or my family, but there is still not enough to go around. I explain to those who received nothing that there is no more left. They say, "fine, that is all right, we understand." They say the right things, they speak beautifully. But at night they sort their fetishes and plan to murder me and my family.

The Absence of Witchcraft Beliefs among the Semai.

Witchcraft is not a concern within Semai communities, even though there are a number of reasons for expecting that it should be: Semai social organization exemplifies the lack of "superordinate social control" that Beatrice Whiting (1950) found to be typical of societies where witchcraft is important; belief in witches is widespread in Southeast Asia, including among groups to whom the Semai are related (LeBar, Hickey, and Musgrave 1964; Benjamin 1968); and the surrounding Malays, from whom Semai have borrowed extensively, have a highly-developed set of witchcraft beliefs (Skeat 1900; Endicott 1970). The Semai, however, appear to be psychologically and culturally resistant to witch beliefs, probably because such beliefs conflict in fundamental ways with central elements of Semai temperament and culture. The centrality of the band as the sole source of nurturance and security is at odds with a belief in witches. The thought that band members are witches dedicated to the destruction of their friends and kinsmen clashes with the image of the group (*hii'*) as protective and nurturant, and would undermine the bedrock of personal security and identity.

Semai beliefs about the supernatural provide indirect support for this interpretation.[17] While the fear of a witch within the band would be intolerably threatening, the Semai are able to believe in malevolent ghosts, the *kicmoic*. Crucially, unlike a witch, the *kicmoic* are *outside* the community of *living* human beings and thereby do not challenge the image of the group as thoroughly benevolent. Absent that crucial distinction, ghosts are like witches in that they are homicidal; they seek to kill humans, especially their kinsmen; they prowl around the houses and claw at the thatch, sometimes calling to their surviving kin; in the daytime, they ride the mists and storm clouds or lurk in the forest in the vicinity of their graves; their icy touch causes illness; the threads they place across the trails near their graves cause fever and weakness; even their stare brings sickness. When a death occurs, they come in droves to feed on the corpse and to draw the new ghost into their society. At these times, the houses must be tightly shuttered at night and the hearth-fires must be kept burning to keep the dead from trying to carry off the living.

Like witches in many cultures, Semai ghosts reverse proper human conduct. Hence they prey on their own kin. They are cannibals and humans are their "meat." Fire is their water, blossoms are their fruit, and night is their element. They fly through the air or through the ground, their back baskets are worn upside-down, and so on. Kennedy (1969) argues that this inversion, commonly seen in beliefs about witches, represents a negation of human values, which is symbolized by the witch.

Among the Semai, ghosts are (or, rather, were) friends and kinsmen. They are therefore ideal objects for both the projection and direct expression of hostility, since they were once those people toward whom hostile feelings were likely to have been felt (cf. Spiro 1952, 1953). Unlike witches, however, ghosts are no longer members of the band and thus give no cause for fear and suspicion of kin and community; the nurturant and benevolent image of *hii'* remains intact.

The psychological necessity of maintaining a separation of the images of ghost and in-group can be seen in a conversation reported by Robarchek (1977b). One of the band members told of having been chased through the forest by a ghost. As background for the story, he described the misty, cloudy day, the grave nearby, and the circumstances of the death of his young kinsman. It was clear from the account that he assumed that it was the ghost of his kin. Later on, Robarchek raised the question of why good people become ghosts. After pondering the question for several minutes, the informant offered the following explanation. "The ghost that we fear," he said, "the one that attacks us if we go near a grave, is not the ghost of the friend or kinsman buried there; rather, it is a foreign ghost, a stranger." He went on to say that "after death the ghost of our co-villager goes elsewhere to live, and some strange ghost from outside comes and takes up residence in the vacant grave. This is the ghost that we fear, the *mara'* that seeks to kill us."

Because this story was at odds with everything else Robarchek was told about ghosts, it is clear that the story was an ad hoc rationalization. Still, the fact that such an explanation was offered is revealing. The discrepant perceptions of ghosts as evil and *hii'* as good (but ghosts were once *hii'*) are ordinarily compartmentalized and evoke no dissonance or threat. When forced to confront the paradox, however, the informant produced a new explanation that again isolated both perceptions, retaining the murderous ghost image (and that of the malevolence of strangers) while protecting the image of the band and its members as nurturant and benevolent.

Summary and Conclusions

The overall contrast in styles of peacefulness between Mehinaku and Semai turns on the fact that the former choose peace as a matter of policy, whereas the latter are oriented toward peacefulness as a state of being. Thus the Mehinaku and their neighbors are capable of intense competition and occasionally even witch killings. The village churns with hostile gossip and accusations. The Mehinaku nonetheless maintain peaceful ties with their neighbors and fellow tribesmen because there are political and institutional incentives that make such relations in their best interests. Prestige is accorded those who work within the peaceful intertribal system; confrontations result in the loss of one's good name; and appearing generous is the hallmark of the good citizen. When these fail to motivate courteous behavior, external sanctions such as the belief in witchcraft, generally supports the system. When it breaks down, such as in the case of open confrontations or witchcraft killings, the openness of the Xingu communities functions as a safety valve: it is always possible to leave the community.

For the Semai the commitment to peacefulness is psychological as well as cultural, with the two systems mutually reinforcing one another. The cultural commitment to peace is buttressed by cognitive and affective orientations and processes that place powerless individuals in a hostile world, that locate security only within the band, that associate anger with fear, and that define concepts of self in terms of generosity and nonaggressiveness. Because of the threat they pose to the image of self and of the group, disputes, quarrels, and even malicious gossip quickly become the objects of formal, organized, therapeutic processes. Conflict between individuals is, for the most part, avoided and defused. Even in a very large and heavily acculturated settlement where consumption of inexpensive Malay palm "toddy" had increased to the point where many Semai men were intoxicated nearly every night, there was little increase in the expression of emotion and virtually no expression of hostility. For the Semai, a sense of self, a conception of reality, and a pattern of affective responses define a context of action where violence is simply not "motivated." Hence it is not ordinarily considered as a behavioral option (cf. Robarchek and Dentan, 1987).

Among the Semai, the path toward peace seems to be a less sophisticated one than that of the Mehinaku. The enveloping group with its powerful claim on the individual forecloses the possibility of departure or even emotional separation. The system of peace therefore relies heavily on such mechanisms as projection, denial, and distortion of feelings and objective reality. Among the Mehinaku, however, peacefulness is more institutionally and interactionally based. The villagers are freer of unreasonable fear and better able to assess with objectivity and even to modify their political system. Interestingly, the adaptation to peace Ervin Staub describes in terms of ego psychology in chapter 5 applies better to the Mehinaku than to the Semai. Reason, self-interest, and empathy motivate the Mehinaku. From the Mehinaku perspective, the Semai peace looks dearly bought. But it must be recognized that the Mehinaku system may be the more fragile achievement. We do not believe they would retain a peaceful society in the face of alcohol intoxication and acculturation, as have the Semai. Even now, the Xingu peace system is periodically breached, and it is even possible (though unlikely) that under the tutelage of a charismatic but negative leader it could be permanently shattered.

The intricacy of the Semai and Mehinaku systems establishes that peace is a puzzle. Surely, it is a great deal more than the absence of violence. Like violence, peace is a dynamic process. It depends on complex practices, values, and ways of thinking and feeling. What is badly needed are additional studies of the relatively few cultures that are reasonably peaceful. Ultimately we can have as full a knowledge of peace as we have of war and violence. In the process we will have discovered a dimension of the human experience that, until relatively recently, has been nearly hidden from our view.

Notes

The coauthors gratefully acknowledge funding from the National Science Foundation, the United States Institute of Peace and the Harry Frank Guggenheim Foundation (Gregor) and from the Harry Frank Guggenheim Foundation, the United States Institute of Peace, Sigma Xi, and the Society for the Psychological Study of Social Issues (Robarchek) in support of their research. The manuscript has greatly benefitted from Bruce Knauft's helpful comments and criticisms.

1. The Mehinaku and the Semai have been the subjects of long-term research by the coauthors. Gregor has conducted research among the Mehinaku for over two years, between 1967 and 1990. The Robarcheks' research among the Semai includes two extended periods of residence with the Semai in 1973–74 and in 1980.

2. The horticultural societies of the tropical world are among the world's most violent: in this setting, it has been argued that warfare may be inevitable, "a necessary and functional correlate of the inter-riverine hunter-horticulture mode of production which, at a certain level of intensity, has no viable alternative" (Bennett Ross 1980: 55).

3. Recent depictions of Semai society as violent (e.g., Knauft 1987, Paul 1978; Konner 1982; Eibl-Eibesfeldt 1978) have been based on incomplete or inaccurate data. See Robarchek and Dentan 1987, Dentan 1988; Robarchek 1989 for evaluation and refutation of these arguments.

4. This description reflects the Semai life way as it existed in 1973–74 and, to a lesser degree, in 1980. In the intervening years the market economy penetrated much more extensively, and this is reflected in a much greater emphasis on commodity production and wage labor and, as a consequence, a dramatic decline in subsistence self-sufficiency.

5. The sole exceptions are the participation of some young men in insurgent groups and some others in "Home Guard" units and an "Aborigine Regiment" organized by the British during the Communist insurgency of the 1950s and 1960s. They were, apparently, not very effective soldiers. See Robarchek and Dentan (1987) for an extended discussion of this episode.

6. For extended discussion of each of these points, see Robarchek 1977a, 1979b and Dentan 1968).

7. The moral emphasis on "generalized reciprocity" carries implications for other modes of "exchange," i.e., "balanced reciprocity" (barter or monetary transactions) and "negative reciprocity" (theft); (Cf.Sahlins 1965). Owing to the explicit calculation of return, barter or monetary transactions within the band are felt to be embarrassing and a little indecent, because such calculation violates the ideal of generosity and nurturance freely given (see Robarchek 1988).

8. Despite the headman's exhortations there are occasional breaches of the ethic of band solidarity and generosity. Theft, for example, does not occur often, but that it occurs at all is paradoxical. It is clearly a breech of sociality and a conflict and anger-producing act. On the other hand, *pehunan* (see below) and the ideal of generosity imply that a material want should be willingly granted. A thief's real offense is that, rather than coming forward and asking openly for what he wants, he steals secretly in the night and, in so doing, foments conflict and hostility within the band. (Cf. Robarchek 1979a for further discussion of the psychosocial implications of theft).

9. None of these data suggests that Semai are a homogenized, faceless mass, or that individual Semai are devoid of individual personalities (see Robarchek 1989). Because of the crucial role of the band as the only refuge from danger, Semai culture deemphasizes individual differences and stresses band unity. The ideal, if not always the absolute reality, of a nurturant, freely giving community, is carefully maintained.

10. There is only one area in which the Semai do make an effort to stand out. Oratorical skill, and especially the ability to argue persuasively, is one of the essential qualities of headmen. Those with ability argue on behalf of their kindreds in *becharaa'*, the formal "hearings" held to resolve disputes with members of other bands. Speaking ability, however, is never the basis for invidious comparisons. Moreover, the primary use of oratory is to seek peaceful solutions to disputes (Robarchek 1979a).

11. In some of the more acculturated lowlands settlements (which are now essentially permanent peasant villages no longer dependent on hunting and swidden agriculture), there are annual festivals involving visiting and formal hosting. These, however, are relatively recent developments.

12. A Semai child of parents from different bands holds rights in both territories and

may ultimately affiliate with either one. This potential is kept open by a pattern of ambilo-cal residence that may continue for many years, often until the children are well on their way to adulthood.

13. The danger of frustration arising in social interactions also includes failure to keep promised appointments. Yet another, and particularly deadly, *mara'* hears those promises and afflicts those whose plans have been frustrated with high fever and rapid death (hall-marks of falciparum malaria).

14. There are several myths in which an Angry Woman Spirit was killed by village marksmen. Her body parts and clothes were appropriated by local witches, who continue to use them as fetishes to assault their fellows.

15. See Robarchek 1979a, and 1989 for detailed analysis and discussions of this process.

16. An anti-gun-control bumper sticker recently seen by one of the authors offered a similar analysis, observing that "an armed society is a polite society."

17. Our discussion assumes that in those societies beliefs in witchcraft are *projective*, that they provide an objectified image through which impulses that are socially disapproved or personally threatening may be expressed (see, for example, Kennedy 1969, Kluckhohn 1944; Nadel 1953; Spiro 1967, 1969).

References

Alland, Alexander, Jr. 1972. *The Human Imperative*. New York: Columbia University Press.

Ardrey, Robert. 1961. *African Genesis*. New York: Dell.

————. 1966. *The Territorial Imperative*. New York: Atheneum.

Benedict, Ruth F. 1934. *Patterns of Culture*. Boston: Houghton Mifflin.

Benjamin, Geoffrey. 1968. Headmanship and Leadership in Temiar Society. *Federation Museums Journal* 12: 1–43.

Bennett-Ross, Jane. 1980. Ecology and the Problem of the Tribe: A Critique of the Hobbesian Model of Preindustrial Warfare. In *Beyond the Myths of Culture*; ed. Eric B. Ross. New York: Academic Press.

Burling, Robbins. *Hill Farms and Paddy Fields*. Englewood Cliffs, N.J.: Prentice-Hall.

Chagnon, Napoleon. 1967a. *Yanomamo: The Fierce People. Natural History* 66:1.

————. 1967b. Yanomamo Social Organization and Warfare. In *War: the Anthropology of Conflict and Aggression,* ed. Morton Fried, Marvin Harris, and Robert Murphy. New York: Natural History Press.

————. 1968. *Yanomamo: The Fierce People*. New York: Holt, Rinehart and Winston.

Chapman, F. Spencer. 1957. *The Jungle is Neutral*. London: Transworld.

Dentan, Robert K. 1968. *The Semai: A Nonviolent People of Malaya*. New York: Holt, Rinehart and Winston.

————. 1988. On Reconsidering Violence in Simple Societies. *Current Anthropology* 29: 624–629.

————. 1992. The Rise, Maintenance and Destruction of a Peaceable Polity: A Preliminary Essay in Political Ecology. In *Aggression and Peacefulness in Humans and Other Primates*, ed. James Silverberg and J. Patrick Gray. New York: Oxford University Press.

Eibl-Eibesfeldt, Irenaus. 1978. *The Biology of Peace and War*. New York: Viking.

Endicott, Kirk. 1970. *An Anaysis of Malay Magic*. Oxford: Clarendon.

Evans-Pritchard, E. E. 1957. Zande Border Raids. *Africa* 27: 217–231.

Fix, Alan G. 1977. The Demography of the Semai Senoi. *Anthropological Papers, Museum of Anthropology*, no. 62. Ann Arbor: University of Michigan.

Freeman, Derek. 1980. *Margaret Mead and Samoa: The Making and Unmaking of an Anthropological Myth.* Cambridge: Harvard University Press.

Gardner, Peter M. 1966. Symmetric Respect and Memorate Knowledge: The Structure and Ecology of Individualistic Culture. *Southwestern Journal of Anthropology* 22: 389–415.

Goldman, Irving. 1963. *The Cubeo: Indians of the Northwest Amazon.* Urbana: University of Illinois Press.

Gregor, Thomas. 1985. *Anxious Pleasures: The Sexual Lives of An Amazonian People.* Chicago: University of Chicago Press.

Harris, Marvin. 1971. *Culture, Man and Nature.* New York: Crowell.

———. 1972. Warfare, Old and New. *Natural History* 813: 18–20.

———. 1977. *Cannibals and Kings.* New York: Random House.

Kennedy, John G. 1969. Psychosocial Dynamics of Witchcraft Systems. *International Journal of Social Psychiatry* 15 (3): 163–178.

Keifer, Thomas M. 1969. Tausug Armed Conflict: The Social Organization of Military Activity in a Philippine Moslem Society. *Philippine Studies Program Research Series,* no. 7. Chicago: Department of Anthropology, University of Chicago.

Kluckhohn, Clyde. 1944. *Navaho Witchcraft.* Cambridge: Papers of the Peabody Museum of Archaeology and Ethnology, Harvard University.

Koch, Klaus-Frederich. 1970. Cannibalistic Revenge in Jale Warfare. *Natural History* 792: 41–50.

Konner, Melvin. 1982. *The Tangled Wing: Biological Constraints on the Human Spirit.* New York: Holt, Rinehart and Winston.

Lathrap, Donald W. 1968. The Hunting Economies of the Tropical Forest Zone of South America: An Attempt at Historical Perspective. In *Man the Hunter,* ed. Richard B. Lee and Irven DeVore. Chicago: Aldine.

———. 1970. *The Upper Amazon.* New York: Praeger.

LeBar, Frank M., Gerald C. Hickey, and John K. Musgrave. 1964. *Ethnic Groups of Mainland Southeast Asia.* New Haven: Human Relations Area Files.

Lorenz, Konrad. 1966. *On Aggression.* New York: Harcourt, Brace and World.

Montagu, Ashley. 1968. *Man and Aggression.* New York: Oxford University Press.

Morey, R. V. and John P. Marwitt. 1975. Ecology, Economy and Warfare in Lowland South America. In *War, Its Causes and Correlates,* ed. M. A. Nettleship, R.D. Givens, and A. Nettleship. The Hague: Mouton.

Murphy, Robert F. 1957. Intergroup Hostility and Social Cohesion. *American Anthropologist* 59: 1018–1035.

Nadel, S. F. 1953. Social Control and Self Regulation. *Social Forces* 31: 265–273.

Otterbein, Keith. 1968. Internal War: A Cross-Cultural Study. *American Anthropologist* 7 (2): 277–289.

Robarchek, Clayton A. 1977a. Frustration, Aggression and the Nonviolent Semai. *American Ethnologist* 4 (4):762–779.

———. 1977b. Semai Nonviolence: A Systems Approach to Understanding. Ph.D. diss., University of California, Riverside.

———. 1979a. Conflict, Emotion and Abreaction: Resolution of Conflict among the Semai Senoi. *Ethos* 7 (2): 104–123.

———. 1979b. Learning to Fear: A Case Study in Emotional Conditioning. *American Ethnologist* 6 (3): 555–567.

———. 1981. The Image of Nonviolence: World View of the Semai Senoi. *Journal of the Federated States Museums,* vol. 24.

———. 1986. Helplessness, Fearfulness, and Peacefulness: The Emotional and Motivational

Contexts of Semai Social Relations. *Anthropological Quarterly* 59, no. (4): 177–183.

———. 1988 How Do We Get Some Meat? (1): Generalized Reciprocity and Semai World View. Paper delivered at the annual meetings of the Central States Anthropological Society, March 24–27, 1988. St. Louis.

———. 1989. Primitive Warfare and the Ratomorphic Model of Mankind. *American Anthropologist* 91 (4): 50–67.

Robarchek, Clayton A. and Robert K. Dentan. 1987. Blood Drunkenness and the Blood-thirsty Semai: Unmaking Another Anthropological Myth. *American Anthropologist* 89 (2): 356–365.

Ross, Eric B. 1978. Food Taboos, Diet and Hunting Strategy: The Adaptation to Animals in Amazonian Cultural Ecology. *Current Anthropology* 19 (1): 1–36.

Sahlins, Marshall. 1965. On the Sociology of Primitive Exchange. In *The Relevance of Models for Social Anthropology*, ed. M. Banton. London: Tavistock.

Skeat, Walter W. 1900. *Malay Magic: Being an Introduction to the Folklore and Popular Religion of the Malay Peninsula*. New York: Dover.

Spiro, Melford. 1952. Ghosts, Ifaluk, and Teleological Functionalism. *American Anthropologist* 54: 497–503.

———. 1953. Ghosts: An Anthropological Inquiry into Learning and Perception. *Journal of Abnormal and Social Psychology* 48: 376–382.

Whiting, Beatrice. 1950. *Paiute Sorcery*. Viking Fund Publications in Anthropology, no. 15.

7

The Aucas, the Cannibals, and the Missionaries: From Warfare to Peacefulness among the Waorani

CLAYTON A. ROBARCHEK AND CAROLE J. ROBARCHEK

■ Radcliffe-Brown once observed that the difference between cultures and biological organisms was that while species are relatively fixed, a culture could, after a brief period of malaise, transform itself as radically as a mouse metamorphosing into an elephant. Such transformations are surely the most fascinating moments in cultural history. Occasionally, they are cause for optimism about the human spirit, as in the blossoming of democracy from dictatorship. In the Robarcheks' study we have an example at a relatively simple level. The Waorani, a small-scale tribal society in Eastern Ecuador, once had a homicide rate that was among the highest known to anthropology. In the space of just a few years they transformed themselves into a relatively peaceful people. What is truly remarkable about the process is that it occurred in the absence of coercion from the outside or significant social change. Rather it was the choice of the Waorani themselves.

The Robarcheks' chapter has connections to other contributions in this volume, including Crenshaw's study of terrorists' decisions to give up violence (chapter 9), and Vasquez's examination of peace making among nations (chapter 10).

ONE OF THE THEMES of the conference that gave rise to this volume was "peace as a positive achievement," and this chapter presents a case study of precisely that. It is a preliminary report of ethnographic research on an Amazonian society that is in the process of attempting, very consciously and deliberately, to transform itself from the most violent on earth into one that is, at least in comparative terms, peaceful. Understanding the contexts and circumstances of this transformation has the potential to enlarge our understanding not only of violence and nonviolence, but of the dynamics of human culture and behavior generally.

The data presented here were collected as part of a broader comparative study of peacefulness and violence in two tropical forest societies: the Semai, hunters and swidden gardeners of the Malaysian rain forest and one of the most peaceful societies known, and the Waorani, a hunting and horticultural people in western Amazonia, who were until recently the most violent society yet described, a society where more than 60 percent of deaths were homicides, mostly resulting from intense internal feuding and external raiding (cf. Yost 1981). Our objective was a controlled comparison of these two hunting and horticultural societies, very similar in terms of their ecological setting, subsistence system, technology, settlement sizes, social organization, and a great many other variables (including, presumably, biology) but at opposite extremes in their attitudes and behaviors regarding violence (cf. Robarchek and Robarchek 1992).

We had previously collected extensive data on the Semai during two field studies in 1973–74 and 1979–80 (some of the results of those studies are reported by Gregor and Robarchek in chapter 6). In 1987, we undertook an intensive one-year ethnographic study to document the psychological, social, cultural, and ecological contexts of warfare and violence among the Waorani. Preliminary comparative analysis reveals that, while the ecological settings, technology, subsistence practices, settlement patterns, kinship, and social organizations of these two societies are indeed remarkably similar, their perceptions of these realities, and thus their motivational contexts of action, are profoundly different. Our published results thus far have focused on defining the contrasting conceptions of the nature of reality, of human beings, and of the relationships among them, and on exploring the implications of these differences for the radically divergent attitudes and behaviors regarding violence that characterize these two societies (C. J. Robarchek 1988; Robarchek and Robarchek 1988, 1989, 1992).

We mention all of this simply as background, since the discussion below will occasionally refer to this research, but the comparative study of Semai and Waorani (data analysis for which is still continuing) is not our primary concern here. In the course of conducting our fieldwork among the Waorani, we came to realize that we were in the midst of a society that was in the process of actively transforming its culture from one premised on warfare to one premised on peace. We decided to seize this rare opportunity to study a people who are striving, consciously and deliberately, to construct a culture of peace. That transformation and its implications—for our understanding of violence as well as peacefulness specifically, and of human psychocultural dynamics in general—are the subjects of this chapter.

The Historical Context

Raiding and warfare have long been endemic in the western Amazon basin, and we can only speculate about the ultimate causes of this widespread culture of war. The earliest accounts, from the beginning of the Spanish colonial era and even before, describe the bellicosity of the inhabitants of the region. Inca attempts at colonization were successfully repelled by the Jivaros and others, as were the early incursions by the Spanish. In 1599 many of the indigenous groups united to drive all colonists from the region, sacking their cities and killing the inhabitants (cf. Harner 1972). In the nineteenth century, the rubber boom brought major dislocations and disruptions to the native peoples. Large numbers of Indians were enslaved to work as rubber collectors and were subjected to brutal mistreatment by the Europeans and their local henchmen. Epidemics of introduced diseases swept through the indigenous populations, entirely wiping out some groups and decimating most of the others. The haciendas established on the major rivers at the foot of the Andes utilized what amounted to Indian slave labor to exploit the alluvial gold deposits in the Andean foothills, and they supported and encouraged intertribal slave raiding. It was in this context that the Waorani culture of war developed, but precisely how or when we cannot say because no references to any group that can be unambiguously identified as Waorani occur before the turn of this century.

The Waorani Culture of War

In this violent milieu, the Waorani, called "Auca" (savages) by their lowland Quichua neighbors, were among the most feared. Until the late 1950s, there were, with few exceptions, no regular peaceful contacts with other groups (most of whom they believed to be cannibals). They and their neighbors raided each other incessantly. Although the Waorani numbered fewer than one thousand and, unlike their neighbors, possessed no firearms, their nine-foot hardwood spears and their deservedly fearsome reputation allowed them to maintain control over an immense territory, some eight thousand square miles of deep valleys and dense rain forest, from which they drove out or killed all who attempted to settle. Although vastly outnumbered, they attacked neighboring groups to steal machetes, axes, and occasionally women. The surrounding groups also raided them for women and children, who were taken to work on the haciendas that persisted in the Andean foothills until the middle of this century.

Scattered in widely dispersed settlements over their vast territory, they also raided each other. Blood feuds and vendettas arising from past killings, from quarrels over marriage arrangements, and from accusations of sorcery were a way of life, even among closely related bands. Based on extensive genealogies collected in the 1970s, Yost (1981) calculated that fully 60 percent of adult deaths over the past five generations were the result of warfare, 17 percent resulting from external warfare and 44 percent from internal war. The genealogies that we collected yielded similar estimates.

Prior to the beginnings of peaceful contacts in the late 1950s and early 1960s, there were a number of scattered subgroups of Waorani, each occupying a separate region within the larger territory. Members of each were hostile to most of the others and often to many of the other bands within their own territories as well. While bonds of kinship and affinity linked the members of settlements in a particular region, for Waorani these were as likely to be sources of conflict as of amity.

Among the Waorani, now as then, there is generalized reciprocity among close kin, especially parents and children and real and classificatory siblings (parallel cousins). Beyond this immediate kindred, however, there is no real obligation to give aid and assistance nor expectation of receiving it. The elderly, when they became a burden, were sometimes speared to death by their own kin, and we have several documented accounts of the spearings of old people by their own grandchildren. Women give birth alone and unattended; snakebite victims may be left in the forest, by their own kin, to fend for themselves. In the event of a raid, all flee for their lives, men abandoning their wives, women their children (see Robarchek and Robarchek 1988, 1989, 1992).

In the past, raids frequently were precipitated by disagreements arising from the Waorani practice of prescriptive bilateral cross-cousin marriage. These marriages were arranged by parents, often by one parent without the knowledge or consent of the other. Thus a father, who may have agreed to marry his daughter to his sister's son, may return to his house during a banana-drinking feast to find that, in his absence, the girl has been married to his wife's brother's son. In the absence of any institutionalized mechanisms for dealing with conflicts or resolving disputes, the anger and animosities generated often led to spearing raids, sometimes even against relatives.

Witchcraft accusations were another common source of lethal hostilities. Because serious illnesses are infrequent, and since most of those bitten by snakes survive, a death from either of these causes is an abnormal event that requires explanation. The explanation that is almost certain to be offered is witchcraft, probably practiced by a relative or a member of a related band who has a grudge against the victim or his kin. Until recently, the typical response was a retaliatory raid on the suspected sorcerer's household, the raiders bursting into the house at night and spearing the sorcerer and as many of his housemates—men, women, and children—as possible.

These killings, in turn, generated their own momentum, and long-term blood feuds developed, motivated by the desire to avenge past killings. Following an attack, the raiders and their families would abandon their houses and fields and retreat into the forest to avoid retaliation. They would establish a new hamlet many miles away, and several years might pass before a telltale footprint betrayed the location of the settlement to hunters from another band and led to a new cycle of killing.

. Although little has been written by anthropologists on the Waorani, they have gained worldwide notoriety in some circles through innumerable church-basement showings of a film describing the killing of five young American missionaries who, in 1956, ferried themselves by small plane onto a sandbar in the Curaray River, where they were promptly speared to death. The story made headlines around the world and set in motion a chain of events that would ultimately lead most Waorani to abandon their traditional hostility to all outsiders and their incessant warfare among themselves (for missionaries' accounts of these events, see Elliot 1957; Wallis 1960).[1]

The End of Warfare

Peaceful relations with the outside world began in 1958 when two Protestant missionary women, Elizabeth Elliot, the wife of one of the slain missionaries and Rachel Saint, the sister of another, aided by two young Waorani women who had fled to the outside some years before to escape the raiding, walked into the forest and made contact with the very kindred that had speared the young missionaries.

This contact initiated a remarkable transition in Waorani culture and behavior. The missionaries (and there were never more than a half-dozen in residence, all but one of whom were women) made the ending of warfare their highest priority, but they had no way of enforcing this goal, since they were completely without coercive authority. No troops or police were on call; the region was and is essentially beyond Ecuadorian military control. For the missionaries to succeed in their objective, the Waorani had to be persuaded to give up internal feuding and external raiding. When the missionaries began to expand their contacts and to act as mediators between hostile groups, most Waorani were quite willing to cease raiding, once they became convinced that the other groups would do the same. One by one, individual bands did, in fact, abandon raiding within a matter of months after contact. While the potential for (and indeed the actuality of) occasional spearings continues (during our field-work, two Catholic missionaries were speared to death by a band that continues to resist contact, and there were a number of disputes that threatened to turn violent), the large-scale pattern of incessant raiding was given up remarkably quickly and easily following the initial contacts.

This transition is even more remarkable in that it occurred, at least in its initial phases, in the absence of other major changes, either within or outside of Waorani society. There was no military conquest; there were no major demographic shifts; the ecological situation had not been altered. The Waorani simply decided to stop killing. The culture of war disappeared when new cultural knowledge—new information and new perceptions of reality—allowed the formulation of new individual and social goals. People responded by choosing courses of action based on what they wanted from this new reality. After generations of warfare and raiding, Waorani were persuaded almost overnight to abandon the pattern. In scarcely more than a decade, virtually the entire society transformed itself from the most violent known into one that is essentially peaceful.

The theoretical implications of this are potentially profound. It suggests, first of all, that, regardless of the origins of the Waorani warfare complex, an intrinsic psychocultural dynamic, rather than extrinsic economic, political, or ecological determinants, was crucial to the maintenance of it. Beyond that, it argues for a perspective on warfare (and on human behavior in general) that sees people not passively responding to ecological or biological determinants external to their own consciousness, but as active participants in their own destinies, as purposeful decision makers in pursuit of particular goals within culturally constituted realities that they themselves are continually constructing and reconstructing.

Culture, Genuine or Spurious

The first paper we delivered after returning from the field (C. J. Robarchek 1988) described the violence and the atomism and individualism of pre-contact Waorani society and brought a response from the audience that we have now come to expect: "They sound like the Ik!"

That observation must be addressed because of the implication that

Waorani culture, as Turnbull (1972) argued in the case of the Ik, was dysfunctional or, to use a label employed in another response to our presentation, "pathological." While the idea that cultures can be pathological or pathogenic has never been clearly formulated as a theoretical proposition (Sapir's *Culture, Genuine and Spurious* [1924], Henry's *Culture Against Man* [1963], and Wallace's analyses of revitalization movements [1956, 1957, 1961] are probably among the most ambitious attempts), there is, nevertheless, a widely held common-sense notion, exemplified by the Ik, that a culture can degenerate to a point where sociality essentially ceases and a dog-eat-dog, devil-take-the-hindmost individualism rules (cf. Calhoun 1972). While we have no reason to question either the accuracy of Turnbull's description of Ik social life or his explanation for its apparent pathology, it is essential that we explicitly consider whether or not a similar diagnosis of cultural pathology is appropriate for the Waorani. If it is, if the spectacular level of homicidal violence that characterized Waorani society was a symptom of cultural degeneration and pathology, then the explanation for the society's current peacefulness is relatively simple: in essence, it is that the culture "recovered" and more "normal" social relations were reasserted. If, on the other hand, Waorani culture was not pathological but was merely one extreme on a continuum of "normal" culture and social relations, then a very different explanation for the origins of the current state of social life is required, one that explicitly addresses the sources and dynamics of sociocultural and psychological continuity and change.

Waorani Culture, Pathological or Normal?

First, it is necessary to clarify the ethnographic record by acknowledging that virtually all of the descriptions of pre-contact Waorani life, ours as well as others', have been subtly and not so subtly biased, and in a consistent direction. The bulk of the published material on the Waorani is contained in several books written by missionaries (or by those who were promoting, or at least were sympathetic to, missionary activities) and directed to a popular audience, (e.g., Wallis 1960, 1973; Elliot 1957). Not surprisingly, these descriptions have consistently (and also fairly accurately) emphasized the contrast between life in the pre- and post-missionary periods and, as a consequence, when they discussed the pre-contact life, they focused on the violence to the virtual exclusion of everything else.

The few anthropological descriptions that exist, our own included, suffer from biases similar in content, if not in form. Since all observation is selective and subjective, no description can completely mirror the reality perceived by its creator (let alone the reality of its subjects), and all descriptions must necessarily abstract, select, and, to some extent, distort. Ours are no exception. It is the violence that gives pre-contact Waorani society its significance in terms of the theoretical questions that occupy us, and that made this society an apt subject for our comparative study. Thus, much of our time in the field was devoted to documenting and attempting to understand the patterning of, and the motives behind, the raids and vendettas. The papers that have thus far resulted have, because of the theoretical issues that they were addressing, stressed the violence at the expense of the rest of the pre-contact culture and social life. As a first step toward understanding pre-contact culture, then, we must attempt to put the violence into perspective.

To see Waorani warfare in relation to the rest of Waorani life, the first thing to recognize is that the violence, while it was certainly a constant threat, was not a constant reality. Years might pass between raids. While variables like group size and average life span are difficult to estimate, it seems that a band consisting of forty people was likely to take or lose one life, on average, every two years. Because organized attacks seldom claimed only a single life, raids were undoubtedly much less frequent than that. Thus, while the cultural and psychological salience of warfare was (and is) great, and while in relative terms the level of killing was astronomically high, most of day-to-day life was spent in the subsistence and social pursuits typical of these sorts of societies everywhere. This pattern has, according to the recollections of the oldest Waorani of their childhoods and of the stories told by their parents and grandparents, per-sisted in much the same form for at least a century, with daily life devoted to hunting, gardening, fishing, arranging marriages, banana-drinking feasts, making love, and all the other activities that signify a nor-mal culturally structured social life.

Waorani and Ik

In his description of the Ik, Turnbull documents the circumstances and historical events that ultimately dehumanized them: powerlessness, dislocation, and deprivation. Additionally, their material condition became so impoverished that life was reduced to an essential struggle for daily survival, leading to a malignant selfishness and a complete break-down of social life. The unexamined Hobbesian image implicit in that description notwithstanding, his account of the process of dehumaniza-tion is compelling, and we want to begin by considering to what degree the Waorani case is similar.

Immediately, however, we are confronted with a paucity of reliable history. Still, it is certainly safe to assume that the Waorani, like other Amazonian peoples, have been suffering, directly or indirectly, the negative effects of European incursions since the colonial period. We can also safely assume that these impacts increased dramatically around the turn of the century with the onset of the rubber boom. The catastrophic effects of that period on other groups in the region are well documented (cf. Harner 1972; see also Ferguson 1990 for a discussion of the impact of European expansion on the peoples of Amazonia generally), and there is no reason to believe that the Waorani were spared suffering similar effects.

There is even some suggestive direct evidence that the Waorani were powerfully affected by this period. A Waorani story purporting to explain how they came to their present territory recalls that their numbers were dwindling as they were captured and eaten by the *kowodi* (the term for all non-Waorani). They fled upriver to escape the cannibals, but some returned and were captured and held prisoner. They were killed, one by one, their flesh eaten, and their blood painted on a magic "thing" that made a loud noise. The survivors escaped and fled far upstream to where they live today. Rachel Saint, who first recorded the story, recalls that when some Waorani were taken to the Summer Institute of Linguistics compound at Limoncocha, they identified the generating plant as matching the description of the *kowodi* "thing" (Saint 1964).

It does not take much imagination to see in this an account of captured Waorani taken as slaves to a jungle rubber-processing operation, where they encountered their first industrial machinery and where many died, and the subsequent flight of the survivors to avoid a similar fate. Such a flight from genocide in some distant region may account for why the Waorani language is apparently unrelated to any of those in the surrounding area and, perhaps, to any other surviving language.

With the establishment of the haciendas in the lower foothills of the Andes, the Waorani were subjected to frequent violent clashes with invaders from surrounding groups, and to periodic slave raids by the hacendados and the Indians in their employ. An elderly Ecuadorian woman, who spent her youth on haciendas owned by her father and husband, recounted to us her experience with a Waorani boy, captured by the lowland Quichua, who was about to be killed because they feared that he was too old to be safely "tamed." She intervened and took him as a house servant, but he soon died. "Those Auca children," she said, "they always died of colds very soon."

There is, thus, abundant direct and indirect evidence that the Waorani were significantly impacted by outside forces, especially during the early years of this century. Were they, however, "deculturated" by the experience? Listening to our Waorani neighbors describe their lives prior to the establishment of the first peaceful contacts, we did not get a picture of the hopelessness, normlessness, and anomie of a society where regularized social life has broken down. Rather, they painted a picture of close-knit groups of kin, allied and divided by a pattern of prescriptive cross-cousin marriage that was rigorously followed. The violence, which was a primary fact of life, was structured in part by the patterns of conflict and alliances thus produced: siblings and parallel cousins were allies, while cross-cousins were potential spouses and affines and potential targets for raiding.

Nor, unlike the Ik, were they physically deprived. The region abounds in game and fish and, even today when the territory of the reserve on which most Waorani live has been reduced to less than ten percent of the pre-contact range, hunting, fishing, and gardening remain highly productive. Their traditional technology (nets, fish poison, spears, blowpipes, and poisoned darts) was so effective at harvesting these resources that it is still used extensively, even though cheap single-shot shotguns are now readily available (cf. Yost and Kelley 1983). Where amicable relations prevailed, groups, then as now, played host to each other for dancing and (nonalcoholic) banana-drinking feasts lasting for several days and nights.[2]

Each band was essentially an island unto itself, perpetually at war with all non-Waorani and periodically or permanently at war with most other Waorani groups as well. It should not, however, be assumed that the Waorani were always the victims of the aggression of outsiders. They often initiated attacks against surrounding Indian groups and others who came within range. Our neighbors described their killing of the five missionaries and recalled raids undertaken against the Quichua to acquire machetes and axes, to kidnap women, and just for excitement and adventure.

The individuals who comprised these bands were, and are, independent and self-reliant. Waorani self-image was and remains highly individualistic and autonomous; both men and women are expected to be self-reliant and independent, and they see themselves as such. While there is sharing and cooperation among close kin, especially siblings and parallel cousins, outside this kindred there is no obligation to give aid nor any real expectation of receiving it. Every person is ultimately responsible for him- or herself. Affectionate and non-punitive socialization produces people, both men and women, who look out on a world that holds few terrors beyond the human threats of witchcraft or raiding and who are fully confident of their own capacities to deal with that world on its own terms.

The total picture presented, while it is most assuredly one of great violence, is not one of social and psychological disintegration and anomie. The inescapable conclusion, although it is perhaps less palatable than an explanation premised on pathology, is that Waorani culture and social life, although they were certainly at one extreme on a continuum of violence, were nonetheless "normal," in the sense that the culture provided a coherent, stable, and meaningful map of the world for the society, defining a social reality where most individuals could find a meaningful place for themselves.

It is quite possible, indeed probable, that this was a relatively new sociocultural configuration that grew out of the dislocations of the late colonial period, but it nonetheless provided a coherent map of reality that allowed the members of the society to make sense of their world and to make their way effectively in it. Nor is this a unique or even an unusual state of affairs. The Plains Indians' case comes easily to mind here as one where a new and highly coherent culture configuration (also, incidentally, a very violent one) was rapidly forged in response to a number of new circumstances, especially the waves of dislocations caused by European settlement of the east coast of North America, the introduction of the horse from the south, and the creation of markets for indigenous products, including slaves (cf. Robarchek 1994). These societies developed, flowered, and were destroyed in a period of little more than two centuries. If the cultures of the Sioux and Cheyenne, the Crow and the Commanche were "genuine," how did they differ from that of the Waorani?

The Waorani Transition from Warfare to Peacefulness

Waorani society was aboriginally, and is today, comprised of a varying number of scattered and autonomous settlements on and off what is now the Auca Reserve. Since most of these settlements are still largely kin-based, most roughly represent the dispersed and usually mutually hostile pre-contact groups and subgroups. This was not then and is not now a unitary "society," although most groups recognize at least distant kin ties to other groups. There is now, of course, a greatly increased frequency of contacts and intermarriage among the members of different groups and settlements due to the cessation of warfare and the fact that most now reside on a single reserve that is much smaller than the pre-contact territory.

The process of "pacification" of these isolated groups has been a long-term one which, although it began in the late 1950s with the first peaceful contacts with one band of the "upriver Auca" subgroup, is not yet entirely completed. There are still several groups living off the reserve, at least two of which continue to resist all contacts.

At first, the missionaries made little headway in trying to convince that first group to become Christians and give up the killing. Crucial to their ultimate success were several young Waorani women who had earlier fled to the outside to escape the vendettas. Some of these had lived with the Quichua for a number of years, and they returned with the missionaries to tell their kinsmen of their lives on the outside—that the kowodi were not cannibals, that there was no raiding, and that people did not live in constant fear for their lives. They urged their kinsmen to accept the teachings of the missionaries so that the killing could end, and it was largely through their mediation that the missionaries' message was heard and accepted (cf. Yost 1981).

By the mid 1960s, a small group of missionaries who were associated with the Summer Institute of Linguistics were seeking and locating hostile bands from the air. One by one, new groups were located and, for several months, small planes dropped gifts of tools, food, clothes, and so on. Later, through loudspeakers lowered from the planes, Waorani already influenced by the missionaries spoke to their hostile kinsmen, assuring them that the vendettas were ending. Finally, when contact could safely be made on the ground, they were approached by relatives from previously contacted bands. Each new group was persuaded to relocate in the area that is now the Auca Reserve, under the assurance that others who had preceded them had also agreed to give up the vendettas. (This strategy was not always successful, however; the first Wao who attempted such a contact was killed almost immediately.)[3] As each new group moved onto the reserve, their commitment to keeping the peace was reinforced by their dependence on the missionaries and the other groups upon whom they relied for food until their own gardens matured. Their resolve was further buttressed by the Christian values and beliefs promulgated by the missionaries. This process continued through the 1970s, when the activities of the SIL were severely curtailed by the Ecuadorian government.

Other factors, of course, quickly came into play. The intensity of the killing had left some bands without potential spouses of the proper kin type, and peaceful contacts with formerly hostile bands opened up a realm of new marriage possibilities with former enemies. Also, as the intensity of the violence declined and peaceful contacts with missionaries and with the surrounding indigenous peoples increased, the Waorani began to acquire the material goods and other advantages that their long isolation had denied them: medical care, iron tools, new foods, shotguns, flashlights, medicines, snakebite antivenins, and so on. Their increasing desire for access to new marriage partners and to these new goods and services reinforced their commitment to ending the violence, once the process was underway.[4]

Nevertheless, it is important to recognize, because of its significance in terms of current dominant theoretical approaches to the explanation of warfare, that, for each new group contacted, the change in behavior was the primary one. Giving up the killing of outsiders was the sine qua non for any subsequent changes—technological, social, cultural, or psychological.

As originally conceived, the comparison of Semai and Waorani was to be on three primary dimensions: the allocation of time and resources (focusing specifically on the material aspects of daily life), social relations, and ideology. It appears that, even today, there has been little fundamental change in any of these three systems. This conclusion is based on our interviews with missionaries who were involved in the initial contacts, interviews with and publications by James Yost (the only other anthropologist to have lived among the Waorani) who witnessed early contacts with some groups in the mid 1970s, and on interviews that we conducted during our residence with and visiting of different bands with differing lengths of residence on the reserve and with varying degrees of commitment to Christianity.

The subsistence system and thus the material pattern of daily life based on swidden horticulture, hunting, fishing and gathering, has remained essentially unchanged. Increasing involvement with the outside money economy has been confined almost entirely to essentially peripheral "luxury" goods: clothes, flashlights, shotguns, aluminum pots, and so on. Commodity production for export is confined to captured animals, mainly baby parrots and monkeys captured while hunting, and to a few handicrafts–primarily hammocks and net bags. Some men occasionally work as laborers, cutting brush for the oil exploration companies that are now penetrating the region, but for most people the vast majority of day-to-day activities remain tied to the traditional subsistence system.

Social organization and social life, including kinship, domestic group composition, marriage patterns, political structure, patterns of work and cooperation, and so on, are virtually identical to those of the pre-reservation period. The basic social, economic, and political unit remains the autonomous household or, more frequently today, house-cluster of parents and married siblings. Within these, patterns of sharing and cooperation are little changed from those described in the earliest missionary accounts and by the Waorani themselves. The range of social relations has, of course, broadened dramatically to include a great many more Waorani as well as other Indians and outsiders.

Ideological continuity is similarly evident. There appears to be little fundamental difference in basic world view assumptions and values between early and late arrivals to the reserve, and informants' accounts of spearing raids and other events from the pre-contact period show similar value sets.[5] Although selected elements of the Christian beliefs and values communicated by the missionaries have been fairly widely adopted (preeminently, the idea that God abhors killing), Christian ideology and cosmology are, for most people, a superficial veneer over the pre-contact consciousness, an overlay on the traditional value system but not a replacement of it (cf. Yost 1981). This can be seen clearly in a tragic and dramatic incident that occurred during our fieldwork, when two Ecuadorian Catholic missionaries were speared to death by a band of Waorani still living off the reserve. The reaction of our Waorani neighbors was, by and large, not horror or revulsion at the violence of the act but, rather, was speculation about whether or not the rumored motive— that the missionaries had been responsible for the disappearance of a Waorani child—was true (it was not) and, for a time, a heightened suspicion of us and our motives for being there.

Individual autonomy continues to be highly valued and, even within the extended family, elders have but limited influence over the actions of their adult kin. All this is well illustrated in a case—not atypical— described to us by an eyewitness, in which three young men—brothers and classificatory brothers—killed their paternal grandmother, bursting into her house and spearing the old woman in her hammock. Their father was furious at the murder of his mother, but did nothing. "What could he do?" our informant observed, "They are his sons." The most recent spearing on the reserve shows a striking similarity: a group of young men speared an old woman, with whom they once had been co-resident, although elders of their group continue to call for an end to the violence.

Creating a Culture of Peace

Although the level of homicidal violence has decreased dramatically, this should not be interpreted as indicating that this has become an inherently peaceful society. While the commitment to giving up large-scale raiding has been honored, occasional spearings have continued over the years, both on and off the reserve. For example, as contacts with surrounding Indian groups stabilized in the 1970s, a group of men from the band with whom we lived (incidentally, one of the first contacted and "pacified") was hired by members of a neighboring Quichua group to kill a suspected Quichua sorcerer (which they did, along with his wife and all his children). We also expect to hear any time of the spearing of an old woman who is widely believed to be a witch, and who expects to be killed. Her family also expects it because, although she "resides" with her daughter and son-in-law, she actually lives alone in a shack about a quarter of a mile away from them. This arrangement is highly unusual and was devised, we suspect, so that when the raiders eventually come, they will not kill the entire family.

Nevertheless, compared to pre-contact times, Waorani life is now very peaceful. Where previously the homicide rate exceeded 60 percent and every adult man had been involved in multiple killings, now very few of the first adult generation since contact have been so involved. Yet, in a cross-cultural perspective, Waorani society remains fairly violent, with a homicide rate we have very conservatively calculated (excluding, for example, any consideration of infanticide) to be at least 57/100,000 per annum over the past twenty years. This is more than five times the rate for the U.S. as a whole in 1980, and about twice the rate of the !Kung, whom Knauft (1987) considered to be quite violent. This should not, however, be allowed to obscure the fact that a dramatic change in behavior has, in fact, taken place—a decrease in homicide rates from near 1,000 per 100,000 to around 60 per 100,000 per annum.

Although the incidence of violence has decreased dramatically, the new peacefulness has few psychological, social, or cultural underpinnings. There is still little structural basis for group solidarity, little sense of group-consciousness, and little concern with group cohesiveness beyond the extended family (Robarchek and Robarchek 1989, 1992). In many societies where there is intense external warfare, mechanisms exist to restrain conflict within the group and to promote internal solidarity so that a united front can be presented to the outside. No such social or cultural mechanisms exist among the Waorani, however. Nothing resembling the fraternal interest groups that Otterbein (1980) found often accompanying external warfare exist here. With bilateral kinship, there are no lineages or clans to provide a framework for mutual obligation and support. With the exception of witchcraft, there is little concern with the "supernatural" and, with no tutelary spirits and few animistic beliefs, there are no communal religious rituals or responsibilities to link people together. There is also no strong gender dichotomy, and thus none of the men's clubs or men's houses so prominent elsewhere in the region to bind individuals into interdependent groups. Every settlement, every kin group, and in the final analysis, every individual remains an independent entity (cf. Robarchek and Robarchek 1992).

With such an "atomized" social system, there is little concern with group cohesion, and thus no social mechanisms for the resolution of disputes and no institutionalized or internalized controls on violence. The pattern of cross-cousin marriage splits the kindred into classificatory siblings, on the one hand, and potential spouses and affines, on the other, the latter being those with whom conflict is most likely to occur. There is no primary reference group beyond the extended family that acts to restrain individual behavior. There are, thus, few constraints, social, cultural or psychological, on the actions of individuals.

In such a context, with no social bases for the creation of mutual interest groups or the suppression of self-interests, few obligations among individuals, few integrating social mechanisms, little expectation of or interest in group cohesiveness, and no mechanisms for resolving disputes, the conflicts that are inevitable in any society—and the anger and hostility that they can engender—were, until recently, given free rein. Any dispute was likely to escalate into a spearing raid which, in turn, called for endless retaliation, and all of this remains a looming possibility.

Waorani themselves recognize that this is a fragile peace with few cultural and social underpinnings. The desire not to be drawn back into the vendettas of the past is very real but, at this point, it is a superimposition on top of the pre-contact consciousness, not a replacement of it. The old pattern remains latent, and the potential for a return to violence is ever-present, as can be seen in a homicide rate that, relative to other societies, remains high, and in the continuing obsession with the raids and killings of the recent past. These are constant topics of conversation, and even the attempt to elicit genealogies invariably calls forth accounts of the violent demise of deceased relatives, told in elaborate, graphic, and gory detail. Avoiding a return to this state is an immediate, pragmatic objective for most of the people, but there has been little time to develop a commitment to values of peacefulness in the abstract or to produce the psychological orientations and the social and cultural institutions necessary to sustain it (cf. chapter 6, Gregor and Robarchek). The endless spearing stories reflect the ambiguity and ambivalence toward violence in the current culture and in individuals' consciousness. They express a guilty fascination with the violence of the recent past, while at the same time keeping

it constantly on view as a reminder of a world to which most people profoundly do not want to return. This preoccupation with violence was, in
fact, one of the few psychocultural similarities that we found to the
Semai, who are also obsessed with the possibility of violence and who see
wholesale slaughter lurking behind every minor conflict (cf. Robarchek
1977, 1989).

In this new culture of peace, lacking as it does other internalized or
institutionalized controls on conflict and violence, Christianity looms
large. While Christian theology has been little assimilated—for most, a
few bible stories and a belief in a God who abhors killing—the cessation
of the killing is directly attributed to the Christian message and to the
women who brought it. "We were down to almost two people," one vet-
eran of many raids told us; "if it had not been for Nimo and Dayume
(Rachel Saint and one of the young Waorani women who first accompanied her into the forest), we would all be dead now." Other attitudes, values, and behaviors promoted by the missionaries have not gained such
widespread acceptance: charity seems notably lacking, sexual access to
spouses of real and classificatory siblings continues, as does at least some
polygyny and infanticide; but for many Waorani, being peaceful and
being Christian are indissolubly linked.

Most of the larger settlements hold Sunday services, which virtually
the entire community attends (almost the only event that brings the entire
community together), usually in a building especially constructed for the
purpose. In most communities, these are entirely under the control and
direction of the Waorani. Individual Waorani, both men and women,
take the lead by leading prayers and reciting Bible stories. There are only
three missionaries, all women, regularly in residence on the reserve; two
of these are Bible translators who live in the village of Tiwaeno for periods of two months or so at a time working with linguistic informants, but
who do no direct proselytizing (although, of course, their responses to
village gossip from their informants certainly conveys attitudes and judgments). The other resides permanently in the largest settlement on the
reserve, which has grown up around her headquarters and which is a
center for acculturation. (She describes herself as "an old-time missionary," and most certainly *does* proselytize.)

In the settlement where we made our headquarters, the meetings—
conducted entirely by Waorani themselves—generally began with the
recitation of one or more Bible stories—Noah and the Ark, Samson and
Delilah—and so on. These seem to be told primarily as literally true
accounts of the past, and there is little attempt to extract morals or messages from them. If there have been reports of a dispute that threatens to

turn violent, a prayer—a public reaffirmation of the community's commitment to peace—is offered to forestall that possibility. There may also be discussion of other problems—illnesses, injuries, snakebites, and so on—that have been rumored or reported on the reserve, and prayers offered for their resolution. The concern with violence, however, is clearly the focus of the entire ritual (cf. Yost 1981). Being Christian and participating in the weekly church services are powerful and public symbols of commitment to the new culture and the new "civilized" self image that both reflects and supports it: "We are not `Auca' (savages)," says an old man, "we are Waorani."[6]

Today, when there are rumors of a dispute anywhere on the reserve, a great deal of concern is expressed everywhere. The participants are urged not to escalate the conflict into violence, and prayers are offered that the killing not begin again. Even when a killing does occur, there is now no retaliation. For example, when a group of young men speared an old woman several years ago, the woman's daughter (the young woman who accompanied the first missionaries into the jungle, now the politically most powerful Waorani woman on the reserve) reportedly refused even to acknowledge that her mother had been murdered. The old woman's brother, himself a renowned killer, said recently, "In the old days, I would have killed them all by now, but we don't spear any more."[7]

Thus, while the potential for (and indeed the actuality of) occasional spearings continues, the large-scale pattern of incessant raiding was given up remarkably quickly and easily. Most individuals, when given the opportunity, agreed to forego old grievances and animosities and to abandon revenge raiding, once they were convinced that others would do the same. Although the culture of war had a momentum of its own that had carried it from generation to generation, when new opportunities and new cultural information were presented, most individuals altered their motivational complexes—and their behavior—in pursuit of different, previously unobtainable goals, such as personal security and access to new goods and to a new pool of potential spouses. The result was that a cultural pattern of intense internal and external raiding that had persisted for at least five generations was abandoned. The rapidity of the transformation—a matter of months for individual bands and less than a decade for virtually the entire society—can be explained only as a consequence of the Waorani's conscious striving to accomplish what they themselves wanted to do—to escape the killing.

According to our informants, they had on many occasions tried to reduce the level of the violence. Individual bands had tried to make peace with their enemies, but the efforts inevitably failed when some long-standing grudge led one or another individual or group to violate the truce. There were no social mechanisms to permit either initial peaceful contacts between enemies or the growth of trust, nor were there any cultural values promoting peacefulness beyond the immediate kindred. Instead, Waorani values promoted individualism and demanded blood vengeance for the deaths of close kin.

Initial peaceful contacts were made possible by the technology of the missionaries, and the alternative value system that they provided urged and facilitated the abandonment of the vendettas. But a desire on the part of the Waorani, independent of the wishes of the missionaries, to end the killing was what made the transformation possible. Further evidence of this is the fact that several groups on the reserve whose members do not see themselves as Christians, and one group off the reserve that was never missionized, have also stopped raiding.

The abandonment of warfare took place prior to changes in the underlying "infrastructure," either techno-environmental or social, which most current theories of warfare (and social science theories generally) see as determining such higher level "superstructural" features as warfare; and it preceded major changes in ideology—such as, world view, self-image, and values—as well. These data run counter to current deterministic theories of warfare and social action generally and instead give support to systems theory-based models such as those proposed by Ervin Laszlo (1969, 1972) and Ludwig von Bertalanffy (1981), who argue that causality in human action systems often proceeds from higher to lower levels of systemic organization.

The Waorani themselves seem to agree. From their perspective, individual decisions and actions could still bring a reversion to the old pattern, and this fear and concern is reflected in the public prayers and frequent exhortations to avoid conflict and violence and, in the cases of the recent killings, to forego retaliation. In documenting this change from violence to peacefulness, we have the opportunity to observe the deliberate creation of a new culture pattern or, possibly, the reversion to the old one. The outcome, in the view of the Waorani, is still in doubt, as they consciously strive to construct a culture of peace.

Conclusion

The major theoretical controversy in the anthropological study of war and peace in preindustrial societies is over the issue of the relative significance of "material" factors (e.g., ecological and biological) versus "motivational" factors (sociocultural and psychological) (see, for instance, Chagnon 1988; Harris 1974, 1979; Ross 1980; Bennett Ross 1980). The data presented here argue for abandoning the unproductive dichotomy of material versus ideological "causes" of warfare in favor of a consideration of the relationships between the options and constraints of the material world, and the cultural and psychological constructions of reality within which human beings are motivated to engage in violence or nonviolence. A number of the contributions to this volume offer support for such an approach, and they show how far we have come theoretically from the "superorganic" conception of culture that informs the various deterministic approaches that have dominated anthropological thinking about war and peace for the past three decades.

The importance of human values and decisions in the construction of peaceful social systems is a thread linking many of the chapters in this volume. Both Staub and Monteville emphasize the centrality of values in the shaping of peaceful ways of life, and Tuzin sees the persistence of the peaceful values of an earlier culture within the Tambaran cult of war (just as we see the persistence of a pre-contact world view and values within the incipient Waorani culture of peace). Tuzin also shows the cyclical transition from war to peace among the Ilahita to be a collective decision, the result of a collective shift of opinion within the society. Crenshaw documents the importance of decisions, transformations of identity, and small-group dynamics in shaping courses of action in terrorist groups.

We have argued here that a crucial factor in the Waorani transition to peacefulness was the incorporation of new information into the individual and cultural schemata that constituted their maps of reality, thus permitting individuals, bands, and ultimately the society as a whole to consciously choose the path of peacefulness. Tuzin's argument that peace and war are each conceivable only from the perspective of the other is clearly relevant here. As in the case of the proverbial fish that could not discover water because it could not imagine an alternative, war (and, thereby, peace) were transparent to the Waorani as long as they were immersed in the culture of war. When the possibility of an alternative state was presented (in the form of new information about the outside world provided by the missionaries and the returned refugees), both war and peace ceased to be transparent, and alternative possibilities could then be consciously entertained. (This may also cast some light on the striking similarity of Semai and Waorani in their obsessive concern with violence, even in times of peace: by keeping the image of war alive, they do not need the reality of it to keep peace from becoming transparent [see also Robarchek 1977, 1989; chapter 6, herein, Gregor and Robarchek]).

Gregor and Robarchek's analysis of Semai and Mehinaku peacefulness emphasizes their psychological, social, and cultural underpinnings
and highlights the significance of the Waorani as a sort of minimalist
counterpoint to these "developed" peace systems. Institutionally unsup-
ported peacefulness such as that of the Waorani is highly unstable and
vulnerable, however, as can be seen in the relative ease of reversion to
warfare and violence described by Gordon and Meggitt for highland
New Guinea (1985). Waorani peacefulness—newly emerged and similarly lacking psychological, social, or cultural underpinnings—is currently being sustained largely by the force of conscious social will; and,
as the Waorani themselves see clearly, the ultimate outcome is still in
question.

The fact remains, however, that the Waorani culture of war was deliberately and decisively abandoned. After generations of warfare and raiding and in the absence of major changes—not only in the material realm
of subsistence practices and available resources but also in the ideological realm of values and world view—the Waorani almost overnight
foreswore warfare. In scarcely more than a decade, the entire society
transformed itself from the most violent known into one that is essentially peaceful.[8] When new cultural knowledge—new information and
new perceptions of reality—allowed the formulation of new individual
and social goals, people responded by choosing courses of action based
on what they wanted from this new reality. When the opportunity to
escape the endless cycle of killing presented itself, they seized and implemented it, a powerful testimony to the capacity of human beings to take
their destinies into their own hands.

Epilogue

In 1992–93, we returned to Ecuador to survey groups of Waorani living off the Reserve. Unhappily, we found, as we had suggested might
happen, that violence is on the increase (although the homicide rate is
still less than one-tenth that of the pre-contact level). In the intervening
years, oil exploration and extraction have begun to have serious impacts
on the Waorani homeland. Most destructive is the continuing construction of pipelines and of the roads necessary to service them. This has led
to a greatly increased frequency of contact with outsiders and to increasing colonization of traditional Waorani lands. Within the past several
years, there have been at least two raids launched against suspected
Quichua sorcerers with whom the Waorani had ongoing relations. In
both cases, the suspected witches and their wives and children were

speared to death. The Ecuadorian government, wary of creating an incident that might attract additional international attention to the exploitation of the region and its inhabitants, possibly jeopardizing the flow of oil, has maintained a strictly hands-off policy.

In another incident, repeated incursions (reportedly promoted by a journalist seeking an adventure story for a European magazine) by an off-reservation band into the territory of the "unpacified" Tageiri (Tage's band), finally resulted in an ambush and the spearing death of one of the invaders. That, in turn, has generated threats of a new vendetta against the Tageiri. The final chapter in the Waorani odyssey obviously remains to be written.

Notes

Initial field research in 1987 and the subsequent comparative analysis of Semai and Waorani data have been supported by research grants from the Harry Frank Guggenheim Foundation. Additional field research in 1992–93 was made possible by research grants from the United States Institute of Peace and the Harry Frank Guggenheim Foundation. We gratefully acknowledge their support and encouragement .

1. We want to thank Dr. Katherine Peeke, Rosie Jung, and Rachel Saint for sharing their recollections of this period of early contacts with us.

2. This is a variant of the ubiquitous *chicha* drink of the western Amazon, but instead of being made of sweet manioc and left to ferment, it is made of mashed and boiled ripe plantains and is drunk fresh.

3. *Wao* is singular, and means *person*; *Waorani* is plural.

4. According to a missionary who came to the reserve during this period as a nurse, sickness was another important factor. The isolated groups of Waorani were very susceptible to introduced illnesses, especially respiratory infections, and each new group was soon swept by illness so that, as she put it, "They were too sick to fight, even if they had wanted to." The tragic error of concentrating so vulnerable a population in one location soon became apparent when a polio epidemic swept through the community causing paralysis and a number of deaths. Following that, a policy of decentralization led to the reestablishment of the pattern of widely scattered hamlets that prevails today over most of the reserve.

5. World view was inferred from two kinds of evidence: cultural data (magical and other religious rituals and beliefs, ethnomedical beliefs, and so on) and individual data (expressions derived from interviews and participant observation). There appears to be little difference in these expressions and beliefs between early and late arrivals to the reserve, or between them and those who remain off the reserve. Informants' accounts of spearing raids and other activities and events from the pre-contact period show similar value sets.

6. Other such public symbolic statements include the abandonment of a string around the waist as the only article of clothing and of the large balsa-wood ear spools, both of which once marked the wearers as "Auca."

7. Our thanks to James Yost for giving us access to the unpublished interview from

which this quote was drawn.

8. The rapid transformations from warfare to peacefulness is, in itself, not unique to the Waorani (see, for instance, Meggitt 1977; Herdt 1987), nor is the sense of relief at having escaped from a long established warfare system (see, for instance, Brown 1986; Herdt 1987; Billings 1991).

References

Bennett Ross, Jane. 1980. Ecology and the Problem of the Tribe: A Critique of the Hobbesian Model of Preindustrial Warfare. In *Beyond Myths of Culture*, ed. Eric B. Ross, pp. 33-60. New York: Academic Press.

von Bertalanffy, Ludwig. 1981. *A Systems View of Man*. Boulder, Colo.: Westview.

Billings, Dorothy. 1991. Cultural Style and Solutions to Conflict. *Journal of Peace Research* 29 (3): 249–262.

Brown, Paula. 1986. Simbu Aggression and the Drive to Win. *Anthropological Quarterly* 59 (4): 165–170.

Calhoun, John B. 1972. Plight of the Ik and Kaiadilt Is Seen As a Chilling Possible End for Man. *Smithsonian* 2 (8).

Chagnon, Napoleon. 1988. Life Histories, Blood Revenge, and Warfare in a Tribal Society. *Science* 239 (Feb. 2, 1988): 985–992.

Elliot, Elisabeth. 1957. *Through Gates of Splendor*. New York: Harper & Brothers.

Ferguson, R. Brian. 1990. Blood of the Leviathan: Western Contacts and Warfare in Amazonia. *American Ethnologist* 17 (2): 237–257.

Gordon, Robert and Mervyn Meggitt. 1985. *Law and Order in the New Guinea Highlands: Encounters with Enga*. Hanover, N.H.: University Press of New England.

Harner, Michael J. 1972. *The Jivaro: People of the Sacred Waterfalls*. Garden City, N.Y.: Doubleday Harris.

Marvin. 1974. *Cows, Pigs, Wars and Witches: The Riddles of Culture*. New York: Random House.

———. 1979. The Yanomamo and the Causes of War in Band and Village Societies. In *Brazil: Anthropological Perspectives*, ed. Maxine L. Margolis and William E. Carter, pp. 121–132. New York: Colombia University Press.

Henry, Jules. 1963. *Culture Against Man*. New York: Random House.

Herdt, Gilbert. 1987. *The Sambia: Ritual and Gender in New Guinea*. New York: Holt, Rinehart and Winston.

Knauft, Bruce M. 1987. Reconsidering Violence in Simple Human Societies: Homicide among the Gebusi of New Guinea. *Current Anthropology* 28 (4): 457–499.

Laszlo, Ervin. 1969. *System, Structure and Experience*. New York: Gordon and Breach.

———. 1972 .*The Systems View of the World*. New York: George Braziller.

Meggitt, Mervyn. 1977. *Blood is Their Argument*. Palo Alto, Calif.: Mayfield.

Otterbein, K. F. 1980. Internal War: A Cross-Cultural Study. In *The War System: An Interdisciplinary Approach*, ed. R. A. Falk and S. S. Kim. pp. 204-223. Boulder: Westview Press.

Robarchek, Clayton A. 1977. Frustration, Aggression, and the Nonviolent Semai. *American Ethnologist* 4 (4): 762–779.

———. 1988. How Do We Get Some Meat? (1): Generalized Reciprocity and Semai World View. Paper delivered before the 65th Annual Meetings of the Central States Anthropological Society, March 24–27, 1988, St. Louis.

———. 1989. Primitive Warfare and the Ratomorphic Image of Mankind. *American Anthro-*

pologist 91 (4): 903–920.

———. 1994. Plains Warfare and the Anthropology of War. In *Skeletal Biology in the Great Plains: An Interdisciplinary View*, ed. Douglas Owsley and Richard Jantz, 307–316. Washington: Smithsonian Institution.

Robarchek, Clayton A. and Carole J. Robarchek. 1988. Reciprocities and Realities: World View, Peacefulness and Violence among Semai and Waorani. Paper presented at the 87th Annual Meetings of the American Anthropological Association, November 16–20, 1988, Phoenix.

———. 1989. The Waorani: From Warfare to Peacefulness. *The World and I* 4 (1): 624–635.

———. 1992. Cultures of War and Peace: A Comparative Study of Waorani and Semai. In *Aggression and Peacefulness in Humans and Other Primates*, ed. James Silverberg and J. Patrick Gray, pp. 189–213. New York: Oxford University Press.

Robarchek, Carole J. 1988. How Do We Get Some Meat? (2): Balanced Reciprocity and Waorani World View. Paper delivered before the 65th Annual Meetings of the Central States Anthropological Society, March 24–27, 1988, St. Louis.

Ross, Eric B. 1980. *Beyond Myths of Culture*. New York: Academic Press.

Saint, Rachel. 1964. Aucas and Cannibals: How the Aucas Came to Ecuador. Norman, Oklahoma: Summer Institute of Linguistics.

Sapir, Edward. 1924. Culture, Genuine and Spurious. *American Journal of Sociology* 29: 401–429.

Turnbull, Colin. 1972. *The Mountain People*. New York: Simon and Schuster.

Wallace, A. F. C. 1956. Revitalization Movements. *American Anthropologist* 58: 264–281

———. 1957. Mazeway Disintegration: The Individual's Perception of Socio-Cultural Disorganization. *Human Organization* 16: 23–27.

———. 1961. *Culture and Personality*. New York: Random House.

Wallis, Ethel. 1960. *The Dayuma Story: Life under Auca Spears*. New York: Harper & Brothers.

———. 1973. *Aucas Downriver*. New York: Harper & Row.

Yost, J. A. 1981. Twenty Years of Contact: The Mechanisms of Change in Wao (Auca) Culture. In *Cultural Transformations and Ethnicity in Modern Ecuador*, ed. N. A. Whitten, pp. 677–704. Urbana: University of Illinois Press.

Yost, J. A. and Patricia M. Kelley. 1983. Shotguns, Blowguns and Spears: The Analysis of Technological Efficiency. In *Adaptive Responses of Native Amazonians*, ed. R. B. Hames and W. Vickers, pp. 189–224. New York: Academic Press.

FIVE

State Systems and
Cycles of Peace and War

8

War, Peace, and the Collapse of a Native American Civilization: Lessons for Contemporary Systems of Conflict

ARTHUR A. DEMAREST

■ In his discussion of primate aggression and reconciliation, Frans de Waal reminds us that enduring biological and cultural systems are homeostatic. They shift from one equilibrium point to another, so that one cannot state with any degree of confidence what their normal state is, other than that of being able to restore themselves. From this perspective, peace and aggression are themselves part of a larger cycle of conflict and restorative mechanisms that alternately damage and repair the social fabric. In chapter 8, Arthur Demarest examines the changing nature of a system of war and peace that maintained the relative stability of the ancient Maya. For over a millennium Maya civilization endured as political relations alternated between culturally constrained war and strong networks of peaceful trade, alliance, and intermarriage. Reconciliation, restitution, and restraint balanced aggression. Professor Demarest documents how, in the case of one Maya region, equilibrium was shattered in the eighth century by an intensification of warfare. He finds specific lessons for contemporary cultures in terms of leadership and relationship to environment. In this compelling essay, he uses data from the archaeological investigations he directs in Guatemala to help solve the mystery behind the collapse of the ancient Maya—one of the major riddles of world cultural history.

STUDIES OF the nature and paths to peace address these issues from the perspectives of a wide range of disciplines and data. The disciplinary bases stretch across psychology, political science, history, ethnography, archaeology, and primatology—in each case with a goal of achieving trans-disciplinary breadth, but with real limitations imposed in each case by the data, methodologies, and perspectives inherent in each scholar's training. Scales of evolutionary and social complexity in recent studies of peace systems range from baboon troops to contemporary industrial states, and the human societies discussed vary from the peaceful Semai and Mehinaku to the warlike Waorani, Yanamamo, and Ik.

I would hope that this chapter might provide an intermediate set of data and arguments on some of these scales. My own researches draw on the data and methodologies of archaeology, history, and ecology, but with the interpretive biases of an anthropologist. The system analyzed here as a springboard for broader interpretations was an archaic state—simple in its technology, pre-market in its economy, but highly stratified. Of greatest potential is the time depth provided by this study. For, as described below, the Classic Maya civilization in the region of study gradually shifted over a millennium from a system of controlled conflict to one of conquest states and finally to one of unrestricted and highly destructive warfare. The functioning and eventual failure of the Classic Maya cultural system may have valuable lessons for present concerns about systems of war and peace. The diachronic perspective provided by Maya history and archaeology allows examination of a conflict-control system affected by many centuries of change in other institutions.

Relevancy: Systems of Peace Versus Systems of Controlled Conflict

Previous studies have concluded that peace, as an absolute state, is very rare in human societies (Otterbein 1970; Sipes 1973; Wiberg 1981; Westing 1982; Gregor 1990, 1994). Violent intrasocietal or intersocietal conflict is characteristic of most areas and periods of the human experience. The most peaceful societies sometimes achieve what Galtung termed "negative peace" through avoidance, isolationism, and/or the occupation of ecologically marginal areas (Galtung 1968). Virtually all relatively "peaceful" societies are small in scale and complexity. Many exemplify what Thomas Gregor (Introduction) has termed "separative peace." Such peace systems provide a fertile source of theory on personal/psychological/attitudinal factors involved in establishing and maintaining peace. Their exceptional nature suggests the limits of possibility and helps formulate general hypotheses regarding structural principles for peace systems that might often be equally applicable to complex societies.

Still, contemporary world problems, as well as regional and ethnic conflicts, more often deal with complex societies or interaction between complex and "simple" political and social groups. The more interactive mechanisms involved in what Gregor has called "sociative peace" and "restorative peace" may be more directly relevant to such complex systems and to problems of peaceful relations today. Also note that most complex societies are already in a state of intermittent warfare (at the very least). Any specific proposal for collective international action in today's world must begin by dealing with circumstances of ongoing intergroup conflict and warfare that we can seek to restrict, control, or limit before moving on to proposals for broader attitudinal change, educational programs, and/or institutional mechanisms to stabilize circumstances of long-term peace.

Thus, I agree with the other authors in this volume that peace studies have been neglected, but I am not surprised that most discussions of peace center upon its presumed opposite of warfare or related forms of violent aggression. I concur with Tuzin's philosophical perspective, expressed in chapter 1, that the two conditions are inseparable; the presence of even the concept of "peace" is built upon a familiarity with war. In this sense, even societies like the Semai and Mehinaku are examples of conflict control systems. They are merely extraordinarily successful in these efforts. Clearly, consideration of peace systems must include research on systems of restraint, limitations, and control of inter-group relations, including warfare. As I hope to convey below, in the case of the Maya, the structural principles involved are often the same, and the lessons of such case studies may be applicable to contemporary problems.

The history of the rise and fall of Maya civilization represents a long-term experiment in the functioning of a culturally adaptive system of warfare. The Maya were never a "peaceful" society, yet for most of Maya history even their most violent confrontations were defined in such a way as to prevent the unraveling of the delicate political order and the ecological foundations of their civilization. The evolution of the society (until about A.D. 600) and its decline (especially from A.D. 750 to 900) are closely linked to the success and failure of its system of conflict. The challenge that the Maya faced, as we face today, was to mitigate a landscape of ongoing conflict between complex societies that were themselves built upon social and political inequality. The possible relevance of the study of the Maya is further increased by the fact that these dramas were played out on the ecological stage of the rain forest, where the activities of human civilization were sometimes near the limits of the environment's capacity to sustain them.

The Classic Maya Civilization:
The Mystery of Its Success and the Lessons of Its Failure

The ancient Maya civilization of Central America has long been known for its spectacular art and architecture, for its achievements in science, and for its development of the New World's only true writing system. During the Classic period florescence (A.D. 300–900) and for nearly a thousand years before, the ancient Maya lords ruled a network of kingdoms in the Peten jungle of northern Guatemala and adjacent portions of Mexico, Belize, and Honduras (see figure 8.1). Many of their capital centers possessed fine stone architecture, palaces, temples, mural and sculptural art, royal tombs, and hieroglyphic stairways. From recent

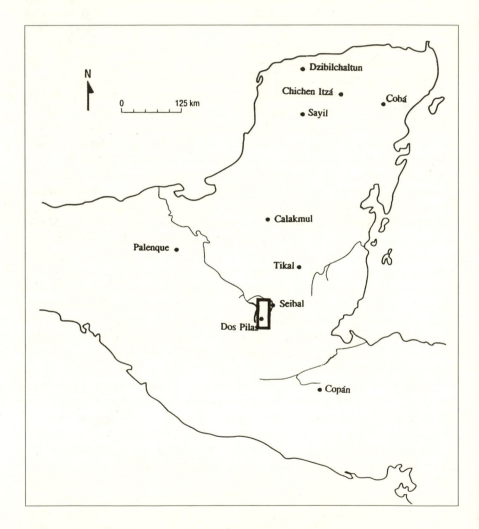

FIGURE 8.1. Map of Mesoamerica showing some major sites of the Maya area and the Petexbatun region (close-up in figure 8.7).

settlement pattern studies and ecological research, we know that some cities had populations of over 40,000 and that they were supported by a complex system of agriculture, which included the use of terraces, canals, and, in some cases, artificially raised fields in swamp zones (Matheny 1976; Turner and Harrison 1983). Hundreds of miles of well-built stone roads formed a network of interaction between these great centers. The recent revolution in Maya hieroglyphic decipherment has now revealed to us a detailed view of the political history of this civilization (e.g., Culbert, ed., 1991).

The Ecological Mystery

The explanation of the rise and the success of the Maya civilization has always presented a challenge to archaeologists and anthropologists interested in cultural evolution (see for example, Adams, ed., 1977). Unlike the more arid environments in which most early states flourished, the Classic Maya culture was one of the few high civilizations that flourished in a lowland jungle. Moreover, their settlement strategy was dispersed rather than nucleated. Most specific models of cultural evolution have emphasized the role of ecological parameters such as geographical circumscription, irrigation in arid environments, and environmental diversity. Yet, the Maya raised their cities and ceremonial centers in seeming contradiction to ecological rationality, achieving their florescence in a dense, subtropical rain forest with generally thin and poor soils, unstable fresh water supplies, few navigable rivers, and *less* environmental diversity or environmental circumscription than most areas of Mesoamerica. Interpreters of ancient Maya culture history have puzzled over a possible relationship between the Maya civilization and its unusual ecological circumstances as a rain forest civilization.

The Mystery of Its Collapse

To scholars and laymen, however, an even more intriguing aspect of the Maya civilization has been the continuing mystery of its collapse. In the southern lowland area of the Peten jungle of Guatemala and Mexico, most of the Maya kingdoms rapidly disintegrated and were gradually covered by the dense rain forest of that region after the ninth century. In many subregions of the southern Maya lowlands, monumental construction ceased, political order disintegrated, and population rapidly declined. Even today, the only traces of human presence in many areas of the Peten jungle are the overgrown ruins of the ancient Maya centers. Despite a century of exploration, the fall of the Maya civilization continues to be one of the enduring mysteries of modern archaeology. Proposed theories for the Maya collapse have emphasized epidemic disease, earthquakes, climatic change, economic competition, invasion, and almost every other possible human or environmental calamity (see, for example, Culbert, ed., 1973, Culbert 1977; Sabloff and Andrews, eds., 1985).

The Thesis

Here, I present a trial synthesis of the results to date of an ongoing six-year, multidisciplinary project that is addressing the questions surrounding the unique success and ultimate failure of this civilization in one region of the Peten rain forest. One preliminary conclusion at this point is of direct relevance to this book's discussion: the two millennia of success and the ultimate failure of southern lowland Maya civilization can only be understood with an appreciation of changes in its system of political competition and warfare. In this speculative reconstruction I will argue that the success of Maya civilization was facilitated by a gradual adaptation to the rain forest environment that included a system of warfare defined to allow political competition and even conquest, but without destructive impact on settlement patterns or field systems. As warfare and elite competition accelerated in the Classic period, Maya civilization in the region of our studies unraveled—with a large hegemony disintegrating into smaller units and eventually into units of lower levels of sociopolitical complexity. By the tenth century, this region, the Petexbatun, was largely abandoned. Limitations placed by rain forest ecology on the Maya system might help explain the impact of increasingly intensive warfare on lowland Maya civilization.

Possible reason for decline

Maya War and Peace: The Archaeological and Historical Evidence

The "Discovery" of the Warlike Maya

Since 1960, archaeology has transformed our understanding of the ancient Maya. Until that time, scholars regarded Maya civilization as an almost ethereal system of ceremonial centers ruled by peaceful priest-kings (e.g., Thompson 1954). As a result of new archaeological methods and techniques, however, we now have a very different view of the Maya (e.g., Webster 1975, 1977; Ball 1977; Demarest 1978; Marcus 1973). Particularly critical to this revolution in Maya archaeology were breakthroughs in Maya hieroglyphic decipherment. The deciphered monuments unmasked the Maya rulers as all-too-human warlords. It appears that the bulk of the Maya hieroglyphic texts actually document the ascent, marriages, alliances, and, especially, the wars of Maya rulers in the Classic period (e.g., Culbert 1988; Culbert, ed., 1991, Marcus 1974, 1976; Mathews 1985).

This new archaeological and hieroglyphic evidence shows that the Maya were as violent as any other state-level society of the New World. This fact is most clearly demonstrable after about A.D. 550, when hieroglyphic texts, art, and iconography indicate almost continual warfare between the elites of adjacent city-states. The violence in Maya society had its roots in a long Mesoamerican tradition of warfare, conquest, and sacrifice (e.g., Baudez and Mathews 1979; Boone, ed., 1984; Freidel 1986; Schele 1984; Demarest 1984; Stuart 1985; Schele and Miller 1986). Most major ceremonial occasions involved rituals of public sacrifice including self-laceration and bloodletting by rulers, as well as sacrifice of captive kings and nobles taken in battle. The price of defeat and capture was public humiliation, torture, and sometimes decapitation. Furthermore, archaeological, textual, and iconographic evidence have shown that the power and prestige of ruling dynasties depended to a large extent on their success in battle, conquest, and intimidation.

The warlike nature of the Maya civilization is now accepted, but that leaves us with several major contradictions in our current views of Maya warfare. Extensive review of mapped Maya settlements (Demarest 1977, 1978) indicates that before the eighth century relatively few sites were fortified or even placed in defensible positions (cf. Webster 1976; Graham 1967). The vast majority of Maya centers display dispersed residential patterns in open, indefensible locations. Prior to the Late Classic period in the Maya area, there is little evidence of burning of settlements, mass sacrifice of war captives, or other manifestations of truly intensive warfare. We can speculate that warfare in the Maya world had, along with other cultural systems, come to achieve a balance between its economic and political benefits and the physical effects of violence and destruction. We can also assume that Maya demographic and economic patterns had similarly come to adapt successfully to the fragility and structural characteristics of their environment and subsistence systems.

The Maya System of Controls on Warfare

In 1978, I argued that such adaptations were aided by a widely held code of ethics or rules of engagement that may have limited the destructive or destabilizing effect of Maya warfare (Demarest 1978). For example, attacks on fields or domestic areas may have been forbidden, with most conflict being channeled into confrontations between elites. Such proposed rules of engagement were seen to have restrained warfare and perhaps set limits that would explain the rarity of fortifications before the eighth century, as well as the Maya's dispersed settlement patterns and the continual extensive peaceful contact among Maya centers (Demarest

1977, 1978). While I observed such norms to be the general case in the Maya lowlands, I speculated that regional variability might reflect more intensive warfare, including fortification systems, that seemed to align with probable ethnic boundaries.

Since the mid-seventies, fifteen years of archaeological and epigraphic research have demonstrated an even greater degree of both regional and chronological variability in Maya warfare (see for example, Chase and Chase 1987, 1989; Chase, Grube, and Chase 1991; Demarest 1990, 1992; Demarest and Inomata 1992; Demarest and Valdes 1994; Freidel 1981, 1986; Freidel, Schele, and Parker 1993; Schele and Freidel 1990; Webster 1976). Furthermore, warfare clearly had a very critical political and economic impact including the tentative definition by archaeological and epigraphic evidence of conquest states based on centers like Caracol (Chase and Chase 1987, 1989; Chase 1992), Dos Pilas (Demarest, Valdes, et al. 1991; Demarest and Valdes 1994; Mathews and Willey 1991), Calakmul (Folan 1992; Marcus 1993; Martin 1993; Martin and Grube 1994), and Tikal (Adams 1986; Adams, ed., 1984; Culbert 1991). These new evidences on Maya warfare correspond well with representations like the famous murals from the palace of the site of Bonampak that display the equipment, rituals, and grim results of Maya wars (Miller 1986). These murals show them to be bloody affairs, ending in torture, sacrifice, and glory for the victors.

Yet in many cases, Maya wars served largely as a mechanism for maintaining an equilibrium between polities of roughly equal size, so-called "peer polities" (Freidel 1986; Hammond 1974, 1991; Mathews 1988, 1991; Renfrew and Cherry, eds., 1986; Sabloff 1986). Maya warfare involved the participation of rulers and subordinates from allied centers. As such, it helped to define larger systems of inter-polity alliance and contact. War helped define and channel inter-center relations and may have helped cement the relations between kingdoms while maintaining clear political boundaries (Freidel 1986). Thus, despite continual conflict and conquests, a *dynamic* equilibrium was maintained because Maya warfare occurred in a broader structured context of relations between city-states, relations which included trade, cohesion in stylistic canons in art and artifacts, extensive systems of exchange and redistribution, inter-center elite marriages, and a shared religious and political ideology (Freidel 1986; Sabloff 1986; Hammond 1991; Demarest 1992). Warfare did affect political power, and, even as in chiefdom level societies, it probably usually involved some degree of economic tribute (see, for example, Carneiro 1990). Yet, some of the destructive effects of warfare were apparently kept in check by interaction networks and by shared values on most aspects of culture, including rules of engagement.

Networks of Dependence: Lowland Maya Conflict and Conflict Control Systems

In all world regions and periods, there is some degree of cultural restraint on war. Highly structured systems that place limits on conflict are common cross-culturally (e.g., Evans-Pritchard 1940; Rappaport 1967). These are the inverse of what Galtung (1968: 487–493, 1981, 1985) called *"positive* peace systems". The dynamic-equilibrium of most Maya warfare not only rested on cultural constraints, but on such positive systems of complex inter-societal interaction and mutual political and economic need—very much like the positive incentives for constraint of conflict that exist today between industrialized, capitalist nations. Such systems are based on cooperation, integration, and the establishment of extensive networks of relationships that crosscut the boundaries of the societies involved. For example, Gluckman (1955:11–20) and Colson (1953) have shown that exchange of goods and services creates common interests among parallel subgroups of potentially conflicting societies. As in modern times, classes of merchants, politicians, astronomers, scribes, and transport specialists had shared interests in limiting truly destructive conflict. Indeed, these class interests were as critical to them as their "national" identity within each kingdom, if not more so. This division of loyalties and interests, together with the positive incentives of economic and intellectual exchanges, created constituencies for peaceful relations, or at least for restraining the most destructive modes of warfare; similar restraints apply to world politics in postnuclear times. Furthermore, interaction between such interest groups helps to create an "international" culture across political boundaries that further discourages disruptive warfare (cf. Teft 1975: 700–703; Galtung 1968; Levine 1961: 13–14; Gregor 1990, 1994, this volume).

Certainly, the Classic-period Maya of the southern lowlands existed in such an elaborate network of inter-society relations. As described above, most of the art, writing, iconography, and finer artifacts of the Maya reflect and celebrate such intense, positive inter-polity interaction. An intense "cultural homology" of elites in the Maya world was created by inter-elite marriages, periodic ritual events and visits, ceremonial exchange of high status goods, inter-center participation in dynastic rites of passage (births, marriages, funerals), exchanges of artisans and scribes, and other forms of inter-elite contact. More cynically viewed, they also marked and reinforced common class interests. Non-elite-level economic exchanges are equally well documented in the Maya area. Trace-element analyses help identify inter-polity networks of exchange in chert, obsidian, and ceramics (e.g., Shafer and Hester 1983, 1986; McAnany 1986; Bishop 1980; Bishop et al. 1986; Ball 1993; Rice 1987), and these imply trade systems that also carried perishable materials such as chocolate beans, salt, feathers, wood, shell, textiles, and even some foodstuffs. Such exchanges also carry all manner of cultural concepts (e.g., Wobst 1977). As a result, shared values within the lowland area even reached to the non-elite level from domestic ceramic styles to household religion (e.g., McAnany 1993). Like the intra-tribal exchange systems of the Mundurucu (Murphy 1957), or the Xingu (Gregor 1990, 1994), the Maya peer-polity networks may have created a setting that encouraged common interests and, implicitly or explicitly, shared definitions of appropriate interaction, including warfare.

Paradoxically, one could even argue that Maya warfare itself often functioned for most of Maya history as an element in such an interactive system. It leveled inter-polity conflicts with a minimum of destructive costs. It allowed for conflict resolution between elites, especially regarding dynastic succession, and allowed the establishment of regional political hierarchies with a low destructive cost to the environment and settlement patterns. The warfare itself was also followed by rituals, public gatherings, and tribute exchanges, often attended by elites of other centers, which brought great prestige and thus economic benefit to the victorious polity. Such benefits included booty, but most importantly they probably included greater access to larger pools of corvée labor. Such greater access to labor was to some extent due to the taking of captives and probably "labor taxes" as tribute from conquered centers. An even more important factor, however, was the increased prestige of the victorious center—enhanced by stone monuments and public ritual—which allowed their rulers to attract labor, satellite centers, and allies (cf. Demarest 1992).

Possible Ecological Bases of Maya Conflict and
Conflict Controls: "Spaceship Peten"

Very few cultures have been able to support very complex societies and large populations on the thin soils and dispersed resources of rain forests. Perhaps the greatest achievement of the Maya was to raise and maintain their city-states in the Peten rain forest for over 1,500 years without destroying its ecology. Note that today the combined efforts of USAID Guatemala and many international agencies still have failed to come up with a subsistence strategy that can parallel the Classic Maya success, even at population levels one-fifth the size of those of the Classic Maya states (Dunning and Demarest 1989).

For decades, archaeologists working in the Maya area believed that the Peten could only have sustained small and scattered populations dependent upon highland-style *rosa* (slash-and-burn) agriculture. This view paralleled the general belief that tropical rain forest ecosystems were homogeneously hostile and unsuitable for anything but the most "primitive" of agricultural practices—a position that we now know to be erroneous. Subsequently, the Tikal research and other studies revealed that the Maya had large populations, more concentrated than previously believed, and that at least some forms of intensive agriculture were present including raised fields, terraces, some canals, and significant non-maize crops, such as tubers and arboriculture (e.g., Haviland 1970; Harrison and Turner 1978). This drove Mayanists to the other extreme. They began to see the Peten, and rain forests in general, as environments of limitless possibilities, and they envisioned intensive agricultural systems across wide stretches of the Peten (e.g., Adams 1980, 1983; Harrison and Turner, eds., 1978).

We now know that the truth about human rain forest ecology lies somewhere between these earlier extreme positions. The rain forest is not a rich, limitless environment, nor is it a poor, homogeneous one—rather, it is a rich, *but fragile*, environment. More recently, these rain forest ecosystems have been recognized to be very complex, and it is this complexity that has presented and continues to present both the greatest problems and opportunities for human occupation of such regions. We are now coming to understand that many traditional agricultural subsistence systems employ knowledge and techniques that are finely tuned to specific environmental conditions in tropical ecosystems, most of which act to preserve the integrity and survival of these habitats (Nye and Greenland 1964). Such traditional technologies include conservative shifting cultivation (slash-and-burn or swidden agriculture), complex multicropping schemes, tree-cropping, and intensive "backyard" gardening (Nations and Nigh 1980; Turner and Harrison 1983). The key to understanding rain forest environments is to appreciate their *dispersed* nature. Animal, plant, and human systems successfully adapt to rain forests by mimicking this dispersed nature and complexity (Nations and Nigh 1980; Dunning and Demarest 1989). Thus, it seems probable that Maya civilization was based upon a complex structure of techniques, each in relatively small units, adapted to the limits and possibilities of specific types of econiches. Dispersion of both residential and field systems was critical to lowland Maya success.

It should be clear from this description that the Maya economic system could only tolerate intensive warfare up to a point. Specifically, the needs of defense could not place too great a burden on their rain forest adaptation. Indeed, it would appear that the ecology required that warfare had to be limited in precisely the way that is reflected in the archaeological evidence: outlying settlements, fields, and population centers had to be protected from raiding. This helps to explain the Maya pattern of generally sprawling, indefensible settlements, fields, and centers for most states in the Maya lowlands, as well as the corresponding historical and iconographic evidence that most warfare was focused on specific dynastic disputes, limited economic goals, or ritual ends. Whatever their economic or political benefits, warfare prior to the Late Classic period (A.D. 600–900) did not involve campaigns of long duration, sieges, or destruction of the economic base of other polities. We can make this assertion based on the general settlement patterns, architecture, and site placements of Maya centers—features that remain the best indicators of modes of warfare and defensive responses. Fortresses do exist (e.g., Webster 1976, 1979; Puleston and Callendar 1967; Graham 1967; Demarest 1977; Rice and Rice 1981). However, they are the exception rather than the rule. The general pattern of Maya settlement suggests a system of warfare with clearly defined rules and controls. The epigraphic and iconographic evidence prior to the late sixth century is consistent with this interpretation (e.g., Culbert, ed., 1991). It may be that the specific level of violence and the modes of conflict of lowland Maya warfare represent yet another element explaining the unique success of Maya civilization in the rain forest—inseparable from its general ecological and economic adaptation.

Speculating even more widely, one might argue that the case of the Maya indicates that there may be some validity to Carneiro's correlation of militarism, circumscription, and cultural evolution (Carneiro 1961, 1970; Webster 1975). The Maya never achieved long-term unification of their tiny polities into larger political units. Perhaps one effect of the naturally dispersed ecology of the lowlands was to discourage the formation of larger, integrative polities through sustained and intensive large-scale conflict. Unlike their highland neighbors, the Maya remained for over a thousand years as a system of smaller states in dynamic equilibrium. Larger alliances and conquest states did form but had little long-term stability (Demarest 1992; Freidel 1981, 1992; Marcus 1993; Martin and Grube 1994; cf. Culbert, ed., 1991).).

The Acceleration of Classic Maya Conflict, A.D. 550–800

After the middle of the Classic period at about A.D. 550, there is increasing evidence of militarism in art and historical texts (e.g., Culbert, ed., 1991; Schele and Freidel 1990). Beginning at the end of the sixth century, some polities in the Maya area such as Tikal, Calakmul, Caracol, and Dos Pilas began to place greater emphasis on territorial absorption in their approach to politics and power. While the general nature of conflict and crosscutting inter-site relations remained in place, militarism began to receive more and more emphasis in art and history. Furthermore, recent hieroglyphic decipherments indicate that inter-site alliances began to alter the regional scale of conflicts (Martin 1993; Martin and Grube 1994; Stuart personal communications 1993, 1994). Finally, by the mid-eighth century, at least in the Petexbatun region, the rules of engagement and control of warfare truly began to break down, impacting on all aspects of the culture. By A.D. 761 defensive considerations began to lead the Maya in the Petexbatun region to change many aspects of the economic, political, and ecological adaptations that had sustained them successfully in the region for many centuries.

The Intensification of Militarism in the Eighth Century:
New Evidence from the Petexbatun Region

From 1989 to 1994, a team of archaeologists, hieroglyphic specialists, geographers, and other scientists conducted a large-scale project exploring the issues of the nature of the Maya peace/conflict system and its eventual disintegration. Focusing from the beginning on issues of war and peace, the Vanderbilt University Petexbatun Regional Archaeological Project consisted of a dozen subprojects that have separately explored Petexbatun regional ecology, nutrition, architecture, defensive systems, settlement patterns, hieroglyphic texts, cave ritual, trade and exchange systems, and so on (Demarest, Inomata, et al, eds., 1991; Demarest et al, eds., 1992; Valdes et al. 1993; Demarest 1990; Demarest, Valdes, et al, eds., 1991; Demarest and Inomata 1992; Wright 1993; Valdes and Demarest 1993; Demarest and Valdes 1994). The initial phases of the project focused on the unusually rich historical evidence and the undisturbed archaeological sites from one remote area of the Peten jungle, to the west of the Pasión River, near Lake Petexbatun (see figure 8.1). There an area of about nine hundred square kilometers includes at least six great centers and many villages with many dozens of hieroglyphic monuments. Excavations, surveys, and hieroglyphic finds in the region have shown that in the Petexbatun in the eighth century Classic Maya civilization rapidly unraveled.

Previously known monuments (Houston and Mathews 1985; Mathews and Willey 1991; Houston 1987) and many new texts discovered in the course of the project (e.g., Symonds et al. in press; Palka et al. in press; Wolley 1990a; Demarest and Valdes 1994), together provide a detailed political history of the Petexbatun zone. In the mid-seventh century the dynasty of one of the Petexbatun centers, Dos Pilas, was involved in well-documented wars against its neighbors. Towards the end of the seventh century, the rulers of Dos Pilas began to establish a regional polity through conquest and alliance. Typical of Maya wars, the conquest of large centers like Seibal was celebrated in hieroglyphic monuments and stairways deciphered by the project's team (Symonds, Arroyo, and Houston 1990). Again, in the normal Maya pattern of the Late Classic period, conquered centers were then incorporated into the Dos Pilas hegemony. These vassal centers would have owed some (as yet uncertain) degree of political subservience and probably provided gifts, tribute, and perhaps even corvée labor or troops for warfare (see Demarest, Escobedo, et al. 1991 for an example of gifts or booty from conquest). It was in this period of political success that most of the large pyramids, palaces, and tombs at Dos Pilas and other Petexbatun centers were constructed and dozens of monuments were erected to glorify the dynasty throughout its realm. Similar changes in warfare have been found at Caracol (Chase and Chase 1987, 1989; Chase 1992) and other centers of the A.D. 600–900 Late Classic period (see Culbert, ed., 1991; Schele and Freidel 1990 for recent summaries of Late Classic political conquests and conflicts).

Political and economic motives may have driven these wars. Efforts to expand the Dos Pilas hegemony run along the Pasion river valley, suggesting that a possible motive for the warfare was competition over the trade routes in exotic, status-reinforcing goods from the highlands. This hypothesis is now being tested by Smithsonian-sponsored neutron activation and exchange systems studies. These studies will plot changes in patterns of trade and distribution of goods as the Dos Pilas hegemony expanded and then collapsed (e.g., Foias, Bishop, and Hagstrum 1991). The elite were probably the major beneficiaries from such military victories. The general population probably did not greatly benefit from success in war (see Chase 1992 for a contrary perspective). Current evidence does indicate ancient population concentration, increased monumental architecture, and richer elite tombs or cave deposits near militaristic centers like Dos Pilas and Caracol. Yet remember that none of these features necessarily benefited the society as a whole. More likely such concentration of wealth in material remains resulted from the increased level of status competition between elites that was characteristic of this period. Tribute from war would primarily benefit the elite, who in the eighth century were deeply engaged in competition for prestige, and the exotics and propaganda needed to translate that prestige into power.

The Bubble Bursts: The Collapse of the Petexbatun Kingdom

The Petexbatun kingdom of Dos Pilas reached its apogee by A.D. 740 to 760. In A.D. 761, the hieroglyphic and archaeological evidence of our project shows that dominated centers turned on their capital, Dos Pilas, and besieged and overran it, defeating its last ruler. The archaeological evidence of the fall of this kingdom includes hastily constructed concentric walls surrounding the main palaces and temples of the Dos Pilas center (figure 8.2). Excavation within these walls uncovered a late-eighth-century village. Surface remains, platforms, and small midden deposits contained thousands of potsherds and artifacts, all dating to the eighth century. The dating, the platforms, and their placement are compatible with the hypothesis of a small impoverished occupation, besieged within the central precinct of Dos Pilas at the end of the Classic period.

The impact of warfare at this time in the Petexbatun can be seen in the nature of defensive constructions. Encircling palisade walls were built by dismantling palace facades and temples. In one case, a defensive wall was placed directly through the center of a palace with the stones of the wall placed against an earlier hieroglyphic stairway (figure 8.3). This one context exemplifies the dramatic nature of the fall of the Petexbatun kingdom: the hieroglyphic stairway, a monument to earlier conquests, was bisected by a crude, rapidly constructed palisade—footed in stones ripped off from the facades of the royal palace itself. With the fall of this center of Dos Pilas came a breakdown in the culturally defined modes of warfare in this region.

After this siege, the Dos Pilas expansion state appears to have broken up into smaller warring polities—first, two or three warring states and, then, even smaller units. In the eighth century, walls of stone and rubble were built to encircle some of the sites, and many of these walls probably supported wooden palisades. Many discoveries in the period of 1989–1994 of the Vanderbilt project testified to the desperate nature of these final years of the Maya civilization in the Petexbatun. One center, Punta de Chimino, has temples, houses, and monuments constructed on a narrow peninsula within Lake Petexbatun (see figure 8.4). Survey revealed a series of fortifications here that were among the most massive in the history of Mesoamerican warfare (Inomata et al. 1989; Wolley and Wright 1990b; Wolley 1991; Demarest, Suasnavar, et al. 1994). The entire Punta de Chimino peninsula was cut off from the mainland in Late Classic times by the excavation of a defensive moat system. Three concentric moats and walls were constructed around the base of the Punta de Chimino peninsula, the innermost being over forty feet deep and cut into solid limestone bedrock. The waters of Lake Petexbatun would have flowed through this moat, making the site an island fortress. The labor invested in the site's defenses included the movement of thousands of square meters of bedrock, a volume several times larger than that of all of the architecture within the site itself (Wolley 1991; Inomata et al. 1989).

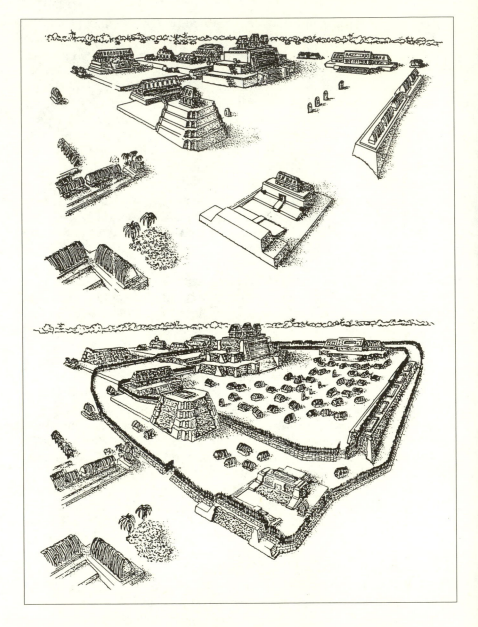

FIGURE 8.2. Perspective views of the cleared or excavated area of the Dos Pilas central plaza and acropolis before A.D. 761 (above) and (below) the concentric palisades and plaza village from the time of the siege and fall of Dos Pilas in A.D. 761. Drawing by LeRoy Demarest.

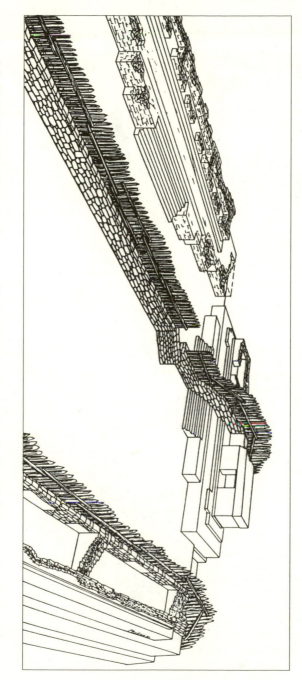

FIGURE 8.3. Reconstruction perspective views of the Dos Pilas central palace in A.D. 761 with defensive walls and palisades running through the palace and over its hieroglyphic stairway. Drawing by Paulino Morales.

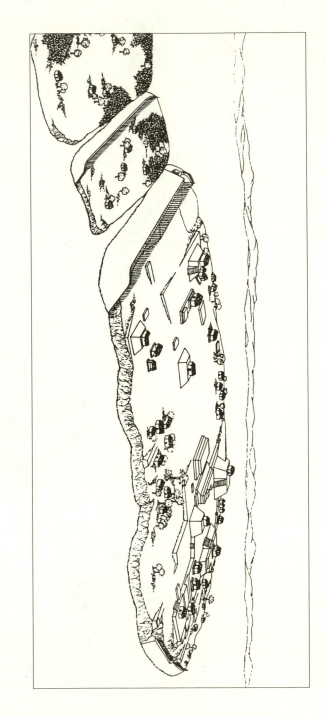

FIGURE 8.4. Perspective reconstruction view of the Punto de Chimino island showing the peninsula defensive systems at the end of the eighth century. Drawing by Sonia Wolff.

From an economic perspective such an expenditure of energy was wasteful and indicates that the Petexbatun political system had shifted to a self-destructive course.

The evidence from Punta de Chimino, Dos Pilas, and now many other sites in the Petexbatun (Demarest, Inomata, et al., eds., 1991; Valdes and Demarest 1993; Demarest and Valdes 1994; Demarest, Suasnavar, et al. 1994) shows that, near the end of the Classic period, this particular region had collapsed into endemic, open warfare. The exhausting expenditure of energy on defense in the period from A.D. 761 to 830 in the Petexbatun reflects an apparent spiraling acceleration and intensification of warfare there. This shift from the norms of ritual, dynastic, and conquest warfare of the Classic Maya to militaristic anarchy occurred over a half century prior to the collapse of southern lowland Maya civilization in most regions. Reconnaissance and excavation along the lake bluffs and at the centers of Punta de Chimino, Tamarindito, and Aguateca (figures 8.5 and 8.6) found that in the late eighth and early ninth century (A.D. 761–830) much of the escarpment of Lake Petexbatun (see figure 8.9) was walled (Demarest, Valdes, et al. 1991; Demarest 1992; Demarest, Inomata, et al, eds., 1991; Demarest, Suasnavar, et al. 1994; Inomata 1991, 1992; Wolley 1991). Some long stretches of walls may have functioned to protect areas of probable agricultural fields and terraces. Farther west, recent surveys and excavations have defined over a dozen hilltop fortresses—some of them tiny walled villages (Demarest, Suasnavar, et al. 1994). Ultimately, siege warfare might have caused over-exploitation of fields and terraces in certain areas, such as near fortified centers.

In overview, one possible hypothetical history of Maya warfare in the Petexbatun would set out a four-stage process:

- Stage 1: (Before the seventh century) Over a millennium of occupation following standard Maya canons, including warfare, defined by commonly held rules of engagement. Economic and political impact, but little destructive cost.
- Stage 2: (Seventh to eighth centuries) Wars of ritual capture, dynastic succession, and conquest intensify in scale and frequency—but all still defined and channeled by common canons and ethics of warfare, as represented in art and epigraphy, and as objectively manifest in still generally dispersed settlement patterns and indefensible site placement.
- Stage 3: (Late eighth to early ninth century) The siege, fall, and abandonment of Dos Pilas in A.D. 761, followed by a period of virtually unrestricted warfare, the construction of defensive works throughout

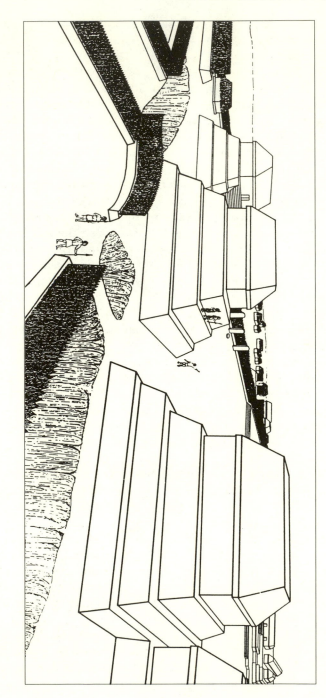

FIGURE 8.5. Reconstruction view of one of the Aguateca inner defenses and gateways. Drawing by Takeshi Inomata.

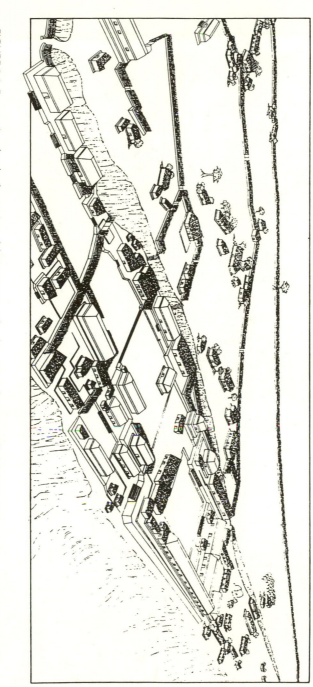

FIGURE 8.6. Perspective sketch of a portion of the Aguateca palisade systems showing walled field and outer defenses in the background. Drawing by Sonia Wolff.

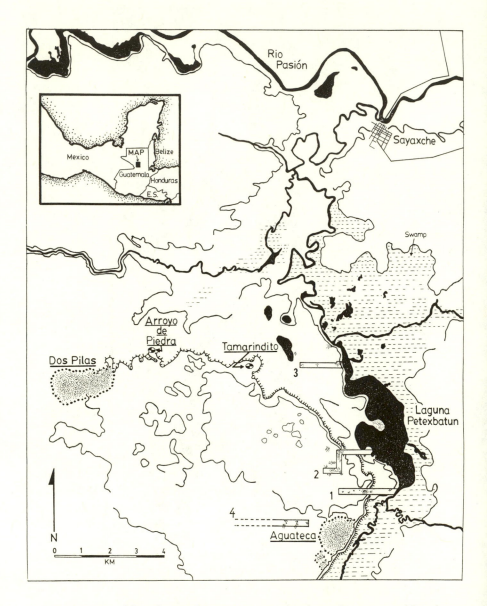

FIGURE 8.7. Map of the Lake Petexbatun escarpment showing major centers and Petexbatun Project Intersite Settlement Survey Transects exploring rural areas, fields, and villages.

the region, and consequent changes in economics, politics, and settlement patterns. Population estimated to fall to about 10 percent of previous levels by end of period.
- Stage 4:(After A.D. 810 to 830) Near abandonment of most of the Petexbatun region, with only tiny squatters' populations of a few families in most centers (dates defined by the presence of Fire Orange ceramics).

By about A.D. 830 abandoned centers, villages, and fields and ruins of long stretches of fortifications testify to the possibility of such a sequence of events.

What we do not yet know is whether the violent fall of the Petexbatun kingdom reflects general processes affecting other regions of the Maya world. Another question is whether destructive warfare might have spread by contagion from the Petexbatun region during its early collapse to other areas—adding to the factors involved in the subsequent ninth-century collapse of most Peten Maya centers.

The Probable Impact of Warfare on Ecology

As noted above, the Maya appeared to have followed the rationale that fits most successful agricultural approaches to rain forest environments: to mimic the diversity and complexity of the rain forest ecosystem. This means that Maya populations, while large, were generally dispersed across the landscape. It also implies that agricultural systems would have included a wide range of techniques, including traditional small-plot swidden (*not* cutting large trees) and using a wide range of fallow times adapted to microvariation in soil conditions. They also probably alternated swidden and fallow areas with small and scattered plots of infield/outfield garden systems, terraces of various types, fruit and ramon nut trees, hunting preserves, tuber fields, etc. (Dunning et al. 1993; Dunning and Demarest 1989; Demarest and Dunning 1990). The guiding principles behind such a system are: (1) small locally sensitive systems; (2) wide dispersion of any one type of field or crop; and (3) a general imitation of the complexity and dispersion of the rain forest environment. The preliminary results of the Petexbatun Ecology subproject directed by Nicholas Dunning indicate that such a system seems to have been the subsistence base in the Petexbatun area prior to the middle of the eighth century (Dunning, et al. 1993).

Yet, as described above, after the fall of Dos Pilas in A.D. 761, the regional landscape shifted to one of walled defensible centers. It should be clear that such a pattern of siege warfare, along with its attendant costs, would have strained the long-successful Maya ecological adaptation to the Peten rain forest. General economic costs would have been great. Local ecological damage also might have occurred near fortified settlements, given the thin soils and steep slopes in most defensible locations. Intensified war, in any of the probable scenarios, would certainly have resulted in disruption of trade, in high labor costs for defensive construction, and in the economic costs of battle itself (e.g., loss of young farmers/warriors and interruption of planting and harvesting schedules). Continuing researches in the Petexbatun region are now more precisely defining the interaction between politics, warfare, and ecology that brought about the end of civilization in the Petexbatun (Demarest and Valdes 1994; Valdes and Demarest 1994; Dunning et al. 1993).

What Went Wrong?
The Lessons of the Failure of Maya Civilization in the Petexbatun

Stable relations provide the context for societies to deal jointly with their economic and ecological adaptations and the long-term problems of such adaptations. Such stable relations can include warfare and conquest, even with some degree of destruction, so long as they are part of a culturally defined system, mutually accepted by all participants, in a state of "dynamic equilibrium." Whatever the precise nature of Maya warfare in the millennium preceding the seventh century, clearly it was well enough adapted to the fragile and complex Maya ecological and economic regime to allow this civilization to maintain populations in the millions in the Peten rain forest—an astonishing achievement. The Maya systems of ecological adaptation, economic decentralization, and culturally defined warfare together achieved a unique success: maintenance of a high civilization in a rain forest environment without the destruction of that fragile ecosystem. Consciously, or unconsciously, restrictions on combat tactics, collateral damage to infrastructure, and duration of conflict may have been critical to that success. It would appear that in the eighth century in the Petexbatun area, changes in conflict control resulted in far more destructive war. Even conquest or tribute would have been rendered useless as rewards if the impact of victory was so destructive. In turn, the societies in this area may have focused on military survival at the expense of their economic systems and ecological adaptations.

Anthropologists have often argued that ecological and/or demographic pressures lead to warfare (e.g., Carneiro 1961, 1970; Rappaport 1967; Vayda 1961, 1969, 1976; Ball 1977; Paulsen 1976). Here we find interactive and simultaneous causes: warfare, economics, and ecology may have changed together, setting the Petexbatun kingdoms on a disastrous course.

Culture-Historical Reconstruction: Elite "Demographic Pressure" and the Breakdown of the Maya Systems of Conflict and Conflict Control

Why did the Petexbatun Maya, like so many societies, change their focus to short-term military demands at the expense of their economies, environment, and, eventually, their own survival? The Vanderbilt Petexbatun Regional Archaeological Project has spent six years seeking the answers to this question, and will continue to explore it in coming years from the perspective of archaeology, ecology, osteology, trade patterns, settlement patterns, hieroglyphic history, and demography. At this point, I believe that we can say that the answer to this question does not lie solely in the realm of ecology or demography as independent variables in culture change. Rather, an understanding of the problems of war and peace in the case of the Maya, as in the case of most complex societies, has to do with power, stratification, and class interests as they impact on the material base of society.

Here I have proposed one initial and highly speculative model for the processes that led to the Late Classic failure of the Maya system of conflict control and the corresponding changes in settlement patterns and ecology that led to the Classic Maya collapse. While it was a complicated process, it could have been initiated by a small number of independent destabilizing variables. One such factor was the demographic expansion of the noble class. Royal and noble polygamy exacerbated this problem. The growth of elites might have been a far greater pressure than general population increase. Maya elites were very expensive to maintain, and the expansion of that privileged class was documented in every aspect of Late Classic material culture, including architecture, settlement patterns, and hieroglyphic history. This class had a vested interest in warfare—an interest that, prior to the Late Classic period, was somewhat contained by Maya norms of warfare and by strong crosscutting cultural ties, shared interests, and shared canons of behavior. As the noble class grew, there may have been increased pressure and competition for limited positions of status and also for the exotic, status-reinforcing goods that marked such positions (jade, quetzal feathers, shell, obsidian, imported polychrome ceramics, etc.).

It is not surprising, then, that the two probable sources of increased warfare in the Late Classic period in the Petexbatun region appear to have been struggles for political position and wars over the trade routes in exotic goods. In the specific case of the Petexbatun, their many wars appear to have had one of two objectives: (1) to monopolize positions of sacred authority for which the Dos Pilas's dynasty was competing with their close relatives at Tikal and with local established elites, and (2) to control the Pasion trade route that brought exotic goods down from the highlands. Note that no society-wide issues of material gain or well-being were involved, nor were there driving subsistence pressures. Archaeologists sometimes naively assume that warfare is undertaken with the rational goal of bettering the polity's general economic condition, and it is even sometimes assumed that manifestations such as monumental architecture and population concentration reflect the benefits of such wars. In the case of the Maya, a growing, self-interested elite might have pursued political gains with increasingly aggressive tactics, increasing frequency of conflict, and a growing disregard for the established Maya canons of war. In pursuit of its own interest, the elite class may have ignored both the cogent economic and political goals of warfare and the ecological reasons for restraints on disruptive forms of conflict.

Implications for Contemporary Systems of Conflict Controls:
Some Subjective Reflections

There are a surprising number of lessons that might be drawn from the long success and final failure of the Maya system of war and peace. Its success was based upon many of the same principles that have already been indicated in contemporary ethnographic studies, including the creation of intersocietal ties that crosscut the boundaries of combatant groups. Resultant restrictions on rules of engagement based on these common interests probably provided a mitigation of tactics of warfare. The fact that such rules of engagement seemed to be specifically appropriate to the maintenance of residential dispersal in the rain forest can hardly be coincidental: it represented either unconscious evolutionary adaptation or a conscious collective strategy for survival. In either case, this strategy was highly successful, and together with their the complex ecological pattern, it allowed the Maya to flourish for nearly two millennia in an environment that today can barely sustain village life.

Obviously the manner in which the Maya system of conflict integrated with its ecological adaptation to a fragile environment has particular relevance for our own struggles today to maintain the world's spiraling populations within its shrinking ecological parameters. But another set of lessons—negative ones—can be read into the probable causes of the collapse of Maya civilization. These relate to the need for:

- mature understanding by political leadership of the ecological and

economic circumstances of the societies they govern;
- leaders willing to act on that knowledge in the best interest of *all* members of their society, rather than in their own individual or class interests;
- political leadership that views both (1) and (2) in a *long-term* perspective.

In the contemporary world, few societies meet these criteria. Until they do, war will continue to be an open-ended threat to human survival.

I would not, however, aspire to the lofty goals of Galtung's "positive peace" concept (1968) or similar exhortations by Barash (1991). In effect, these scholars argue that peace can only be achieved when there is general social and economic justice. I would draw from the Classic Maya a different lesson. Maya society, even a thousand years before the collapse, was never just, and was certainly highly stratified. Yet its forms of warfare were well attuned to its economic, settlement, and ecological systems—which, in turn, were well adapted to the rain forest. In the case of the Maya, leaders accepted some degree of restriction on the political and economic burdens they placed on their society's infrastructure and environment. In this case economic and ecological rationality, not political justice, were the ultimate pressure for controls on war. When these parameters were ignored in the eighth century in the Petexbatun, the entire cultural system collapsed in a state of endemic war. Today, the ruined and overgrown palaces, temples, and fortresses of the region remind us of the potentially terrible cost of war waged in the pursuit of elite wealth and power.

References

I wish to thank the H. F. Guggenheim Foundation, and its Director, Karen Colvard, for the funding, institutional support, and advice that made possible the research described in this chapter. The Vanderbilt Petexbatun Regional Archaeological Project was also supported by grants from The National Geographic Society, The National Endowment for the Humanities, the Swedish International Development Authority, the U.S. Institute of Peace, USAID, Vanderbilt University, and private donors. The project was carried out under the supervision of the Instituto de Antropologia e Historia of the Republic of Guatemala. On behalf of all of the scientists on the project we wish to thank these institutions and their staff, as well as the generous individual supporters, whose help allowed us to complete the six years of field research of the project.

Adams, Richard E. W. 1980. Swamp, Canals, and Locations of Ancient Maya Cities. *Antiquity,* 54: 206–214.

———. 1983. Ancient Land Use and Culture History in the Pasion River Region. In *Prehistoric Settlement Patterns: Essays in Honor of Gordon R. Willey,* ed. Evon Z. Vogt and Richard M. Leventhal, pp. 319–335. Albuquerque: University of New Mexico Press.

———. 1986. Rio Azul. *National Geographic,* 169: 420–451.

Adams, Richard E. W., ed. 1977. *The Origins of Maya Civilization.* Albuquerque: University of New Mexico Press.

———. 1984. *The Rio Azul Archaeological Project: 1984 Preliminary Report.* San Antonio: Center for Archaeological Research of the University of Texas at San Antonio.

Ball, Joseph W. 1977. The Rise of the Northern Maya Chiefdoms: A Socioprocessual Analysis. In *The Origins of Maya Civilization,* ed. Richard E. W. Adams, pp. 101–132. Albuquerque: University of New Mexico Press.

———. 1993. Pottery, Potters, Palaces, and Politics: Some Socioeconomic and Political Implications of Late Classic Maya Ceramic Industries. In *Lowland Maya Civilization in the Eighth Century A.D.,* ed. Jeremy A. Sabloff and John S. Henderson, pp. 243–272. Washington, D.C.: Dumbarton Oaks Research Library and Collection.

Barash, David B. 1991. *Introduction to Peace Studies.* Belmont, Calif.: Wadsworth.

Baudez, Claude F. and Peter Mathews. 1979. Capture and Sacrifice at Palenque. In *Tercera Mesa Redonda de Palenque.* Vol. 4. Ed. M. G. Robertson, pp.31–40. Palenque, Mexico: Pre-Columbia Art Center.

Bishop, Ronald L. 1980. Aspects of Ceramic Compositional Modeling. In *Models and Methods in Regional Exchange,* ed. Robert E. Fry, pp. 47–66. SAA Papers No. 1. Washington, D.C.: Society for American Archaeology.

Bishop, Ronald L., Marilyn P. Beaudry, Richard M. Leventhal, and Rober J. Sharer. 1986. Compositional Analysis of Classic Period Painted Ceramics in the Southeastern Maya Area. In *The Southeast Maya Periphery,* ed. Patricia A. Urban and Edward M. Schortman. pp. 143–167. Austin: University of Texas Press.

Boone, Elizabeth H., ed. 1984. *Ritual Human Sacrifice in Mesoameria.* Washington, D.C.: Dumbarton Oaks Foundation, Trustees for Harvard University.

Carneiro, Robert L. 1961. Slash and Burn Cultivation Among the Kuikuru and Its Implications for Cultural Development in the Amazon Basin. In *The Evolution of Horticultural Systems in Native South America: Causes and Consequences,* ed. J. Wilbert, pp. 47–68. Caracas: Sociedad de Ciencias Naturales La Salle.

———. 1970. Theory of the Origin of the State. *Science* 169: 733–738.

———. 1990. Chiefdom-level Warfare as Exemplified in Fiji and the Cauca Valley. In *The Anthropology of War.* ed. Jonathan Haas, pp. 190–211. School of American Research Advanced Seminar Series. Cambridge: Cambridge University Press.

Chase, Arlen F. 1992. Elites and the Changing Organization of Classic Maya Society. In *Mesoamerican Elites: An Archaeological Assessment,* ed. Diane Z. Chase and Arlen F. Chase, pp. 30–49. Norman: University of Oklahoma Press.

Chase, Arlen F. and Diane Z. Chase. 1987. Investigations at the Classic Maya City of Caracol, Belize: 1985–1987. *Pre-Columbian Art Research Institute Monograph No. 3.* San Francisco: Pre-Columbian Art Research Institute.

———. 1989. The Investigation of Classic Period Maya Warfare at Caracol, Belize. *Mayab* 5: 5–18.

Chase, Arlen F., Nikolai Grube, and Diane Z. Chase. 1991. *Three Terminal Classic Monuments from Caracol, Belize.* Research Reports on Ancient Maya Writing, no. 36. Washington, D.C.: Center for Maya Research.

Colson, Elizabeth. 1953. Social Control and Vengeance among the Plateau Tonga. *Africa* 23: 199–211.

Culbert, T. Patrick. 1977. Maya Development and Collapse: An Economic Perspective. In *Social Process in Maya Prehistory*, ed. N. Hammond, pp. 509–530. London: Academic Press.

———. 1988. Political History and the Maya Glyphs. *Antiquity* 62: 135–152.

———. 1991. Polities in the Northern Peten, Guatemala. In *Classic Maya Political History: Hieroglyphic and Archaeological Evidence*, ed. T. P. Culbert, pp. 128–146. Cambridge: Cambridge University Press.

Culbert, T. Patrick, ed. 1973. *The Classic Maya Collapse*. Albuquerque: University of New Mexico Press.

———. 1991. *Classic Maya Political History: Hieroglyphic and Archaeological Evidence*. School of American Research Advanced Seminar Series. Cambridge: Cambridge University Press.

Culbert, T. Patrick and Don S. Rice, eds., 1990. *Pre-Columbian Population History in the Maya Lowlands*. Albuquerque: University of New Mexico Press.

Demarest, Arthur A. 1977. Regional Patterning of Lowland Classic Fortifications. In a paper presented to the Harvard Seminar on Mesoamerican Archaeology. Cambridge: Harvard Tozzer Library.

———. 1978. Interregional Conflict and "Situational Ethics" in Classic Maya Warfare. In *Codex Wauchope: A Tribute Roll*, ed. M. Giardino, B. Edmunson, and W. Creamer, pp. 101–111. New Orleans: Tulane University.

———. 1984. Mesoamerican Human Sacrifice in Evolutionary Perspective. In *Ritual Human Sacrifice in Mesoamerica: A Conference at Dumbarton Oaks, October 13th and 14th, 1979*, ed. Elizabeth Boone, pp. 227–247. Washington, D.C.: Dumbarton Oaks Research Library and Collection.

———. 1990. Conclusiones: Resume de los Resultados de la Segunda Temporada. In *Proyecto Arqueologico Regional Petexbatun: Informe Preliminar #2—Segunda Temporada*, ed. Arthur A. Demarest and Stephen D. Houston, pp.607–626. Guatemala: Instituto de Antropologia e Historia de Guatemala.

———. 1992. Archeology, Ideology, and Pre-Columbian Cultural Evolution: The Search for an Approach. In *Ideology and Pre-Columbian Civilizations*, ed. Arthur A. Demarest and Geoffrey W. Conrad, pp. 135–158. Santa Fe: School of American Research Press.

Demarest, Arthur A. and Nicholas P. Dunning. 1990. Ecologia y Guerra en la Region de la Pasion: Resultados y Planes del Subproyecto Ecologico. In *Proyecto Arqueologico Regional Petexbatun: Informe Preliminar #2—Segunda Temporada*, ed. Arthur A.Demarest and Stephen D. Houston. Guatemala: Instituto de Antropologia e Historia de Guatemala.

Demarest, Arthur A., Hector Escobedo, Juan Antonio Valdes, Stephen Houston, Lori E. Wright, and Katherine F. Emery. 1991. Arqueologia, eqigrafia y el descubrimento de una tumba real en el centro ceremonial de Dos Pilas, Peten, Guatemala. *Utz'ib* 1, no. 1: 14–28.

Demarest, Arthur A. and Takeshi Inomata. 1992. Conclusiones Generales Para la Temporada 1992 del Proyecto Arqueologico Regional Petexbatun. In *Proyecto Arqueologico Regional Petexbatun: Informe Preliminar #4—Cuarta Temporada*, ed. Arthur A. Demarest, Takeshi Inomata, and Hector Escobedo, pp. 370–383. Guatemala: Instituto de Antropologia e Historia de Guatemala.

Demarest, Arthur A., Takeshi Inomata, and Hector Escobedo, eds., 1992. *Proyecto Arqueologico Regional Petexbatun: Informe Preliminar #4—Cuarta Temporada*. Guatemala: Instituto de Antropologia e Historia de Guatemala.

Demarest, Arthur A., Takeshi Inomata, Hector Escobedo, and Joel Palka, eds., 1991. *Proyecto Arqueologico Regional Petexbatun: Informe Preliminar #3—Tercera Temporada*. Guatemala: Instituto de Antropologia e Historia de Guatemala.

Demarest, Arthur A., J. S. Suasnavar, Claudia Wolley, Matt O'Mansky, Josh Hinson, Erin Sears, and Cora Rasmussen. 1994. Reconocimiento de Sistemas Defensivos del Petexbatun: La Evidencia Material de la Guerra. *VIII Simposio de Investigaciones Arqueologicas en Guatemala*. Guatemala: Museo Nacional de Arqueologia y Etnologia.

Demarest, Arthur A. and Juan Antonio Valdes. 1993. Proyecto Arqueologico Regional Petexbatun: Resultados y Perspectivas de la Cuarta Temporada. *VI Simposio de Investigaciones Arqueologicas en Guatemala*. Guatemala: Museo Nacional De Arqueologia y Etnologia.

————. 1994. Regresion Politica y el Colapso de la Civilizacion Maya en la Region Petexbatun. *VII Simposio de Investigaciones Arqueologicas en Guatemala*. Guatemala: Museo Nacional de Arqueologia y Etnologia.

Demarest, Arthur A., Juan Antonio Valdes, Takeshi Inomata, Joel Palka, Hector Escobedo, James Brady, Nicholas Dunning, Thomas Killion, Antonia Foias, Christopher Beekman, Oswaldo Chinchilla, Robert Chatham, Inez Verhagen, Laura Stiver, and Kim Morgan. 1991. Conclusiones Preliminares e Interpretacions de la Temporada de Campo de 1991. In *Proyecto Arqueologico Regional Petexbatun: Informe Preliminar #3—Tercera Temporada*, ed. Arthur A. Demarest, Takeshi Inomata, Hector Escobedo, and Joel Palka. Guatemala: Instituto de Antropologia e Historia de Guatemala.

Dunning, Nicholas P., Estuardo Secaira, and Arthur A. Demarest. 1991. *The Petexbatun Region and the Peten: A Legacy of Human Impact*. Guatemala: The United States Agency for International Development (USAID).

Dunning, Nicholas P. and Arthur A. Demarest. 1989. *Sustainable Agricultural Systems in the Petexbatun, Pasion, and Peten Regions of Guatemala: Perspective From Contemporary Ecology and Ancient Settlement*. Guatemala: The United States Agency for International Development (USAID).

Dunning, Nicholas P., Leonel E. Paiz, Timothy Beach, and James Nicholas. 1993. Investigacion de Terrazas Agricolas en Petexbatun: Temporada de 1993. In *Proyecto Arqueologico Regional Petexbatun: Informe Preliminar 5—Quinta Temporada*, ed. Juan Antonio Valdes, Antonia Foias, Takeshi Inomata, Hector Escobedo, and Arthur Demarest, pp. 171–182. Guatemala: Instituto de Antropologia e Historia de Guatemala.

Evan-Prichard, E. E. 1940. *The Nuer*. Oxford: Oxford University Press.

Foias, Antonia E., Ronald L. Bishop, and Melissa Hagstrum. 1991. Analisis de la Ceramica de la Region de Petexbatun. In *Proyecto Arqueologico Regional Petexbatun: Informe Preliminar 3, Tercera Temporada*, ed. Arthur Demarest, Takeshi Inomata, Hector Escobedo, and Joel Palka, pp. 749–756. Guatemala: Instituto de Antropologia e Historia de Guatemala.

Folan, William J. 1992. Calakmul, Campeche: A Centralized Urban Administrative Center in the Northern Peten. *World Archaeology* 24, no. 1: 158–168.

Freidel, David A. 1981. Continuity and Disjunction: Late Postclassic Settlement Patterns in Northern Yucatan. In *Lowland Maya Settlement Patterns*, ed. Wendy Ashmore, pp. 311–332. Albuquerque: University of New Mexico Press.

————. 1986. Maya Warfare: An Example of Peer Polity Interaction. In *Peer Polity Interaction and Socio-Political Change*, ed. Colin Renfrew and John F. Cherry, pp. 93–108. England: Cambridge University Press.

————. 1992. Children of the First Father's Skull: Terminal Classic Warfare in the Northern Maya Lowlands and the Transformation of Kingship and Elite Hierarchies. In

Mesoamerican Elites: An Archaeological Assessment, ed. Diane Z. Chase and Arlen F. Chase, pp. 99–117. Norman: University of Oklahoma Press.

Galtung, Johan. 1968. Peace. In *International Encyclopedia of Social Sciences* 2: 487–496.

———. 1981. Social Cosmology and the Concept of Peace. *Journal of Peace Research* 18: 183–189.

———. 1985. Twenty-Five Years of Peace Research: Ten Challenges and Some Responses. *Journal of Peace Research* 22, no. 2: 141–158.

Gluckman, Max. 1955. *Custom and Conflict in Africa.* Glencoe, Ill.: Free Press.

Graham, Ian. 1967. *Archaeological Exploration in El Peten,* Guatemala. Middle American Research Institute, Tulane University, Publication 33. New Orleans: Tulane University.

Gregor, Thomas. 1990. An Uneasy Peace: Intertribal Relations in Brazil's Upper Xingu Valley. In *The Anthropology of War,* ed. Jonathan Haas, pp. 105–124. A School of American Research Advanced Seminar. Cambridge: Cambridge University Press.

———. 1994. Symbols and Rituals of Peace in Brazil's Upper Xingu. In *The Anthropology of Peace and Non-violence,* ed. Leslie Sponsel and Thomas Gregor, pp. 241–257. Boulder, Colo.: L. Rienner.

Hammond, Norman. 1974. The Distribution of Late Classic Maya Major Ceremonial Centers in the Central Area. In *Mesoamerican Archaeology: New Approaches,* ed. Norman Hammond, pp. 313–334. Austin: University of Texas Press.

———. 1991. Inside the Black Box: Defining Maya Polity. In *Classic Maya Political History,* ed. T. Patrick Culbert, pp. 253–284. Cambridge: Cambridge University Press.

Harrison, Peter D. and B. L. Turner II, eds., 1978. *Pre-Hispanic Maya Agriculture.* Albuquerque: University of New Mexico Press.

Haviland, William A. 1970. Tikal, Guatemala and Mesoamerican Urbanism. *World Archaeology,* 2: 186–198.

Houston, Stephen D. 1987. The Inscriptions and Monumental Art of Dos Pilas, Guatemala: A Study of Classic Maya History and Politics. Ph.D. diss., Yale University. Ann Arbor: University Microfilms.

Houston, Stephen D. and Peter Mathews. 1985. *The Dynastic Sequence of Dos Pilas, Guatemala.* San Francisco: Pre-Columbian Art Institute, Monograph 1.

Inomata, Takeshi, Kevin Johnston, Stephen Houston, and Antonia Foias. 1989. Registro y Rescate en Punta de Chimino. In *Proyecto Arqueologico Regional Petexbatun: Informe Preliminar #1—Primera Temporada,* ed. Arthur Demarest and Stephen Houston, pp. 130–154. Guatemala: Instituto de Antropologia e Historia de Guatemala.

Levine, Robert. 1969. Anthropology and the Study of Conflict. *The Journal of Conflict Resolution,* 5: 3–15.

Levine, Robert and Donald Campbell. 1972. *Ethnocentrism: Theories of Conflict, Ethnic Attitudes, and Group Behavior.* New York: John Wiley.

Marcus, Joyce. 1973. Territorial Organization of the Lowland Classic Maya. *Science* 180: 911–916.

———. 1974. The Iconography of Power Among the Classic Maya. *World Archaeology* 6: 83–94.

———. 1976. *Emblem and State in the Classic Maya Lowlands: An Epigraphic Approach to Territorial Organization.* Washington, D.C.: Dumbarton Oaks.

———. 1993. Ancient Maya Political Organization. In *Lowland Maya Civilization in the Eighth Century A.D.,* ed. Jeremy A. Sabloff and John S. Henderson, p. 111–171. Washington, D.C.: Dumbarton Oaks.

Martin, Simon. 1993. Site Q: The Case for a Maya Super-Polity. Unpublished manuscript.

Martin, Simon and Nikolai Grube. 1994. Evidence for Macro-Political Organization

Amongst Classic Maya Lowland States. Unpublished manuscript.

Matheny, Ray. 1976. Maya Lowland Hydraulic Systems. *Science* 193: 639–646.

Mathews, Peter. 1985. Maya Early Classic Monuments and Inscriptions. In *A Consideration of the Early Classic Period in the Maya Lowlands*, ed. Gordon Willey and Peter Mathews, pp. 5–54. Institute for Mesoamerican Studies. Albany: State University of New York.

———. 1988. The Sculpture of Yaxchilan. Ph.D. diss., Yale University. Ann Arbor: University Microfilms.

———. 1991. Classic Maya Emblem Glyphs. In *Classic Maya Political History: Hieroglyphic and Archeological Evidence*, ed. T. Patrick Culbert, pp. 19–29. School of American Research Advanced Seminar Series. Cambridge: Cambridge University Press.

Mathews, Peter and Gordon R. Willey. 1991. Prehistoric Polities of the Pasion Region: Hieroglyphic Texts and Their Archaeological Setting. In *Classic Maya Political History: Hieroglyphic and Archaeological Evidence*, ed. T. Patrick Culbert, pp. 30–71. Cambridge: Cambridge University Press.

McAnany, Patricia A. 1986. Lithic Technology and Exchange Among the Wetland Farmers of the Eastern Maya Lowlands. Ph.D. diss., University of New Mexico. Ann Arbor: University Microfilms.

———. 1993. The Economics of Social Power and Wealth Among Eighth Century Maya Households. In *Lowland Maya Civilization in the Eighth Century A.D.*, ed. Jeremy A. Sabloff and John S. Henderson, pp. 65–89. Washington, D.C.: Dumbarton Oaks.

Miller, Mary E. 1986. *The Murals of Bonampak*. Princeton: University Press.

Murphy, Robert F. 1957. Intergroup Hostility and Social Cohesion. In *American Anthropologist* 5: 1018–1035.

Nations, James and R. B. Nigh. 1980. The Evolutionary Potential of Lacondon Maya Sustained Yield Tropical Forest Agriculture. *Journal of Anthropological Research* 36, no.1: 1–26.

Nye, P. H. and D. T. Greenland. 1964. Changes in the Soil After Cleaning a Tropical Forest. *Plant and Soil* 21: 101–112.

Otterbein, Keith. 1970. *The Evolution of War: A Cross-Cultural Study*. New Haven: HRAF Press.

Palka, Joel, David Stuart, and Stephen D. Houston. In press. 9. Dos Pilas Panel 19: A Classic Maya Initiation Rite. *Research Reports on Ancient Maya Writing*. Washington, D.C.: Center for Maya Research.

Paulsen, Allison C. 1976. Environment and Empire: Climatic Factors in Prehistoric Andean Culture Change. *World Archaeology* 8: 121–132.

Puleston, Dennis E. and D.W. Callender, Jr. 1967. Defensive Earthworks at Tikal. *Expedition* 9, no. 3: 40–48.

Rappaport, Roy. 1967. Ritual Regulation of Environmental Relations Among a New Guinea People. *Ethnology* 6: 17–30.

Renfrew, Colin and John F. Cherry. 1986. *Peer Polity Interaction and Socio-Political Change*. Cambridge: Cambridge University Press.

Rice, Prudence M. 1987. Economic Change in the Lowland Maya Late Classic period. In *Specialization, Exchange, and Complex Societies*, ed. E. M. Brumfiel and T. K. Earle, pp. 76–85. Cambridge: Cambridge University Press.

Rice, Don S. and Prudence M. Rice. 1981. Murrala de Leon: A Lowland Maya Fortification. *Journal of Field Archaeology* 8: 271–288.

Sabloff, Jeremy A. 1986. Interaction Among Classic Maya Polities: A Preliminary Examination. In *Peer Polity Interaction and Socio-Political Change*, ed. Colin Renfrew and John F. Cherry, pp. 109–116. Cambridge: Cambridge University Press.

Sabloff, Jeremy A. and E. Wyllys Andrews V, eds., 1986. *Late Lowland Maya Civilization: Classic to Postclassic.* A School of American Research Advanced Seminar Series. Albuquerque: University of New Mexico Press.

Schele, Linda. 1984. Human Sacrifice Among the Classic Maya. In *Ritual Human Sacrifice in Mesoamerica*, ed. E. Boone, pp. 6–48. Washington, D.C.: Dumbarton Oaks.

Schele, Linda and Mary E. Miller. 1986. *The Blood of Kings: Dynasty and Ritual in Maya Art.* Fort Worth: Kimbell Art Museum.

Schele, Linda and David Freidel. 1990. *Forest of Kings: The Untold Story of the Ancient Maya.* New York: Morrow.

Shafer, Harry J. and Thomas R. Hester. 1983. Ancient Maya Chert Workshops in Northern Belize, Central America. *American Antiquity* 48: 519–543.

———. 1986. Maya Stone-tool Craft Specialization and Production at Colha, Belize: Reply to Mallory. *American Antiquity* 51: 158–166.

Sipes, R. G. 1973. War, Sports, and Aggression: An Empirical Test of Two Rival Theories. *American Anthropologist* 75: 64–86.

Stuart, David. 1985. The "Count of Captives" epithet in Classic Maya Writing. In *Fifth Palenque Round Table*, vol. 3, 1983, ed. Merle Greene Robertson and Virginia M. Fields, pp. 97–102. San Francisco: The Pre-Columbian Art Institute.

Symonds, Stacey, Barbara Arroyo, and Stephen Houston. 1990. Operacion DP11: Investigaciones en el Palacio de Dos Pilas. In *Proyecto Arqueologico Regional Petexbatun Informe Preliminar #2, Segunda Temporada 1990*, ed. Arthur A. Demarest and Stephen D. Houston, pp. 235–276. Guatemala: Instituto de Antropologia e Historia de Guatemala.

Symonds, Stacey, Stephen D. Houston, David Stuart, and Arthur A. Demarest. In press. Dos Pilas Hieroglyphic Stairway 4: An Important War of the late Classic Period. In *Research Reports on Ancient Maya Writing.* Washington, D.C.: Center for Maya Research.

Teft, S. 1975. Warfare Regulation: A Cross-cultural Test of Hypotheses. In *War, Its Causes and Correlates*, ed. M. A. Nettleship, R. Dalegivens, and A. Nettleship. The Hague: Mouton.

Thompson, J. Eric S. 1954. *The Rise and Fall of Maya Civilization.* Norman: University of Oklahoma Press.

Turner II, B. L. and Peter D. Harrison. 1983. Pulltrouser Swamp and Maya Raised Fields: A Summation. In *Pulltrouser Swamp*, ed. B. L. Turner and Peter D. Harrison, pp. 246–270. Austin: University of Texas Press.

Valdes, Juan Antonio and Arthur A. Demarest. 1993. Conclusiones Generales de la Temporada de Campo de 1993. In *Proyecto Arqueologico Regional Petexbatun: Informe Preliminar #5—Quinta Temporada*, ed. Juan Antonio Valdes, Antonia Foias, Takeshi Inomata, Hector Escobedo, and Arthur Demarest, pp. 189–192. Guatemala: Instituto de Antropologia e Historia de Guatemala.

Valdes, Juan Antonio, Antonia Foias, Takeshi Inomata, Hector Escobedo, and Arthur A. Demarest, eds., 1993. *Proyecto Arqueologico Regional Petexbatun: Informe Preliminar #5—Quinta Temporada.* Guatemala: Instituto de Antropologia e Historia de Guatemala.

Vayda, Andrew P. 1961. Expansion and Warfare Among Swidden Agriculturalists. *American Anthropologist* 63: 346–358.

———. 1969. The Study of the Causes of War, with Special Reference to Head-Hunting Raids in Borneo. *Ethnohistory* 16: 14–21.

———. 1976. *War in Ecological Perspective: Persistence Change and Adaptive Processes in Three Oceanic Societies.* New York: Pleum.

Webster, David L. 1975. Warfare and the Evolution of the State: A Reconsideration. *American Antiquity* 40: 464–470.

————. 1976. *Defensive Earthworks at Becan, Campeche, Mexico: Implications for Maya Warfare*. Middle American Research Institute, Publication 41. New Orleans: Tulane University.

————. 1977. Warfare and the Evolution of Maya Civilization. In *The Origins of Maya Civilization*, ed. R. E. W. Adams, pp. 335–372. Albuquerque: University of New Mexico Press.

————. 1979. *Cuca, Chacchob, Dzonot Ake: Three Walled Northern Maya Centers*. Occasional Papers in Anthropology, no. 11. University Park: Pennsylvania State University.

————. 1993. The Study of Maya Warfare: What It Tells Us About the Maya and What It Tells Us About Maya Archaeology. In *Lowland Maya Civilization in the Eighth Century A.D.*, ed. Jeremy A. Sabloff and John S. Henderson, pp. 415–444. Washington, D.C.: Dumbarton Oaks.

Webster, David L. and Ann Corrine Freter. 1989. The Demography of Late Classic Copan. In *Pre-Columbian Population History in the Maya Lowlands*, ed. T. Patrick Culbert and Don S. Rice. Albuquerque: University of New Mexico Press.

Westing, A. 1982. War as Human Endeavor: The High-Fatality Wars of the Twentieth Century. *Journal of Peace Research* 3: 261–264.

Wiberg, Hakan. 1965. *A Study of War*. Chicago: University of Chicago Press.

————. 1981. JPR 1964–1980—What Have We Learned About Peace? *Journal of Peace Research* 18, no. 2: 111–148.

Wobst, H. Martin. 1977. Stylistic Behavior and Information Exchange. In *For the Director: Research Essays in Honor of James Bennett Griffin*, ed. E. E. Cleland, pp. 317–334. Anthropological Papers, vol. 61. Ann Arbor: Museum of Anthropology, University of Michigan.

Wolley, Claudia. 1991. Sondeos en Punta de Chimino: Un Centro Fortificado del Clasico Tardio y Terminal. In *Proyecto Arqueologico Regional Petexbatun: Informe Preliminar #3, Tercera Temporada*, ed. Arthur Demarest, Takeshi Inomata, Hector Escobedo, and Joel Palka, pp. 558–587. Guatemala: Instituto de Antropologia e Historia de Guatemala.

Wolley, Claudia and Lori Wright. 1990a. Operacion DP7: Investigaciones en el Grupo L4–4. In *Proyecto Arqueologico Regional Petexbatun: Informe Preliminar #2, Segunda Temporada*, ed. Arthur Demarest and Stephen Houston, pp. 44–65. Guatemala: Instituto de Antropologia e Historia de Guatemala.

————. 1990b. Punta de Chimino: Sondeos en el Sistema Defensivo. In *Proyecto Arqueologico Regional Petexbatun: Informe Preliminar #2, Segunda Temporada*, ed. Arthur Demarest and Stephen Houston, pp. 423–437. Guatemala: Instituto de Antropologia e Historia de Guatemala.

Wright, Lori. 1993. Investigaciones Osteologicas en la Petexbatun: Reporte Interino IV. In *Proyecto Arqueologico Regional Petexbatun: Informe Preliminar 5, Quinta Temporada*, ed. Juan Antonio Valdes, Antonia Foias, Takeshi Inomata, Hector Escobedo, and Arthur Demarest, pp. 151–160. Guatemala: Instituto de Antropologia e Historia de Guatemala.

9 Why Violence Is Rejected or Renounced: A Case Study of Oppositional Terrorism

MARTHA CRENSHAW

■ The Robarcheks' discussion of the Waorani (chapter 7) is an extraordinary case study of a society that gave up violence. Arguably, a mass society parallel of the Waorani experience is that of politically radical groups that give up violence. These groups operate from different motives and in a wholly different cultural and social milieu from the Waorani. Nonetheless, the comparison is of theoretical interest in that for both the Waorani and the terrorists, aggression may test the limits of social cohesion. Typically, the violent act is reinforced by the culture of the group, justified in terms of prosocial goals (see chapter 1, Tuzin) and encapsulated so that nonviolent relations are possible with members of the community. But as in the case of the Waorani, terrorists may follow a path back to peace. Professor Crenshaw tells us that the transition to peace occurs for a variety of reasons, from suppression by the state to moral revulsion over the terrorist act. The possibility of radical change among those radically committed to violence justifies profound optimism. In that possibility we see human choices for peace in a setting where we would least expect to find it.

SCHOLARS USUALLY ask why violence occurs rather than why it does not (see, for example, Merkl 1986, and Reich 1990; exceptions are Ross and Gurr 1989, and Licklider, ed., 1993). This study is an attempt to fill that gap by addressing two questions related to the governance of the modern state and the management of the international system. First, this chapter asks why political actors reject terrorism as a method of opposition to the state or to the international society of states when it appears to be an available option for resistance. Second, it asks why oppositions abandon or renounce terrorism after its initiation as a form of political action. This question is also posed by the Robarcheks with regard to the Waorani, and my answer, like theirs, is nondeterministic. It stresses the voluntary quality of such decisions.

Furthermore, my argument about political terrorism applies to specific cases, not to patterns of general decline in the measurable incidence of terrorism over time. Its focus is on decision making in political organizations acting in the context of particular historical settings and cultures. The complexity of each case is emphasized, and no predictions are offered about the future of terrorism in aggregate terms. A further note of caution: this analysis of terrorism as a form of radical opposition to the status quo is not meant to deny that some governments use terrorism to control their citizens or to impose their values on other states. The rejection or repudiation of terrorism as a means of social and political control is an important subject, but it is beyond the scope of the present analysis.

It is also important to acknowledge that the concept of terrorism is both ambiguous and controversial. The term is often used in a careless or pejorative way for rhetorical reasons. My analysis is based on the premise that terrorism is simply one form of political violence. The method, not the identity or ideology of the user, determines whether or not an action can be defined as terrorism. Terrorism involves the use or threat of physical harm in order to achieve a disproportionately large psychological effect. It is demonstrative or propagandistic violence without significant military value, directed against symbolic rather than utilitarian targets. States as well as nonstates may use terrorism as a political weapon, although in this case I am concerned with oppositional rather than repressive violence.

This analysis considers the rejection or abandonment of terrorism from the point of view of the actors using it, in effect, as a problem of political decision making. Although my interpretation resembles that of the Robarcheks in their analysis of the Waorani, it differs from most other approaches to political violence. For example, a common assumption is that oppositional terrorism ends only when governments militarily defeat groups practicing terrorism or that terrorism fails to emerge because potentially violent actors in society are deterred by the prospect of punishment or retribution. Actually government policies intended to suppress terrorism (or the potential for terrorism) constitute only one of the many factors that influence the decisions of groups embracing terrorism. Groups can maintain their integrity and organizational continuity while abandoning terrorism. Nor does the answer lie simply in conditions. In the same context different organizations or different factions within movements make different choices. Furthermore, the possible reasons for the initiation of terrorism, such as lack of access by minorities to the political arena, need not be those that groups or individuals consider in their decisions to abandon it.

This argument about the autonomy of political actors and the importance of their choices is developed from three theoretical frameworks that are not always seen as compatible. One is the view that terrorism is the result of strategic choice. A second approach focuses on terrorism as the outcome of internal organizational politics. A third view of the problem draws on theories of psychological motivation and group interaction. A combination of these theories is needed to explain why political organizations either reject terrorism at the outset of a conflict or abandon the strategy after having practiced it.

If terrorism is instrumental behavior, the answer to my questions is relatively simple. Decisions result from calculations of relative costs and benefits. Methods of resistance are chosen because of their utility compared to other alternatives. Behavior is thus primarily a reaction to external considerations. Likely effectiveness in achieving long-term interests is the chief criterion for choices. Terrorism is thus purposeful in terms of ultimate political objectives. However, explanations based on psychological and organizational considerations suggest that the choice of terrorism as a method is only indirectly related to the pursuit of ideological ends. From this perspective, it is critical to understand how organizations form, what binds their members together, and how leaders and followers interact. Organizational integration and disintegration may be the keys to behavior. Organizational cohesion depends on psychological incentives for participation, which in turn require justifications for the use of terrorism that go beyond political effectiveness. Decisions about using terrorism are based not only on the anticipation of government response and the likelihood of achieving a desired outcome but on disputes over strategy and divergent perceptions of conditions, particularly the likelihood of acquiring popular support and moving to mass action. Collective belief systems and values and loyalty to the group are as important as interests. Self-image and concepts of identity help determine beliefs about the appropriateness of violence. Thus organizational and psychological costs and benefits are part of a mixture of considerations that do not exclude strategic logic. Decisions to avoid terrorism may be based on misperception and misconception as much as on accurate appreciation of conditions and especially of the reactions of other actors—the government, the public, and rivals for leadership of the opposition.

The Initial Rejection of Terrorism

What reasons do opposition groups offer for rejecting terrorism in situations where it was a realistic alternative? The following examples, which are illustrative but not exhaustive, are taken from conflicts where terrorism was largely avoided, but also from those where one group rejected terrorism while another embraced it. The arguments that political actors make against terrorism can be summarized in terms of the following general themes.

Terrorism is rejected as a matter of principle because it is elitist and does not involve the masses.

This is a condition that violates an essential philosophical and moral principle stating that the masses must be engaged in the struggle for political change. This view is usually an offshoot of revolutionary socialism or nationalism. Collective action is seen as morally preferable and only secondarily as more efficient. The preference for mass action is sufficiently strong to overcome the recognition that collective action is not feasible, at least not in the foreseeable future. The group does not see itself as acting for the people, only as acting with them. This conception of the appropriate role of a revolutionary or nationalist party is often based on ideas of the future. Costs and benefits are perceived in long rather than short terms. That is, even if the opposition succeeds through terrorism in securing immediate goals (e.g., demoralization of the adversary), the long-term outcome will not be satisfactory because the people will not have taken part in their own liberation.

Gandhi, for example, argued that terrorism in the struggle for Indian independence was elitist. Reliance on terrorism would mean that British rule would only be replaced by that of another small minority. Although Parekh (1986: 192–193) argues that Gandhi was wrong to assume that terrorism does not require community support or that nonviolence avoids elitism, Gandhi clearly felt that noncooperation, civil disobedience, and fasting were preferable because they engaged the masses in the struggle. Interestingly, a British government assessment of the decline of terrorism in India in 1936 (Government of India, 1937) concluded that Gandhi's campaigns actually stimulated upsurges of terrorism, whereas "improvement" was due not only to tougher laws and prosecutions of the terrorists but to the conversion of the terrorists to communism and socialism, ideologies that stressed mass involvement.

In the late nineteenth and early twentieth centuries, debates within communist or Marxist-Leninist movements in Russia and Germany over the use of terrorism were bitter. Arguments over terrorism split the Russian revolutionary movement, especially during the early twentieth century when Lenin vigorously attacked the Socialist-Revolutionary Party for its endorsement of terrorism (Newell 1981). Lenin's 1902 *What Is To Be Done?* criticized terrorism as a form of spontaneous release of indignation for intellectuals who were unable or unwilling to take on the task of organizing the masses. He demanded to know why terrorism should be expected to incite mass resistance if all the cruelties associated with the tyranny of the czarist regime had not. Opponents of terrorism insisted that mass organization had to precede a violent confrontation with the regime and that terrorism would only reinforce the passivity of the population.

Leaders of the German Communist Party under the Weimar Republic insisted that terrorism would weaken and divide the proletariat and that it would distract the party from organizing the masses (Rosenhaft 1982). The opponents of terrorism thought that genuine revolution was impossible without mass involvement, a belief they adhered to with surprising tenacity despite the growing realization that a socialist revolution was unlikely in Germany in the 1930s. That is, the likelihood of the success of alternatives to terrorism was not a decisive factor in the decision to reject it.

A question that has often puzzled researchers is why terrorism did not emerge in France in the early 1970s when it did in comparable circumstances in Germany and Italy. A leader of the Gauche Prolétarienne (GP), which was the major radical organization of the post-1968 period, explained French "exceptionalism" in terms of group beliefs (Liniers 1985). Members of the GP did not regard themselves as heroes or professional revolutionary elites. Their faith in the masses kept them from approving individual actions. Although in retrospect it became clear that the group had misperceived the nature of "people's war" in Vietnam, a key source of inspiration, at the time they were convinced that only popular uprisings could start a revolution (Liniers 1985: 180–181). Furthermore, they overestimated the likelihood of collective action, thinking that the radical left had some influence over the workers and that spontaneous revolution might eventually erupt. To them the apparent linking of worker and student protest in May 1968 was an encouraging precedent (see also Geismar 1981). Thus the rejection of terrorism was based on miscalculation and misperception.

Terrorism is rejected because its costs will be excessive.

This judgment may be based on considerations of timing or calculations about the appropriate stage for violence; for example, the organization is still too weak and should wait to challenge the regime until it is able to defend itself against government retaliation. Terrorism is thought likely to provoke repression that the organization cannot survive. This is a particularly interesting argument because terrorism is often characterized as the "weapon of the weak." Also paradoxical is the fact that government repressiveness that increases the cost of popular mobilization is often thought to motivate terrorism, which requires only small numbers. Yet some revolutionaries perceive government strength as an obstacle to using terrorism (at least early in the life of an organization).

The costs of terrorism may also be perceived in terms of its impact on the achievement of political goals. Oppositions always have to juggle short- and long-term interests. For example, resorting to terrorism may be seen as likely to preclude eventual compromise, necessitated by the power of the government or by the strength of popular opposition to what revolutionaries or nationalists want. De Nardo (1985) argues that in a revolutionary movement both terrorists (who together with the proponents of mass mobilization are absolutists or "purists") and advocates of compromise are similarly impatient; they want to see immediate results. But compromisers may actually be realists, while the terrorists see no need to form a coalition with other groups in society. Compromisers or "reformist pragmatists" understand that they need support from constituencies who will be alienated by terrorism. Their conceptions of strategy differ accordingly.

These arguments against terrorism also reveal that radicals need not see mass mobilization and terrorism as mutually exclusive, as De Nardo suggests. Terrorism is often thought to be appropriate *only* when the organization is ready to mobilize mass violence. It is seen as the catalyst for revolution.

In South Africa the African National Congress formed its military wing, the "Spear of the Nation," in 1961. But terrorism was deliberately rejected as a form of armed struggle because the ANC sought a negotiated political settlement, not the destruction of the government (Howe 1989). The founding ANC leaders believed that terrorism would only cause bitterness and alienate South Africa's powerful white minority, whose reactions to terrorism were expected to be excessive. Terrorism might also cause the frontline states to deny sanctuary to the ANC (Howe 1989: 174). Furthermore, terrorism was not considered likely to bring about a revolution, only turmoil. "A radical ANC pursuing terrorism would short-circuit attempts to achieve other prerequisites for a successful uprising" (Davis 1987: 210). Unlike the Pan African Congress, an anti-apartheid organization willing to use terrorism against civilians, ANC leaders seemed quite sensitive to the costs of terrorism.

In the 1930s, leaders of the German Communist Party also feared that terrorism would only provoke repression (Rosenhaft 1982: 350). They also hoped to attract some of the Nazi rank-and-file and feared that the use of terrorism would make this impossible (355–356).

Most of Lenin's objections to terrorism were based on considerations of expediency. He thought terrorism likely to provoke repression before the revolutionary organization was prepared to meet it. Since terrorism had not worked in the past, in the days of the People's Will revolutionaries who assassinated the Czar in 1881, there was no reason to think it would work in the future. Despite Lenin's objections, however, when terrorism appeared to be successful in Russia, Marxists were reluctant to condemn it.

Many Irish nationalists were distressed when a small faction, the "Irish National Invincibles," assassinated the British chief secretary for Ireland and his under secretary in Phoenix Park in Dublin in 1882. They were aware of the political damage terrorism could do to the nationalist movement (primarily by discrediting moderates such as Charles Stewart Parnell) and to the likelihood of a repressive British reaction. Interestingly, radicals in Ireland were more likely to reject terrorism than were Irish-American nationalists in the United States. Opponents of terrorism argued that it was only appropriate in a genuinely insurrectionary situation; otherwise it would result in the destruction of all nationalist opposition. It was premature, in fact "mad, criminal, and suicidal" before the masses were organized and armed (O'Brien and Ryan 1953: 4–10). Various opponents labeled it as "imprudent," "foolish," and "immoral" (O'Brien and Ryan 1948: 143 and 323). Some feared a British reaction that would drive Irish public opinion away from the nationalists.

Terrorism may also be costly as a strategy if its implementation is botched. Incompetence by inexperienced and ill-trained aspirant terrorists damages an organization's credibility. Terrorism may be the weapon of the weak, but it is not suitable for amateurs. As William Mackey Lomasney said apprehensively of the Irish nationalist "Skirmishers" who wanted to bomb targets in London in the 1880s, "The amount of folly and bungling in connection with these attempts is simply disgraceful" (quoted in O'Brien and Ryan 1948: 44). Similar problems of incompetent implementation of a terrorist strategy plagued the right-wing Secret Army Organization during the last years of the Algerian war (1961–62).

Terrorism is undesirable because it cannot be controlled by the leaders of the organization.

Escalation will lead to adverse effects on audiences, but more importantly on the group itself. Militarization of the movement is a likely outcome of a terrorist strategy. Terrorism has a tendency to escalate, so that it no longer serves its original strategic purpose, and it corrupts the organization using it, thus altering its character. Such militarization in turn would affect the nature of a future government should the opposition come to power. This view also reinforces the argument that terrorism is potentially too costly in the long term, since uncontrolled terrorism can only divide society and prevent compromise with the government.

Gandhi advanced this argument in the 1920s (Parekh 1986). So, too, did ANC leaders in the 1960s and 1970s (Howe 1989: 173). With regard to the left in France, Alain Geismar (1981: 51) refers to the "repulsive image" of the Japanese Red Army, whose violence was turned inward and resulted in self-destruction through torture and killing of group members. These expectations represent a form of social learning. The experiences of other radical groups made an impression on the French left, and not all these impressions were favorable.

In organizations that reject terrorism, the leadership often resists pressures from the rank and file. Successful rejection of terrorism may thus require a strong leadership that is both committed to its views and capable of imposing them on their followers. This argument is applicable to the ANC's experience as a resistance organization. Davis (1987: 122) points to discipline breakdowns in the Spear of the Nation's underground units in South Africa in 1985–1986, which led to unauthorized attacks on civilians. (See also Howe 1989: 168–170). In 1931 the German Communist Party issued a resolution condemning "individual" terrorism, which it continued to reaffirm as late as 1933. This "Leninist orthodoxy" was not popular with party members, who confronted the strong determination of the leadership. A member of the Central Committee was even expelled from the Politburo and publicly condemned for criticizing the party's anti-terrorist line. While party theoreticians and publicists developed negative stereotypes of "terrorists," their constituencies continued to support terrorism as a defense against Nazi violence (Rosenhaft 1982: 356–360).

Similarly, the Gauche Prolétarienne in France in the 1970s was only able to enforce the decision to reject terrorism because the leadership could control the organization (an ironic factor, since the group itself was philosophically "anti-organization") (Liniers 1985: 213–223). The leaders, the original "founders" who had been in power since May 1968, were able to resist pressures from below. This "oligarchy" deliberately decided to dissolve the organization in 1974, a measure that took them about a year to implement.

What effect does competition among groups have on decisions to reject terrorism? In terms of organizational theories of political action, the existence of rivals is often thought to make the problem of "exit" more severe, since radicals can always move to another organization with similar goals (see Crenshaw 1988). Leaders who are unable to retain the loyalty of their followers offer violence as an incentive to prevent dissolution of the organization and the flight of its members to other rival groups. Perhaps terrorism is easier to reject when there are no rivals. Liniers (1985) and Geismar (1981) explain that the Gauche Prolétarienne "occupied the space" of the radical Left in France. The GP and its armed clandestine section had a monopoly on the violence of the extreme Left. Anyone attracted to terrorism in the 1969–1973 period would have joined the GP, which played the role of a "pied piper" (Liniers 1985: 151). Yet in South Africa, the fear that the government might choose to negotiate with Buthelezi's Inkatha movement apparently helped prevent the ANC from turning to terrorism. The existence of a rival led to moderation, not extremism. The violence that has occurred during the transition to majority rule has targeted rival groups rather than the government or the white minority. It is also well to remember that Gandhi rejected terrorism even though other factions of the independence movement were using it.

Terrorism, especially indiscriminate violence against civilians, is morally wrong, even if its benefits exceed its costs.

This view is often related to the existence of moral reference groups, such as the European Resistance movements of the second world war. Furthermore, terrorism is expected to alienate international public opinion because it is perceived as morally wrong. This view is also connected to self-conceptions of legitimacy. It is not strongly related to expectations of the likely success of potential alternatives; some people would rather be losers who played fair. That is, universal values inhibit the resort to terrorism. Not only does the group maintain these values, but it perceives the wider audience as reacting in the same terms. The group does not believe that audiences will agree that the ends justify the means.

' This argument is not characteristic of early twentieth-century Marxism, perhaps because at that time terrorism referred primarily to selective assassinations of government leaders, not to violence against civilians in the mode of the nineteenth-century anarchists. The public reaction to terrorism may not have been as negative as it is today, as the nature of terrorism has changed to be less discriminating and more destructive. The meaning of the term has also changed, reflecting changes in the political context.

Gandhi saw the choice of means as a moral, not a pragmatic, choice. To him, terrorism was less courageous than nonviolent resistance. He did, however, distinguish between offensive and defensive violence. The

People's Will in Russia considered terrorism noble because it spared ordinary people, the masses, the suffering of costly and futile rebellion. The terrorists regarded their actions as a form of self-sacrifice. Yet the ANC's sensitivity to public opinion is one reason for the rejection of terrorism in favor of sabotage. Davis (1987: 121–122) notes that

since the exile leadership sought to portray the ANC as a principled and responsible contender for power, it imposed restrictions against terrorist tactics that specifically target noncombatant whites. President Tambo even went to the extent of signing a protocol of the Geneva Convention which legally bound the ANC to avoid attacks on civilian targets and to 'humanitarian conduct of the war,' marking the first time a guerrilla group had ever done so. The hoped-for result would be a growing sense among whites that black resistance cannot be stopped, and that things might not be so bad if the ANC were to have a hand at governing.

The leaders of the Gauche Prolétarienne also note that the philosophical principles that led them to reject terrorism—an antiorganizational bias, a depreciation of the role of revolutionary intellectuals, confidence in the masses, and the subordination of military to political action—were based on a set of moral ideas that included a strong element of antifascism. Their chief reference group was the French Resistance. This sort of role modeling may have contributed to their refusal to cooperate with or emulate Palestinian terrorism (Liniers [1985: 212] says of this reference, "Je ne vois pas quel autre mot employer"). West European groups were asked to perform "anti-Zionist" actions as payment for weapons from radical Palestinian factions. The GP refused and even went so far as to condemn the 1972 Munich Olympics attack, which cost them support since most of their "worker base" was Arab (Liniers 1985: 197–203, 207–213; Geismar 1981: 49–59).

In this respect the press may be an inhibiting factor. Although most analysts see publicity as encouraging terrorism, groups that are sensitive to international public opinion may avoid terrorism because it will be communicated to audiences whose approval and assistance they seek. Howe (1989: 180) thinks that increased press attention reduces the temptation to use terrorism. Paradoxically, however, Davis (1987: 122–123) thinks that the South African government's monopoly over communications gave it the power to interpret ANC violence as inept or accidental. Even if the ANC had been successful in attacking civilian targets, their message would not have gotten across because of Pretoria's "propagandist acumen." Thus there was no point in using terrorism. Press censorship reduced its benefits.

Decisions to Abandon Terrorism

The question of why oppositions abandon a strategy of terrorism is intriguing because such reversals seem to be unusual. They are certainly poorly documented. Insufficient data are available on individual motivations for forming and joining terrorist undergrounds (Della Porta 1995), but even less is known about decisions to abandon terrorism in radical organizations. Franco Ferracuti (1990: 63) notes that "what happens in the minds of terrorists who decide to abandon terrorism is not known. The material available consists of a few interviews and autobiographies in which real motives lie hidden beneath rationalizations and self-serving reinterpretations of reality."

Whereas an instrumental approach to violence suggests that decisions to abandon terrorism are based on calculations of its diminishing utility, organizational and psychological interpretations of terrorist behavior imply that terrorism is rarely abandoned as long as the organization using it continues to exist. After a campaign of terrorism starts, psychological pressures and organizational politics are likely to encourage the continuation of violence even if it becomes counterproductive in an instrumental sense. A group may not perceive mounting costs, decreasing benefits, or emerging alternatives. Decision makers may lack the cognitive capacity to judge the consequences of their actions. They fail to consider new information and new opportunities. In psychological terms it is painful to reverse a decision already taken, especially if that decision was costly.

In democracies, an internal dynamic that encourages the continuation of violence is likely to be established in the early period of an underground group's existence, when the government is still trying to come to grips with the challenge to its authority. The group is pushed into an isolated underground life by having adopted illegality, but government pressure is not yet so constrictive as to pose a serious threat to its survival. As external pressure mounts, the group becomes more isolated from society, and it becomes more cohesive and inner-directed. Terrorism may no longer possess a strategic utility, but it serves the critical function of maintaining the group. It may become justifiable as defense against government repression or revenge for persecution.

These organizational and psychological pressures may explain why changes in the political conditions that made terrorism seem appropriate or even necessary at the outset of a conflict may not reduce violence. The process of terrorism can become independent of original motivations. For example, in Spain, Basque terrorism intensified after the transition to democracy, which resulted in political reforms as well as the establishment of nonviolent alternatives for political participation. Terrorism also persisted in the Philippines after the fall of Ferdinand Marcos.

This analysis will consider three general sets of reasons for abandoning terrorism. First, groups may cease to practice terrorism because it has succeeded in fulfilling its original purposes. Second, organizations may abandon terrorism because its utility declines. Third, new alternatives that are preferable to terrorism may become available or more attractive. Explaining these decisions exclusively on the basis of calculations of objective costs and benefits, that is, as purposive in terms of external goals, is too simple. Among the costs and benefits of terrorism are organizational coherence and maintenance, depending on the psychological, social, and material benefits the organization can offer members. If resorting to terrorism produces internal disintegration that threatens the existence of the organization, then leaders may abandon it regardless of external results.

Terrorism may be abandoned because it has accomplished its purpose.

In considering this possibility, the analyst must distinguish between short-and long-term interests of organizations.

Claims that terrorism succeeded in attaining ultimate objectives are often made in the cases of the Front de Libération Nationale (FLN) against the French in Algeria (1954–1962) and the Irgun and LEHI against the British during the Palestine Mandate (1937–1948). In both cases conflicts in which terrorism played a part resulted in fundamental political change. However, in neither instance can one say that terrorism alone would have been sufficient to assure the success of resistance to foreign rule, and it is difficult to demonstrate even that terrorism was necessary to the outcome. Urban terrorism in Algeria may have been counterproductive. The majority of Jewish opinion in Palestine disapproved of terrorism, and the Haganah (the armed defense force of the official Jewish Agency) openly fought the Irgun.

Although leaders of the Irgun and Lehi acquired positions of power in Israel some thirty years after independence, and the FLN instituted single-party rule in Algeria that lasted for over twenty-five years, practitioners of terrorism do not typically emerge on top, even when the revolutionary or nationalist movement wins the struggle. In Iran, for example, the secular mujahideen turned against Khomeini after the Shah was overthrown. That is, the revolution succeeded, but the new religious state was hostile to the faction most prone to use terrorism. The mujahideen then embarked on a campaign of terrorism against the

Khomeini regime.

Organizational theory suggests that organizations exist primarily to maintain and enhance themselves and that over time organizational maintenance replaces political purpose as the group's aim. Clearly the success of terrorism must be measured in terms of the accomplishment not only, or even primarily, of long-term political interests involving fundamental political and social change but of proximate objectives. Winning public attention, arousing popular support, blocking paths to compromise, visibly intimidating public officials, and other signs of incremental progress may be sufficient to maintain an organization in the absence of ultimate success. Attaining proximate goals can provide critical emotional rewards for individual participation, such as satisfying demands for vengeance. This conception of success implies that terrorism may continue because it is effective, but also that it may be abandoned when a short-term objective, such as political recognition, has been reached.

It is worth noting that in most theories of insurgency, especially those of the 1960s, terrorism is regarded as the first stage of revolution, to be followed by guerrilla warfare and then conventional warfare. It is meant to be abandoned after having worked to gain control of a population and draw attention to the cause (e.g., Campbell 1968: 296).

The case of the PLO is instructive. By 1974 Arafat had abandoned what he defined as international terrorism. He renounced it more explicitly in 1988, at American insistence, although it is doubtful that the two parties had accepted a common definition of terrorism. Abu Iyad, for example, the late second in command to Arafat who was assassinated in 1990 by a rival Palestinian faction, expressed these definitional ambiguities in his 1978 autobiography (Abou Iyad 1978: 156). He insisted that revolutionary violence and terrorism were distinct. The latter, in his view, consisted of individual attacks divorced from organizational interests and strategic conceptions. Terrorism is subjectively motivated and designed to substitute for mass action. Revolutionary violence, by contrast, occurs in the context of a large and structured movement. It is meant to give the movement new spirit during periods of defeat. It becomes superfluous when the movement scores political successes. Accordingly, the Black September organization was not a practitioner of terrorism, nor was their attack on Israeli athletes during the 1972 Munich Olympics an act of terrorism.

Nevertheless, excluding a brief return to terrorism in 1985, and a refusal to condemn the Palestine Liberation Front in 1990, Arafat's position against international terrorism was consistent. The PLO's emphasis was on political processes over armed struggle (of which terrorism was a key expression) after the 1973 war, despite the fact that every move toward compromise produced disunity within Palestinian ranks. The 1985 lapse was probably "merely an improvised and essentially local reply to specific and immediate problems" due to intra-Palestinian rivalry over the leadership of the PLO (Merari and Elad 1986: 99). Arafat may have recognized the costs of terrorism in terms of damage to the PLO's profile in international public opinion, since he desperately wanted a respectable image and a political settlement with Israel. Yet one of the most important reasons for the abandonment of terrorism was the PLO's new acceptability in Western Europe. Terrorism may have transformed the PLO into a political entity with not only diplomatic recognition but significant legitimization. The decision to refrain from terrorism was "a brilliant political stroke" (Merari and Elad 1986: 91) because only renouncing terrorism could safeguard PLO gains (95). (See in general chapter 5 "Conclusion: A Cost-Benefit Accounting," 89–95) Nevertheless the PLO did not succeed in translating these achievements into a satisfactory political outcome in the long run. Diplomacy was a viable alternative to terrorism, but it failed to turn recognition into legitimacy. Thus Arafat's initial calculations did not necessarily change. Furthermore, not all Palestinian factions agreed with Arafat. They continued to use terrorism, which undermined his diplomatic strategy. In 1990 the United States broke off its incipient "dialogue" with the PLO because Arafat would not condemn a subordinate organization's thwarted attack that was suspected of having been directed against Israeli civilians. Thus the perception of terrorism as having attained its objectives was not uniform within the Palestinian movement.

Organizations may abandon terrorism because its costs increase and/or its benefits decline.

Abandonment may occur even though the strategy has not secured either short-term or long-term interests because perceptions of costs and benefits may change independently of objective measures.

A key determinant of the high cost of terrorism is the government response. An efficient coercive policy could make terrorism too dangerous and unproductive to continue. The American policy of "no concessions" to terrorist demands is based on this premise. If terrorism is always punished and never rewarded, its users will presumably be deterred. At the outset of a campaign of terrorism an opposition organization may underestimate the government's capabilities and strength of will. Governments usually take time to organize an effective response to terrorism, especially if they are taken by surprise and unprepared for violent dissent (a matter not just of intelligence capabilities but political culture). Security bureaucracies are reorganized and centralized, intelligence capabilities are improved, punitive legislation is enacted, and more resources are devoted to combating terrorism and defending the vulnerable points of society. However, as Gurr (1990) notes, in liberal democracies deterrence and punishment work best in combination with other processes; abandonment is rarely the result solely of coercive government policies.

For example, consider the Canadian declaration of martial law in Québec in order to counter the terrorism of the Front de Libération du Québec (FLQ). Hewitt (1984) notes in a comparison of Canada, Northern Ireland, and Spain that the greater the number of imprisoned terrorists, the lower the level of violence. Yet Fournier (1982) argues that police repression did not prevent the FLQ from reemerging as a powerful political force in 1972. Ross and Gurr (1989) concur. In Britain, the enactment of the Prevention of Terrorism Acts "had no immediate discernible effect" (Walker 1986: 175). The moderation of terrorism that followed was due to a change in IRA strategy. In addition, as terrorism has become increasingly internationalized, it is harder for governments to increase costs because it is easier for terrorists to evade capture. Merari and Elad (1986: 83) conclude that "in the final analysis, it is difficult to evaluate the direct influence of Israel's measures on the conduct of Palestinian terrorism outside of Israel."

Nevertheless, the government response may contribute to the internal costs of terrorism by provoking organizational disintegration, involving the breakdown of the incentives that the leadership of an organization can offer followers and the dissolution of the psychological bonds that promote solidarity and help provide moral justification for terrorism. Government arrests or assaults may deprive an organization of key leaders who are irreplaceable. In West Germany and Italy the first generation of imprisoned leaders tried to maintain control over the outside organization and came into conflict with the second generation leadership, whose sources of authority were less ideological than pragmatic. They were less adept at framing objectives or elaborating doctrine than at organizing operations. The suicides of the founding members of the Red Army Fraction after the failure of the hijacking at Mogadishu in 1977 signaled the beginning of decline, although remnants of the organization persisted into the 1990s. However, the imprisonment or death of colleagues can also bind militants to the group. Those left outside cannot surrender as long as their comrades are resisting from the inside. Government coercion may help maintain the organization by promoting cohesion and confirming their hostility toward the outside world. Paradoxically, what appears to be military "defeat" may be a source of organizational strength.

Other costs associated with terrorism may be more significant than the direct or indirect penalties that governments can exact, especially in democracies. One of the most important costs is the withdrawal of popular support. The attitudes of an initially sympathetic community on which any underground organization depends may change as a result of both terrorism (especially if it escalates and becomes more random) and the government response, which raises the cost of participating in violent opposition. In a comparison of terrorism in the United States and Canada, Ross and Gurr (1989; see also Gurr 1990: 92–101) refer to this phenomenon as "backlash." Although the public's fear of government repression may contribute to a negative reaction to terrorism, initially a disproportionate government response may make the public more sympathetic. The behavior of the challenging organization matters significantly to public attitudes. For example, the FLQ's abduction and murder of Pierre Laporte alienated nationalists. Ross and Gurr (1989: 414) agree that the murder "helped swing public opinion among Québecois away from the FLQ and toward more conventional forms of political participation." Similarly, in Italy, the Red Brigades lost public support after the kidnapping and murder of Aldo Moro in 1978. The downfall of the Tupamaros of Uruguay may have begun with the kidnapping and murder of Dan Mitrione. In India, the decline of terrorism in Bengal in 1934 was attributed not only to police pressure but to public rejection of the terrorists because they had tried to assassinate the Governor: "Certainly the unequivocal and unqualified condemnation of this outrage by the nationalist press was unparalleled in the history of terrorism in Bengal" (Government of India 1937: 61). Tololyan (1988) argues that Armenian terrorism declined because the radical organizations lost legitimacy in the eyes of Armenian diaspora communities, on whose acquiescence they depended. In his view, the Armenian terrorist organizations, the Armenian Secret Army for the Liberation of Armenia (ASALA), and the Justice Commandos of the Armenian Genocide miscalculated the tolerance of the diaspora for terrorism. Early successes led them to be overconfident about their ability to manipulate public opinion. As terrorism became more indiscriminate, public support diminished.

At the beginning, underground organizations may miscalculate the susceptibility of the public to the appeals of violent extremism. Left-wing extremist groups in Germany and Italy, for example, failed to comprehend that the working classes on whom they wished to base the revolution would not support their efforts. In Germany realization of the absence of support was slow, due in part to the social isolation and ideological rigidity of the underground groups. In Italy, the Red Brigades enjoyed a much higher level of support and operated in an atmosphere of generalized low-level violence, with more extensive connections to social movements.

Terrorism may also become too costly if it results in a withdrawal of support from foreign governments. Many undergrounds, especially those with international operations, depend on governments for funds, weapons, documents, technical assistance, and asylum. When Palestinian terrorism began to target moderate Arab governments, financial aid to the PLO decreased. Saudi unhappiness may have contributed to Arafat's renunciation of international terrorism in 1974. Arafat would surely have recalled that unauthorized terrorism from the PFLP provoked the Jordanian civil war in 1970, which led to the expulsion of Palestinians.

Another cost of terrorism is related to the need of the organization's leaders to maintain the loyalty of militants. Morale may suffer not only because of government pressure but through an onset of disillusionment and demoralization that Ross and Gurr (1989) describe as "burnout." Group solidarity and cohesion break down and individual members begin to abandon both group and strategy. Abandoning terrorism may then be the only way for the leadership to prevent individual "exit." The tension caused by constant danger and recognition of waning popular support puts a strain on political conviction. Self-doubt may also be a result of the escalation of terrorism. For example, Hans-Joachim Klein (1980), a former West German terrorist, claimed that the experience of participating in a terrorist action (the seizure of OPEC ministers in Vienna in 1975) convinced him to abandon the underground. He was unable to adjust to a set of beliefs he regarded as callous and cynical with regard to human life. He felt that for the group violence became its own end.

The benefits of terrorism may also decrease regardless of the costs. The targets of terrorism may adapt. A population may become numbed, for example, and immune to psychological manipulation. They may not reject the terrorists but may no longer respond because terrorism has become routine. Governments that initially give in to ransom demands may cease doing so when the external costs (financial, diplomatic, political, etc.) become too high. Germany is a case in point. In terms of domestic politics, appearing "weak" on terrorism was a serious disadvantage for the Socialist Party in the 1970s. Media coverage may decrease as audiences tire of yet another terrorist spectacular. As terrorism becomes less unusual, it also has less publicity value. Multinational corporations improve security for their executives or move their operations to safer climates, and large monetary ransoms become harder to acquire.

The availability of new options is a third reason for abandoning terrorism.

Alternatives to terrorism, whether violent or nonviolent, may emerge with or without government intervention.

Opportunities for collective action, such as mass protest or revolution, may occur independently of government actions. Alternatively, government repression may be a catalyst for the sort of mass mobilization that makes terrorism unnecessary, or a transition to democracy may permit effective legal opposition. The nineteenth-century anarchist movement turned from violence to anarchosyndicalism and to emphasis on the general strike rather than on individual terrorism, as the working classes became more active and also as governments and society became more tolerant of worker protest. It seems logical that larger and more diversified groups, for whom terrorism is only a subsidiary means, would be more likely to switch to alternative strategies for political change when they become available. They are likely to have more resources and more options than small groups that depend exclusively on terrorism. However, collective action and terrorism are not mutually exclusive alternatives. Sometimes the prospect of collective violence encourages the use of terrorism as a catalyst to mass mobilization, which happened in Russia after the near revolution of 1905. Similarly, FLN terrorism during the Battle of Algiers (1957) may have reflected optimism and the anticipation of victory over the French, not desperation over the failure of rural guerrilla warfare.

The nonviolent alternatives to terrorism usually involve cooperation with the government, on a collective or individual level. A government offer to negotiate, grant amnesty, or permit democratic participation may create new options for the organization as a collective entity, regardless of the costs associated with continuing terrorism. Terrorism may then become less attractive in comparison to other alternatives, although it is important to remember that the decision to cooperate with the government carries risks for radical oppositions in protracted conflicts. For example, if a formal offer to negotiate requires the prior demobilization of opposition forces, then it may be answered with violence to demonstrate that defeat is not eminent and to gain a better bargaining position. Moreover, the acceptance of compromise may provoke violence from more intransigent factions and split the organization. In Spain, for example, the issue of negotiation with the government has split the Basque organization ETA. If the government cannot protect its interlocutors, they will be reluctant to enter into cooperative ventures.

There are a number of instances of government offers of participation in addition to amnesty (which affords the opportunity for the individual to return to society without penalty but not necessarily to pursue political activity). In Venezuela, the government legalized the Venezuelan Communist Party in 1968 and the Movement of the Revolutionary Left (MIR) in 1973 (the MIR had rejected a 1969 amnesty offer, and its own splinter group rejected the 1973 offer.) In 1982 in Colombia, the government offered a unilateral and unconditional amnesty to the four major revolutionary organizations and in 1984 signed a cease-fire with the major rural-based insurgent organization, the Armed Revolutionary Forces of Colombia (FARC). The other violent opposition organizations rejected the offer, while the FARC established a political party (the Union Patriotica) that contested elections. In 1988, another major organization, the M-19, accepted another peace plan and joined the government, participating in deliberations to draw up a new constitution. In the meantime, the FARC returned to the opposition. One reason for this change of course may have been that hundreds of Union Patriotica candidates were assassinated by shadowy right-wing groups, probably linked to drug cartels or the military. According to Americas Watch, M-19's acceptance of the peace plan was related to organizational weakness (M-19 is an urban organization and lacks the peasant support the FARC can muster) and to a "tarnishing of M-19's image" after the Palace of Justice episode, when the Chief Justice and ten members of the Supreme Court were killed during a hostage-taking (Americas Watch 1989: 12). It was also important to the M-19 that the government offered not just participation in the existing political system but a role in forming a new one through democratic means.

In contrast to such offers of accommodation, which permit maintenance of the organization, other policies provide alternatives to terrorism for the individual rather than the group. For example, the Italian government's policies of encouraging "repentance" as well as strengthened security measures are credited with reducing the terrorism of the Red Brigades in the 1980s. According to Weinberg and Eubank (1987), coercive measures enacted by the government in 1978 and 1980 reinforced the state security apparatus and broadened the scope of the state's control. Even membership in an association promoting violence became a crime. Yet "another section of the 1980 law stimulated less debate but proved to be more important than the above in bringing about the terrorist groups' elimination"; it was "the extension of leniency in return for disassociation that had the greatest impact" (129). The Italian policy essentially dealt with terrorism by encouraging individual exit from the group. Reduced prison sentences were offered in exchange for information that would enable the government to dismantle the underground structures of the Red Brigades. Militants who were already becoming disillusioned, bored, or remorseful were attracted to the offer. By 1989, 389 terrorists had repented (130). Thus the costs of continuing terrorism mounted while "exit" became easier. Both developments hastened the process of internal disintegration.

Ferracuti (1990) suggests that in Italy terrorists who "repent" are less stable and well adjusted than those who refuse to abandon terrorism. The founders of organizations and originators of terrorist strategies are the least likely to give up. It may be the case that whereas the rank and file press for terrorism at the beginning of a conflict, they are the first to abandon it under pressure. Ferracuti points out that the decision to abandon terrorism may reflect a reappraisal of self-interest after recognizing the failure of terrorism rather than a change of attitude toward the use of violence. Yet somehow the incentives that have bound individuals to the group and followers to leaders break down. Commitment, affective ties, and identification with the group weaken. Perhaps militants are no longer able to continue violence because they can no longer dehumanize the enemy, see themselves as heroic, or otherwise justify their behavior in moral terms. The analogies that support violence no longer hold up, such as the fantasy that they are engaged in a "war" with the government. Their isolation from society may somehow be lessened, thus forcing them to recognize the absence of mass support. On the other hand, decline may occur not so much when the general population rejects terrorism as when a supportive radical subculture either disappears or repudiates the extremist minority that is using terrorism. The social movement out of which the faction using terrorism originated may have disbanded, depriving the terrorists of a supportive milieu and a pool of potential recruits (see Della Porta 1992).

Conclusions

In order to understand the rejection of violence as a strategy of political resistance, it is helpful to focus on the decisions made by organizations in opposition to the state. Groups as well as individuals make choices about the use of terrorism that contribute significantly to outcomes. This analysis has distinguished the initial rejection of terrorism at the outset of a campaign of resistance from the abandonment of terrorism, whether or not the underlying conflict that originally led to terrorism has been resolved. A combination of instrumental, organizational, and psychological reasons explains both types of decision.

Initial decisions to reject terrorism depend on assessments of its likely consequences. One frequently expressed reason for rejection is that mass action is more highly valued. A second reason refers to considerations of expediency: based on expectations of likely consequences, the costs of terrorism will be too high. It will provoke repression from the government that will destroy all opposition and discourage popular involvement. The use of terrorism will preclude eventual compromise and foreclose other options more likely to succeed. The opportunity costs are excessive. A third set of reasons concerns the effects of terrorism on the internal dynamics of the organization; it is likely to lead to a loss of control that results in militarization and political corruption. Last, terrorism may be unacceptable because it is thought to be morally wrong, even if it should be likely to involve the masses, defeat the government, or invigorate resistance.

Decisions to abandon terrorism depend on the lessons learned from experience. A reason for early abandonment of terrorism is the perception that it has worked to produce a satisfactory outcome, primarily in the short run. Conversely, a second reason is that terrorism has failed; the group recognizes that it has insufficient utility. The government may have made participation in terrorism too dangerous for the individual, so that recruitment is impossible. Militants may perceive that terrorism, especially if it has escalated to random attacks on civilian targets, alienates the public rather than precipitating mass revolt. Foreign governments may have withdrawn their assistance. Governments and businesses may have begun to resist demands in hostage seizures. Militants may have become disillusioned and demoralized.

A last set of possibilities for the abandonment of terrorism involves a change in conditions rather than attitudes. On the one hand, collective action in another form may have become a possibility. Collective action may involve the use of violence, but it may also be peaceful if the government offers opposition organizations the opportunity to participate in the political process. The government may also open up alternatives for the individual to exit from the group, through amnesty and reintegration programs.

These reasons are not mutually exclusive in each case. Government offers of cooperation, for example, may coincide with policies that make the resort to terrorism more costly. Coercive policies may be most effective when they occur in a context of public loss of sympathy with terrorist methods, more the result of terrorist miscalculation than government efforts. A government's offer of negotiations may provide the recognition that persuades oppositions to abandon terrorism because it has succeeded. The perception that terrorism has worked in the short run may coincide with the opening of alternatives for long-term change.

From the government's point of view, these developments are characterized by high levels of uncertainty. It is clear that many of the consequences of terrorism, those anticipated at the outset or realized later by experienced opposition leaders, are independent of government control. Violence may be rejected or abandoned because of misperceptions or miscalculations. The processes by which outcomes are realized are complex and involve interactions among many different political actors under changing circumstances. The use of terrorism automatically involves the public, always as audience and often as victim, and the sensitivity of the public is greatest in democracies.

This volume is generally concerned with the conditions for peace and transitions from war to peace. Unfortunately, the rejection or abandonment of terrorism does not necessarily lead to positive peace. Political actors may reject or abandon terrorism because they prefer other forms of political violence or because they fear that any resistance to authority will meet violent repression. A shift to peaceful opposition may still provoke violence from the state. The government that adopts a conciliatory policy may inadvertently signal that terrorism works. Thus the alternative to terrorism is not always nonviolence, and the choice of a nonviolent strategy is not always reciprocated by one's opponent. The choice of peaceful methods does not guarantee a peaceful result.

References

Abou Iyad [Salah Khalaf]. 1978. *Palestinien sans patrie*. Paris: Fayolle.

Americas Watch. 1989. *The Killings in Colombia*. New York: An Americas Watch Report.

Campbell, Arthur. 1968. *Guerillas*. New York: John Day.

Crenshaw, Martha. 1988. Theories of Terrorism: Instrumental and Organizational Approaches. In *Inside Terrorist Organizations*, ed. David C. Rapoport, pp. 13–31. New York: Columbia University Press.

Davis, Stephen M. 1987. *Apartheid's Rebels: Inside South Africa's Hidden War*. New Haven: Yale University Press.

De Nardo, James. 1985. *Power in Numbers*. Princeton: Princeton University Press.

Della Porta, Donatella. 1992. Political Socialization in Left-wing Underground Organizations: Biographies of Italian and German Militants. In *Social Movement and Violence: Participation in Underground Organizations*, ed. Donatella della Porta , 259–290. Greenwich, Conn.: JAI.

———. 1995. Left-wing Terrorism in Italy. In *Terrorism in Context*, ed. Martha Crenshaw, pp. 105–159. University Park: Pennsylvania State University Press.

Ferracuti, Franco. 1990. Ideology and Repentance: Terrorism in Italy. In *Origins of terrorism: Psychologies, Ideologies, Theologies, States of Mind*, ed. Walter Reich, pp. 59–64. Cambridge: Woodrow Wilson International Center for Scholars and Cambridge University Press.

Fournier, Louis. 1982. *F.L.Q.: Histoire d'un mouvement clandestin*. Montréal: Québec/Amérique.

Furet, François, Antoine Liniers, and Philippe Raynaud. 1985. *Terrorisme et démocratie*. Paris: Fayard.

Geismar, Alain. 1981. *L'Engrenage terroriste*. Paris: Fayard.

Government of India. Home Department, Intelligence Bureau. [1937] 1974. *Terrorism in India: 1917–1936*. Reprint. Delhi: Deep Publications.

Gurr, Ted Robert. 1989. Political Terrorism: Historical Antecedents and Contemporary Trends. In *Violence in America. Vol. 2, Protest, Rebellion, Reform*, ed. Ted Robert Gurr, pp. 201–230. Newbury Park, Calif.: Sage.

———. 1990. Terrorism in Democracies: Its Social and Political Bases. In *Origins of Terrorism: Psychologies, Ideologies, Theologies, States of Mind*, ed. Walter Reich, pp. 86–102. Cambridge: Woodrow Wilson International Center for Scholars and Cambridge University Press.

Hewitt, Christopher. 1984. *The Effectiveness of Anti-Terrorist Policies*. Lanham, Md.: University Press of America.

Howe, Herbert M. 1989. Government and Opposition Terrorism in South Africa. In *The Politics of Terrorism: Terror as a State and Revolutionary Strategy*, ed. Barry Rubin, pp. 153–181. Baltimore: The Johns Hopkins Foreign Policy Institute.

Klein, Hans-Joachim. 1980. *La mort mercenaire: Témoignage d'un ancien terroriste ouest-allemand*, trans. Jean and Béatrice Balard. Paris: Seuil.

Licklider, Roy, ed. 1993. *Stopping the Killing: How Civil Wars End*. New York: New York University Press.

Liniers, Antoine. 1985. Objections contre une prise d'armes. In *Terrorisme et démocratie*, ed. Furet et al., pp. 137–224. Paris: Fayard.

Merari, Ariel and Elad Shlomi. 1986. *The International Dimension of Palestinian Terrorism*. Tel Aviv: Jaffee Center for Strategic Studies, study no. 6. Boulder, Colo.: Westview.

Merkl, Peter H.. ed. 1986. *Political Violence and Terror: Motifs and Motivations*. Berkeley: University of California Press.

Newell, David Allen. 1981. The Russian Marxist Response to Terrorism: 1878–1917. Ph.D. diss., Stanford University.

O'Brien, William and Desmond Ryan, eds. 1948–1953. *Devoy's Post Bag*. 2 vols. Dublin: C. J. Fallon, Ltd.

Parekh, Bhikhu. 1986. Gandhi's Theory of Non-Violence: His Reply to the Terrorists. In *Terrorism, Ideology and Revolution: The Origins of Modern Political Violence*, ed. Noel O'Sullivan, pp. 178–202. Boulder, Colo.: Westview.

Reich, Walter, ed. 1990. *Origins of Terrorism: Psychologies, Ideologies, Theologies, States of Mind*. Cambridge: Woodrow Wilson International Center for Scholars and Cambridge University Press.

Rosenhaft, Eve. 1982. The KPD in the Weimar Republic and the Problem of Terror during the 'Third Period,' 1929–33. In *Social Protest, Violence and Terror in Nineteenth- and Twentieth-century Europe,* ed. Wolfgang J. Mommsen and Gerhard Hirschfeld, pp. 342–366. New York: St. Martin's.

Ross, Jeffrey Ian, and Ted Robert Gurr. 1989. Why Terrorism Subsides: A Comparative Study of Canada and the United States. *Comparative Politics* 21: 405–426.

Tololyan, Khachig. 1988. Cultural Narrative and the Motivation of the Terrorist. In *Inside Terrorist Organizations,* ed. David C. Rapoport, pp. 217–233. New York: Columbia University Press.

Walker, Clive. 1986. *The Prevention of Terrorism in British Law.* Manchester: Manchester University Press.

Weinberg, Leonard and William Lee Eubank. 1987. *The Rise and Fall of Italian Terrorism.* Boulder, Colo.: Westview.

10 Understanding Peace: Insights from International Relations Theory and Research

JOHN A. VASQUEZ

■ According to the Oxford English Dictionary, one of the earliest printed uses of the word *peace* in the English language is "After grete werre cometh good pees." Vasquez points out that the conclusions of wars, especially costly wars, provide a uniquely fluid time in which nations can rethink what happened to them. "Peace," he notes, "is learned through pain." A successful peace is not negative achievement. It is a positive and rational process that not only depends heavily on perceived self interest, but also on issues of legitimacy and morality. It works because it provides structures that allow states to make international decisions and allocate resources among themselves. Even in this, however, peace and war bear a close relationship: "Peace is maintained by providing functional equivalents to war."

Like most of our other authors, Vasquez is optimistic about the human condition. The peace-making process is a conscious one in which past experience is used to construct a more successful future. If nonhuman primates can reconcile, if tribes like the Waorani can choose peace, if even terrorists can put down their arms, surely nations can construct an enduring peace.

IT CANNOT be automatically assumed that peace and war between modern nation-states is the same phenomenon as peace and war between small communities or interpersonal violence within communities. The issues over which individuals fight are often different from those over which collectivities battle. Likewise, persistent raids on small settlements by neighbors, like those characteristic of the Waorani (see chapter 7, Robarchek and Robarchek), seem to have a different dynamic from the wars of organized states. Although such differences preclude easy generalizations, the differences themselves naturally lead one to ask how peace and violence in one domain may be different from peace and violence in other domains. The field of peace studies has not been sufficiently interdisciplinary to make such a comparison possible with all its proper caveats and cautionary notes. Rather than make such an attempt, this chapter will present an overview of existing understandings about peace in international relations theory and research. It is hoped that such an overview will make clear the broad differences and similarities and lay the foundation for a more systematic comparison.

What can international relations theory and research tell us about peace? The first thing to keep in mind is that there is not much scientific *knowledge* about interstate peace. There has not been much research on peace per se, but the findings and hypotheses that do exist are suggestive. In addition, there are some important insights in the literature that should inform contemporary efforts to build peace. The first part of this chapter will review these insights to see how peace should be conceptualized. Next, the characteristics of peaceful systems that have been identified by empirical research will be examined. The chapter closes with a brief discussion of the relationship between peace and war.

The Concept of Interstate Peace

Within peace studies there are two different approaches to defining peace. One takes a broad perspective and focuses on peace as a tranquility that embodies certain positive characteristics and values (such as justice, equality, respect, etc.) that make the society generally free of violence and conflict. Donald Tuzin's vision of peace (chapter 1) takes this approach. Galtung (1969) refers to this as positive peace. A society such as the Semai that are generally free of violence and aggression (see chapter 6, Gregor and Robarchek) approaches this ideal. One of the problems with the idea of positive peace is that it can become so broad that it becomes a synonym for The Good. Peace, instead of becoming one value among several, becomes a way of combining all values in a symphony of ethical perfection.

A second approach is to look at interstate peace in very narrow terms—namely, relations (between states) that are free of war or the threat of war. Sometimes peace in this sense refers to worldwide peace, but it can also mean simply peace between the most powerful states or just avoiding catastrophic world wars. Galtung (1969) and others call this negative peace. The term *negative* refers to the fact that this view of peace emphasizes the absence of war without looking at whether the situation is the result of a deeper satisfaction of values or the result of oppression and dominance. One of the problems with the term *negative*, however, is that it tends to denigrate what many people (particularly those at war) regard as an important objective, in and of itself. Rather than use the concepts of negative and positive peace, this chapter will refer to a minimal peace and a deeper peace.

The focus in this chapter is on minimal peace because, given existing knowledge, that seems a feasible goal that will permit many states to attain at least some peace. Conversely, a deeper peace involves so many different values and goals that it will be much more difficult to develop a strategy for attaining it. This does not mean that such a strategy should be unattempted, but simply that the latter task is different from and more difficult than the one attempted here.

If, at minimum, interstate peace is defined as the absence of large amounts of collective violence, then this has important implications for what is possible on the global stage and for how to bring about peace. One implication is that peace does not require the absence of all conflict. There is no need to assume a harmony of interests in order to have a war-free system of state interaction. It is not necessary to eliminate conflict, particularly disagreement, in order to have peace, but only to keep groups from trying to resolve their disagreements through the use of lethal violence. Of course, a deeper peace will be one that rules out even the possibility of the use of violence (see Rock 1989; chapter 6, herein, Gregor and Robarchek).

Taking the minimal definition of peace, the problem of constructing interstate peace can be intellectually framed in two ways. The first envisions a world system where the probability of war, especially war among major states, is greatly reduced. This characterization relies on a systemic perspective. The second relies more on a perspective of interaction—one that looks at relations between two or more states. Here the question would be how to reduce greatly the probability that political actors will engage in violence with each other to achieve their ends.

Traditionally, international relations theory has provided some important insights from both of these perspectives. Considered on a purely rational (or strategic) basis, political actors will not resort to violence to achieve their ends if there are more efficient, less costly, and more legitimate ways of attaining their ends (cf. Crenshaw's discussion of terrorism in chapter 9). Peace can be maintained, then, by providing functional equivalents to war.

War, as Margaret Mead (1940) noted some time ago, can be seen as a social invention for handling certain situations. A society learns from its wisdom and folklore that when confronted with certain situations (with characteristics X, Y, Z), war is the appropriate response (Vasquez 1993: 31–32). The realist culture of the modern global system (i.e. the belief system that emphasizes realpolitik or power politics) has provided an intellectual guide or cognitive map to political actors that tells them when and over what they should go to war.

War occurs because within realist culture it is an institution by which binding political decisions can be made. To the extent that there are other ways of making authoritative decisions, it can be expected that war will be less frequent, especially because these alternative mechanisms will probably be less costly and morally preferred. To learn peace, states must learn that the situations for which realist culture prescribes war can be handled in a more effective fashion.

In this sense, beliefs are critical. A change in beliefs about violence, as Robarchek and Robarchek (chapter 7) show, can bring about a dramatic change in behavior. Beliefs, however, can also follow a change in behavior (see chapter 5, Staub), so getting states to resolve disputes in a nonviolent manner can lead to a change in beliefs about the efficacy of war.

The dominant realist culture has underestimated the possibility of peace by seeing international politics as a constant struggle for power.[1] To deny or try to change this fundamental fact is viewed by them as idealistically naive and dangerous, a conclusion they support by pointing to the failure of the League of Nations (Carr 1939; Morgenthau 1948). In their effort to avoid illusions, however, realists have overlooked an obvious fact; namely, there have been thousands of important political decision made in the modern global system, but comparatively few wars (Singer and Small 1982: 59–60). This means that global political actors have found ways of resolving issues in the absence of government without going to war. If the mechanisms bringing about these decisions can be identified, then some important insights can be gained about how to prevent war and maintain peace.

A review of the period since the Napoleonic Wars reveals that, at least among major states, wars cluster within distinct periods (Houweling and Siccama 1985), which means that efforts to reach global decisions without resorting to war may also cluster. Empirical research has shown that these peaceful periods have a rich global institutional context in which major states have established rules for the conduct of relations and for resolving disputes (see Wallensteen 1984; Väyrynen 1983). In addition, states, during these periods, have established a body of international law and working norms that circumscribe the use of force and war, thereby limiting its impact while legitimizing and making it part of the system. Peace appears to occur when there is a working political system, even if there is no government.

It can be assumed that the key element in an effective political system would include providing institutions that are the functional equivalent of war. At the domestic level, government has been the main functional equivalent. Understanding that government and war provide some of the same functions elucidates what would be needed in a working political system that was based neither on government nor war. If we view war as a social invention (Mead 1940), then we must also see government, and politics itself, as a social invention. Everyday politics (like party politics or diplomacy) is distinguishable from war in that it is an interdependent system of decision making, whereas war is an attempt to escape that interdependence. Government is useful because it not only institutionalizes interdependencies, but provides ways of breaking stalemates to which equal interdependencies are prone. War is not simply an act of violence but a way of conducting politics. Like government, it also is a way of breaking stalemates, but unlike government it provides a unilateral solution for the resolution of issues, and this has been the main reason why actors have found it so attractive, despite its costs.

Government and war are functional equivalents, and in the West since Hobbes, this has been generally accepted as a truth. Nevertheless, government alone does not prevent war; only *effective* government avoids war. Even here, however, it is clear that certain issues arise that cause governments that had been previously effective to falter and collapse. Issues like slavery, which touch upon fundamental ways of organizing life, are not easily resolved by government, especially when divisions are along sectional (territorial) lines. Questions of social justice that linger for decades likewise can explode (see Burton 1990). Government cannot always avoid war, and the breakdown of government usually forebodes war.

It would be erroneous to assume that there are no social inventions between the extremes of effective government and war that are available to conduct politics. There are many institutional arrangements short of formal government through which politics can be conducted (see Rosenau and Czempiel 1992). Peace reflects and is the outcome of a kind of governance; i.e., the presence of peace indicates that conflicts of interest are being controlled by an invisible exercise of authority and not subject solely to the unilateral behavior of contenders. In this sense, peace involves political rule. Political rule without government has often been tried in the history of the global system, providing a historical record that can be examined to determine the factors associated with its success. The more successful systems have not been rationalistically drafted with pen and paper and then implemented, but have evolved through *praxis* and a process of conflictive and cooperative interactions (Rummel 1979: 331).

One would expect that a successful global political system would, like government, institutionalize interdependent decision making but would, like war, provide a set of rules permitting political actors to break stalemates by escaping that interdependence. Also, like both government and war, effective global political systems would establish a context in which actors, even if they lose, feel constrained to accept the outcome of the system's institutions. Actors are likely to accept such outcomes for the same reasons they accept negative outcomes from government or from war, namely, that the attempt to employ alternative institutions is too costly or uncertain, that generally the overall rewards of the system outweigh the specific loss, or that the actor has no choice—either because the system provides no other options and/or the actor is incapable (militarily or ideologically) of pursuing the legitimate or illegitimate options that might be available.

From the above analysis, it should be clear that peace is something that is consciously constructed and not something that just appears in the absence of violence. How well it is made determines how long it will last; for it is the success or failure of a peace in creating a global political system that will determine the frequency of war in the presence of intractable issues. Peace is a historically determined process, a social construction of a political system—complete with rules of the game, allocation mechanisms, and decision games. Each historical period (and its global culture) has its own form of war and its own form of peace, and the nature of its peace will determine whether war can be avoided for a long or short period of time.

With the conclusion of a major war comes a peace settlement that resolves the outstanding issues between the parties, typically with the defeated acceding to the position of the victor. It is the *acceptance* of this practice—that the loser accede to the general positions of the victor on the issues in dispute—that makes war serve as an authoritative allocation of value. After major wars, the peace settlement typically establishes a system for resolving future disputes and conducting relations among states. Sometimes this will be done formally in a treaty and by the creation of international organizations. At minimum, the way in which the peace settlement is arranged and the new status hierarchy it reflects create precedents for how the system is to be governed in the future. In a limited dyadic war, a peace settlement has similar consequences but is confined to shaping the relationship between the two parties.

Peace, of course, reflects the interests of those who create it. A peace usually distributes stakes and resolves issues to institutionalize a status quo that will be enforced by (as well as reflect) the dominant balance of forces (Gilpin 1981, Rummel 1979). Its rules and procedures create a mobilization of bias (Bachrach and Baratz 1962) in favor of those who created the system. The end of a war gives rise to a structure of expectations about how actors will behave toward one another and how issues will be resolved (Rummel 1979: 368, 372, 375). A structure of expectations shapes behavior in that it provides a framework by which actors understand and perceive each other (Rummel 1979: 114). This structure evolves as interaction gives rise to patterns of behavior. In the new peace, the status quo mirrors and is enforced by a balance of interests, capabilities, and wills (Rummel 1979: 268, 317–318). The mutual willingness of all sides to accept the outcome of a war and the new status quo is a result of their common perception that the nature of this balance would make further contention unprofitable (Rummel 1979: 318).

In these various ways a peace embodies an inchoate political system, and it is the ability of this political system to resolve *new* issues and accommodate new actors that will determine how long the peace will last. It cannot be supposed as Rummel (1979), Gilpin (1981), and, to a lesser extent, Modelski (1978) do, that a change in the balance of powers or the rise of a challenger to the hegemon will result in a new major war. Although these analyses provide some important insights about how peace ends a specific war and about the foundation of power upon which that peace rests, their realist emphasis on the power foundation makes them overlook the extent to which a peace and a structure of expectations do more than resolve the issues that led to a war and give rise to a new status hierarchy. The rise of new actors and changes in capabilities will, of course, place new demands on the political system, but whether those demands will result in a breakdown of the system and a major new war depends on the nature of those demands (the type of issue being raised) and the characteristics of the political system (e.g., the existence of procedures and institutions able to handle highly salient issues, especially territorial issues).

The rise of new powerful actors, however, does not have to mean that a peace system will break down. Realists ignore the most important variable cluster at the systemic level, namely, the global institutional context the peace has created. If the global institutional context is important, then some peace systems should be much more effective than others in the face of secular changes in power. In fact, certain types of peace have been fairly successful in avoiding a repeat of the war, while others have actually promoted a war's recurrence (see Doran 1971).

Because they see anarchy and power politics as prevailing, realists underestimate the possibility of peace. Waltz (1959, 1979) argues that a structure of anarchy makes war possible, and because anarchy is endemic, power politics dominates. However, if the structure of the system is not always anarchic, then power politics behavior might wane and war might not be the main way of resolving fundamental issues.

The conventional wisdom is that the global system is fundamentally anarchic, but is this the case? If one means by anarchy the absence of hierarchical domestic-type government, then it is, but if one means the absence of all governance and order, then it is not. Despite the analogy to domestic government, most realists, including Waltz, use the term *anarchy* to mean not simply the absence of hierarchical government but the presence of a Hobbesian state of nature.

Since 1495, anarchy-as-a-state-of-nature, while present at times in the modern global system, has not been as pervasive as Waltz (1979) would have us believe (see Bull 1977; Alker 1996). Indeed, as David Campbell (1989: 104) astutely observes, the defining characteristic of the international system since the sixteenth century has been capitalism, not anarchy. To see the modern global system as "anarchic" is to hide the historical fact that an arbitrary system of organization (i.e., nation-states and a capitalist world economy) evolved at a particular period of history and has been guided by clear principles of order that make this system much more of a society than a state of nature. The fact that international capitalism is consonant with a multiplicity of states relating to each other on the basis of an interstate anarchy (i.e., in the absence of legal hierarchy), rather than empire (Braudel 1966; Wallerstein 1976; Ashley 1987), makes clear that interstate "anarchy" is a constructed and contingent condition, rather than an eternal verity of world politics.

Waltz underestimates the amount of order in the system because he treats the anarchy/order distinction as a dichotomy when it is better seen as a continuum. Major wars have given rise to political orders, and most wars are not fought in a condition of anarchy but within a regional or global order that shapes the way in which the war is fought (see Bull 1977). The kind of anarchy Waltz and Hobbes talk about only emerges with the complete breakdown of a political system, which occurs only during world wars in the global system and civil wars and social revolutions in domestic systems.

The extent to which a global system can avoid war is a function of the extent to which it has an ordered structure. It can be argued, all other factors being equal, that the more ordered the global structure the fewer wars, the less intense the wars that occur, and the fewer the military confrontations. A system can be considered *ordered* to the extent that actors are constrained from unilaterally imposing their issue preferences on others. In an ordered political system, actors officially recognize and feel it necessary to follow certain rules of the game, and institutions exist for the resolution of issues.

Available empirical evidence concerning the conditions of interstate peace support these general assertions correlating political orderliness and the reduction of warfare. If we examine peaceful periods, then identifying the general factors and specific correlates associated with peace becomes possible.

The Empirical Characteristics of Peaceful Periods

Is it possible to avoid war, or is humanity condemned to an incessant struggle for power? Some interesting findings demonstrate that the frequency of war varies in different periods and systems; there are cases where political actors do not exhibit the kind of power-politics behavior involved in the steps to war. Realism is incorrect in asserting that all periods are a struggle for power.

Peter Wallensteen's (1984: table 2, 246) analysis of peace systems provides evidence to show that when major states make concerted efforts to work out a set of rules to guide their relations (what he calls "universalist policies"), no wars among major states are fought, military confrontations are drastically reduced, and even wars and confrontations between major and minor states are somewhat attenuated. Conversely, when major states do not (or are unable to) create an order based on acceptable rules and fall back on "particularist policies" based on unilateral actions, war breaks out periodically among them and confrontations increase twofold. Specifically, he finds that from 1816 to 1976, in universalist periods, there are no wars between major states, but in particularist periods there were ten wars. In universalist periods, there are twenty-four militarized disputes between major states compared to forty-nine militarized disputes in particularist periods.

The definition of univeralist policies given by Wallensteen implies that periods of peace are associated with establishing certain "rules of the game" that are used to make binding decisions and to resolve disputes. Universalist policies may also be connected with certain procedures—such as third-party mediation or conferences among major states—that can manage crises and/or reduce tensions in relations. Rules and norms set up expectations about general standards of behavior that not only control escalation if crises should develop, but push actors to deal with disputes by making them try certain measured actions before turning toward more drastic action. Universalist policies try to reduce and eliminate certain types of behavior, particularly unilateral acts, while establishing certain preferred means of interaction.

Norms and "rules of the game" are important because they provide ways of adjudicating disagreements.[2] How rules of the game shape behavior and help avoid war can be seen by looking at what Wallensteen calls *particularist policies*. When these policies dominate, unilateral actions and practices guide states. There are few or no means to adjudicate disagreements. Actors in an interdependent decision making situation can reach agreement through making a bargain (each trading something to get what they can), if the friendship-hostility level of their relationship permits. Otherwise, there are few norms, mechanisms, or institutions (formal or informal) in particularist periods for the resolution of persistent conflicts of interest. In such a global or regional context, a stalemate over a crucial issue leads actors to take unilateral acts to resolve the dispute in their favor. This leads to a focus on questions of power and capability, which leads in the modern global system to an adoption of realist perspectives and power politics.

Unilateral actions, particularly when they are associated with power politics, seem to be the key factor distinguishing periods of extensive warfare from periods of peace. When rules govern behavior and establish a structure of expectations that political actors will not act on their own to secure their issue positions, then confrontations are reduced and wars cease among major states. However, in the absence of rules, political actors seem to have little choice but to take unilateral action or give up their issue position.[3]

Periods of peace are most likely distinguished by other characteristics, but Wallensteen's research on those other factors is exploratory and needs further detailed investigation. Nevertheless, he does find that peaceful periods are clearly associated with conscious attempts to separate major states geographically so that they do not border each other. This is usually done through the creation of buffer zones. In particularist periods, just the opposite occurs. Territory separating major states is seen as a vacuum that needs to be filled and over which rivals compete (Wallensteen 1984: 247, 250). Since territorial issues are the most likely to end in war (Vasquez 1993: chapter 4; see also Holsti 1991), Wallensteen's observation probably indicates that the practices and procedures available for dealing with territorial questions are an important measure distinguishing peaceful periods from more war-prone periods.

Because serious disputes over territorial contiguity can lead to war, efforts that reduce those disputes, especially by eliminating the contiguity, will reduce the probability of war. Thus, one of the ways in which rules of the game probably produce peaceful relations is by establishing practices for handling the territorial disputes between major states. The diplomats of the one hundred years of peace between 1815 and 1914 were particularly adept in this regard. Not only did they employ the practice of buffer zones in the core of Europe but also in the periphery to manage colonial claims and rivalries.

In the nineteenth century creating buffer zones was only one practice used to handle territorial questions; equally important was the practice of *compensation* (see Morgenthau 1960: 179–180; Craig and George 1983: 34; Lauren 1983: 33). Compensation embodies the principle that among major states, especially rivals, advantages given to one state must be offset by advantages given to competing states. Territorial distributions and allocations of spheres of influence often followed this principle in the nineteenth century. Thus, if one major state won new territory by taking over a weaker political actor, other major states were entitled to compensation. Clearly, such rules go a long way toward avoiding war between major states. Without such rules other major states have to either acquiesce or take unilateral action. The practice of compensation made such a choice unnecessary and kept hostility within manageable bounds.

The practice of buffer zones and compensation illustrates that peaceful relations can be consciously built. It must be remembered, however, that such practices typically are part of a broader system of rules and understandings. In the nineteenth century, the use of buffer zones and compensation reflected the workings of an inchoate political system created at the Congress of Vienna for the settlement of the French Revolutionary and Napoleonic wars. The Concert of Europe was a conscious attempt to govern the world and manage relations among major states. Although it broke down midway through the century (see Rosecrance 1973: 36–38), it created a set of precedents and rules of the game that served the system right up to 1914.

Thus, the legacy of the Concert seems to have been critical in avoiding war in the scramble for Africa in the late-nineteenth century. Through a series of interactions and subsequent conferences, like that at Berlin (1884–1885), the major states were able to handle important territorial questions without fighting wars with one another. In Africa, as in other areas before, this peace allowed the major states to divide the world among themselves and to fight wars of inequality without the fear of interference. In this case, as in others, it should not be assumed that peace will necessarily enhance the net balance of values. In the nineteenth century, peace in one area of the world established the foundation for war, dominance, and social injustice in another.[4]

Nevertheless, the likelihood of peace increases to the extent major states develop practices and a system for dealing with territorial issues. Practices that succeed in handling territorial questions are likely to be associated with rules that can handle other issues as well, so that peaceful systems will tend to take on the characteristics of a political system that is governed by an elite.

In conjunction with the establishment of rules of the game, a second characteristic of peaceful periods, according to Wallensteen (1981), is the absence of messianism and expansionist ideologies. In peaceful periods, there is more of a willingness to tolerate differences (cf. Craig and George 1983: 33–35). States are basically satisfied with the status quo, and change is confined to the margins. Classical realism, long recognizing that moral and ideological issues dealing with how life should be lived are warprone, has extolled rules developed to keep such issues off the agenda. Realist prescriptions and rules about noninterference in the internal affairs of other nation-states, conducting diplomacy prudently so as not to overextend one's power or threaten the vital interests of another, as well as the need to make foreign policy on the basis of interests rather than morality (see Kennan 1951; Morgenthau 1960: 3–14) can be understood in this light.

The occurrence of social revolutions and civil wars shows that certain political issues can place too great a demand on even the most established political system, i.e., government. On these kinds of issues, no one believes they can afford to lose; therefore, if in any given procedure they lose, they will turn to another procedure whereby they think they might win. Ultimately, one side is apt to break out of the system and engage in unilateral action to secure its issue position. If this analysis is correct, it means that the political stability and peacefulness of certain periods is related to the absence of life-and-death issues that are likely to produce unilateral action if permitted a prominent place on the international agenda. Ideologies and religions that seek exclusive rights to institutionalize their way of life on a territory obviously raise fundamental issues of life and death.

Whether peace can be maintained depends on the ability of the political system to establish a structure that encourages the disputants to use the rules of the game to settle their differences. When a political system fails to resolve an issue, actors must give up or take matters into their own hands. The kinds of unilateral actions typically favored constitute the core of Wallensteen's particularist periods.

During particularist periods, states rely on alliance making and arms buildups. Wallensteen (1984: 248) argues that, because in universalist periods attention is focused on diplomatic resolution of problems, there is likely to be less emphasis on military buildup and a reduction in the importance of alliances. He finds this to be the case in three of his four univeralist periods, the exception being the early detente period of 1963–1976.[5] In contrast, three of the four particularist periods show a rapid arms buildup, the exception being 1849–1870 (Wallensteen 1984: 248). Likewise, Wallensteen finds alliance systems to be loose in peaceful periods and tight (in that allies make stronger commitments to each other) in particularist periods. Most universalist periods have loose alliance systems, the only possible exception being 1963–1976, but even this shows a breakdown in blocs with the defection of France from NATO and of China from the Eastern bloc. Three of the four particularist periods show tight alliance structures, with the 1849–1870 period again being the exception.

According to Wallensteen (1984: 248), there appears to be an interaction between alliances and arms buildups. When no major allies can be had (usually because the world has been polarized), then the only way to increase capability is through military buildup. Alliance polarization would be expected to encourage military buildups, and Wallensteen finds this to be the case in 1896–1918, 1933–1944, and in the post-1945 era.

This delineation of the characteristics of particularist periods provides significant additional evidence that realist practices (i.e., alliances and military build-ups) are associated with war, and peaceful systems are associated with an emphasis on other practices.[6] Peaceful systems are exemplified by the use of practices like buffer states, compensation, and concerts of power that bring major states together to form a network of institutions that provide governance for the system. The creation of rules of the game that can handle certain kinds of issues—territorial and ideological questions—and/or keep them off the agenda, seems to be a crucial variable in producing peace.

Several studies by Kegley and Raymond (1982, 1984, 1986, 1990) that are operationally more precise than Wallensteen's (1984) analysis provide additional evidence on the import of rules and norms. Kegley and Raymond show that when states accept norms, the incidence of war and military confrontation is reduced. They find that peace is associated with periods in which alliance norms are considered binding and the unilateral abrogation of commitments and treaties illegitimate. The rules imposed by the global political culture in these periods result in fewer militarized disputes and wars between major states. In addition, the wars that occur are limited wars, kept at lower levels of severity, magnitude, and duration.

To measure the extent to which global cultural norms restrain major states, Kegley and Raymond look at whether international law and commentary on it see treaties and alliances as binding. They note that there have been two traditions in international law—*pacta sunt servanda*, which maintains that agreements are binding, and *clausa rebus sic stantibus*, which says that treaties are signed "as matters stand" and that any subsequent change in those circumstances permits a party to withdraw unilaterally. One of the advantages the Kegley-Raymond studies have over Wallensteen (1984) is that they are able to develop reliable measures of the extent to which in any given half-decade the tradition in international law emphasizes the *rebus* or *pacta sunt servanda* traditions. This indicator is important not only because it focuses on the question of unilateral actions, but because it can serve as an indicator of how well the peace system is working. The *pacta sunt servanda* tradition implies a more constraining political system and robust institutional context, which should provide an alternative to war.

Examining the 1820–1914 period, Kegley and Raymond (1982: 586) find that in half-decades when treaties are considered nonbinding *(rebus)*, wars between major states occur in every half-decade (100 percent), but when treaties are considered binding *(pacta sunt servanda)*, wars between major states occur in only 50 percent of the half-decades.[7]

In their analysis of militarized confrontations (from 1820 to 1914) they also find that there is a negative relationship between binding norms and the frequency and size of disputes (Kegley and Raymond 1984: 207–211). In periods when the global culture accepts the *pacta sunt servanda* tradition as the norm, the number of military disputes goes down and the number of major states involved in a dispute decreases. Although the relationship is of moderate strength, it is not eliminated by other variables, namely alliance flexibility. As Kegley and Raymond (1984: 213) point out, this means "that in periods when the opportunistic renunciation of commitments" is condoned, militarized disputes are more likely to occur and to spread. The finding that norms can reduce the frequency and scope of disputes strongly suggests that rules can permit actors to control and manage disputes preventing contagion and escalation into war. These findings are consistent with Wallensteen's (1984) and suggest that one of the ways rules help prevent war is by reducing, limiting, and managing disputes short of war.

Even though alliance norms and the legal tradition governing commitments may be important, it is unlikely that, in and of themselves, they would have such an impact on the onset of war; rather, the presence of such norms is an indicator of a much broader consensus (on rules of the game) that diminish unilateral action. In a subsequent analysis, Kegley

and Raymond (1986: 217–224) use the notion of rules to explain their findings and to account in detail for actual historical practices. They conclude
that a consensus among major states about rules is a precondition for the
avoidance of war (Kegley and Raymond 1986: 223). Interestingly, they
note that an essential element in avoiding war is to set up rules that "permit, but place limits on, the uses of force short of war" (Kegley and Raymond 1986: 223; see also Kegley and Raymond 1994).

They also provide evidence to support the claim, made earlier in this
chapter, that such rules develop from peace settlements concluding the
last major war. They find that norm formation is associated with the outbreak of violence, but that the force of these rules erodes with time. They
suggest that the horrors of war make leaders establish rules so as to avoid
war but as memory fades and new generations and political actors
emerge, the salience of the rules wanes, especially in the face of new
issues (Kegley and Raymond 1986: 224). Leaders then need to relearn
their painful lessons about the acceptability of war as a way of handling
disagreement.

Väyrynen's (1983) study of the role of economic cycles and power
transitions in wars among major states provides one last piece of evidence supporting the view that rules are important for establishing
peace. Väyrynen finds war less frequent among major states when the
system of "political management" of interstate relations restrains unilateral actions. When alliances and institutionalized norms are in place as
retraining forces—as in a system managed by a concert of states or institutionalized regional or global organizations—then wars among major
states are less frequent. When the system is unrestrained—as in a balance
of power system in which management is based solely on calculations of
distribution of power—war is more frequent. On the basis of a historical
analysis, Väyrynen (1983: 402–410) classifies 1854–1871, 1890–1914, and
1920–1939 as unrestraining. If we place his nine wars in these periods, we
see that seven of his nine major wars occur when the system is unrestraining—the Seven Weeks' War (1866), Franco-Prussian War
(1870–1871), Russo-Japanese War (1904–1905), World War I (1914–1918),
Russian Civil War (1917–1921), Soviet-Japanese War (1939), and World
War II. If we eliminate the questionable cases of the Russian Civil War
and Soviet-Japanese War (1939)—the former being a civil war and the latter actually a sideshow—then five of seven wars since 1815 have occurred
in unrestraining periods. Only two wars occur when the political management of the system has been restraining—the Crimean War
(1853–1856) and the Korean War (1951–53)—and the Korean War was
unwanted by both major states (the U.S. and China). Although Väyry-

nen's (1983: 403) measurement of the political management variable is post hoc and his study is concerned primarily with the role of economic cycles, his analysis implies that the ability of a political system to restrain allies and adversaries by setting up norms and rules to resolve disputes is an important factor in reducing the probability of war.

Each of these studies suggests that one of the keys to peace is getting major states to control their unilateral actions in favor of some set of rules that will allow them to contend over certain issues while leaving other more highly salient (and less resolvable) issues off the political agenda. When major states have been unable or unwilling to institutionalize such rules, they have had to rely on their own unilateral actions, which in the modern global system means they have relied on the practices of power politics to gain their ends. War is a way of making authoritative decisions unilaterally. Since force and war are costly ways of making decisions, it can be assumed that war will decrease when alternative ways of making authoritative decisions exist. Likewise, it is plausible to assume that when there is a strong global order, rules and norms will limit war, even when it occurs, by restricting the situations under which it can be initiated and circumscribing how it may be fought. Many of these ideas about peace have been circulating for some time; what is significant about the above studies is that they provide systematic quantitative evidence to support these conclusions.

On the basis of the above review of this quantitative evidence, the following inductions can also be made about the characteristics associated with peace. In peaceful periods, rules of the game have been created and norms are not unilaterally abrogated. The system as a whole restrains the contention of actors by offering them practices other than power politics for the resolution of issues. In particular, practices—like buffer states, compensation, and concerts of power—that permit states to deal with territorial issues have been implemented. Issues involving severe threats to territory, especially to the core territory of major states, and certain life and death issues are kept off the agenda through the creation of a tolerable status quo and the avoidance of messianism. In addition, it can be inferred from Doran's (1971) study that the system must permit the status quo to change in order to accommodate new actors and new issues that come to the fore after the system has been created (see also Doran 1991). As peace research extends to periods prior to 1816 and to non-Western civilizations, it will be possible to determine just how generalizable these inductions are. Wallensteen's (1984) identification of periods of general peace provides an important first step in creating data for that purpose.

Assuming that avoidance of war at the domestic, regional, or global level involves the creation of a political system or regime capable of making decisions, then how long a peace will last following a major war depends upon its success in creating an order that institutionalizes procedures for the resolution of political demands. In this way, the global institutional context has a direct impact on whether and when war will occur. The global institutional context, which is created by the previous interactions of states, forms a structure that either encourages or discourages war. This is the primary way in which war is embedded in peace and vice versa (cf. chapter 1, Tuzin).

Conclusion

Kenneth Waltz (1959: chapter 6; 1979: 111; 1988: 41–44) argues that the condition of anarchy provides a structure that makes war permissible. Because anarchy provides few ways of making authoritative decisions, it follows that when certain issues are present, war is more likely than in a structure where there are a variety of ways of making authoritative decisions. In other words, a rich global institutional context should provide a structure that will make war less probable. A system's structure can be seen as ranging from one of little order (e.g., anarchy) to one that is highly ordered (e.g., government in stable societies). Force and war tend to be more frequent in a condition of anarchy simply because when no practices permitting binding decisions are available, unilateral practices dominate by default. War is less frequent in an ordered system that provides more efficient means of resolving issues, particularly when norms proscribe and deprecate the use of violence.

The structure of any system, whether it be global or domestic, must be seen not as something that is inherent in nature but as something socially constructed by the combination of practices employed by political actors. Structure is historically contingent and reflects the informal institutionalization of previous practices.

Some peace systems have been more successful in avoiding future war than others (contrast the Concert of Europe [1815] with Versailles [1918]). Some succeed because they manage to avoid war-threatening issues, and they probably are able to do that because they have consciously established a set of practices to keep those issues from arising.[8] It has already been seen how the nineteenth-century practices of buffer states, compensation, and the use of concerts of power did this. Sometimes systems succeed by being able to deal with political relations in a manner that controls hostility and avoids actions that are apt to escalate to war. The "long peace" of the Cold War that avoided a direct war between the U.S. and the USSR was of this type (see Gaddis 1987).

Peace systems do not collapse so much as they decay. War, especially war between equals, does not break out at the initial stages of contention over an issue. The onset of war must be seen as occurring only after actors have failed to resolve their issues by following the nonviolent practices of joint decision making that the prevailing rules have presented as the most legitimate. War emerges from a process by which actors shift from one nonviolent practice to the next. As these fail to resolve the issue, actors entertain unilateral solutions. In the modern global system, these solutions have been the practices of power politics. As these fail to resolve the issue, actors shift from one practice of power politics to another, gradually learning that war is the only answer.

So long as disputants are willing to accept some authoritative resolutions and the losses they imply, then relations can be successfully managed. As issues take on a more symbolic, even transcendent, quality (e.g., a battle between good and evil), actors are wont to reject any interim disposition, thereby increasing hostility and frustration. The fear and threat associated with salient security issues drives the actors toward the unilateral actions made available by realist practices. Zero-sum perceptions are bred, and the entire concatenation of global and domestic factors associated with war come into play (see Vasquez 1993: chapters 5 and 6).

In general, the process of war involves not so much the abandonment of all rules as the breakdown of the nonviolent political system and a complete switch to and reliance upon a unilateral system of coercion and force. Only by knowing whether peace has produced a political system able to resolve issues is it possible to assess the probability of war. The outbreak of war does not follow cycles (see Singer and Cusack 1981; Small and Singer 1982: 150–156; Levy 1983: 137) because *when* a war will occur depends not so much on inexorable shifts of capability (Gilpin 1981; Organski and Kugler 1980; Modelski 1978; and Thompson 1988) but on how well the peace system created after the last major war can manage existing issues and new issues that arise.

It seems that people can learn to conduct politics on a more peaceful basis; herein lies some hope for humanity. The creation of new ways of handling issues comes about after existing practices have failed to resolve issues or have resolved them at great human cost. The capacity for insight and learning provides a way of restructuring the cognitive map to provide better channels and new paths, although clearly such changes are difficult to bring about and occur rarely. Prolonged stalemates like that of the Cold War or great conflagrations like World War I break the bond between existing habits and the expectation of value satisfaction. Failure that results in great human suffering promotes a search for new ways of doing things, not only because leaders and intellectuals begin to learn to think differently but because domestic political forces push aside those who are committed to the old ways of doing things. It is not an accident that the creation of new global systems and practices is associated with the conclusion of the major world wars of the past and the creation of new domestic political systems is associated with revolution and civil war. Peace is learned through pain and the domestic reaction to that pain.[9]

Learning occurs through a search for new practices and through the examination of historical precedents (Vasquez 1976: 304–305; Mansbach and Vasquez 1981: 302). The negative example of the immediate past is instrumental in developing new practices that attempt to avoid the disastrous consequences of the former way of conducting politics. Rationalistic schemes can become utopian as in Wilsonianism. More lasting norms are apt to come out of a process of mutual probing that tacitly works out how major states will treat each other. This in turn may produce an atmosphere where more creative practices can be born. The exact manner in which effective new social inventions come about is an area that needs considerable investigation.

* * *

Three conclusions about the relationship of peace to the causes and avoidance of war can be derived from the analysis of this chapter. First, the global institutional context, like any structural variable, must be seen as a fundamental permissive cause that either allows or (generally) prevents a certain kind of behavior from occurring. A system that lacks rules and is unordered is going to have few ways of resolving issues, forcing states to rely on unilateral actions. During certain periods and in certain regions, the lack of order in the system along with a realist culture has permitted war to occur. However, because this structure has been constant for all actors within certain periods, it cannot explain why most dyads have not been engaged in constant warfare. A structure may encourage war, but specific wars are brought about by interactions that increase hostility. These interactions are characterized by unilateral actions, but even their use is not a sufficient condition for war. Rather, they must be seen as putting actors on a course, where, in the presence of the right kinds of issues, states take steps that produce the domestic political environments and increased hostility that are congenial to the kinds of crises that trigger war (see Vasquez 1993: chapter 5).

Second, no global institutional context in and of itself can cause war, but certain global institutional contexts can eliminate the conditions in which disputes and practices related to war become ingrained and highly functional. The importance of the kind of structure a peace system establishes for maintaining peace cannot be overestimated. The structure of the system determines how long war can be delayed and the type of war that will predominate. Some peace settlements structure the system so as to reduce the probability of future war. A structure that has one kind of disposition of stakes, rules and practices, and distribution of capability is likely to have a different war profile from a peace settlement that structures these factors in a different manner. In working political systems, war as an alternative is avoided or delayed for a long time or highly restrained and ritualized. Learning why some postwar systems fail can help us uncover the flaws within a political structure that might be avoided in constructing a new peace system.

Third, peace is not simply a negative phenomenon but the active creation of relationships that permit actors to contend over issues whose resolution will enhance or harm their value satisfaction. Nations not only learn how to go to war; they also learn how to construct a peace. Just as there is a culture of war that shapes behavior, so, too, is there a culture of peace that guides relations. If peace is to be maintained among equals, then institutions for resolving issues must be created and nonviolent ways of contending for stakes must be learned (see Vasquez et al. 1995). The end of the Cold War has provided an opportunity to create a lasting system of peace among the major states in the system, something that has not been successfully done since the nineteenth century. Meanwhile, the emergence of ethnic wars and civil violence has increased the need to find new ways of resolving conflict in weaker states. The emerging consensus on rules of the game among the strongest states in the system— U.S., Russia, China, Britain, France, Japan, and Germany—can, if properly constructed, provide a modicum of peace and contain wars between weaker actors. With the emergence of a new global order, it is now politically possible to utilize some of the insights of international relations inquiry to construct a theoretically sound peace for the twenty-first century. Humanity need not be condemned to a world of war.

Notes

Parts of this chapter draw from John A. Vasquez, *The War Puzzle* (Cambridge: Cambridge University Press, 1993), chapter 8.

1. For an analysis of the role of realism in the intellectual history of international relations inquiry, see Vasquez (1983). The exemplar of realism and the book credited with shifting the field from Wilsonian idealism to realism is Morgenthau (1948).

2. Even though such rules and norms may be part of a conscious policy by one or more of the actors, it is probably a mistake to imply, as Wallensteen does, that the rules themselves are policies *per se*. They can be nothing more than informal understandings set up after the last major war to demark the bounds of normal relations among major states. Because it is the rules rather than policies that shape behavior, instead of speaking about universalist periods one might speak of periods in which rules of the game have been established.

3. Typically, wars are preceded by periods of unilateral behavior, but is this of causal significance, simply descriptive of some deeper phenomenon, or perhaps even tautological? Wallensteen (1984: 246) raises the last possibility by recognizing that because his demarcation of universalist policies is based on the assessment of historians, they might be quicker to identify an order when there are no major-state wars. Yet he points out that in his classification this has not been the case, noting that none of his periods of universalism end in war. His criteria identify periods of particularism, and only at a much later date, the earliest being in the sixth year of a particularist period, does war erupt (Wallensteen 1984: 246, 256, note 4). This shows that Wallensteen's criteria for particularist and universalist periods are separate from his dependent variables.

4. Wallensteen (1984: 247–248), for example, points out that both British and French extension into the Middle East in the 1880s and 1920s, as well as the scramble for Africa in the early 1880s, occurred in universalist periods, but that decolonization occurred in the particularist and tense period of the early Cold War.

5. In the long run, however, this was not an exception, because Soviet-American arms control agreements eventually led to a relaxation of the Cold War and its decline with the rise of Gorbachev.

6. For additional evidence on the empirical association between realist practices and war see Vasquez (1993: chapter 5).

7. The statistical association (Cramer's V) for this relationship is .66. When the sample is expanded to include all states in the central system, Cramer's V is .44, indicating that global norms have more impact on preventing war between major states. Nevertheless, among central system states between 1820 and 1939, war occurred in 93 percent of the half-decades where the *rebus* tradition dominated and in only 60 percent of the half-decades where the *pacta sunt servanda* tradition dominated.

8. For an intriguing analysis that argues for the use of conflict resolution techniques to resolve issues before they become intractable and thereby take them off the agenda before they are prone to violence see Burton (1995).

9. States and regions that suffer highly costly wars may develop a negative attitude against war in general, which can raise their provocation threshold (see Mueller 1989).

In this sense, it would be interesting to see if the Semai accounts of the danger of violence are in fact based on historical experience (see chapter 6, Gregor and Robarchek). Similarly, this analysis suggests that people like the Waorani, who become receptive to nonviolence (chapter 7, Robarchek and Robarchek), may do so because of casualties suffered in previous battles.

References

Alker, Hayward R., Jr. 1996. The Presumption of Anarchy in World Politics. In *Rediscoveries and Reformulations: Humanistic Methodologies for International Studies*, ed. H. Alker, Jr. Cambridge: Cambridge University Press.

Ashley, Richard K. 1987. The Geopolitics of Geopolitical Space: Toward a Critical Social Theory of International Politics. *Alternatives* 12 (October): 403–434.

Bachrach, Peter, and Morton Baratz. 1962. The Two Faces of Power. *American Political Science Review* 56 (December): 947–952.

Braudel, Fernand. 1966. *The Mediterranean and the Mediterranean World in the Age of Philip II*, trans. Sian Reynolds, 1973. New York: Harper and Row.

Bull, Hedley. 1977. *The Anarchical Society*. New York: Columbia University Press.

Burton, J. 1990. *Conflict: Resolution and Provention*. New York: St. Martin's

———. 1995. Conflict Provention as a Political System. In *Beyond Confrontation: Learning Conflict Resolution in the Post-Cold War Era, ed.* John A. Vasquez, James Turner Johnson, Sanford Jaffe, and Linda Stamato. Ann Arbor: University of Michigan Press.

Campbell, David. 1989. Security and Identity in United States Foreign Policy: A Reading of the Carter Administration. Ph.D. diss., Australian National University.

Carr, E. H. 1939 [1964]. Reprint. *The Twenty Years' Crisis*. New York: Harper and Row.

Craig, Gordon A., and Alexander L. George. 1983. *Force and Statecraft*. New York: Oxford University Press.

Diehl, Paul. 1985. Contiguity and Military Escalation in Major Power Rivalries, 1816–1980. *Journal of Politics* 47 (4): 1203–1211.

Doran, Charles F. 1971. *The Politics of Assimilation: Hegemony and Its Aftermath*. Baltimore: Johns Hopkins University Press.

———. 1991. *Systems in Crisis: New Imperatives of High Politics at Century's End*. Cambridge: Cambridge University Press.

Gaddis, J. L. 1987. *The Long Peace*. New York: Oxford University Press.

Galtung, Johan. 1969. Violence, Peace, and Peace Research. *Journal of Peace Research* 6 (no. 3): 167–191.

Gilpin, Robert. 1981. *War and Change in World Politics. Cambridge.* Cambridge University Press.

Grotius, Hugo. 1625 [1925]. *The Law of War and Peace*, trans. Francis W. Kelsey. Carnegie Endowment for International Peace.

Houweling, Henk W., and Jan G. Siccama. 1985. The Epidemiology of War, 1816–1980. *Journal of Conflict Resolution* 29 (December): 641–663.

Kegley, Charles W, Jr., and Gregory A. Raymond. 1982. Alliance Norms and War: A New Piece in an Old Puzzle. *International Studies Quarterly* 26 (December): 572–595

———. 1984. Alliance Norms and the Management of Interstate Disputes. In *Quantitative Indicators in World Politics: Timely Assurance and Early Warning*, ed. J. D. Singer and Richard J. Stoll, pp. 199–220. New York: Praeger.

———. 1986. Normative Constraints on the Use of Force Short of War. *Journal of Peace Research* 23 (September): 213–227.

———. 1990. *When Trust Breaks Down: Alliance Norms and World Politics*. Columbia: University of South Carolina Press.

———. 1994. *A Multipolar Peace? Great-Power Politics in the Twenty-first Century*. New York: St Martin's.

Kennan, George F. 1951. *American Diplomacy, 1900–1950*. Chicago: University of Chicago Press.

Lauren, Paul Gordon. 1983. Crisis Prevention in Nineteen-Century Diplomacy. In *Managing U.S.-Soviet Rivalry*, ed. Alexander L. George, pp. 31–64. Boulder, Colo.: Westview.

Levy, Jack S. 1983. *War in the Modern Great Power System, 1495–1975*. Lexington, Ky.: University Press of Kentucky.

Mansbach, Richard W., and John A. Vasquez. 1981. *In Search of Theory: A New Paradigm for Global Politics*. New York: Columbia University Press.

Mead, Margaret. 1940. Warfare is Only an Invention—Not a Biological Necessity. *Asia* 40 (8): 402–405.

Modelski, George. 1978. The Long Cycle of Global Politics and the Nation-State. *Comparative Studies in Society and History* 20 (April): 214–235.

Morgenthau, Hans J. 1948, 1960. *Politics Among Nations: The Struggle for Power and Peace*. First and Third editions. New York: Knopf.

Mueller, J. 1989. *Retreat from Doomsday: The Obsolescence of Major War*. New York: Basic Books

Organski, A. F .K., and Jacek Kugler. 1980. *The War Ledger*. Chicago: University of Chicago Press.

Rosenau, James N., and Ernst-Otto Czempiel, eds. 1992. *Governance without Government: Order and Change in World Politics*. Cambridge: Cambridge University Press.

Rosecrance, Richard. 1973. *International Relations: Peace or War?* New York: McGraw Hill.

Rummel, Rudolph J. 1979. *War, Power, Peace. Understanding Conflict and War*, vol. 4. Beverly Hills: Sage.

Singer, J. David, and Thomas Cusack. 1981. Periodicity, Inexorability, and Steersmanship in International War. In *From National Development to Global Community*, ed. R. Merritt and B. Russett, pp. 404–422. London: George Allen & Unwin.

Small, Melvin, and J. David Singer. 1982. *Resort to Arms: International and Civil Wars, 1816–1980*. Beverly Hills: Sage.

Thompson, William R. 1988. *On Global War: Historical-Structural Approaches to World Politics*. Columbia: University of South Carolina Press.

Vasquez, John A. 1976. A Learning Theory of the American Anti-Vietnam War Movement. *Journal of Peace Research* 13 (no. 4): 299–314.

———. 1983. *The Power of Power Politics: A Critique*. New Brunswick, N.J.: Rutgers University Press.

———. 1993. *The War Puzzle*. Cambridge: Cambridge University Press.

Vasquez, John A., James Turner Johnson, Sanford Jaffe, and Linda Stamato, eds. 1995. *Beyond Confrontation: Learning Conflict Resolution in the Post–Cold War Era*. Ann Arbor: University of Michigan Press.

Väyrynen, Raimo. 1983. Economic Cycles, Power Transitions, Political Management and Wars Between Major Powers. *International Studies Quarterly* 27 (December): 389–418.

Wallensteen, Peter. 1984. Universalism vs. Particularism: On the Limits of Major Power Order. *Journal of Peace Research* 21 (no. 3): 243–257.

Wallerstein, Immanuel. 1976. *The Modern World-System: Capitalist Agriculture and the Origins of the European World Economy in the Sixteenth Century* (text ed.). New York: Academic Press.

Waltz, Kenneth N. 1959. *Man, The State, and War*. New York: Columbia University Press.

———. 1979. *Theory of International Politics*. Reading, Mass.: Addison-Wesley.

———. 1989. The Origins of War in Neorealist Theory. In *The Origin and Prevention of Major Wars*, ed. R. Rotberg and T. Rabb, pp. 39–52. Cambridge: Cambridge University Press.

SIX

The Future of Peace

11 Peace, Justice, Freedom, and Competence in a Changing World

KENNETH E. BOULDING

■ Kenneth Boulding passed away in 1993 after a long and distinguished career. He had a profound and creative impact on the Harry Frank Guggenheim Foundation conference that produced the papers that constitute the chapters of this book. His own contribution, perhaps the last of his posthumously published papers, is a typically lucid and wide-ranging essay. Social change, he maintains, provokes a process of "adaptive learning," by which competence to deal with new situations increases. Peace depends on our ability to manage these situations, as well as the ideologies that emerge from and give way to change. Above all, we need to maintain a respectful balance between the beliefs of right and left, so that power is exercised through moral legitimacy rather than through threats and coercion. From mutual respect should emerge a "dialectics of learning" rather than a "dialectics of struggle." The recent development of peace research as a discipline is a manifestation of a new competence and brings promise for realistic management of conflict and a more peaceful world.

IN 1985 I wrote a paper, "Peace, Justice, Freedom, and Competence," from which this present chapter is derived.[1] At that time I think nobody would have accurately predicted what the world would look like some years later. One should never underestimate the enormous importance of low-probability events in human history. It is a fundamental principle that no matter how low the probability of an event, if we wait long enough it will happen. When there is an empty niche in an ecosystem, whether biological or social, it is not surprising that a mutation or migration takes place that fills it, like rabbits in Australia. When this happens, of course, the world can change dramatically, as it has done in recent years. On the other hand, the old French quip about *plus ça change*, "the more things change, the more they are the same thing," also hovers in the wings. It is not uncommon to find that change is less than we think. Nevertheless, it is hard to deny that the changes have been very striking, especially in the Soviet Union, and even more so in Eastern Europe. The collapse of Marxism as an ideology and the desire for democratic political institutions and reasonably free markets certainly looks like an enormous change. Saddam Hussein, however, has demonstrated that the total international system of the world has not changed that much, and the peace dividend certainly seems to have gone down the drain. The rise of Islam, divided as the Islamic world is, could well create the next great polarization.

In the 1985 paper I argued that peace, justice, and freedom are hard to define but are closely related. Each word indeed covers a spectrum of different concepts and meanings. Each concept, however, represents a certain dichotomizing of human experience and social reality. There is a fuzzy, but very significant distinction in human organizations and behavior between peace and not peace, between justice and not justice (or injustice), and between freedom and not freedom. All important distinctions are fuzzy, however, and fuzzy sets dominate the real world. All human taxonomies are somewhat arbitrary and tributes to the limitations of language. The distinction between war and peace is perhaps the sharpest. Most historians can say whether two countries were at war or at peace with each other on a given date, though there are some ambiguities.

It is much harder to draw the line between what is just and what is unjust. Justice itself has two very different meanings. One is that people get what they deserve, of which the concept of equity is a subset, that similar cases should have similar rewards or punishments. But justice also has quite a different meaning, that people should get what they need. This is distributional or "commensal" justice, which may be quite incompatible with the first meaning. The distinctions between freedom and not freedom may be even harder to draw. The distinctions among "freedom to," that is, to do what we want, and "freedom from," from what we regard as illegitimate restrictions on "freedom to," and even "freedom of," such things as speech and religion, all add to the terminological and taxonomic confusion.

The events of the late 1980s and early 1990s have not much changed my mind in regard to these fundamental principles. In fact, if anything they have reinforced the views I held in 1985. In this interval I published *Three Faces of Power* (1989), which develops all these ideas somewhat further, looking at the first face of power in terms of threat power, used mainly by governments, the military, and police, although by no means unknown in the family, corporations, or even universities. The second face, economic power, which is what the rich have more of than the poor, is a result of a very long process of economic growth or decline, and the distribution of thrift or luck. The third face is integrative power, which is the power of legitimacy, loyalty, affection, prestige, love, and so on. This I argue, especially in the long run, is the dominant form of power, because without legitimacy threat power is very weak, and economic power precarious.

I must confess that the events of the last few years have confirmed most of my previous views, although they have also raised some very interesting questions which I did not discuss in the earlier work. The transformations in the Soviet Union and in the Eastern European countries underscore the basic weakness of the threat system, whether directed against external potential enemies in the case of national-defense organizations, or directed toward internal enemies in the case of the KGB and the FBI, in the face of an overwhelming collapse of legitimacy. I have argued, indeed, that for any single element in the dynamics of the world, especially of social systems, the rise and fall of legitimacy is about the best candidate, though how this happens is often very puzzling. In my own lifetime I lived through the collapse of the legitimacy of empire, which in England certainly nobody questioned, even when I was in high school, and now the collapse of Marxism, and especially Marxism-Leninism, as an ideology. History is a continuum of examples: the collapse of papal legitimacy in the Reformation in northern Europe, the collapse of absolute monarchy or its transformation into constitutional monarchy after 1688, and the collapse of the legitimacy of financial institutions and private enterprise in the first half of this century in the Communist world, now apparently being restored. Legitimacy is a complex system, partly because it involves two processes acting in opposite directions, that is, both positive payoffs and negative payoffs. Positive payoffs perceived as such usually reinforce legitimacy. The fun that the British have with the royal family clearly reinforces the legitimacy of constitutional monarchy.

But the failure of expected payoffs may destroy legitimacy, and this perhaps is the major factor in the collapse of Marxism. One thing an ideology must do is to be successful and to offer hope. certainly in the early part of this century communism offered hope to a great many people, who thought it would lead to a better world, without the pathologies of capitalism in terms of unemployment, the business cycle, and a sense of disempowerment of the worker caused by the rise of the labor market. By the late eighties, these great hopes had been cruelly disappointed. After some initial success in organizing society, centrally planned economies came to be viewed as repressive, threat-dominated societies, ruthless dictatorships, and in the end had a very disappointing economic record—gross inefficiency, empty stores, long queues, and so on. This disillusionment goes back to Solidarity in Poland. Once the old order reached a certain point, it collapsed very rapidly. This collapse had practically nothing to do with the Cold War or with Reagan's rearmament, which was actually fairly moderate. It was certainly not created by the CIA. It was almost 100 percent internal disillusionment.

One wonders a little whether the same thing might not happen in the capitalist militarized world. The financial system, especially in terms of debt burdens, and the general collapse of the debt system, is getting out of hand. In the United States especially, the military, while declining on the whole for the last forty years, has severely damaged the productivity of the economy, simply through the "brain drain" into the military, the absence of which has given Japan and even Germany a great advantage. The spectre of 1929–1933, when capitalism teetered on the edge of total collapse, has not quite disappeared, although we certainly know how to manage these processes today better than we did in the 1930s. The stock market collapse of 1987 had practically no perceptible impact on the overall economy—a great contrast with 1929!

The extremely dangerous situation in the Middle East and the collapse of the "peace dividend" illustrates the basic instability of the current system of unilateral national defense, but it also suggests some hopes for the future in the restoration of the legitimacy of the United Nations, however fragile. The instability of unilateral national defense and deterrence is something still haunting us. The great problem with unilateral national defense organizations is that they have to have an enemy to justify their budgets and become legitimate. Consequently, they are not particularly skilled at conflict management. What we must learn if we are to survive is that the use of threat, unless it is very limited and carefully done, tends to destroy the legitimacy on which the power of threat systems depends. Thus, the United States has severely damaged its legitimacy in the world system, even by such exercises as Grenada and Panama, after which our ultimatum to Saddam Hussein for conquering Kuwait (which could almost be described as an improbable leftover from the British Empire) takes on an air of hypocrisy and unreality. It may be impossible to be both a great power and a good power, for greatness erodes goodness and creates an increasing sense of illegitimacy, and so erodes itself. The evidence for this in human history is overwhelming. Threat is not an ultimate determinant of the power structure, except when its use is highly limited. It tends to weaken the total structure of power, in both its economic and its integrative components.

A curious problem not prominent five years ago, but which has come to the forefront, at least in my own mind, results from the extraordinary collapse of Marxism as an ideology and as a hope for the future. This collapse has created what I tend to call the "wing problem." A bird has to have both a right wing and a left wing to fly properly, though which is right and which is left depends whether one is looking at it from above or from below. If one wing is damaged, the poor bird may only be able to fly in circles. Both a vigorous right wing and a vigorous left wing are necessary if the bird is to steer itself and control its direction of flight.

One should never push an analogy too far, but there is a certain temptation to look at the wing analogy in social and, especially, in political systems, not so much in economic systems, which seem to be driven by the good old single propeller of utility or, as the left wing might say, by greed. To date, however, the most benign or even perhaps the most competent political systems seem to involve two parties, "wings," which are actually very much alike in their overall structure and ideology, with one somewhat to the left and the other somewhat to the right, like the Democrats and the Republicans in the United States, the Conservatives and the Liberals in nineteenth-century England, and so on. I must confess that I have never understood why some societies, especially the English-speaking ones, tend to produce two-party systems, whereas Latin societies seem to have a strong tendency to produce multiparty systems, which seem to lapse either into incompetent government or into dictatorship. The analogy of the airplane, and of the difference between an airplane and a bird, is rather tempting, for where there is a single motive force, whether this is a propeller or a jet, the wings have to become rigid and virtually identical. This is a system which the biosphere certainly never produced in its solutions to the problem of flight.

The virtue of wings is that they may create a learning process that strengthens both wings. Whether or not this is true of birds I do not know. Watching a buzzard soar with such small movements of one wing or the other, one has a feeling that the process by which a bird learns to fly has something to do with the interaction of messages that each wing sends to the brain. In political life the learning process is clearer. In a successful two-party system, a great deal of learning takes place within each party, and each learns from the other. This is the virtue of elections, that the party out of office learns from the experience of the party in office, so that there is a strong tendency for elections not to return the party that has been in office too long and has not learned enough. Power tends to destroy the learning process. Power tends to cover up and hide mistakes and corrupts the information system, particularly where the power is strongly imbued with threat. Lord Acton's famous law that power corrupts has a good deal to do with the fact that power corrupts the information system and the learning process. In hierarchies especially, there is a strong tendency for only information that will please a superior to be passed on. So that as we go up the hierarchy, there is an increasing error in the images of the more powerful. The decay of empires governed by a small class using threat as the major source of power is one of the great lessons of history. An unpleasant but often surprisingly effective substitute for a two-wing system is military defeat, as it frequently results in cultural and economic expansion on the part of the defeated party. The stagnation of the Ottoman Empire and the extraordinary learning explosion in Europe after 1453 is a striking example. There are some exceptions to this rule, which may depend on differences in the adaptability of different cultures, but the examples of it are very striking.

The collapse of the Marxist left may partly be the result of a failure of what might be called the "adaptive learning process," which led to catastrophic learning and disillusionment. Events certainly support the principle of the ultimate instability of error. If people believe something that is not so, they are more likely to change it than if they believe something that is so. I have sometimes called this the principle of the "outability of truth." The truth is that the Marxist theory of class struggle, the labor theory of value and production, and so on, while it had a certain luminosity and gave illusions of understanding, is far too simple to deal with an increasingly complex real world. The subcultures of the human race are immensely complex and cannot be reduced to the concept of class, even though the concept is meaningful. The workers of the world have not united and never will. They are too diverse in both their interests and their cultures. Capitalism can certainly produce some pathological institutions and processes, as the Great Depression clearly showed, but the Marxist-Leninist substitute of central planning has had much greater pathologies, as we saw in Stalin and Ceauşescu. The idea that getting rid of property and private trade would somehow produce a society governed by comradeship was a total illusion. Getting rid of trade produced societies dominated by threat not by love, as we saw both in the National Socialism of Hitler and the equally brutal socialism of Stalin. There is what might be called an "upchuck principle," that the intake of enough informational garbage produces a regurgitation. Another version of this principle is Keynes's' law that there is no evil as bad as a moderate evil, because you do not do anything about it. On the more positive side there is Lincoln's great principle that you cannot fool all the people all the time.

It is hard not to worry a little bit, however, about whether the collapse of the left has created something of a vacuum. In the United States the decline of the left is offset somewhat by the partial collapse of the fundamentalist right, the so-called "moral majority," and the discredited television preachers, but there remains the question as to how we move toward a creative left and a creative right, which between them can develop a learning process toward more realistic images of the complexity of the world and also value systems that are closer to "true" values, or a least less subject to valuational error.[2]

As error is probably easier to detect than truth, we might ask ourselves, What was uncreative or value-erroneous in the traditional images of the world, in both what might be called the "old left" and the "old right"? A source of what might be called "uncreative ideology," which is common to both wings, is the concentration on the hatred of evil rather than on the love of good. An important spectrum of human character and attributes is that which has the avoiders at one end and the approachers at the other, avoiders being those who go away from what they do not like and approachers being those who go toward what they do like (Brown 1957). For some reason, which is not at all clear to me, political advocates and activists often seem to fall more in the avoiders end of this spectrum, even though avoidance seems to lead to more psychological problems and anxieties than approaching.[3] The avoidance syndrome urges the belief that all we have to do is get rid of evil and that will produce good automatically. This neglects the fact that getting rid of one evil easily creates a vacuum or an empty niche in the social system, into which another evil expands. Prohibition in the United States is a good example. In trying to get rid of the social evil of drunkenness, Prohibition damaged the culture of the moderate social and rather ritualistic use of alcohol, which in small quantities is fairly benign, and developed a culture of speakeasies, crime, and disrespect for the law. And while in the short run it may have diminished cirrhosis of the liver, in the long run it seems to have made drunkenness an even more intractable problem. Alcoholics Anonymous, on the other hand, by concentrating on giving alcoholics a new image of themselves, pointing toward what is good rather than away from what is evil, has been much more successful, though perhaps on too small a scale, in dealing with the social problems of alcoholism.

Looking now at the old left, which ranges from John R. Commons and Sidney and Beatrice Webb and the Fabians through the more radical labor movement to the dedicated Communists, we see again a spectrum from the approachers to the avoiders. John R. Commons wanted to save capitalism by making it good. The same could be said of the Webbs. The left wing of the labor movement was a little more concentrated on denouncing the vices of capitalism. What might be called the middle-class quasi-Marxists, who were fairly prominent in peace-movement organizations during the sixties and seventies, tended again to be more conscious of the evils of capitalism in regard to unemployment and equality, intractable poverty, greed and extravagance, consumerism, and perhaps a sense of impotence in the face of the invisible hand than they were aware of any practical alternative. As we move toward the real Communists, however, a certain paradox appears. Because of the existence after 1917 of a Communist state in the Soviet Union, Western communists tended to see all good in the Soviet Union and wanted everybody simply to move toward it. Even the Webbs fell for this in their book on the Soviet Union in the twenties. Perhaps the most striking example of this issue-altering pro-Soviet sentiment was the 180 degree switch in the American Communists' attitude toward the Second World War after Hitler's invasion of the Soviet Union.[4]

On the right wing, we again see something of a spectrum. On one side we have what might be called the old-fashioned conservatives who like the world the way it is and want to preserve it, so that they tend to be approachers rather than avoiders. It is not perhaps surprising that these kinds of conservatives may well have produced more social change than the radicals. After the Second World War, however, a new form of what might be called the "shrill right" developed, of which Joseph McCarthy perhaps was an early example. He was fortunately discredited, though we find a similar attitude in the television evangelists. Here again, the "shrill rightists" were dominated by the hatred of what they perceived as evil, especially the evils of Communism, its belief in class hatred, its destruction of individual freedom, and a tendency for planning to turn into dictatorship, with 1 percent of the people doing the planning and 99 percent being planned. The Communist use of deceit, especially in the twenties and thirties, the "boring from within" strategy, and the subservience of the USSR., may also have helped to create an anti-Communist attitude dominated by the hatred of evil. Oddly enough, much of the initial appeal of Hitler to the German people was also the building up of an evil to hate. He built on the defeat in World War I, the hyperinflation of 1923, and the unemployment of the Great Depression by pinning these evils onto an imaginary conspiracy of the Jews.

Some of the pathologies of both right and left derive from the belief in the ultimate efficacy of the power of threat. We see this on the left in the belief in class war. To some extent, this is an offshoot of a dialectical approach to human history, which, of course, goes back to Hegel and the belief that all good things happen by struggle. I have argued myself that dialectical processes, while they exist, are rather minor interruptions in the long process of nondialectical evolution, both biological and social, and that Darwin's "struggle for existence" is a poor metaphor for the immensely complicated process of ecological interaction, which may involve both competitive and cooperative relationships among species, but rarely involves conscious struggle. Conscious struggle is, of course, more significant in societal evolution but, again, is only a part, and often not a very large part, of the ongoing process of social ecology and inter-action, and the cumulative learning process.

On the right wing, we have a belief in nationalism and military strength, that is, destructive power, and in being a "great power." There is a great deal of evidence that this is a distorted and incomplete picture of the real world. The use of threat easily destroys the legitimacy of the threatener, which itself undermines the power to exercise the threat. Ter-rorism, illegitimate threat, has rarely been effective in achieving the social changes desired by the terrorists themselves, simply because terrorism reinforces the resistance to social change. If it had not been for IRA ter-rorism giving the British the firm conviction that they were right, Ireland might have been unified a long time ago. The evidence that empire crip-ples the development of imperial power is very strong (Boulding and Mukerjee 1972). There are many cases in which military defeat has pro-duced economic and cultural development on the part of the defeated power, which suggests that the world is much more complex than the simplistic belief in threat would indicate.

The ultimate source of these defects of both the old right and the old left is likely to be a reliance on simplistic and inadequate images of the complexity of the total social system, even the total system of the world, and unrealistic views, as a result, of what constitutes "betterment." There is likely to be a combination here of unrealistic images of what we might call "factual dynamics" coupled with the unexamined value systems of what is believed to be better rather than worse. To pursue an image of betterment that does not correspond to reality is all too likely to result in things going from bad to worse rather than from bad to better. Pursuing a phantom easily gets us lost in the woods.

On the left side, the development of Marxism into a secular, quasi reli-gion has led to unrealistic images of the world. The image, for instance, that all the product of society is produced by the working class, as implied in the labor theory of value and of production, is unrealistic. Labor produces very little unless it is in some sense "employed." It may be self-employed, in which case the worker is productive because the worker is himself or herself an employer, but this can only operate on a small scale. In order to produce "riches" (there may be some illusions about what these constitute), workers have to be employed for a wage either by private employers or by the state. The exploitation theory that has been a great appeal of Marxism—that the worker produces everything but does not get everything, having to share the product with the capitalist—can easily be turned on its head. The worker does no more than extract the raw materials from the ground unless the workers' activity is organized by an employer, whether public or private, who has to have control of capital in order to pay a wage.

A fallacy of the left that is tied in with the exploitation theory is the belief that government is an intrinsically nonexploitative employer, which is in turn somewhat derived from the belief that society is an organism that has to be directed by a head. This neglects the ecological aspect of the world, both the biosphere and the sociosphere, which is governed by something very similar to Adam Smith's "invisible hand." An ecosystem has no mayor. It is governed by the mutual interaction of all its parts. This does not rule out the possibility that the human race can assume some kind of governance over the ecosystem, just as agriculture distorts the natural ecosystem in favor of human values, making corn grown instead of weeds. Government is a form of social agriculture engaged in diminishing crime and increasing happiness. But like the farmer, it has to recognize that it works within the limits of an essentially ecological world. The failures of central planning and its appalling ecological effects now being revealed is a good example of the illusion of a too organismic approach to the complexities of the total world system.

On the side of the right, we tend to find the belief that there are no pathologies of the free market and a belief that government should be confined to threat systems and the substitution of inter-nation war for class war. Here again, there is something of an organic fallacy, seeing the nation state as a sacred organism to be preserved at all costs, instead of as a public convenience, designed for narrow and specific functions.

Can we then think of moving toward a "new left" and a "new right" that will make the bird fly again? Perhaps this is too fanciful. But in a situation as unprecedented as the one in which we find ourselves, perhaps being fanciful is the only road ahead. Let us then fancy a "New Left," which would keep the old-left concern for the poor and the powerless and for the dispossessed, but which would pursue change without the self-pity that puts all the blame for evil on others, an attitude all too likely to perpetuate poverty. This new left would raise an image of "empowerment" to increase self-respect in the search for creative power in the personal and local environment. This would not exclude a little preaching at the rich, a demand for a kind of "grants economy," which would help to raise those who are too poor to raise themselves, but it would see inequality not as a phenomenon to be dispensed with in a flash of redistribution, but a problem long developing through relative changes in learning and accumulation that can only be solved over the years by expanding learning and accumulation. I have often inveighed against the false metaphor of the "pie," which is baked as a unit and then divided up. A better image would be innumerable little tarts, all growing up at different rates with some spooning from one to another.

The questions are: (A) How does the "spooning" make the recipients grow faster? (B) Can there be a deeper understanding of the essential ecological nature of complex systems in society, with their innumerable interactions and what might be called an "echo effect," where an action in one place echoes and re-echoes all over the system, so that it is very hard to say what the ultimate consequences are? Attempts to solve problems by governmental threat is a particularly good example of this phenomenon. The consequences of governmental action are frequently extraordinarily different from what was intended. (C) Can there be an emphasis on what might be called creative conflict, the sort of conflict that turns the image of an enemy, abstract and inhuman, into a human opponent, in which the conflict is turned into a positive-sum game from which both parties can benefit rather than, as so often happens, into a negative-sum game in which both parties lose? (D) Can there be a willingness to sacrifice a little justice? This is a very difficult problem, as the relation between freedom and justice is very complex. Obviously criminal justice implies a loss of freedom for the people in jail and a very great loss of freedom for those executed. Whether justice is promoted by prohibiting various forms of business freedom is a tricky question. The United States has felt that justice was served by limiting monopoly power (there is a strong case for this), though exceptions can be made to it. The Communist countries believed that justice was served by limiting all freedom of private enterprise, but this seems to be a very doubtful proposition. The question as to whether it is unjust to limit the freedom of expression runs into difficulties. About all we can say is that justice and freedom have to be balanced, but that this is a precarious and difficult process. It is rather interesting that one of the first peace organizations was the Women's International League for Peace and Freedom, whereas today peace organizations are much more inclined to talk about justice. Somehow we have to keep both these balls in the air, even if it takes a little juggling.

Can we then envision a new right that would interact creatively with the new left but would stress things that the new left tends to forget? The right, at least in the United States, tends to be associated with individualism and even selfishness. There is a good deal to be said for stressing the importance and sovereignty of the individual, and there is a good deal to be said for self-love, provided that it is combined with compassion in the sense of the larger community of the human race. No good comes out of self-hatred, which is a common disease of the left, and even less good comes out of a self-love that does not encompass a larger self than the person and that does not ultimately include the larger neighborhood of the whole planet in some degree.

A new right should have something of a critical watchdog approach toward the role of government, but it cannot really afford to be too anarchistic and needs to have a realistic understanding of the role of government in correcting the pathologies of individual behavior and private organizations. It is ironic that the "old right" tended to be identified with nationalism and a very unconservative worship of the national state. The right can argue profitably that the near should be dear and that love starts with a neighbor, but to love everybody equally is not to love anybody very much. The right needs now, however, to stress the importance of law and legitimacy and be critical of the reliance on threat. This would lead to an emphasis on creative conflict, in which the welfare of the opponent is not denied. This perhaps would lead to a recognition of the essentially conservative nature of peace and the radically disruptive effects of war and violence. The new right might be concerned to sacrifice some freedom in the interest of justice, although it should certainly stand up for freedom. Here it faces the same dilemma that we notice in the case of the new left.

What all this suggests is that we are looking for a dialectics of learning rather than a dialectics of struggle. One of the hopeful signs emerging from this search has been the development of the peace-research movement in the last thirty or forty years, which essentially defines peace as creative conflict and a learning process as over against the old dialectic that cannot live without an enemy. This is a worldwide movement, mainly among academics but increasingly penetrating into the world both of the activists and of government. The foundation of the International Peace Research Association in 1964–1965 was a landmark.

The very name of the American section, the Consortium on Peace Research, Education and Development (COPRED) (formed in 1970), indicates a deep commitment not only to pure academic research but also to its applications in education and in public policy. The formation of a number of government peace research organizations, such as the United States Institute for Peace, is symptomatic also that this movement is being taken seriously, though not seriously enough even in the councils of the powerful. This has gone hand in hand with the development of what might be called a whole new professional discipline of conflict resolvers and managers, going back to the American Arbitration Association in the nineteenth century, and now represented in the National Conference on Peacemaking and Conflict Resolution. The peace research, education, and development movement, as it might be called, is still in its infancy, but it offers perhaps one of the greatest promises for a more realistic political approach to conflict and also for the prospect of mobilizing the world in the face of the enormous environmental problems that are likely to descend upon us in the not-too-distant future.

Notes

This chapter is published by permission of the Archives, University of Colorado at Boulder Libraries.

1. The paper was published: *Zygon* 21, no. 4 (December 1986): 519–533.

2. The idea that there is "truth" in value bothers the positivists, but there is no doubt that values are evaluated, both by individuals—who ask themselves, "Am I wanting the right things?"—and by the larger society that evaluates the value systems of subcultures of which it disapproves. We do not have to postulate an ultimate truth in values to establish the principle that the detection of error in values is a common human experience.

3. For a more detailed explanation, see K. E. Boulding, *Conflict and Defense* (New York: Harper, 1962, pp. 1882; reissued: Lanham, Maryland: University Press of America, 1988).

4. When I was studying the labor movement in 1943, I visited the Office and Professional Workers in New York, which had been taken over by the Communists, as were perhaps ten other unions. I picked up a pamphlet on why you should join the union, the last page of which said, "Most of all, if you join the union you will be helping America in the great war against Nazism," and so on. I noted that the last page was rather thick, so I pried it open and found a new last page had been pasted over an old last page, which began, "Most of all, if you join the union you will help to keep America out of an imperialist war." It is not surprising that this switch threw a good many people out of the Communist bandwagon.

References

Boulding, K. E. 1989. *Three Faces of Power*. Newbury Park, Calif: Sage

Boulding, K. E. and T. Mukerjee. 1972. *Economic Imperialism*. Ann Arbor: University of Michigan Press.

Brown, Judson S. 1957. Principles of Intrapersonal Conflict. *Journal of Conflict Resolution* 1: 135–154.

CONTRIBUTORS

KENNETH E. BOULDING was a former president of the American Economics Association and the American Association for the Advancement of Science and the author of numerous books, including *The World as a Total System* (Sage, 1985). Until his death in 1993 at the age of eighty-three, he was Distinguished Professor of Economics, Emeritus, at the University of Colorado at Boulder.

MARTHA CRENSHAW is Professor of Political Science at Wesleyan University. Her research has focused on the problem of political terrorism, and she is the author of *Terrorism and International Cooperation* (Westview Press, 1989).

ARTHUR A. DEMAREST is the Ingram Professor of Anthropology at Vanderbilt University. He has directed archaeological projects in Central America since 1976. He has a particular interest in pre–Columbian religion, warfare, and political systems. Among his many books on the subject is *Ideology and Precolumbian Civilizations* (University of Washington Press, 1992).

FRANS B. M. DE WAAL is Professor of Psychology at Emory University and Research Professor in Behavioral Biology at the Yerkes Regional Primate Research Center. His studies of primate behavior include *Peacemaking Among Primates* (Harvard University Press, 1989).

THOMAS GREGOR is Professor and Chair of Anthropology at Vanderbilt University. He has conducted extensive field work with the Mehinaku Indians of Brazil, which is the basis of numerous scientific publications, including *Anxious Pleasures: The Sexual Lives of an Amazonian People* (University of Chicago Press, 1987).

BRUCE M. KNAUFT is Professor and Director of Graduate Studies in the Department of Anthropology at Emory University. He is the author of *Good Company and Violence: Sorcery and Social Action in a Lowland New Guinea Society* (University of California Press, 1985).

313

CAROLE J. ROBARCHEK is a research associate in anthropology at Wichita State University. She has conducted field research among the Malaysian Semai and the Ecuadorian Waorani, and her articles have appeared in both Malaysian and American journals.

CLAYTON A. ROBARCHEK is Associate Professor and Chair of Anthropology at Wichita State University. He has conducted long-term comparative research among the Semai of Malaysia and the Waorani of Ecuadorian Amazonia. His articles on violence and nonviolence have appeared in major journals and in numerous edited volumes.

LESLIE E. SPONSEL, Professor of Anthropology at the University of Hawaii, is a founding member of the Spark M. Matsunaga Institute for Peace, the author of many scientific articles, and the editor of *Indigenous Peoples and the Future of Amazonia: An Ecological Anthropology of an Endangered World* (University of Arizona Press, 1995).

ERVIN STAUB is Professor of Psychology at the University of Massachusetts, Amherst. He has studied for many years the determinants and development of helping behavior and altruism, on the one hand, and of harm-doing, aggression, and violence, on the other. He is the author of *The Roots of Evil: The Psychological and Cultural Origins of Genocide* (Cambridge University Press, 1989).

DONALD TUZIN is Professor and Chair of Anthropology at the University of California, San Diego. In addition to numerous papers on Melanesian topics, he is the author of *The Ilahita Arapesh: Dimensions of Unity* (University of California Press, 1976).

JOHN A. VASQUEZ, Professor of Political Science at Vanderbilt University, is a specialist in international-relations theory and peace research. His publications include *The War Puzzle* (Cambridge University Press, 1993).

INDEX

A NATURAL HISTORY OF PEACE

was composed electronically using Palatino types, with display types in
Optima. The book was printed on acid-free, Glatfelter Supple Opaque
Recycled Natural paper, bound and with covers printed in three colors by
Thomson-Shore, Inc. Book and cover designs are the work of Gary Gore.
Published by Vanderbilt University Press Nashville, Tennessee 37235.